GRIMMY: THE HORRORS OF GLOBAL WORMING

BY MIKE PETERS

TOR®

A TOM DOHERTY ASSOCIATES BOOK
NEW YORK

This is a work of fiction.
All the characters and events portrayed in this novel are either fictitious
or are used fictitiously.

GRIMMY: THE HORRORS OF GLOBAL WORMING

TM and Copyright © 2000 by Grimmy, Inc.

A Tor Book
Published by Tom Doherty Associates, LLC
175 Fifth Avenue
New York, NY 10010

www.tor.com

Tor® is a registered trademark of Tom Doherty Associates, LLC.

ISBN 0-312-87326-3

First Edition: April 2000

Printed in the United States of America

0 9 8 7 6 5 4 3 2 1

This book is dedicated to a giant in cartooning:
Chuck Jones

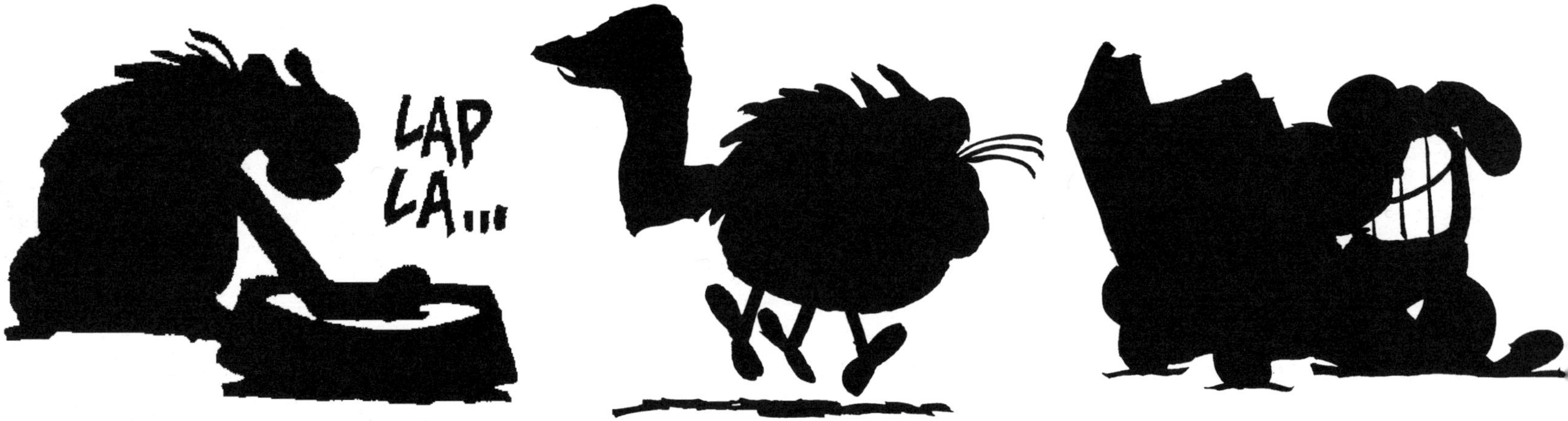
LAP LA...

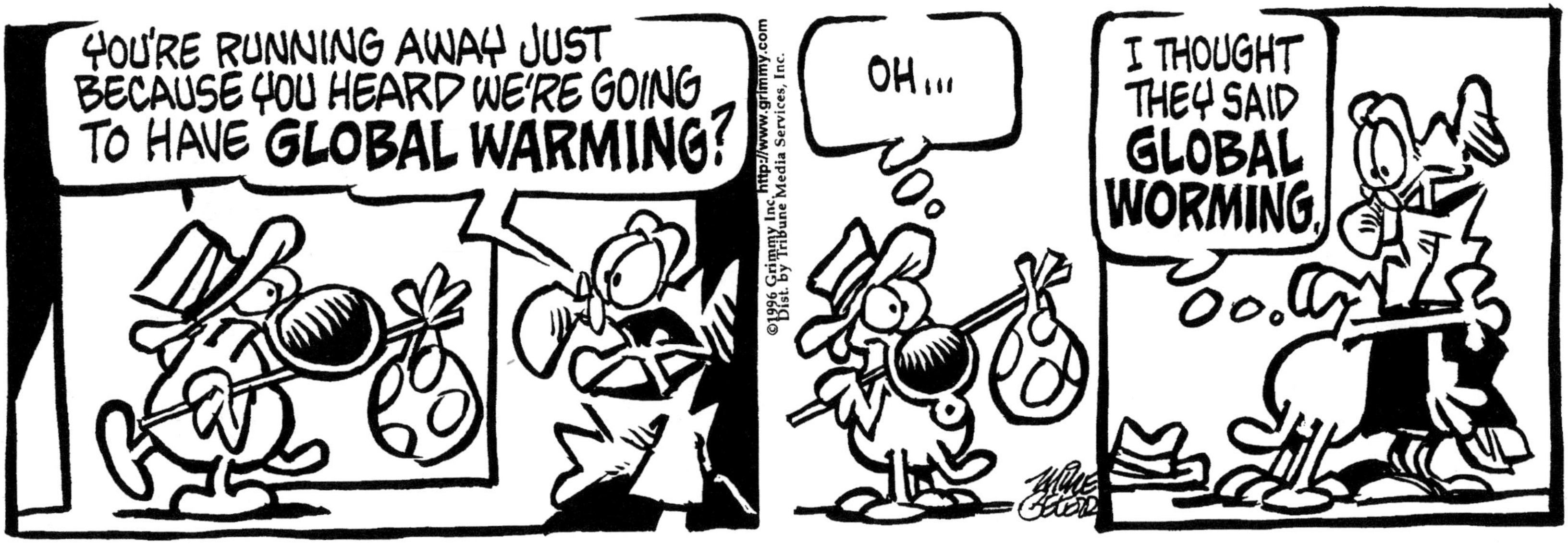
YOU'RE RUNNING AWAY JUST BECAUSE YOU HEARD WE'RE GOING TO HAVE GLOBAL WARMING?
©1996 Grimmy Inc. http://www.grimmy.com Dist. by Tribune Media Services, Inc.
OH...
I THOUGHT THEY SAID GLOBAL WORMING.

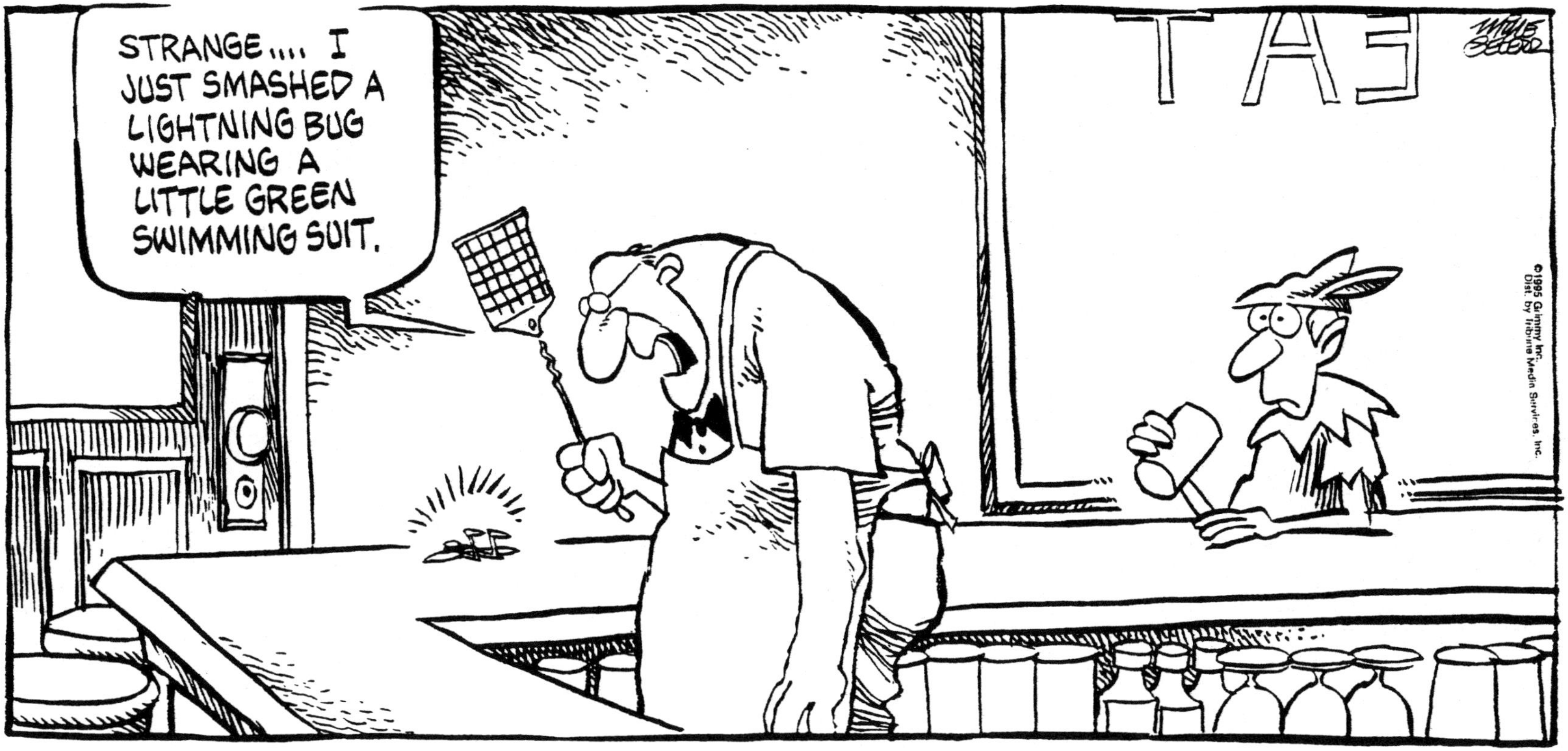
STRANGE.... I JUST SMASHED A LIGHTNING BUG WEARING A LITTLE GREEN SWIMMING SUIT.
EAT
©1995 Grimmy Inc. Dist. by Tribune Media Services, Inc.

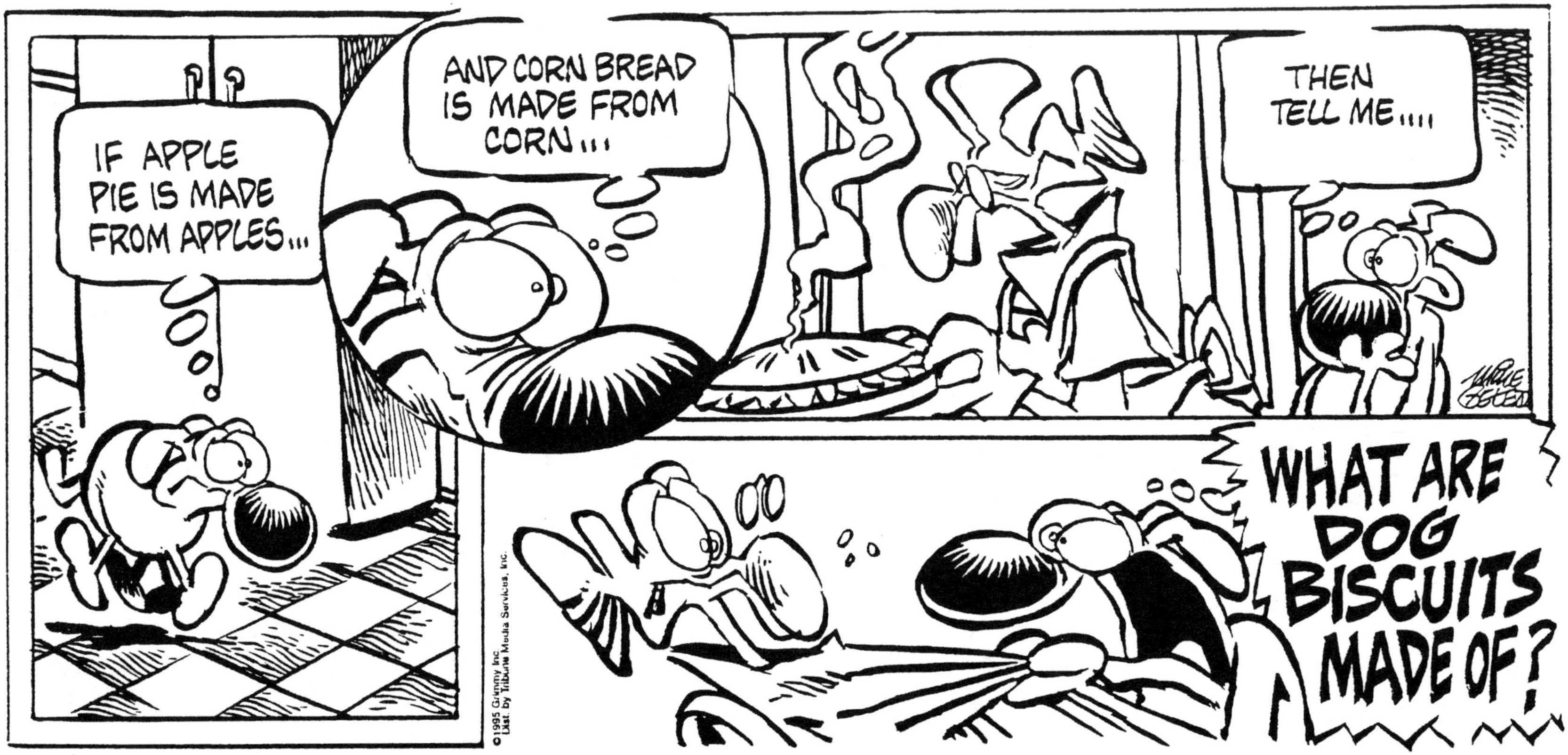
IF APPLE PIE IS MADE FROM APPLES...
AND CORN BREAD IS MADE FROM CORN...
THEN TELL ME....
WHAT ARE DOG BISCUITS MADE OF?

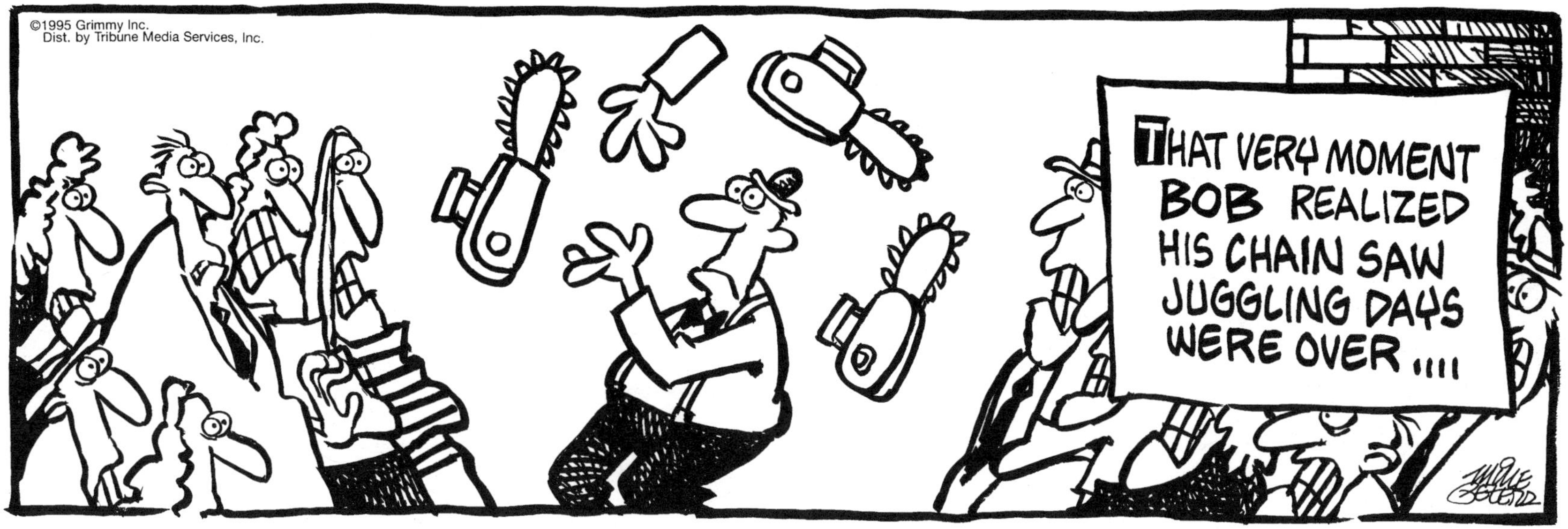
©1995 Grimmy Inc.
Dist. by Tribune Media Services, Inc.
THAT VERY MOMENT BOB REALIZED HIS CHAIN SAW JUGGLING DAYS WERE OVER....

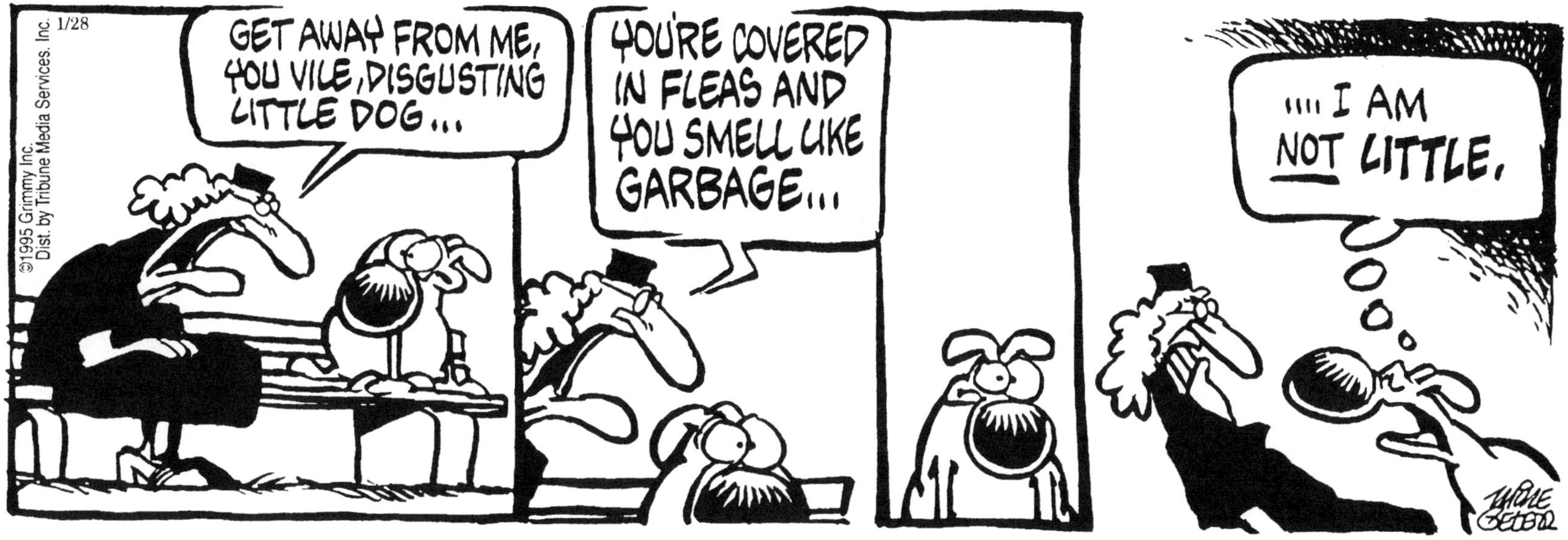
©1995 Grimmy Inc.
Dist. by Tribune Media Services, Inc.
1/28
GET AWAY FROM ME, YOU VILE, DISGUSTING LITTLE DOG...
YOU'RE COVERED IN FLEAS AND YOU SMELL LIKE GARBAGE...
....I AM NOT LITTLE.

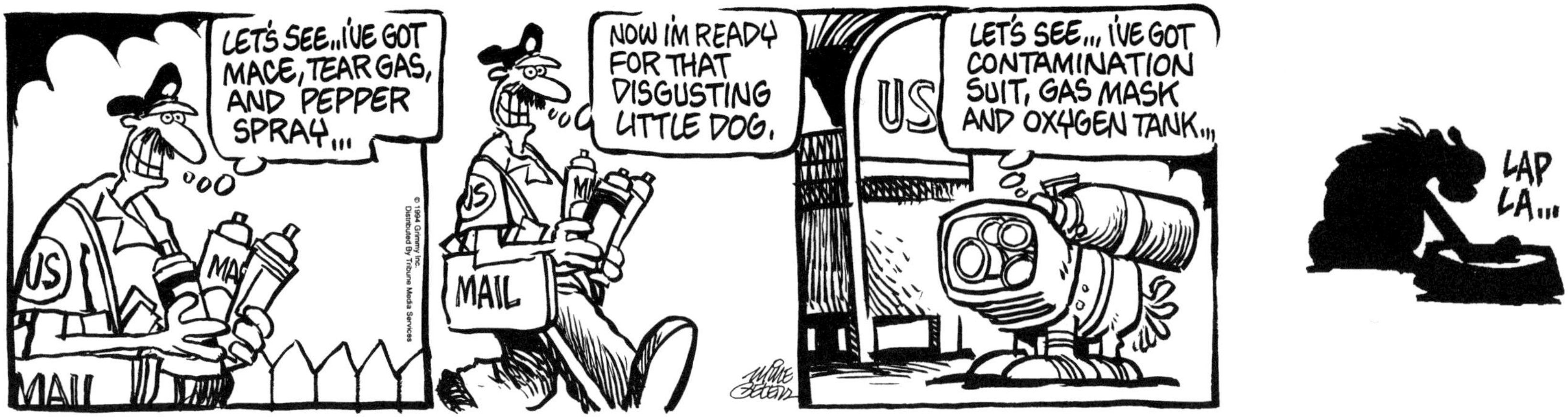
LET'S SEE...I'VE GOT MACE, TEAR GAS, AND PEPPER SPRAY...
© 1994 Grimmy Inc.
Distributed By Tribune Media Services
NOW I'M READY FOR THAT DISGUSTING LITTLE DOG.
LET'S SEE... I'VE GOT CONTAMINATION SUIT, GAS MASK AND OXYGEN TANK...
LAP LA...

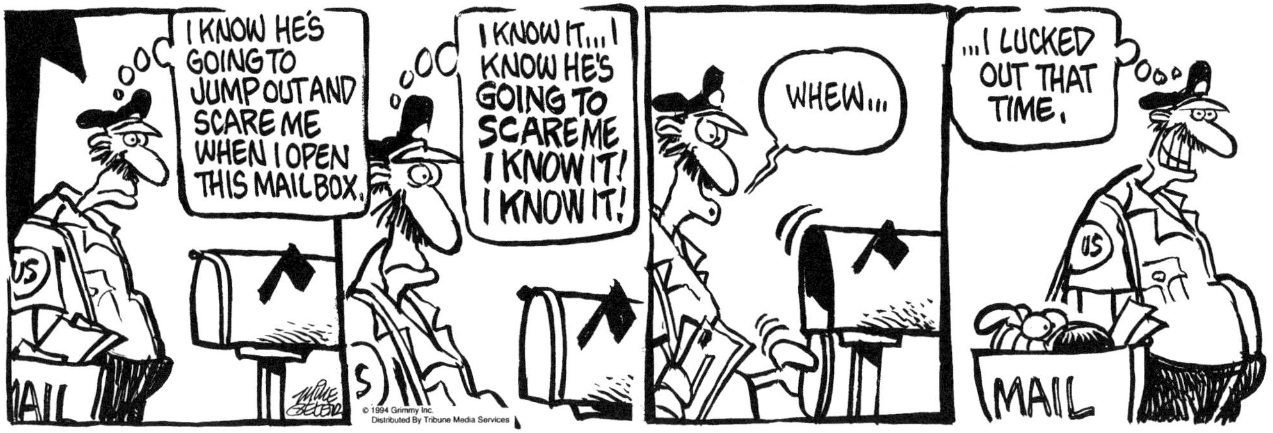
I KNOW HE'S GOING TO JUMP OUT AND SCARE ME WHEN I OPEN THIS MAILBOX.
I KNOW IT... I KNOW HE'S GOING TO SCARE ME I KNOW IT! I KNOW IT!
© 1994 Grimmy Inc.
Distributed By Tribune Media Services
WHEW...
...I LUCKED OUT THAT TIME.

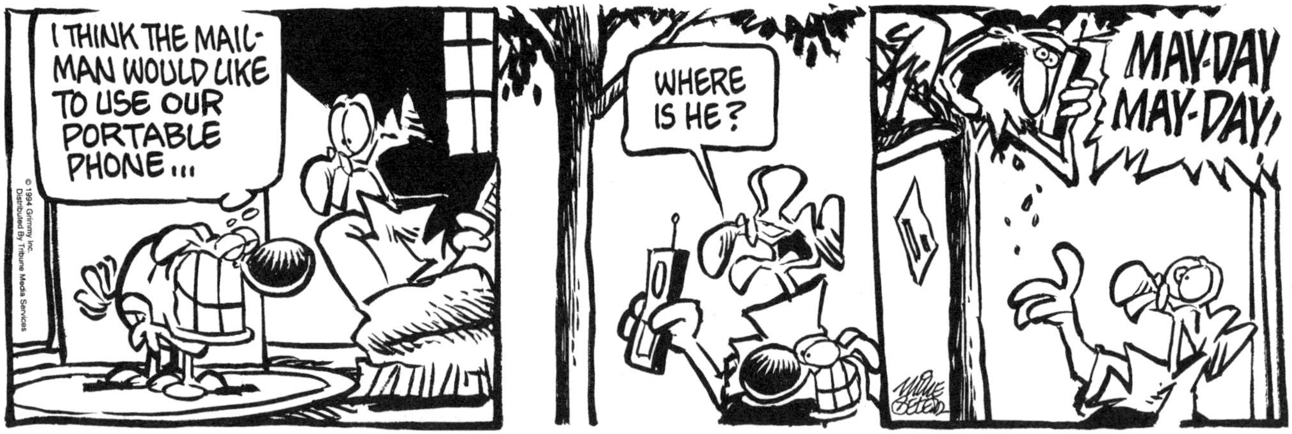
I THINK THE MAIL-MAN WOULD LIKE TO USE OUR PORTABLE PHONE...
© 1994 Grimmy Inc.
Distributed By Tribune Media Services
WHERE IS HE?
MAY-DAY MAY-DAY!

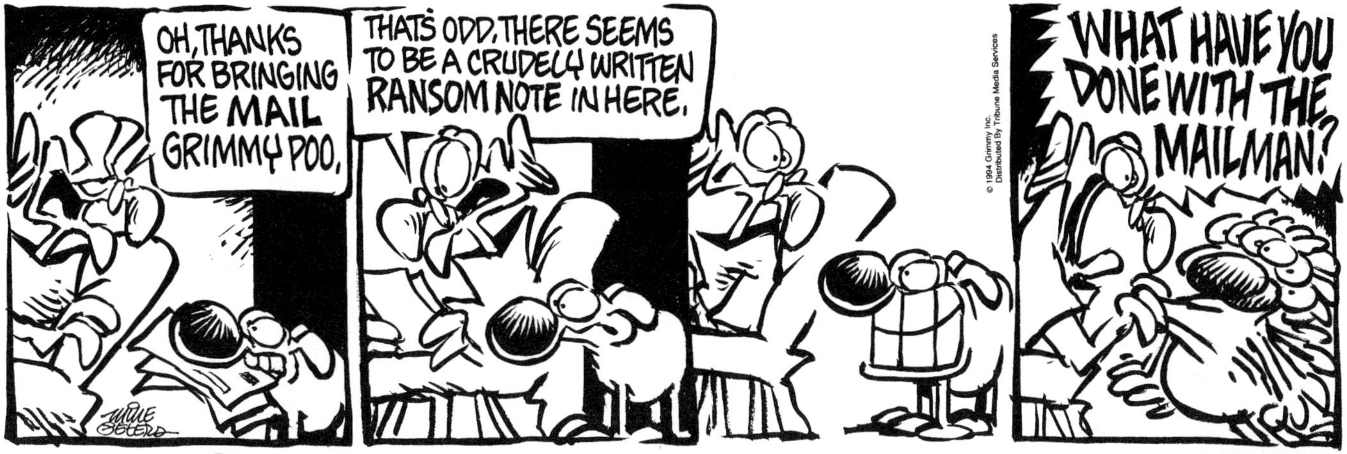
OH, THANKS FOR BRINGING THE MAIL GRIMMY POO.
THATS ODD, THERE SEEMS TO BE A CRUDELY WRITTEN RANSOM NOTE IN HERE.
© 1994 Grimmy Inc.
Distributed By Tribune Media Services
WHAT HAVE YOU DONE WITH THE MAILMAN?

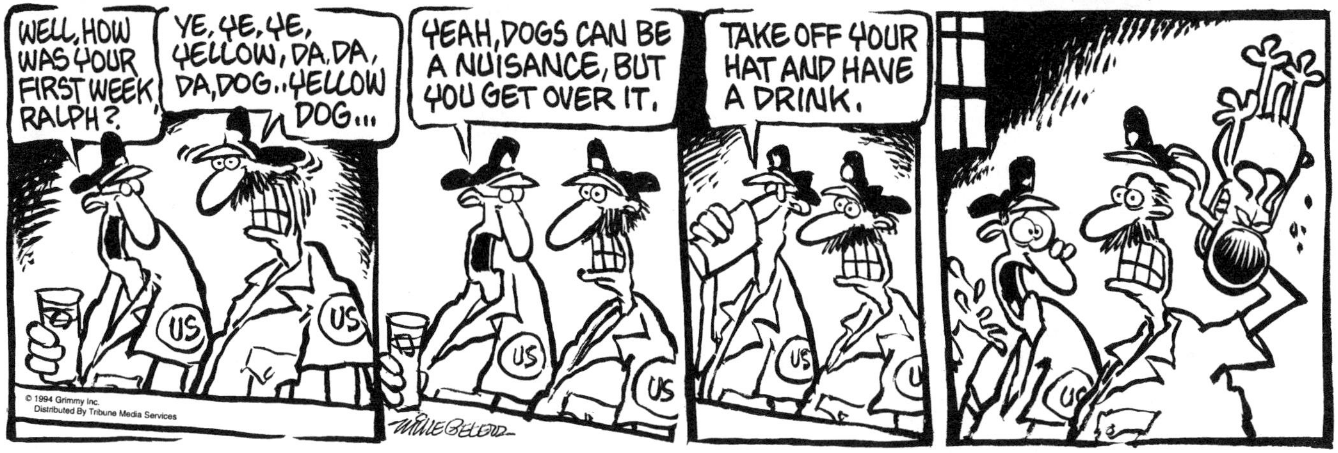
WELL, HOW WAS YOUR FIRST WEEK, RALPH?
YE, YE, YE, YELLOW, DA, DA, DA, DOG.. YELLOW DOG...
© 1994 Grimmy Inc.
Distributed By Tribune Media Services
YEAH, DOGS CAN BE A NUISANCE, BUT YOU GET OVER IT.
TAKE OFF YOUR HAT AND HAVE A DRINK.

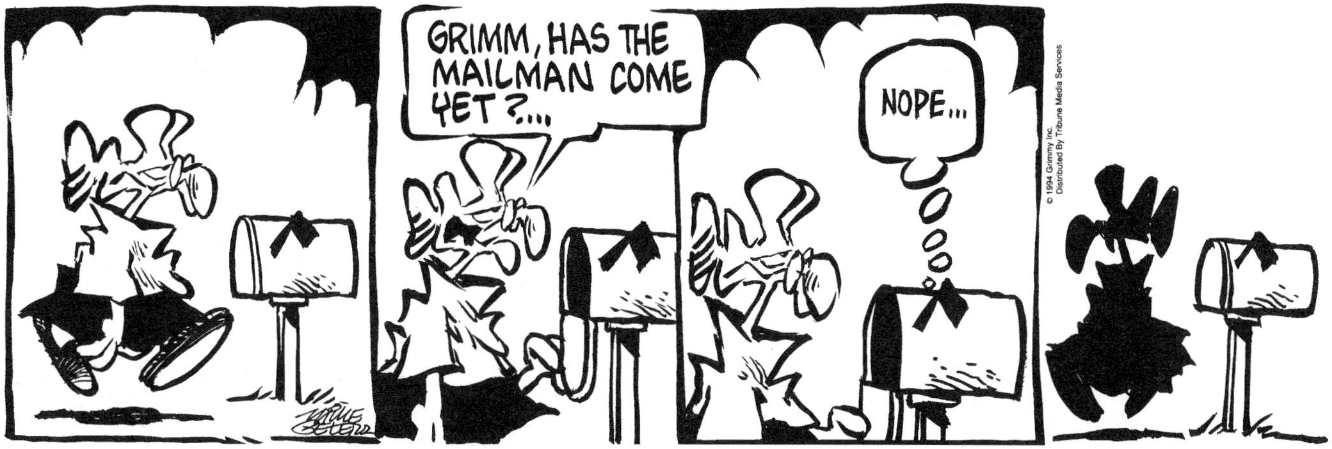
GRIMM, HAS THE MAILMAN COME YET?...
NOPE...
© 1994 Grimmy Inc.
Distributed By Tribune Media Services

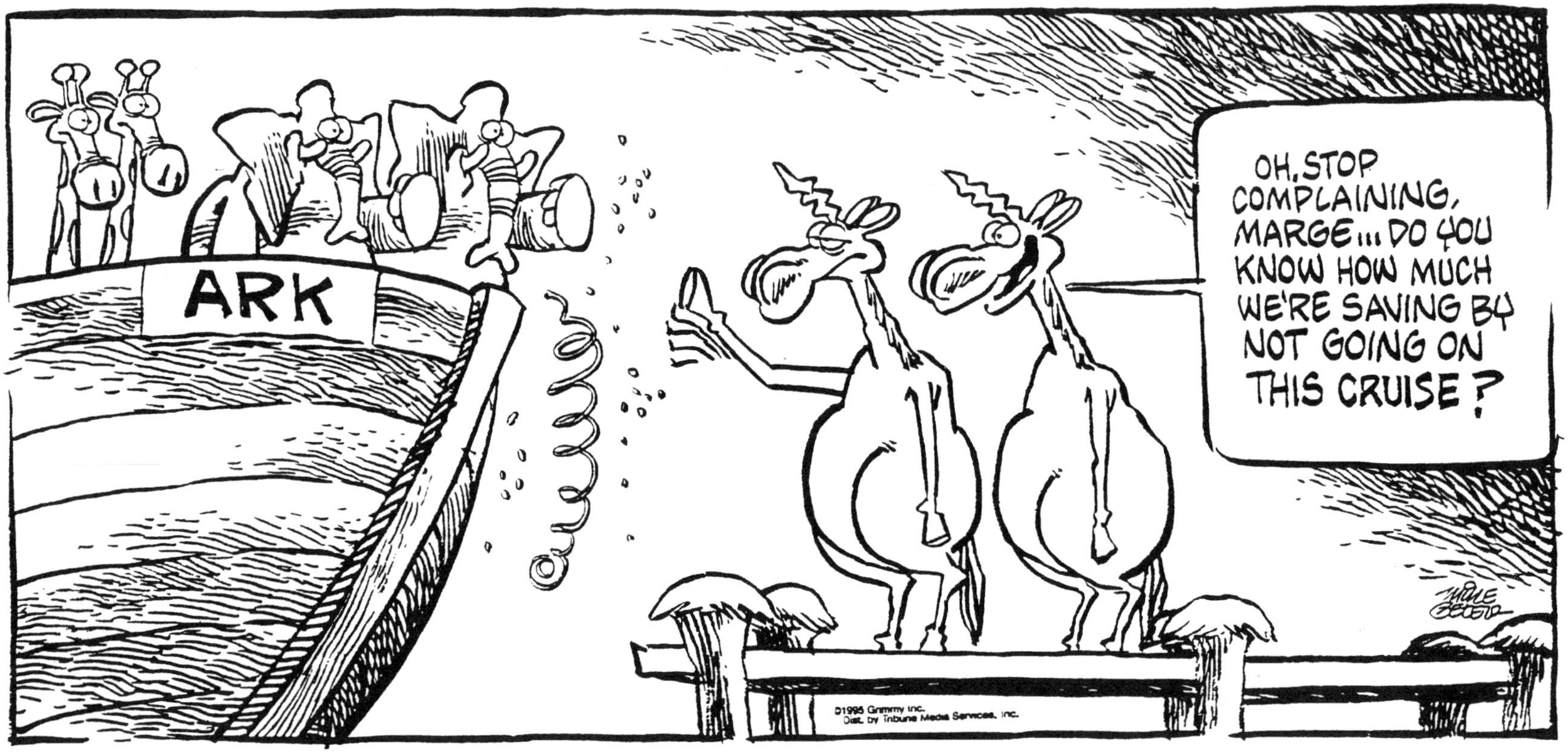
ARK
OH, STOP COMPLAINING, MARGE... DO YOU KNOW HOW MUCH WE'RE SAVING BY NOT GOING ON THIS CRUISE?
©1995 Grimmy Inc.
Dist. by Tribune Media Services, Inc.

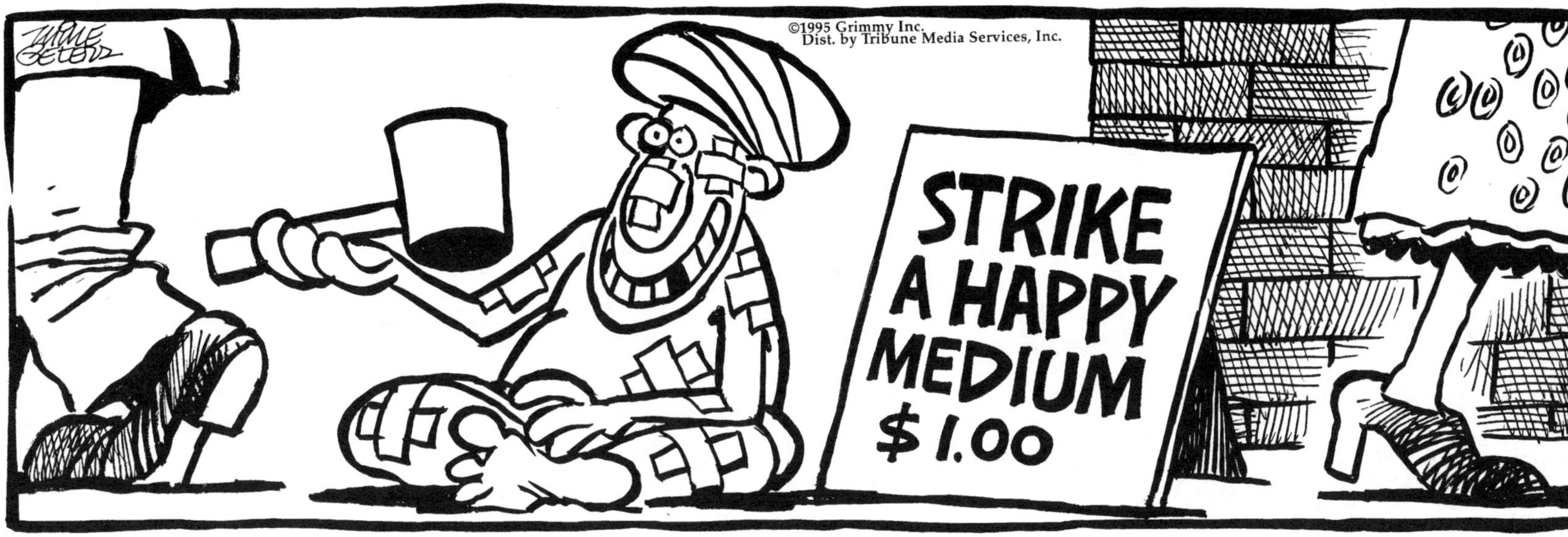
©1995 Grimmy Inc.
Dist. by Tribune Media Services, Inc.
STRIKE A HAPPY MEDIUM $1.00

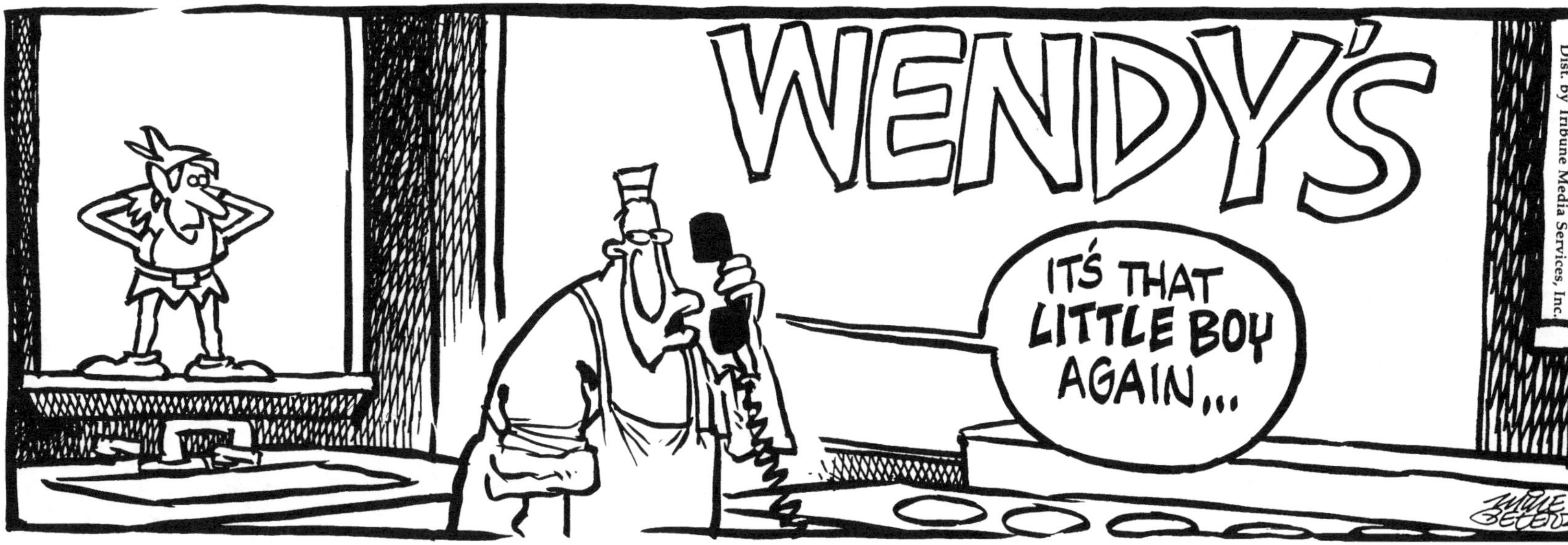
WENDY'S
©1995 Grimmy Inc.
Dist. by Tribune Media Services, Inc.
IT'S THAT LITTLE BOY AGAIN...

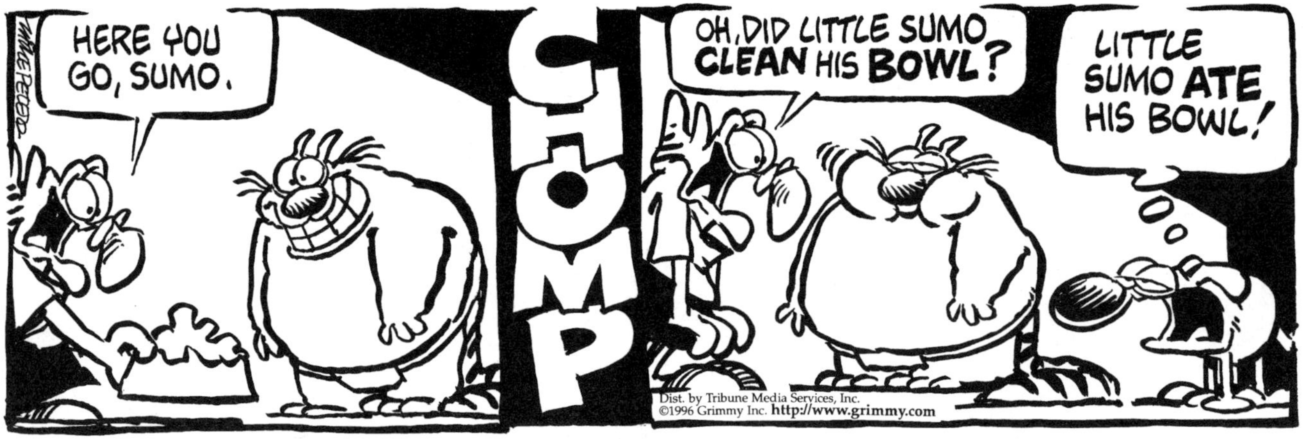
HERE YOU GO, SUMO.
CHOMP
OH, DID LITTLE SUMO CLEAN HIS BOWL?
LITTLE SUMO ATE HIS BOWL!
Dist. by Tribune Media Services, Inc.
©1996 Grimmy Inc. http://www.grimmy.com

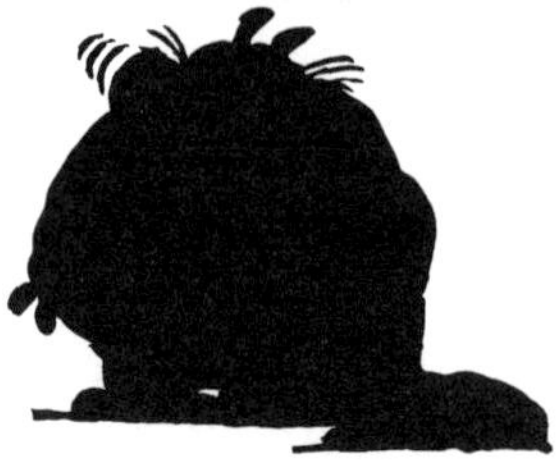

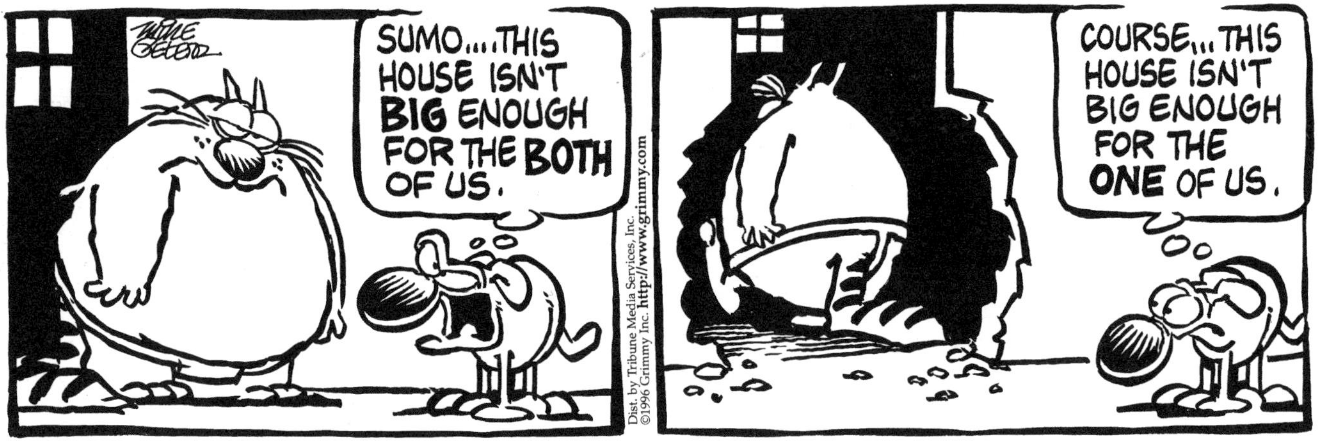
SUMO.... THIS HOUSE ISN'T BIG ENOUGH FOR THE BOTH OF US.
Dist. by Tribune Media Services, Inc.
©1996 Grimmy Inc. http://www.grimmy.com
COURSE... THIS HOUSE ISN'T BIG ENOUGH FOR THE ONE OF US.

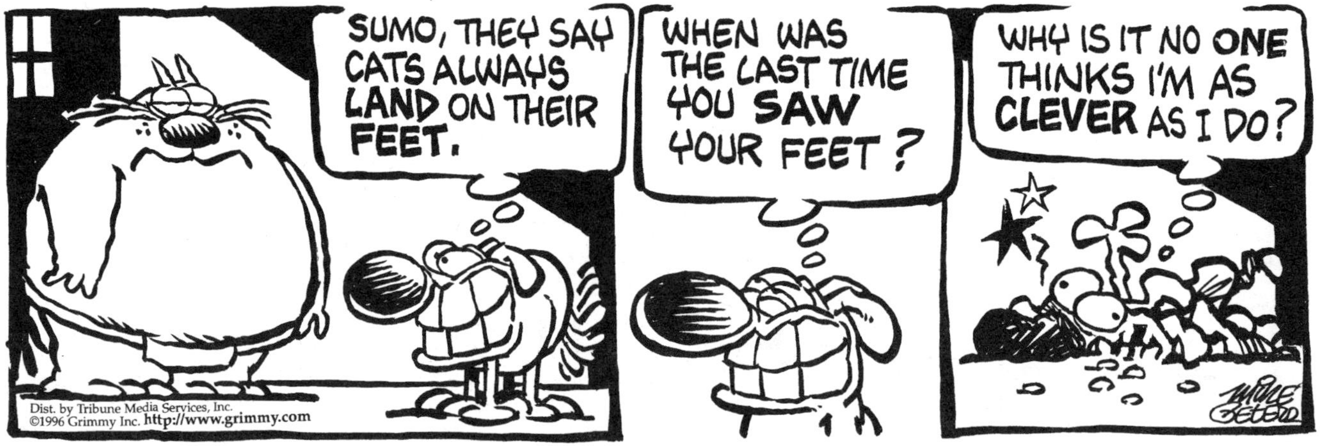
SUMO, THEY SAY CATS ALWAYS LAND ON THEIR FEET.
WHEN WAS THE LAST TIME YOU SAW YOUR FEET?
WHY IS IT NO ONE THINKS I'M AS CLEVER AS I DO?
Dist. by Tribune Media Services, Inc.
©1996 Grimmy Inc. http://www.grimmy.com

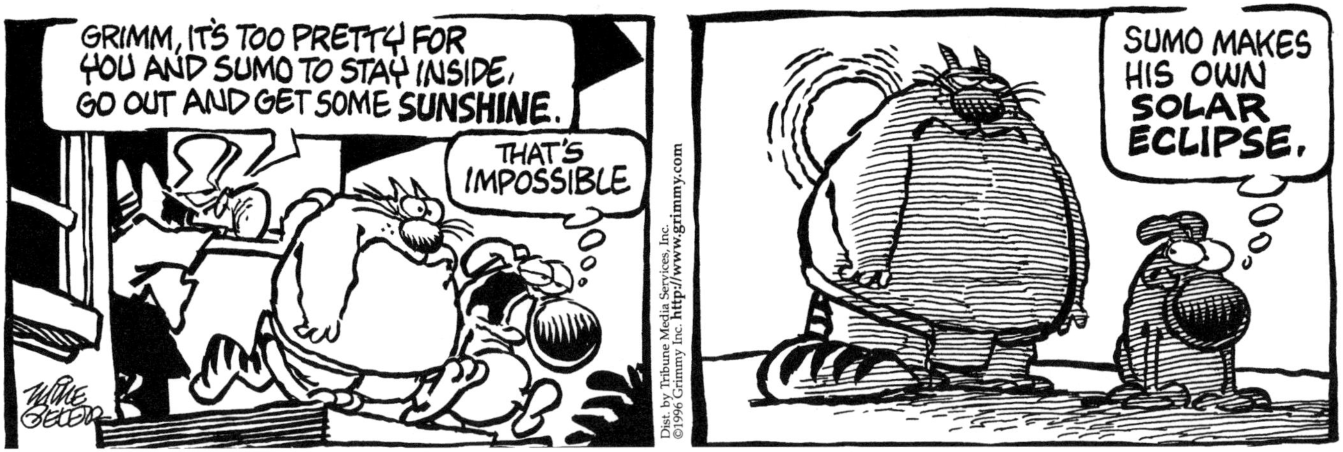
GRIMM, IT'S TOO PRETTY FOR YOU AND SUMO TO STAY INSIDE, GO OUT AND GET SOME SUNSHINE.
THAT'S IMPOSSIBLE
SUMO MAKES HIS OWN SOLAR ECLIPSE.

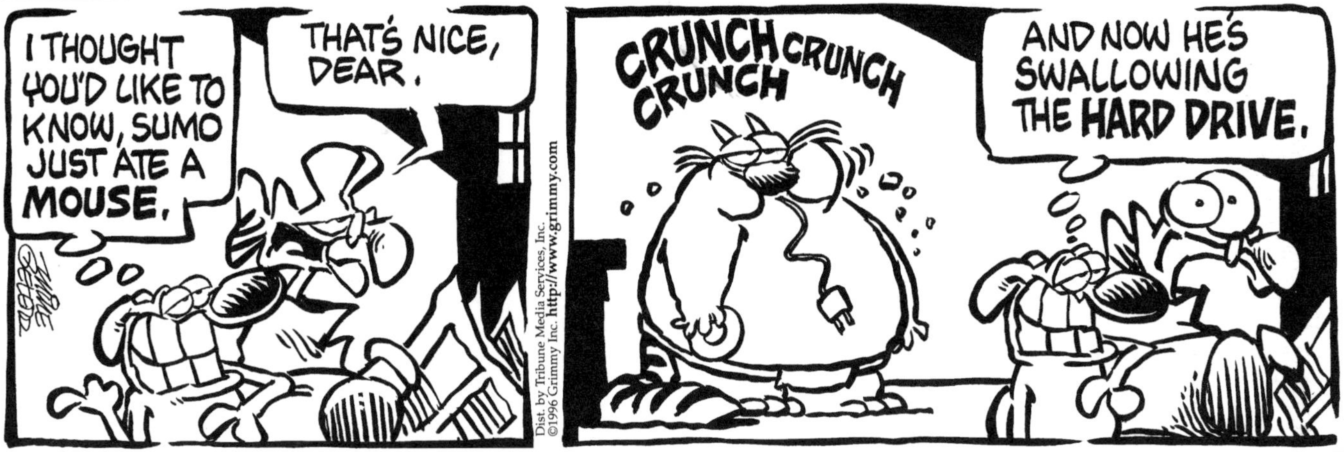
I THOUGHT YOU'D LIKE TO KNOW, SUMO JUST ATE A MOUSE.
THAT'S NICE, DEAR.
CRUNCH CRUNCH CRUNCH
AND NOW HE'S SWALLOWING THE HARD DRIVE.

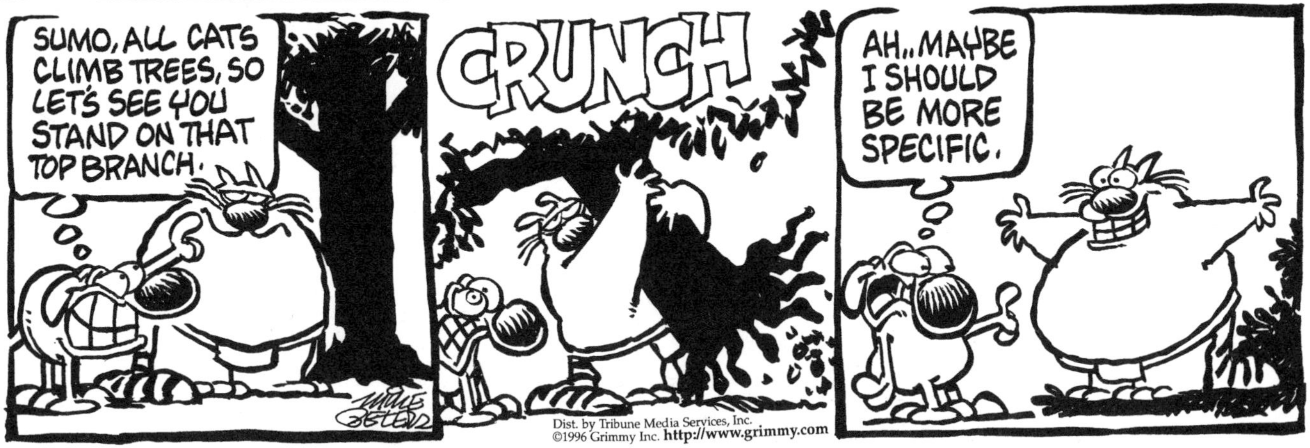
SUMO, ALL CATS CLIMB TREES, SO LET'S SEE YOU STAND ON THAT TOP BRANCH.
CRUNCH
AH.. MAYBE I SHOULD BE MORE SPECIFIC.

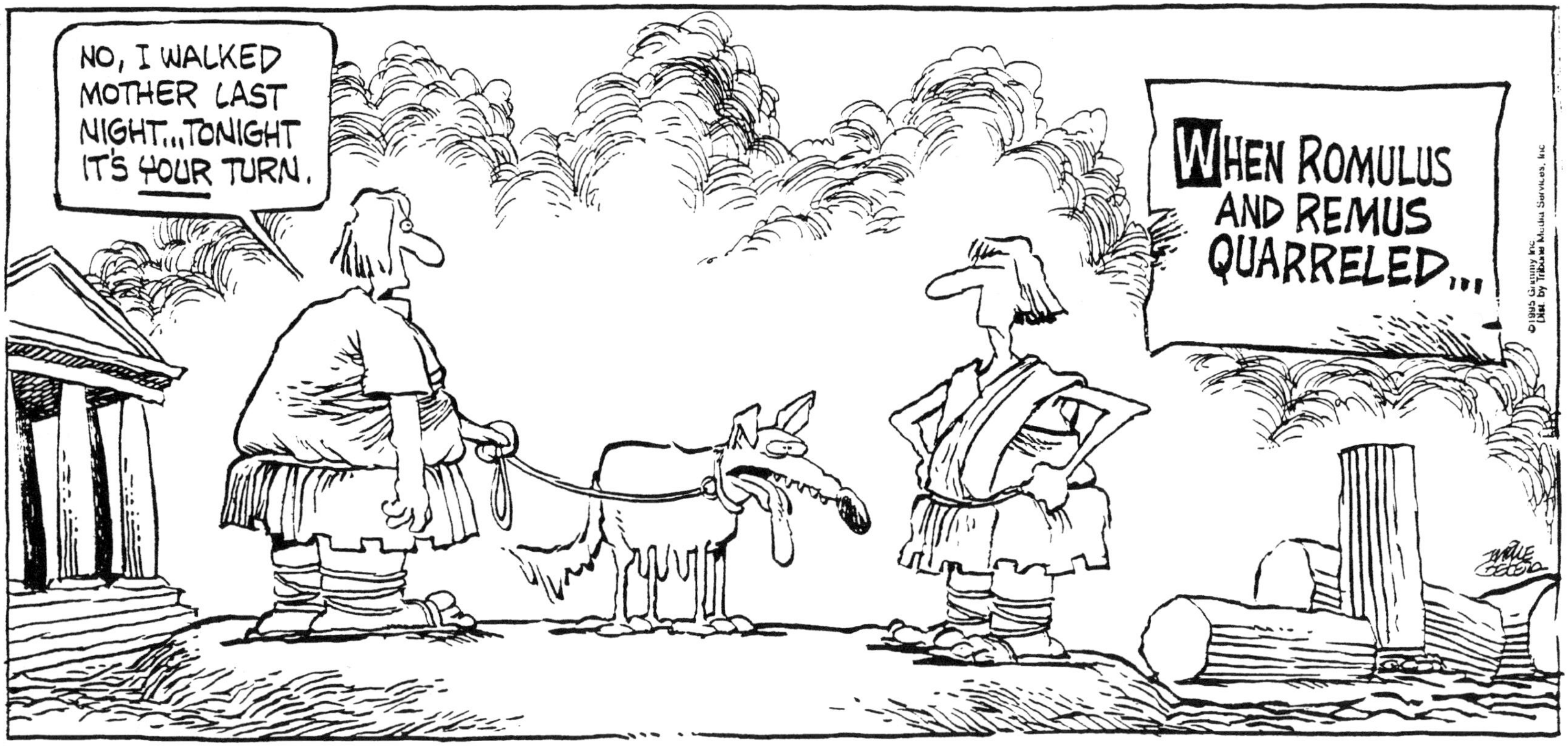
NO, I WALKED MOTHER LAST NIGHT...TONIGHT IT'S YOUR TURN.
WHEN ROMULUS AND REMUS QUARRELED...

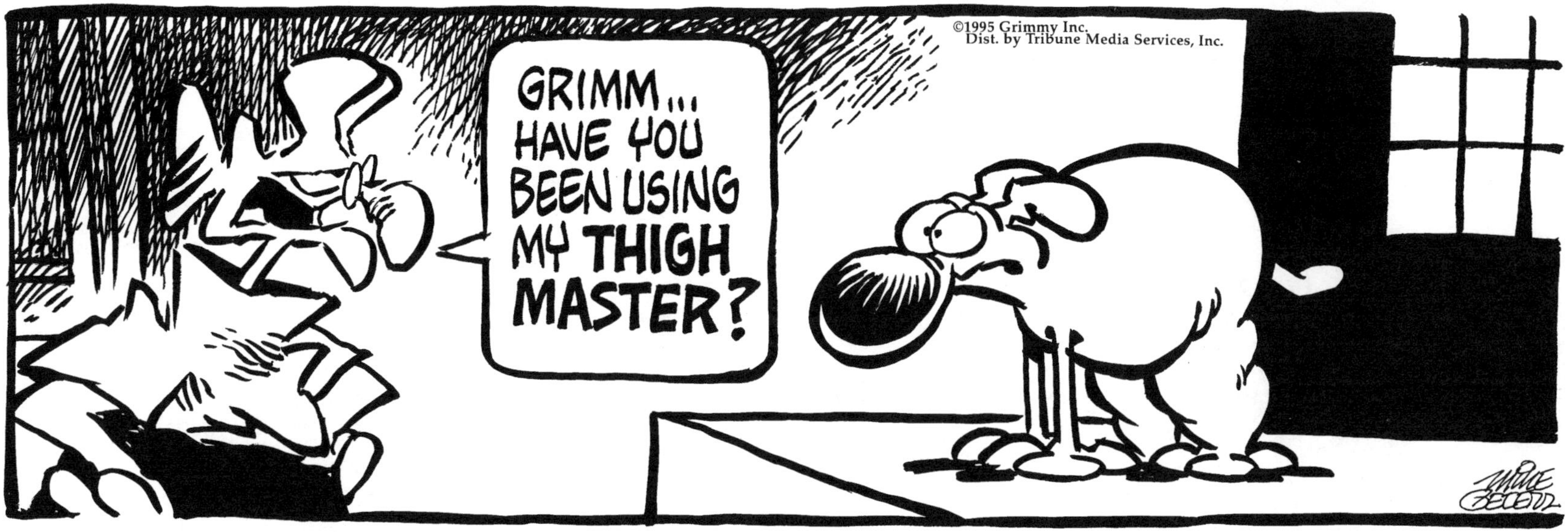
©1995 Grimmy Inc.
Dist. by Tribune Media Services, Inc.
GRIMM... HAVE YOU BEEN USING MY THIGH MASTER?

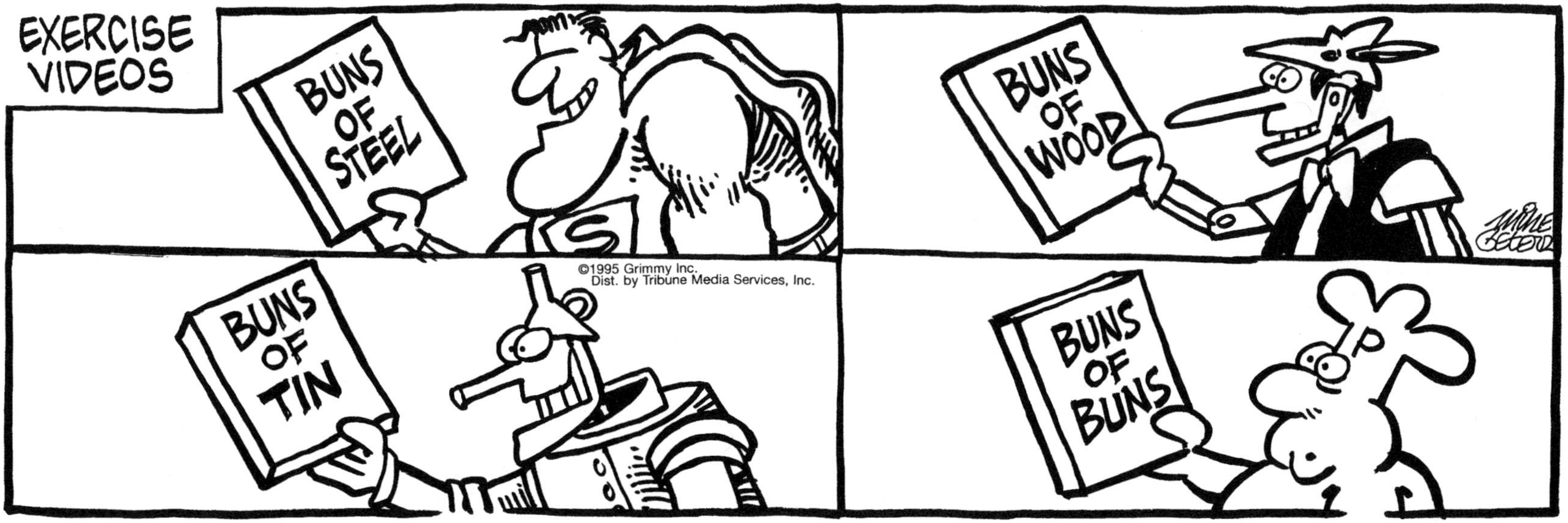
EXERCISE VIDEOS
BUNS OF STEEL
BUNS OF WOOD
©1995 Grimmy Inc.
Dist. by Tribune Media Services, Inc.
BUNS OF TIN
BUNS OF BUNS

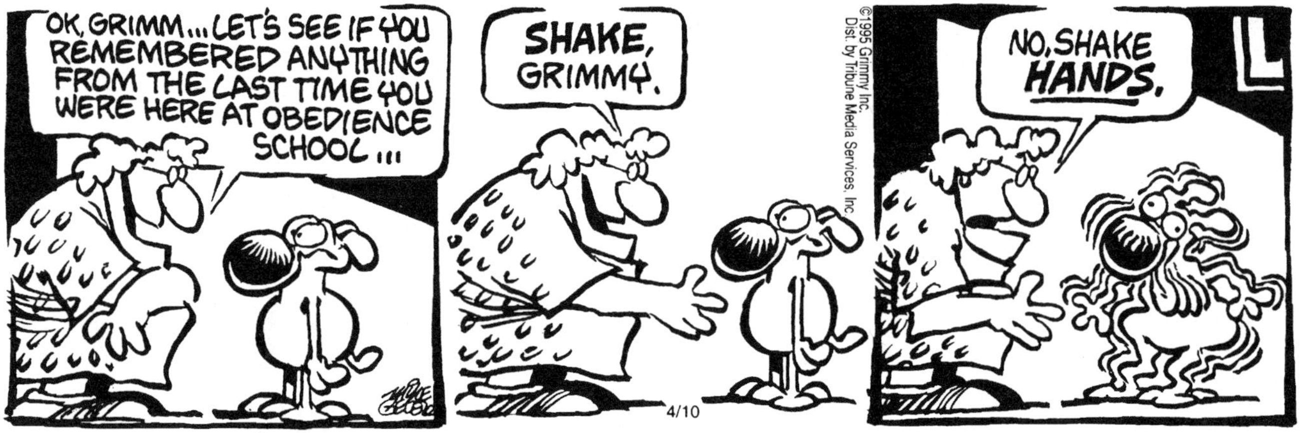
OK, GRIMM... LET'S SEE IF YOU REMEMBERED ANYTHING FROM THE LAST TIME YOU WERE HERE AT OBEDIENCE SCHOOL...
SHAKE, GRIMMY.
4/10
©1995 Grimmy Inc.
Dist. by Tribune Media Services, Inc.
NO, SHAKE HANDS.

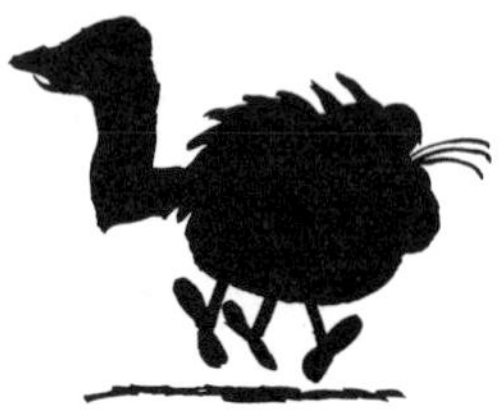

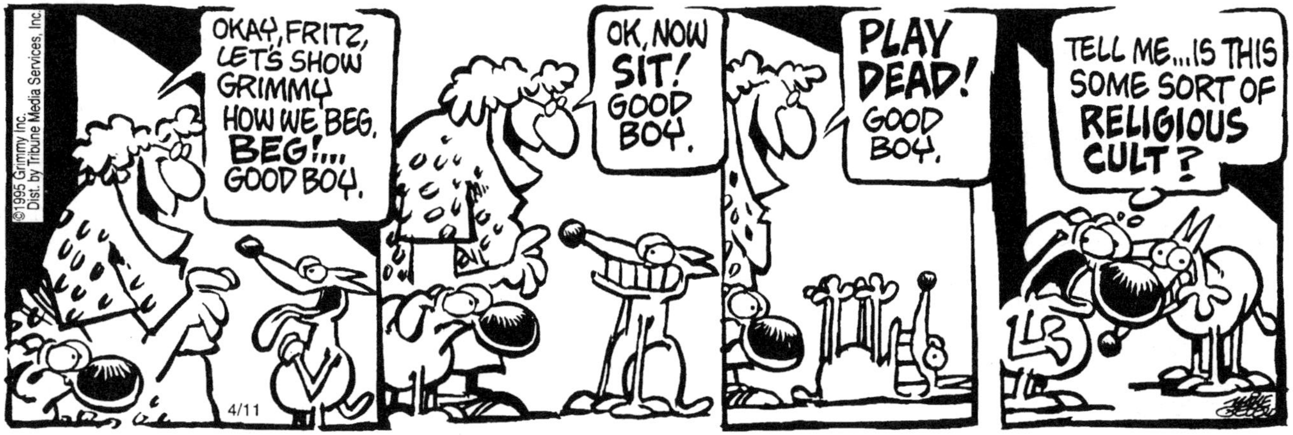
©1995 Grimmy Inc.
Dist. by Tribune Media Services, Inc.
OKAY, FRITZ, LET'S SHOW GRIMMY HOW WE BEG. BEG!... GOOD BOY.
4/11
OK, NOW SIT! GOOD BOY.
PLAY DEAD! GOOD BOY.
TELL ME... IS THIS SOME SORT OF RELIGIOUS CULT?

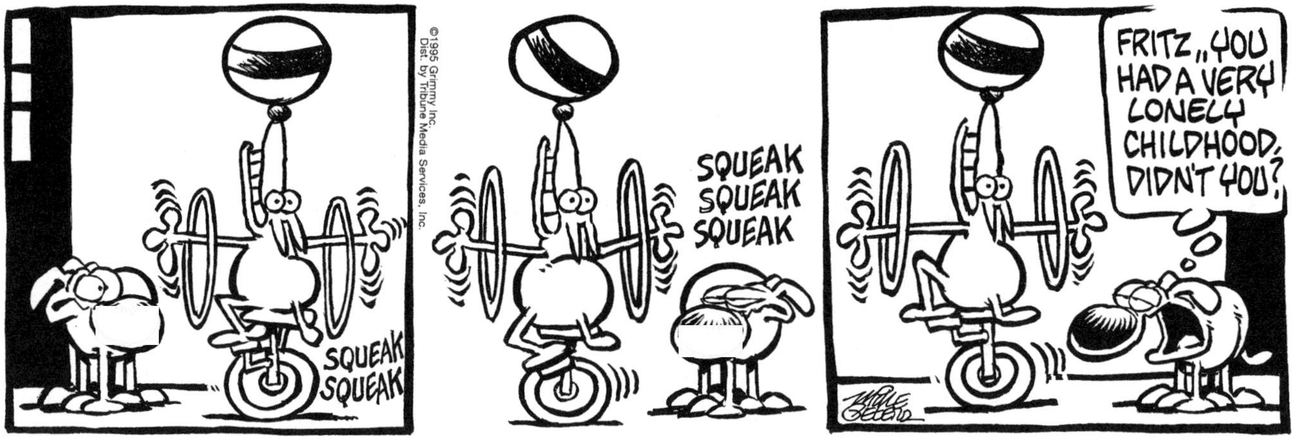
SQUEAK SQUEAK
©1995 Grimmy Inc.
Dist. by Tribune Media Services, Inc.
SQUEAK SQUEAK SQUEAK
FRITZ,, YOU HAD A VERY LONELY CHILDHOOD, DIDN'T YOU?

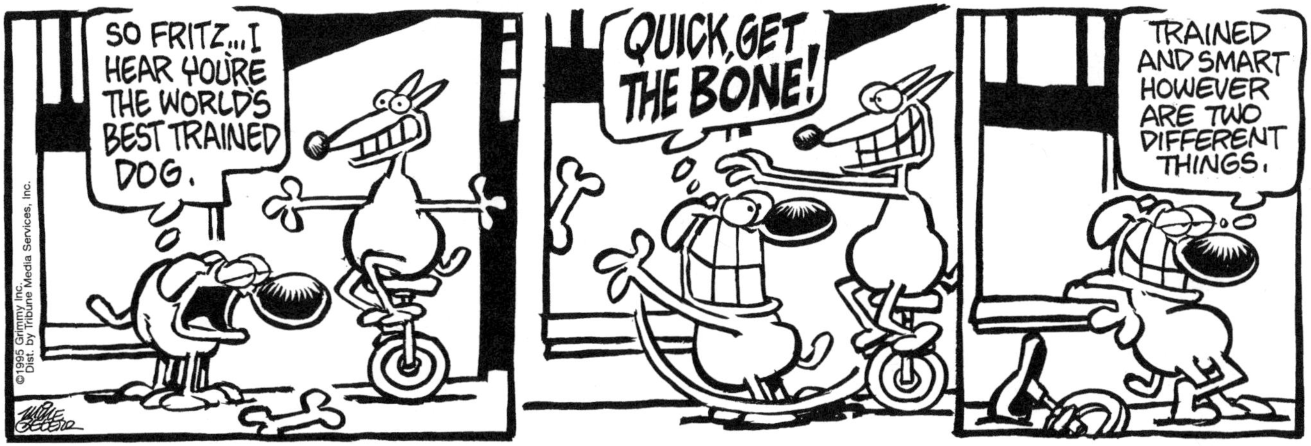
SO FRITZ... I HEAR YOU'RE THE WORLD'S BEST TRAINED DOG.
©1995 Grimmy Inc. Dist. by Tribune Media Services, Inc.
QUICK, GET THE BONE!
TRAINED AND SMART HOWEVER ARE TWO DIFFERENT THINGS.

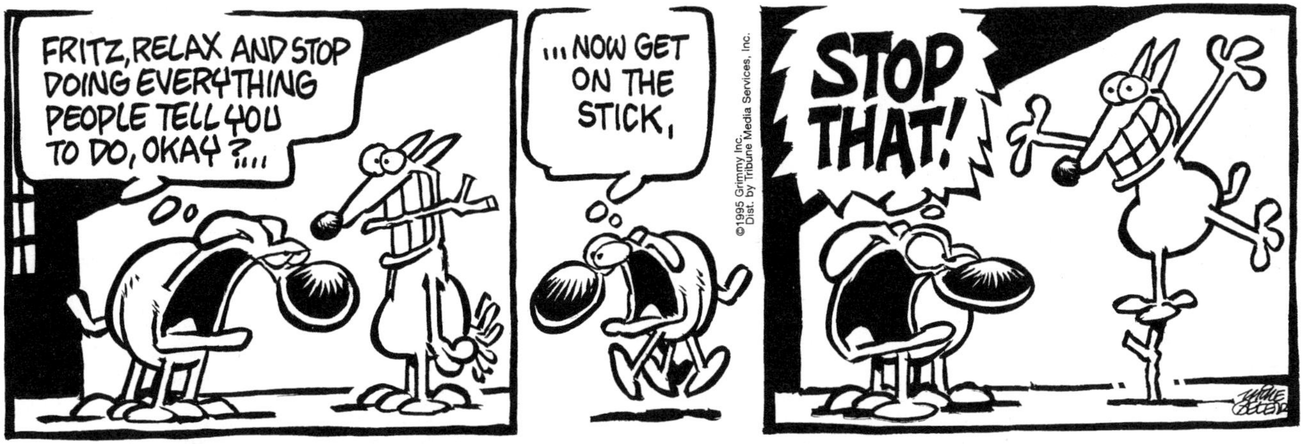
FRITZ, RELAX AND STOP DOING EVERYTHING PEOPLE TELL YOU TO DO, OKAY?...
...NOW GET ON THE STICK.
©1995 Grimmy Inc. Dist. by Tribune Media Services, Inc.
STOP THAT!

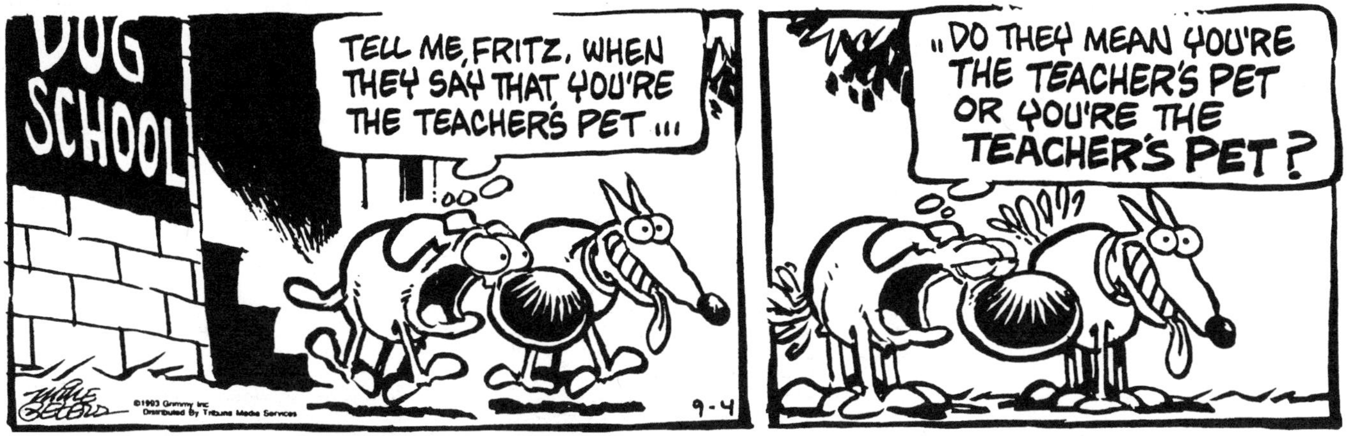
DOG SCHOOL
TELL ME, FRITZ, WHEN THEY SAY THAT YOU'RE THE TEACHER'S PET...
©1993 Grimmy Inc Distributed By Tribune Media Services
9-4
...DO THEY MEAN YOU'RE THE TEACHER'S PET OR YOU'RE THE TEACHER'S PET?

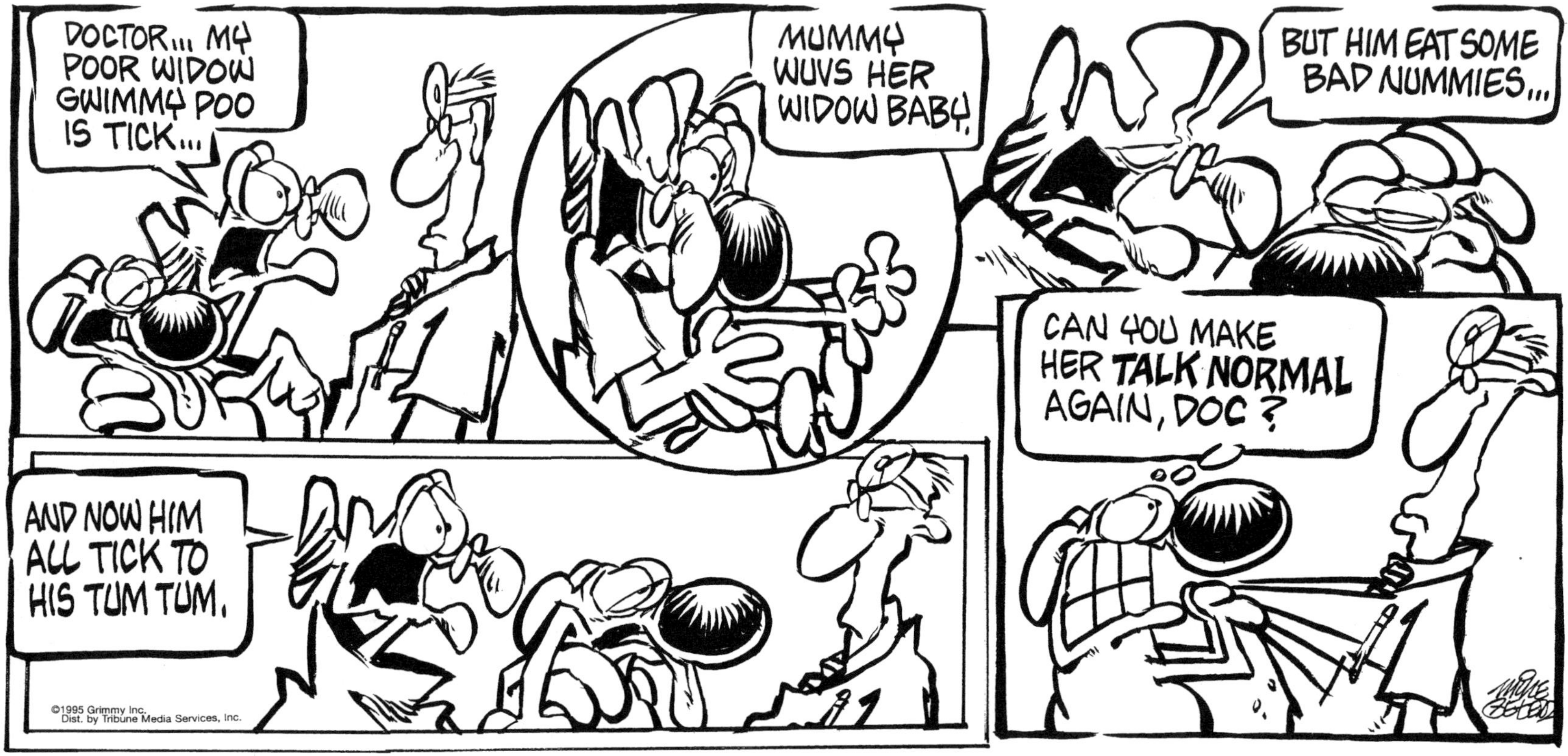

DOCTOR... MY POOR WIDOW GWIMMY POO IS TICK...
MUMMY WUVS HER WIDOW BABY.
BUT HIM EAT SOME BAD NUMMIES...
AND NOW HIM ALL TICK TO HIS TUM TUM.
CAN YOU MAKE HER TALK NORMAL AGAIN, DOC?
©1995 Grimmy Inc.
Dist. by Tribune Media Services, Inc.

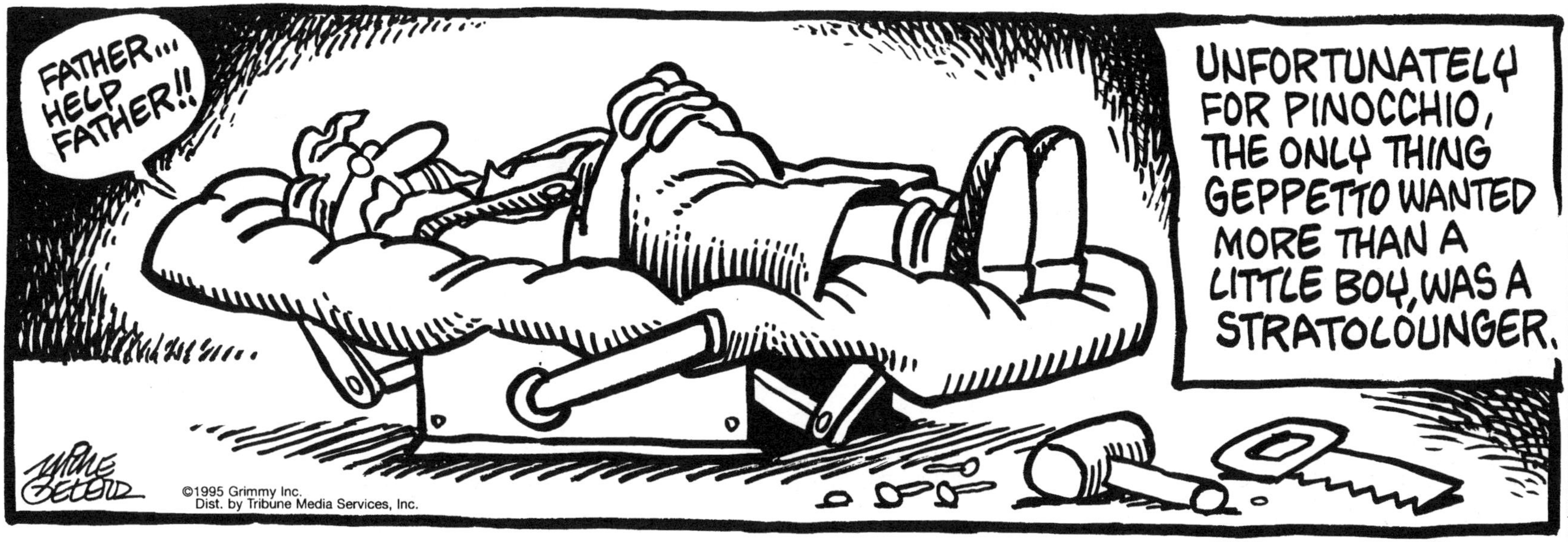
FATHER... HELP FATHER!!
UNFORTUNATELY FOR PINOCCHIO, THE ONLY THING GEPPETTO WANTED MORE THAN A LITTLE BOY, WAS A STRATOLOUNGER.
©1995 Grimmy Inc.
Dist. by Tribune Media Services, Inc.

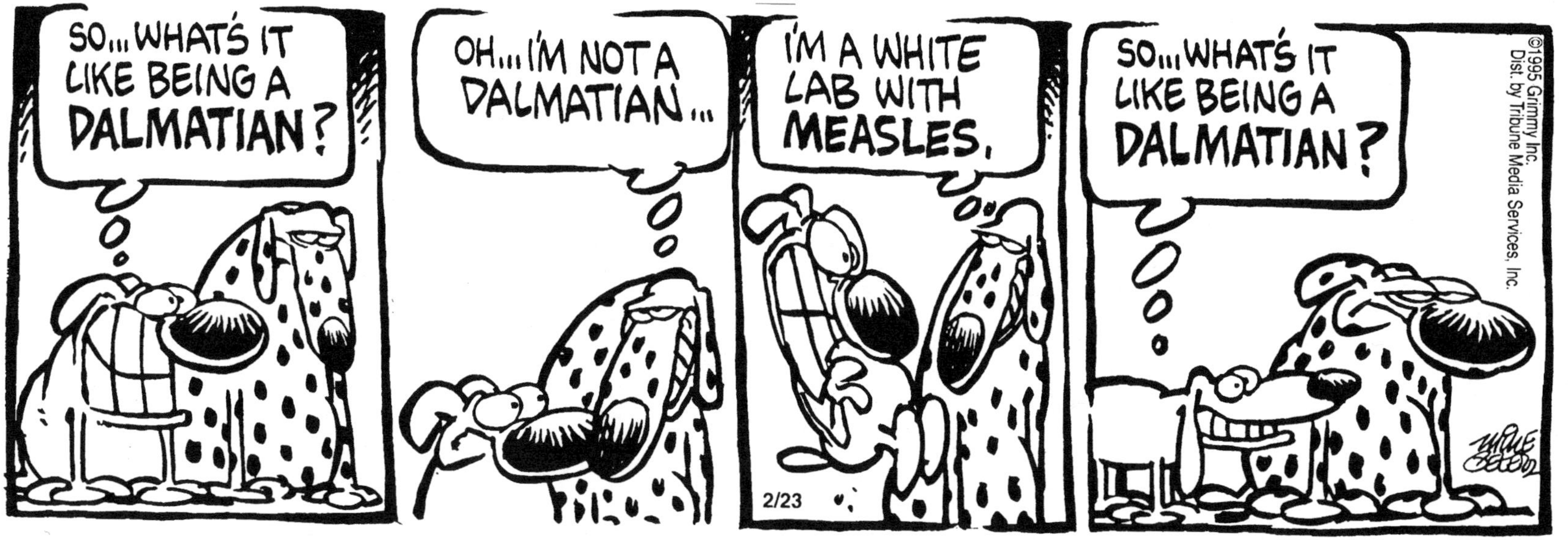
SO... WHAT'S IT LIKE BEING A DALMATIAN?
OH... I'M NOT A DALMATIAN...
I'M A WHITE LAB WITH MEASLES.
2/23
SO... WHAT'S IT LIKE BEING A DALMATIAN?
©1995 Grimmy Inc.
Dist. by Tribune Media Services, Inc.

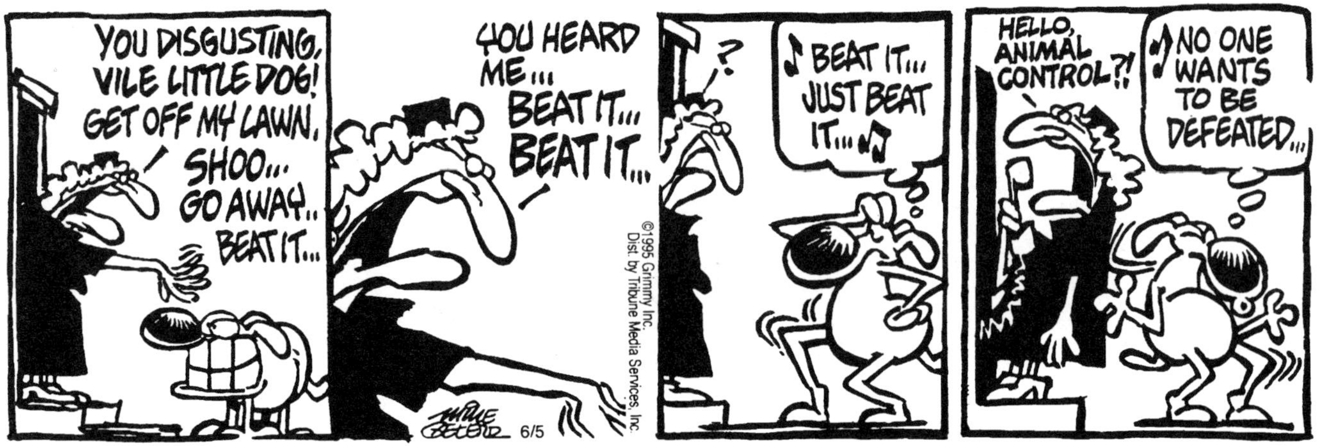

YOU DISGUSTING, VILE LITTLE DOG! GET OFF MY LAWN.
SHOO... GO AWAY.. BEAT IT...
YOU HEARD ME... BEAT IT... BEAT IT...
©1995 Grimmy Inc. Dist. by Tribune Media Services, Inc.
MIKE PETERS 6/5
?
♪ BEAT IT... JUST BEAT IT... ♫
HELLO, ANIMAL CONTROL?!
♪ NO ONE WANTS TO BE DEFEATED...

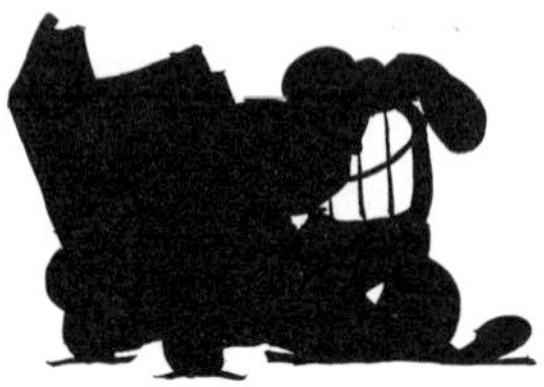

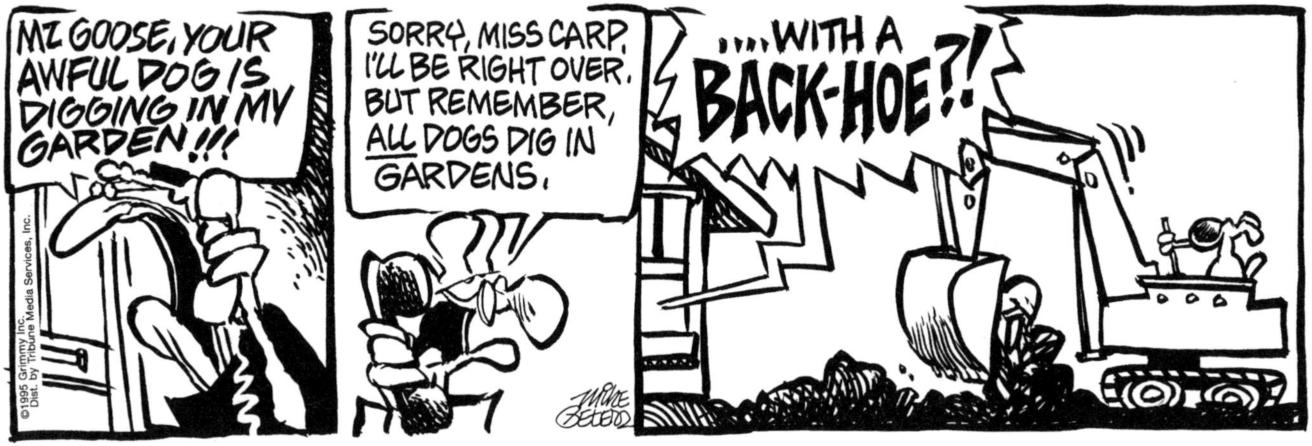

MZ GOOSE, YOUR AWFUL DOG IS DIGGING IN MY GARDEN!!!
©1995 Grimmy Inc. Dist. by Tribune Media Services, Inc.
SORRY, MISS CARP, I'LL BE RIGHT OVER. BUT REMEMBER, ALL DOGS DIG IN GARDENS.
MIKE PETERS
....WITH A BACK-HOE?!

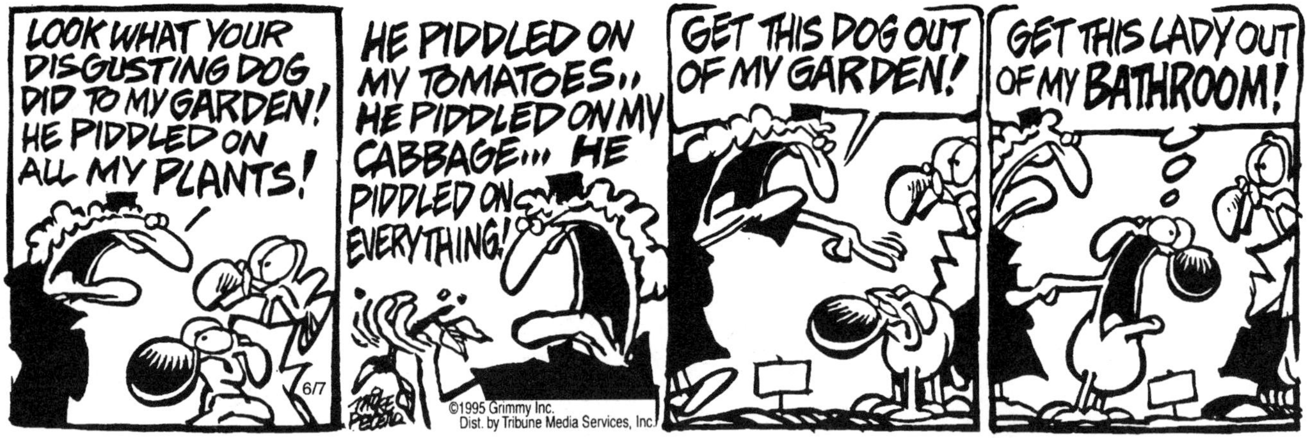

LOOK WHAT YOUR DISGUSTING DOG DID TO MY GARDEN! HE PIDDLED ON ALL MY PLANTS!
6/7
HE PIDDLED ON MY TOMATOES.. HE PIDDLED ON MY CABBAGE... HE PIDDLED ON EVERYTHING!
MIKE PETERS
©1995 Grimmy Inc. Dist. by Tribune Media Services, Inc.
GET THIS DOG OUT OF MY GARDEN!
GET THIS LADY OUT OF MY BATHROOM!

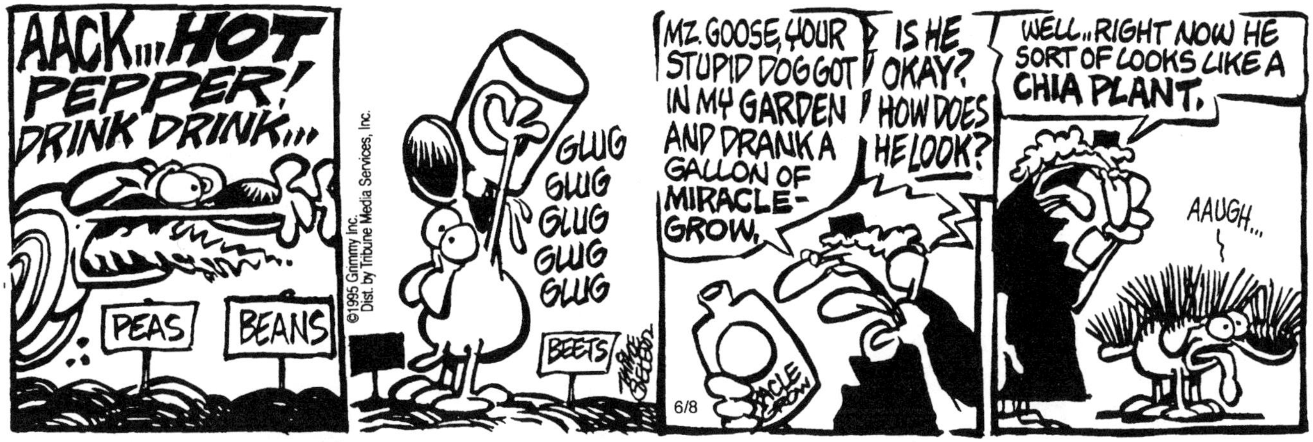
AACK... HOT PEPPER! DRINK DRINK...
PEAS
BEANS
©1995 Grimmy Inc. Dist. by Tribune Media Services, Inc.
GLUG GLUG GLUG GLUG GLUG
BEETS
6/8
MZ. GOOSE, YOUR STUPID DOG GOT IN MY GARDEN AND DRANK A GALLON OF MIRACLE-GROW.
IS HE OKAY? HOW DOES HE LOOK?
WELL.. RIGHT NOW HE SORT OF LOOKS LIKE A CHIA PLANT.
AAUGH...

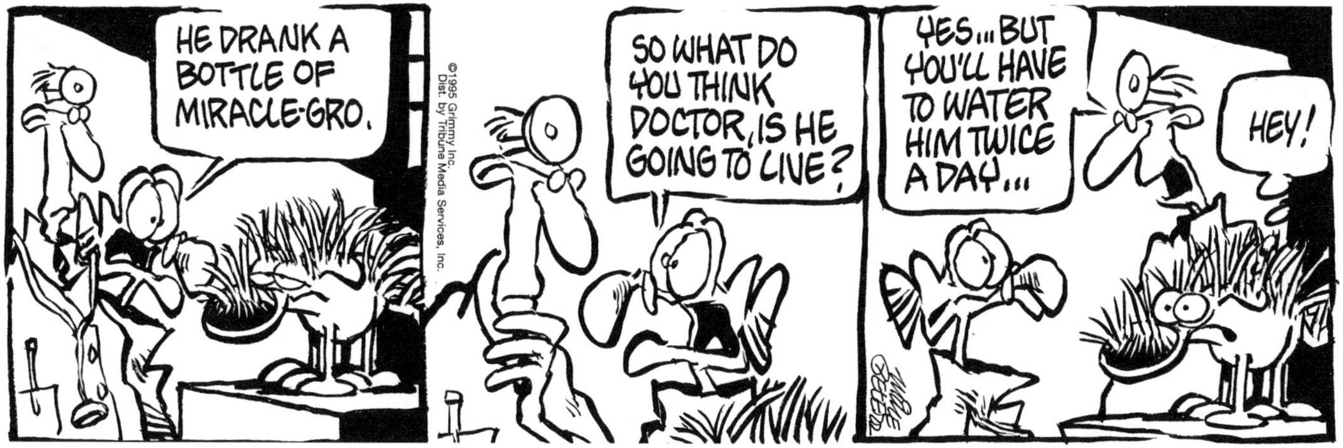
HE DRANK A BOTTLE OF MIRACLE-GRO.
©1995 Grimmy Inc. Dist. by Tribune Media Services, Inc.
SO WHAT DO YOU THINK DOCTOR, IS HE GOING TO LIVE?
YES... BUT YOU'LL HAVE TO WATER HIM TWICE A DAY...
HEY!

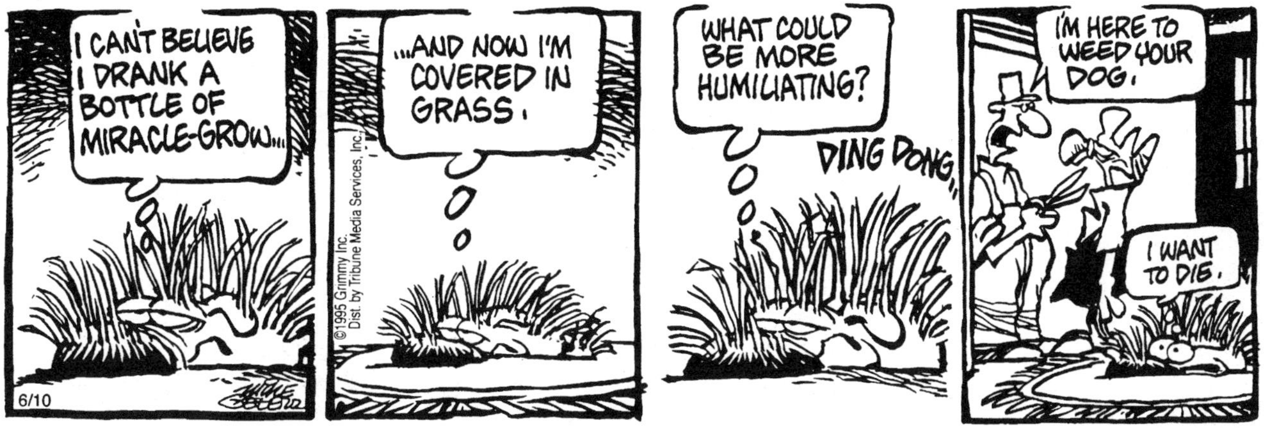
I CAN'T BELIEVE I DRANK A BOTTLE OF MIRACLE-GROW...
6/10
...AND NOW I'M COVERED IN GRASS.
©1995 Grimmy Inc. Dist. by Tribune Media Services, Inc.
WHAT COULD BE MORE HUMILIATING?
DING DONG..
I'M HERE TO WEED YOUR DOG.
I WANT TO DIE.

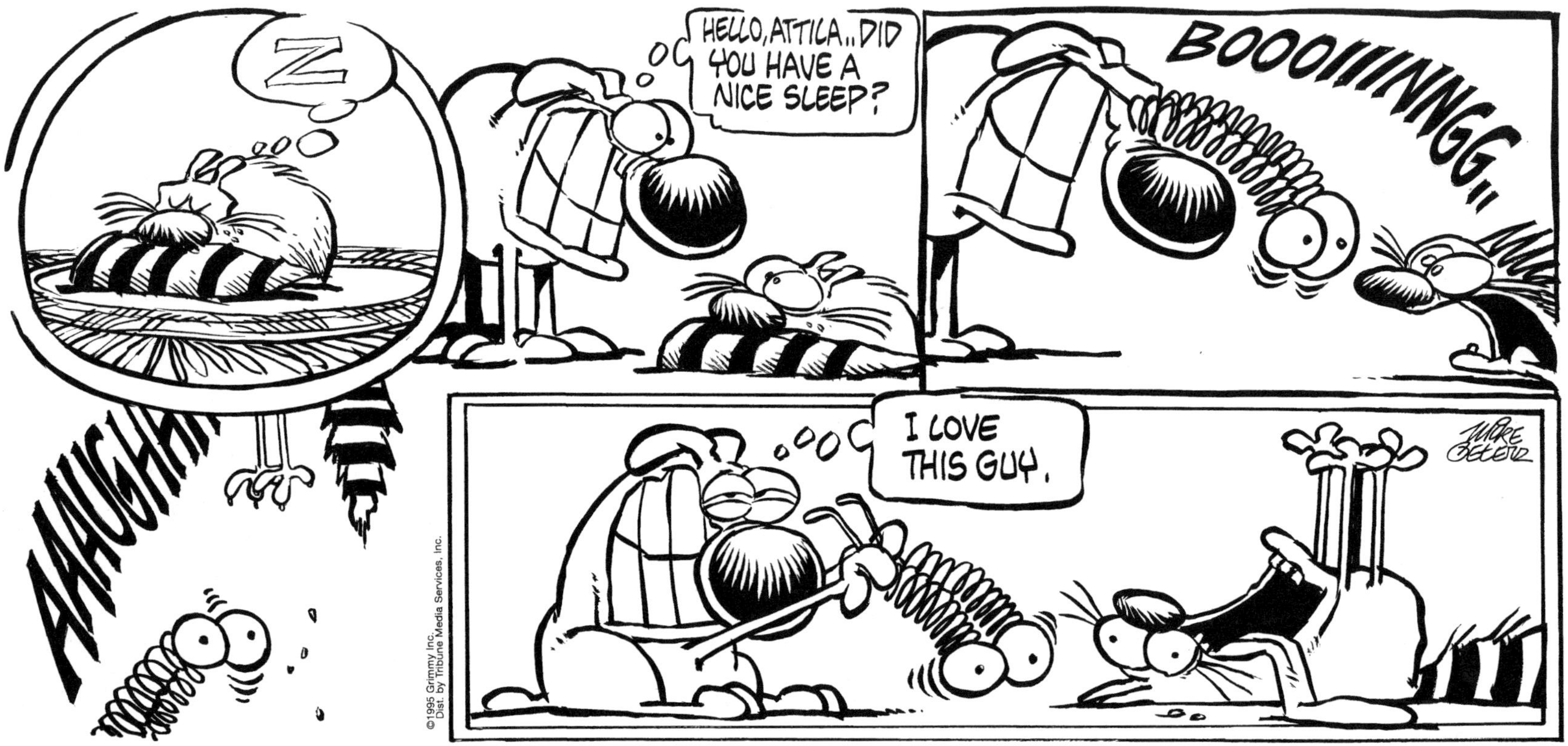
Z
HELLO, ATTICA.. DID YOU HAVE A NICE SLEEP?
BOOOIIIINNGG..
AAUGHH
I LOVE THIS GUY.
MIKE PETERS

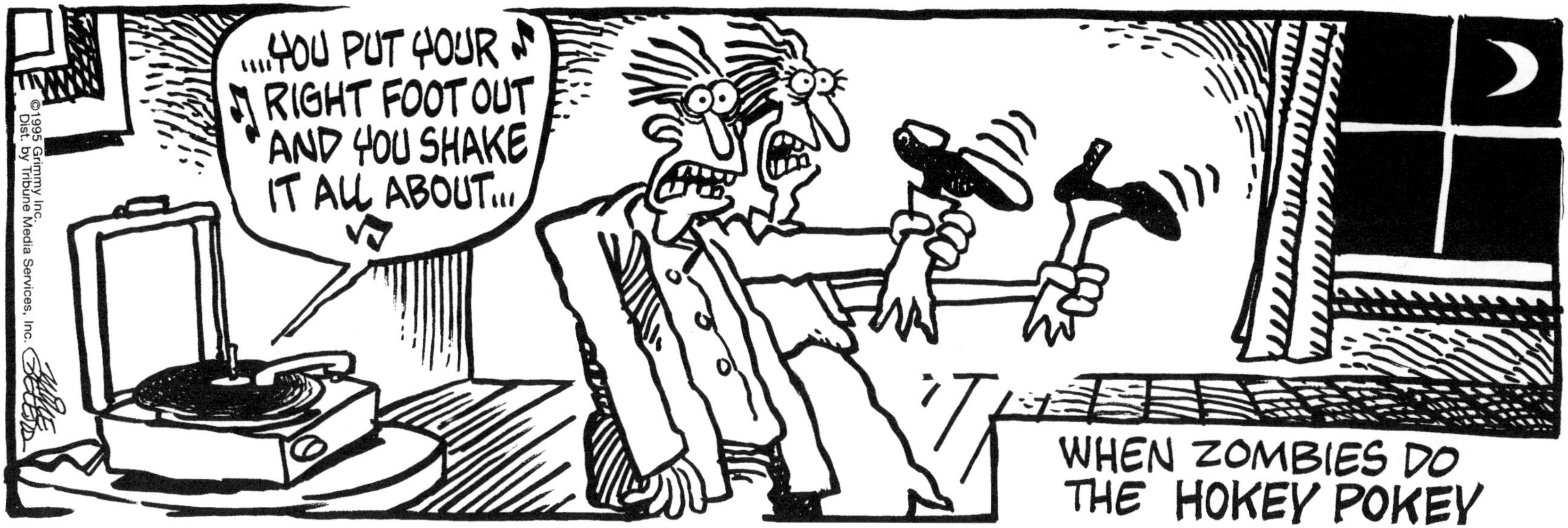
©1995 Grimmy Inc.
Dist. by Tribune Media Services, Inc.
....YOU PUT YOUR RIGHT FOOT OUT AND YOU SHAKE IT ALL ABOUT...
WHEN ZOMBIES DO THE HOKEY POKEY

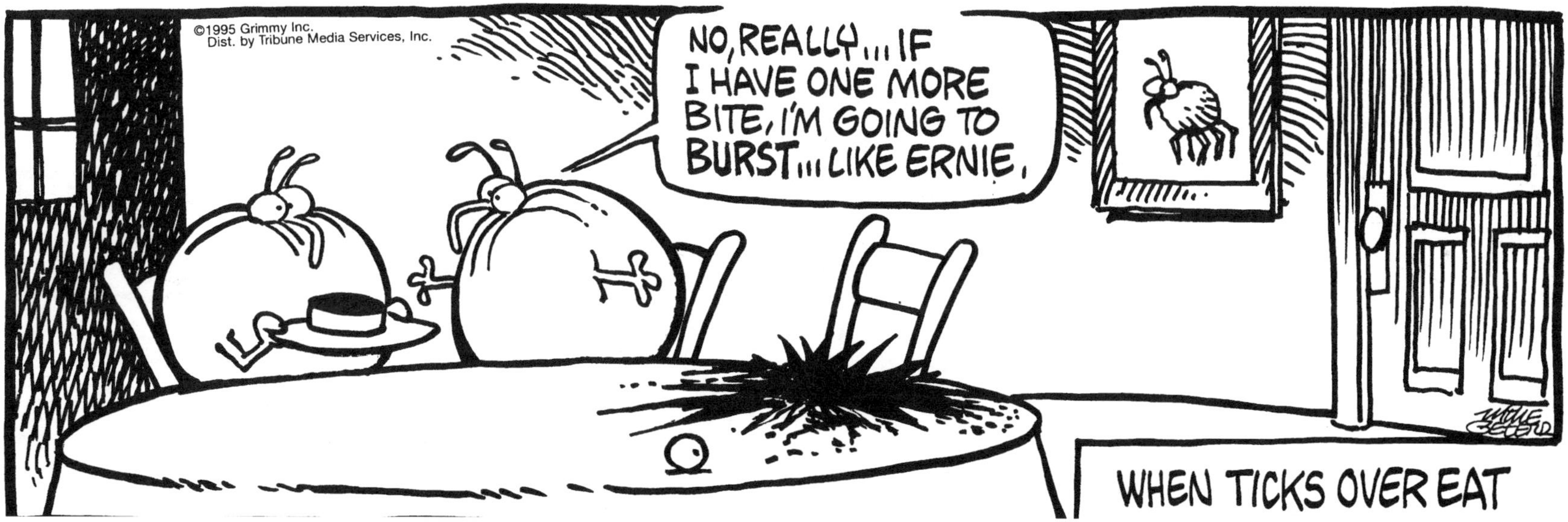
©1995 Grimmy Inc.
Dist. by Tribune Media Services, Inc.
NO, REALLY... IF I HAVE ONE MORE BITE, I'M GOING TO BURST... LIKE ERNIE.
WHEN TICKS OVER EAT

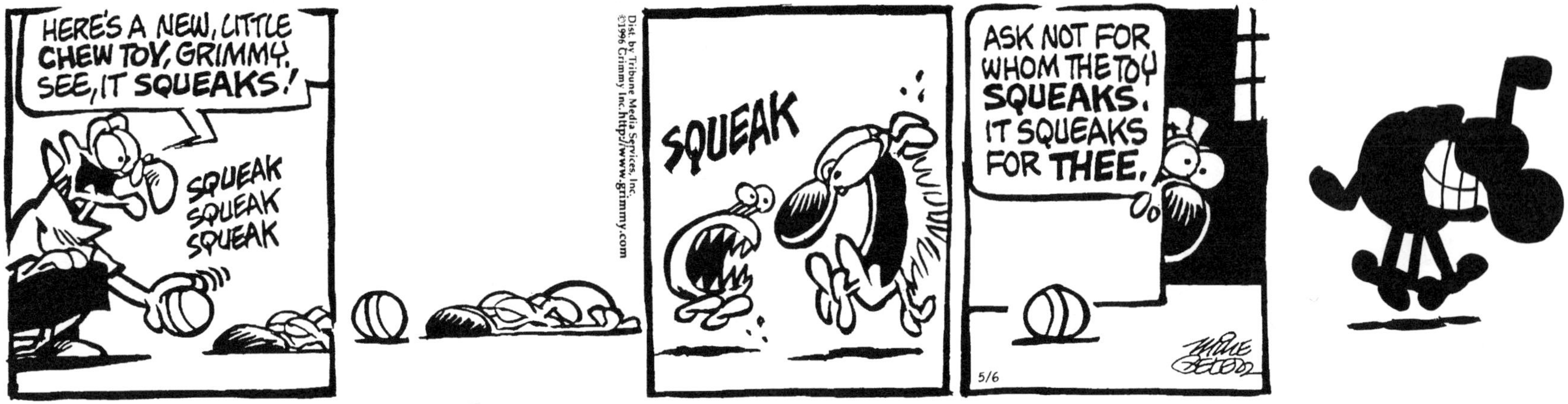
HERE'S A NEW, LITTLE CHEW TOY, GRIMMY. SEE, IT SQUEAKS!
SQUEAK SQUEAK SQUEAK
Dist. by Tribune Media Services, Inc. ©1996 Grimmy Inc. http://www.grimmy.com
SQUEAK
ASK NOT FOR WHOM THE TOY SQUEAKS. IT SQUEAKS FOR THEE.
5/6

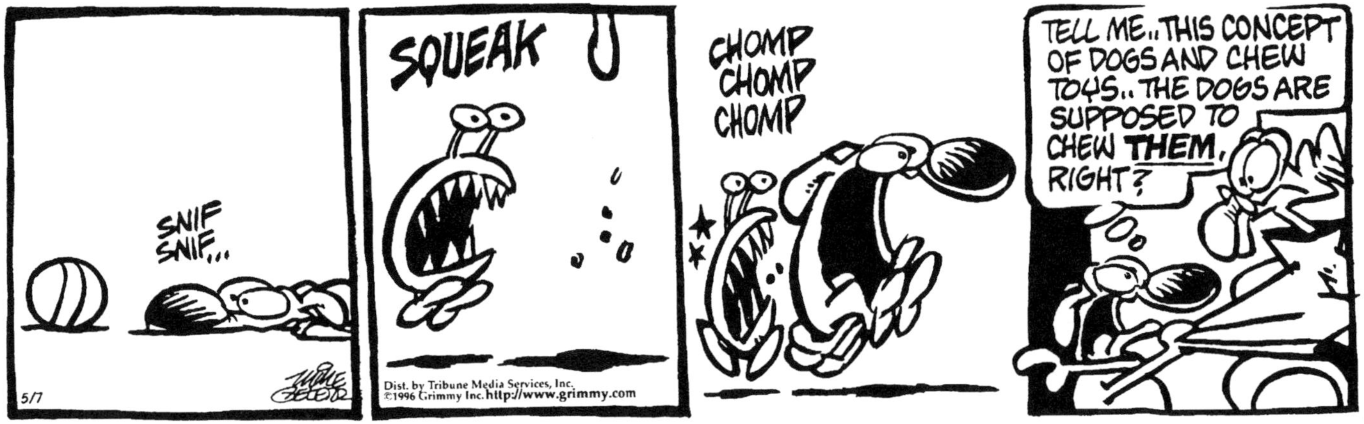
SNIF SNIF...
5/7
SQUEAK
Dist. by Tribune Media Services, Inc. ©1996 Grimmy Inc. http://www.grimmy.com
CHOMP CHOMP CHOMP
TELL ME.. THIS CONCEPT OF DOGS AND CHEW TOYS.. THE DOGS ARE SUPPOSED TO CHEW THEM, RIGHT?

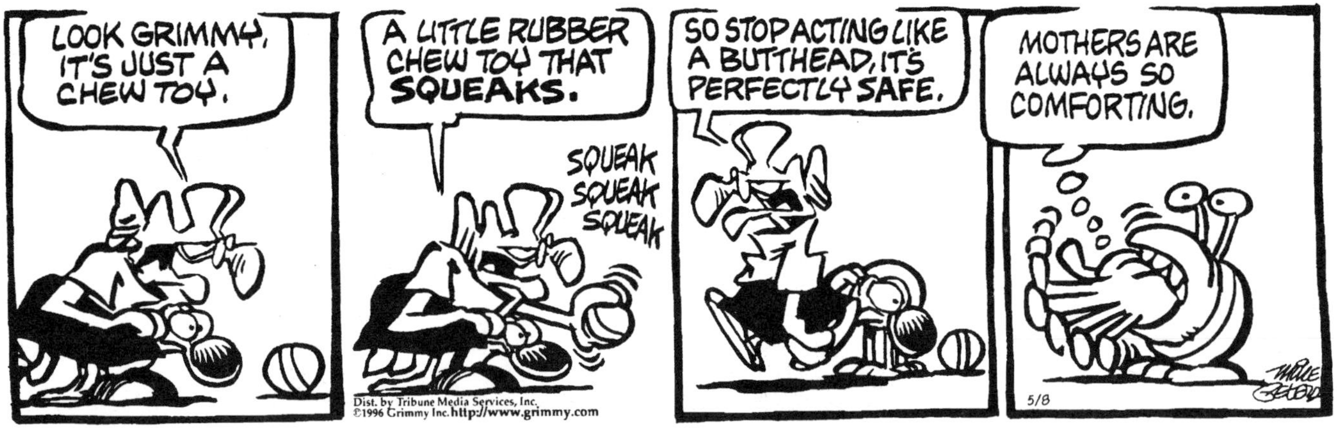
LOOK GRIMMY, IT'S JUST A CHEW TOY.
A LITTLE RUBBER CHEW TOY THAT SQUEAKS.
SQUEAK SQUEAK SQUEAK
Dist. by Tribune Media Services, Inc. ©1996 Grimmy Inc. http://www.grimmy.com
SO STOP ACTING LIKE A BUTTHEAD, IT'S PERFECTLY SAFE.
MOTHERS ARE ALWAYS SO COMFORTING.
5/8

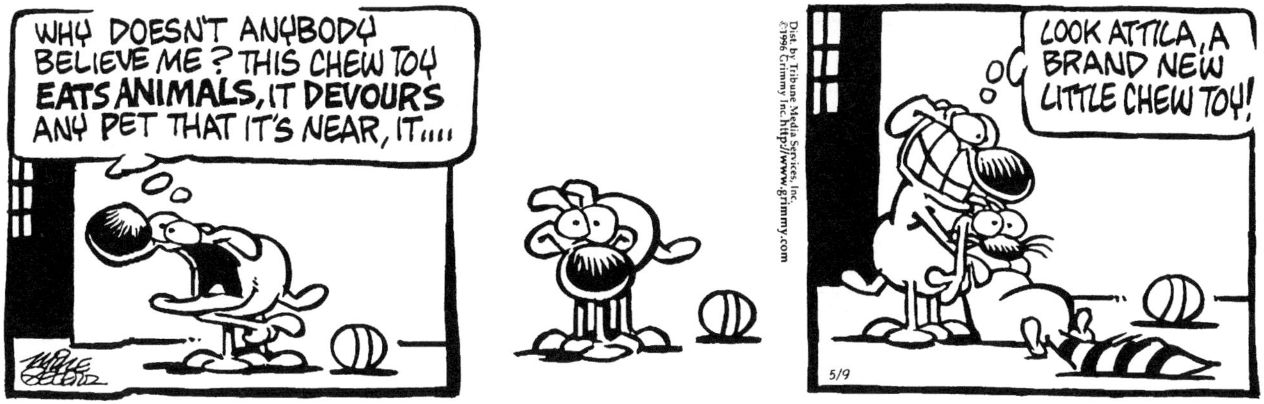

WHY DOESN'T ANYBODY BELIEVE ME? THIS CHEW TOY **EATS ANIMALS**, IT **DEVOURS** ANY PET THAT IT'S NEAR, IT....
Dist. by Tribune Media Services, Inc. ©1996 Grimmy Inc. http://www.grimmy.com
LOOK ATTILA, A BRAND NEW LITTLE CHEW TOY!
5/9

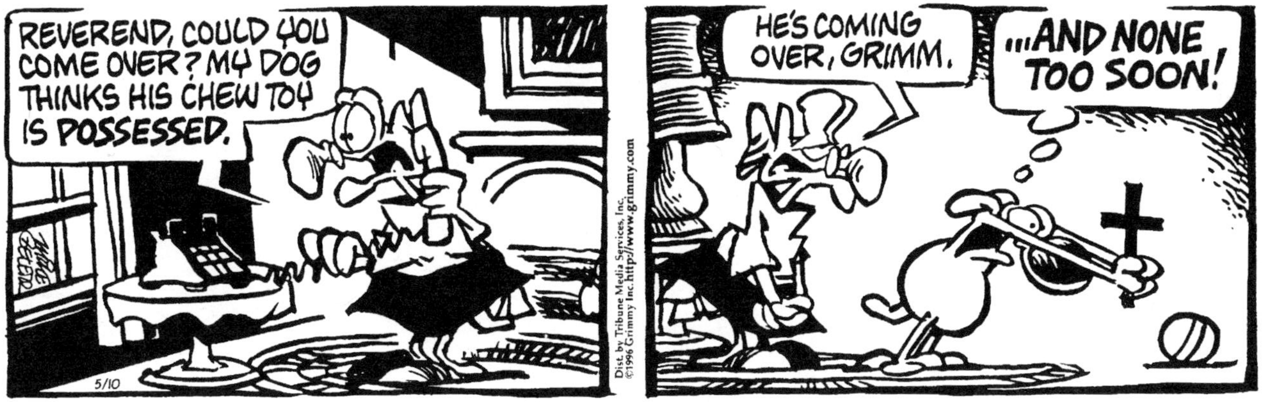

REVEREND, COULD YOU COME OVER? MY DOG THINKS HIS CHEW TOY IS **POSSESSED**.
5/10
Dist. by Tribune Media Services, Inc. ©1996 Grimmy Inc. http://www.grimmy.com
HE'S COMING OVER, GRIMM.
...AND NONE TOO SOON!

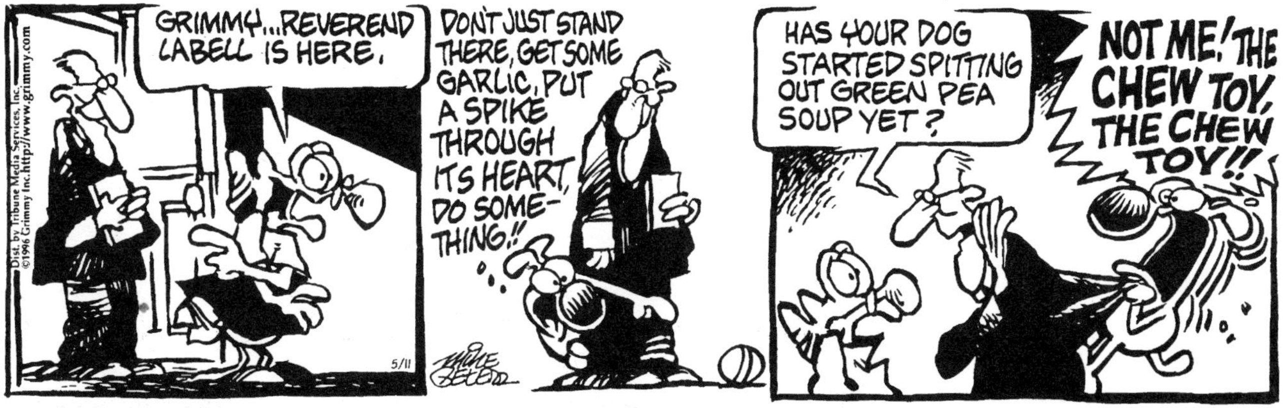

Dist. by Tribune Media Services, Inc. ©1996 Grimmy Inc. http://www.grimmy.com
GRIMMY...REVEREND LABELL IS HERE.
5/11
DON'T JUST STAND THERE, GET SOME GARLIC, PUT A SPIKE THROUGH ITS HEART, DO SOME-THING!!
HAS YOUR DOG STARTED SPITTING OUT GREEN PEA SOUP YET?
NOT ME! THE CHEW TOY, THE CHEW TOY!!

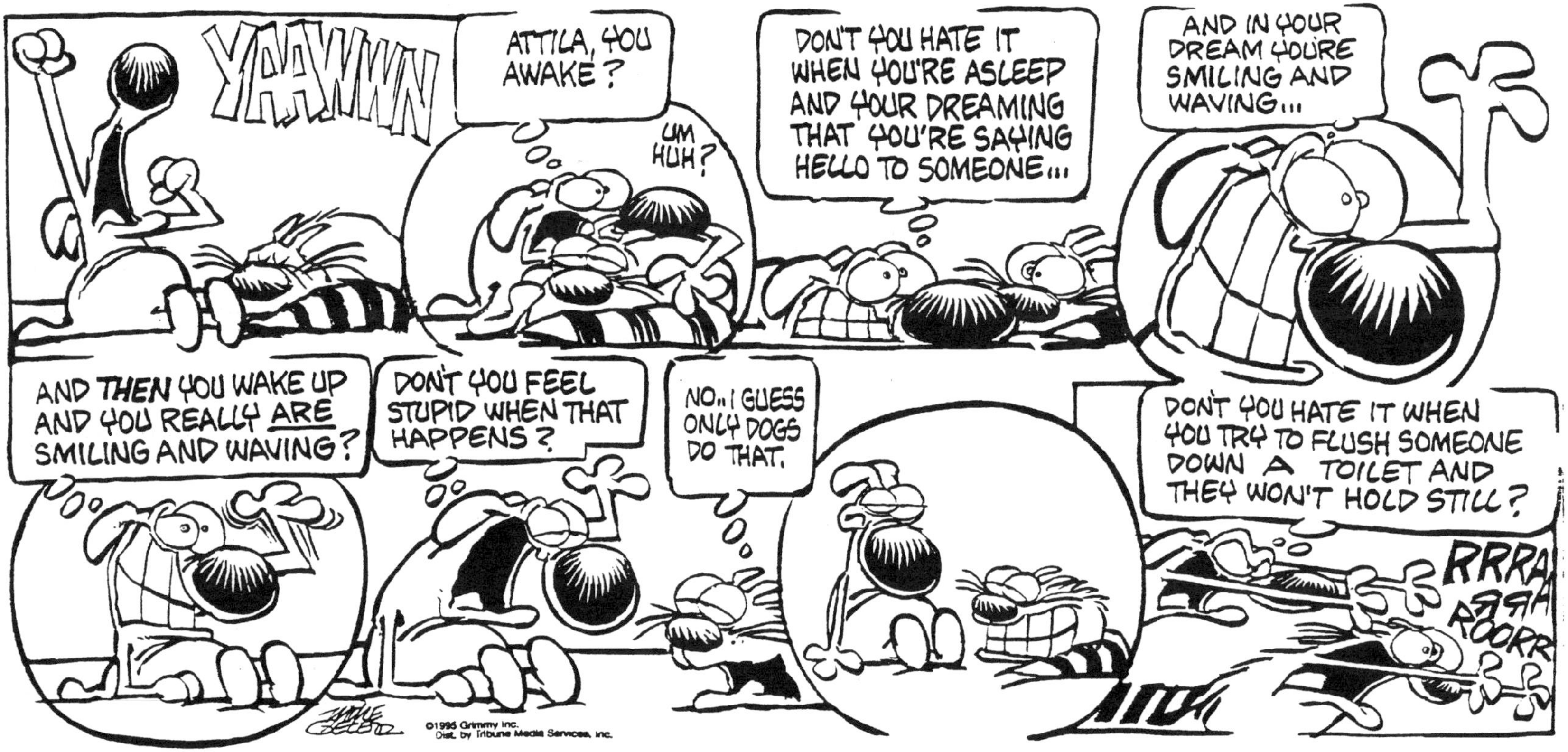
YAAWWN
ATTILA, YOU AWAKE?
UM HUH?
DON'T YOU HATE IT WHEN YOU'RE ASLEEP AND YOUR DREAMING THAT YOU'RE SAYING HELLO TO SOMEONE...
AND IN YOUR DREAM YOU'RE SMILING AND WAVING...
AND **THEN** YOU WAKE UP AND YOU REALLY ARE SMILING AND WAVING?
DON'T YOU FEEL STUPID WHEN THAT HAPPENS?
NO.. I GUESS ONLY DOGS DO THAT.
DON'T YOU HATE IT WHEN YOU TRY TO FLUSH SOMEONE DOWN A TOILET AND THEY WON'T HOLD STILL?
RRRAAHH ROORR
©1995 Grimmy Inc.
Dist. by Tribune Media Services, Inc.

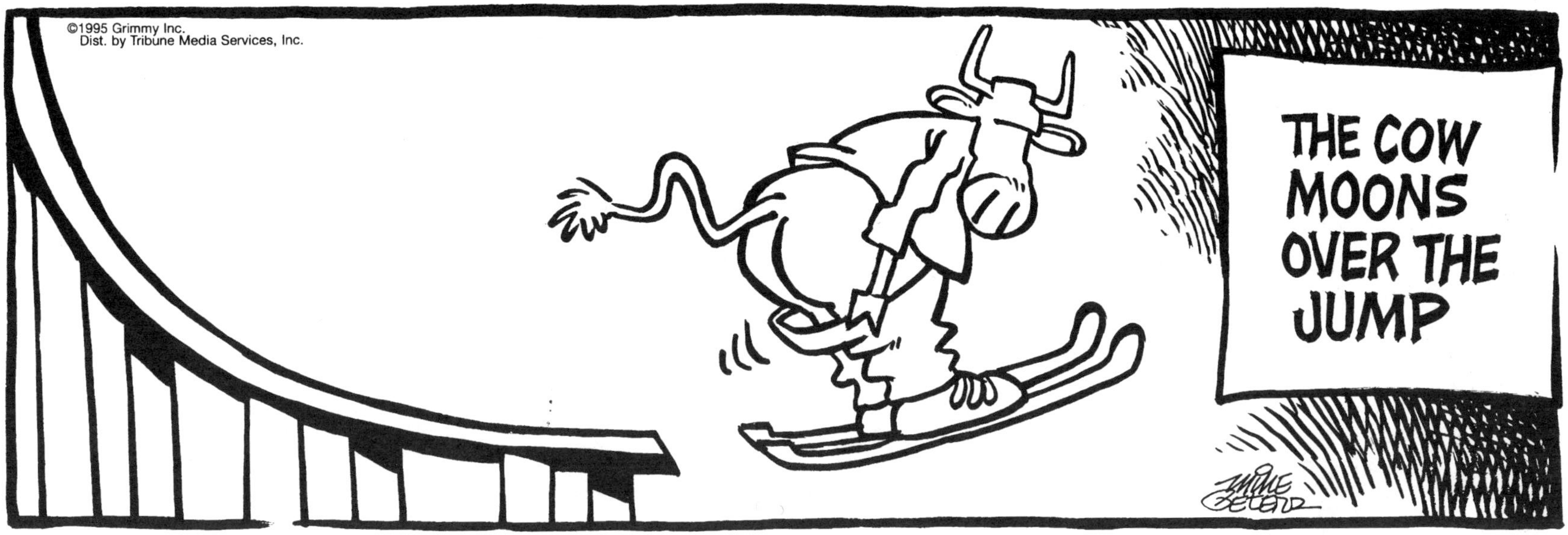
©1995 Grimmy Inc.
Dist. by Tribune Media Services, Inc.
THE COW MOONS OVER THE JUMP

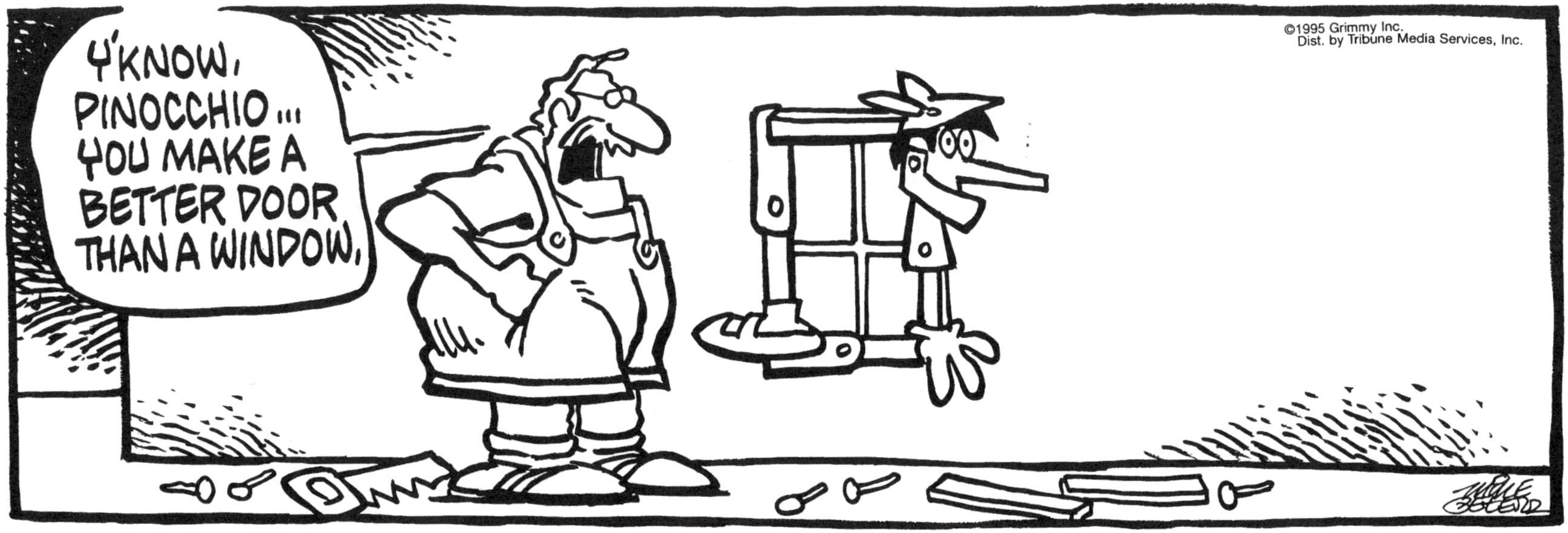
Y'KNOW, PINOCCHIO... YOU MAKE A BETTER DOOR THAN A WINDOW.
©1995 Grimmy Inc.
Dist. by Tribune Media Services, Inc.

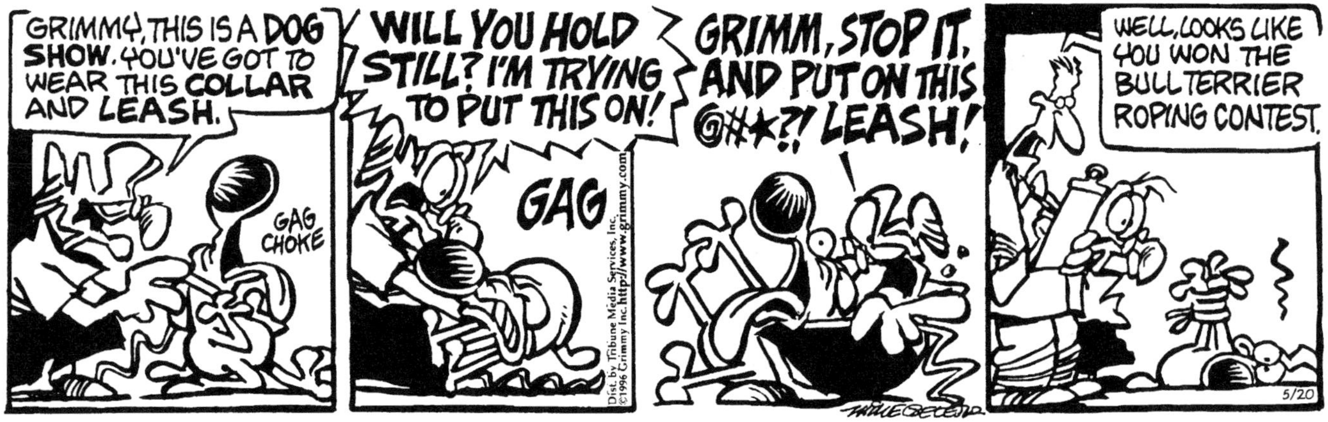
GRIMMY, THIS IS A DOG SHOW. YOU'VE GOT TO WEAR THIS COLLAR AND LEASH.
GAG CHOKE
WILL YOU HOLD STILL? I'M TRYING TO PUT THIS ON!
GAG
Dist. by Tribune Media Services, Inc. ©1996 Grimmy Inc. http://www.grimmy.com
GRIMM, STOP IT, AND PUT ON THIS @#*?! LEASH!
WELL, LOOKS LIKE YOU WON THE BULL TERRIER ROPING CONTEST.
5/20

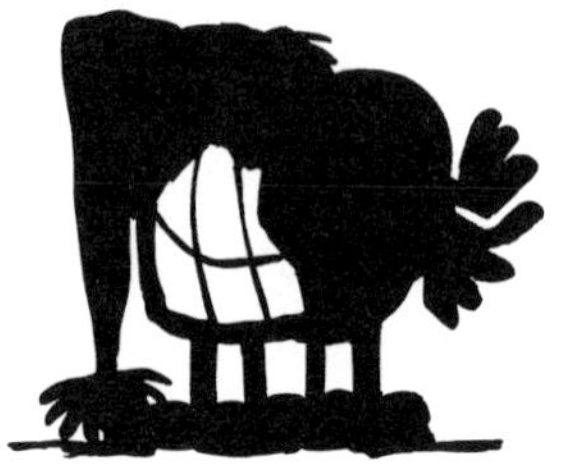

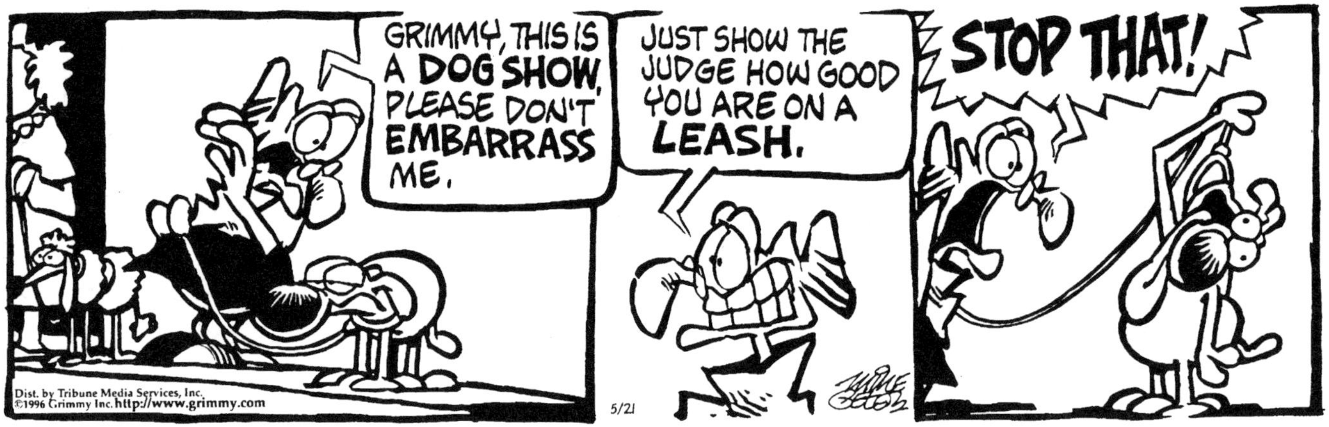
GRIMMY, THIS IS A DOG SHOW. PLEASE DON'T EMBARRASS ME.
Dist. by Tribune Media Services, Inc. ©1996 Grimmy Inc. http://www.grimmy.com
5/21
JUST SHOW THE JUDGE HOW GOOD YOU ARE ON A LEASH.
STOP THAT!

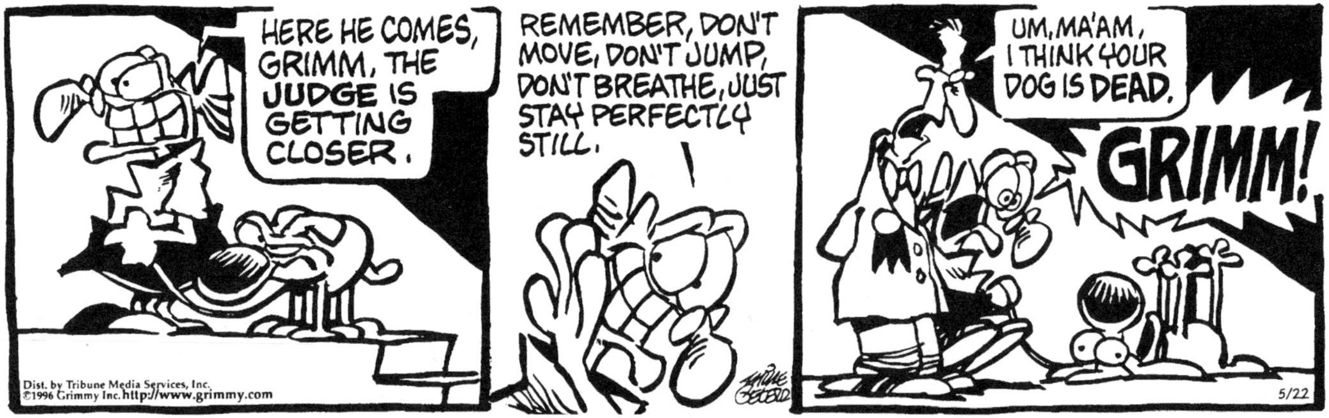
HERE HE COMES, GRIMM, THE JUDGE IS GETTING CLOSER.
Dist. by Tribune Media Services, Inc. ©1996 Grimmy Inc. http://www.grimmy.com
REMEMBER, DON'T MOVE, DON'T JUMP, DON'T BREATHE, JUST STAY PERFECTLY STILL.
UM, MA'AM, I THINK YOUR DOG IS DEAD.
GRIMM!
5/22

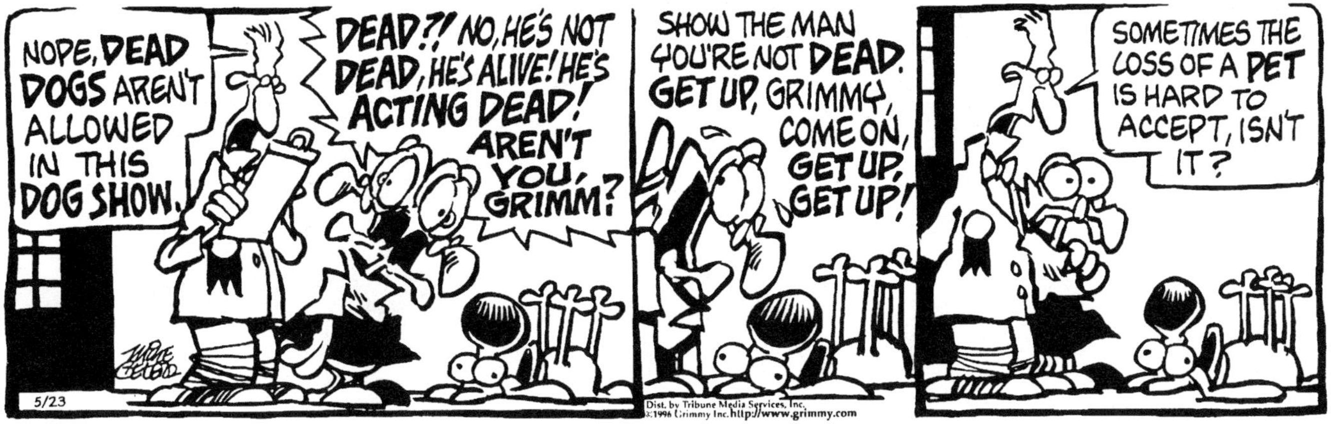
NOPE, DEAD DOGS AREN'T ALLOWED IN THIS DOG SHOW.
DEAD?! NO, HE'S NOT DEAD, HE'S ALIVE! HE'S ACTING DEAD! AREN'T YOU, GRIMM?
SHOW THE MAN YOU'RE NOT DEAD. GET UP, GRIMMY, COME ON, GET UP, GET UP!
SOMETIMES THE LOSS OF A PET IS HARD TO ACCEPT, ISN'T IT?
MIKE PETERS
5/23
Dist. by Tribune Media Services, Inc. ©1996 Grimmy Inc. http://www.grimmy.com

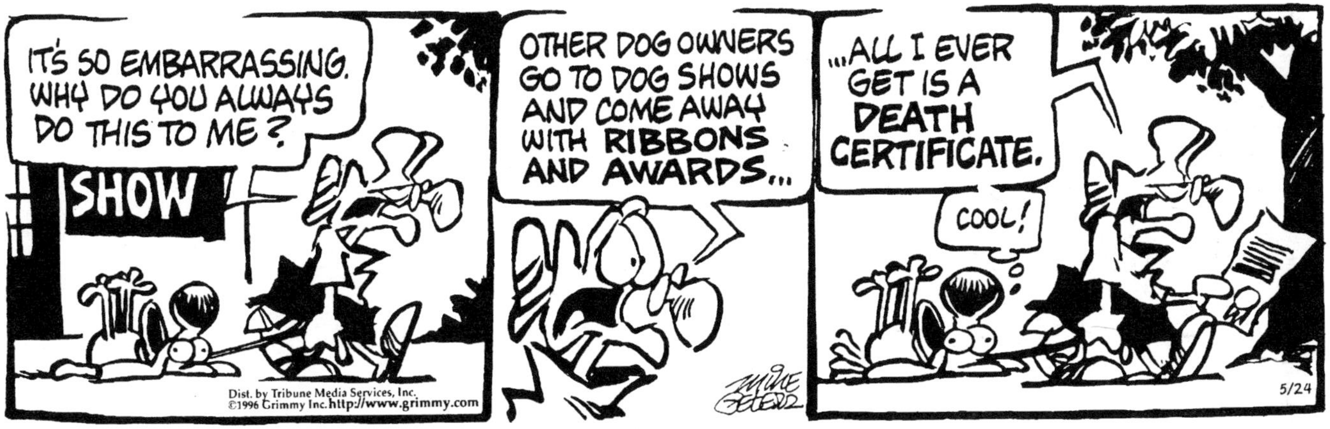
IT'S SO EMBARRASSING. WHY DO YOU ALWAYS DO THIS TO ME?
SHOW
OTHER DOG OWNERS GO TO DOG SHOWS AND COME AWAY WITH RIBBONS AND AWARDS...
...ALL I EVER GET IS A DEATH CERTIFICATE.
COOL!
Dist. by Tribune Media Services, Inc. ©1996 Grimmy Inc. http://www.grimmy.com
MIKE PETERS
5/24

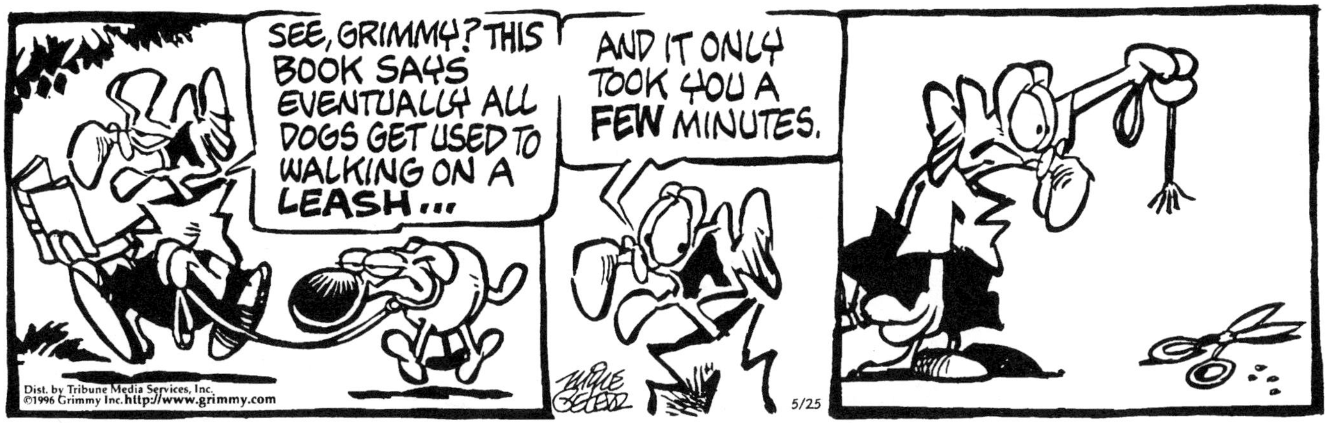
SEE, GRIMMY? THIS BOOK SAYS EVENTUALLY ALL DOGS GET USED TO WALKING ON A LEASH...
AND IT ONLY TOOK YOU A FEW MINUTES.
Dist. by Tribune Media Services, Inc. ©1996 Grimmy Inc. http://www.grimmy.com
MIKE PETERS
5/25

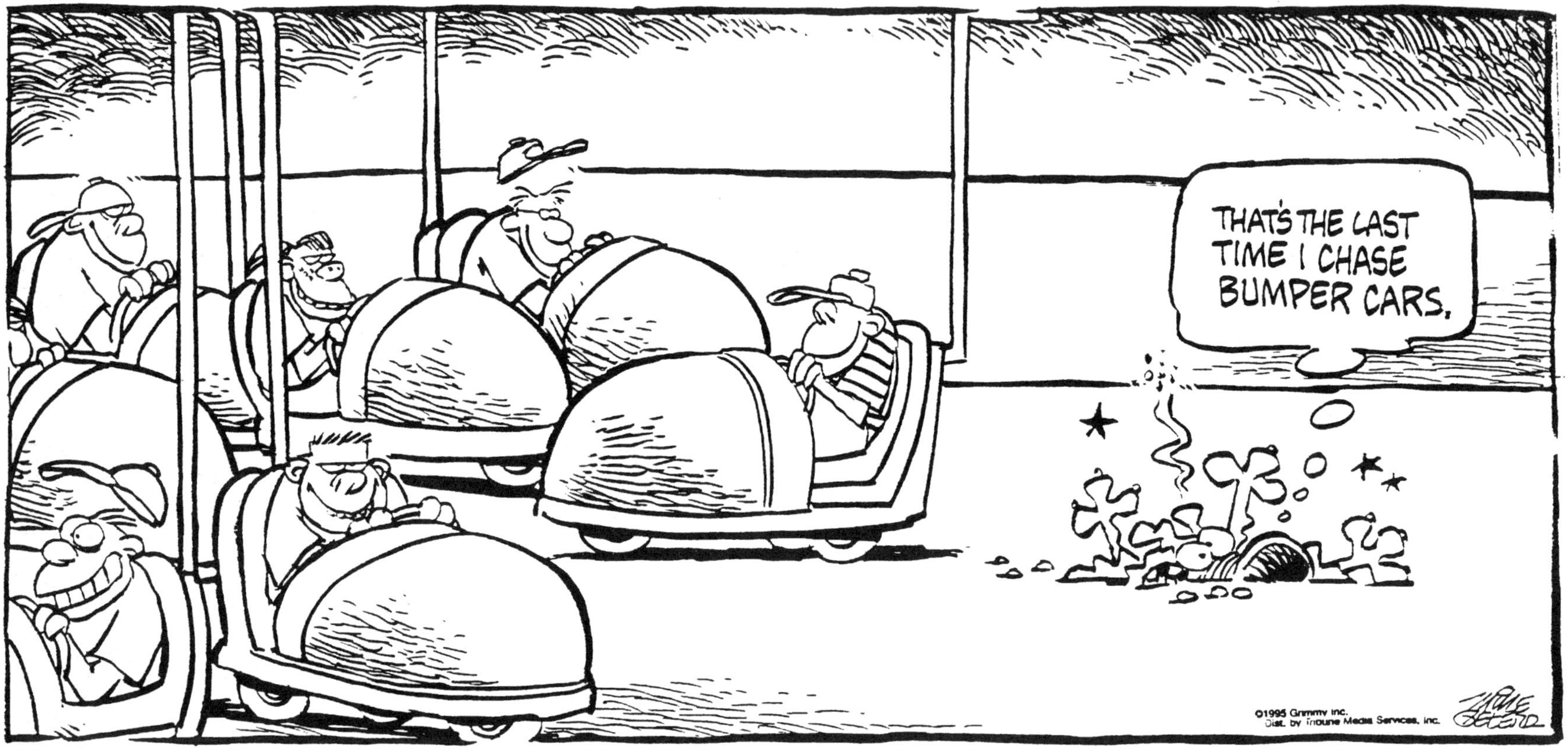
THAT'S THE LAST TIME I CHASE BUMPER CARS.
©1995 Grimmy Inc.
Dist. by Tribune Media Services, Inc.

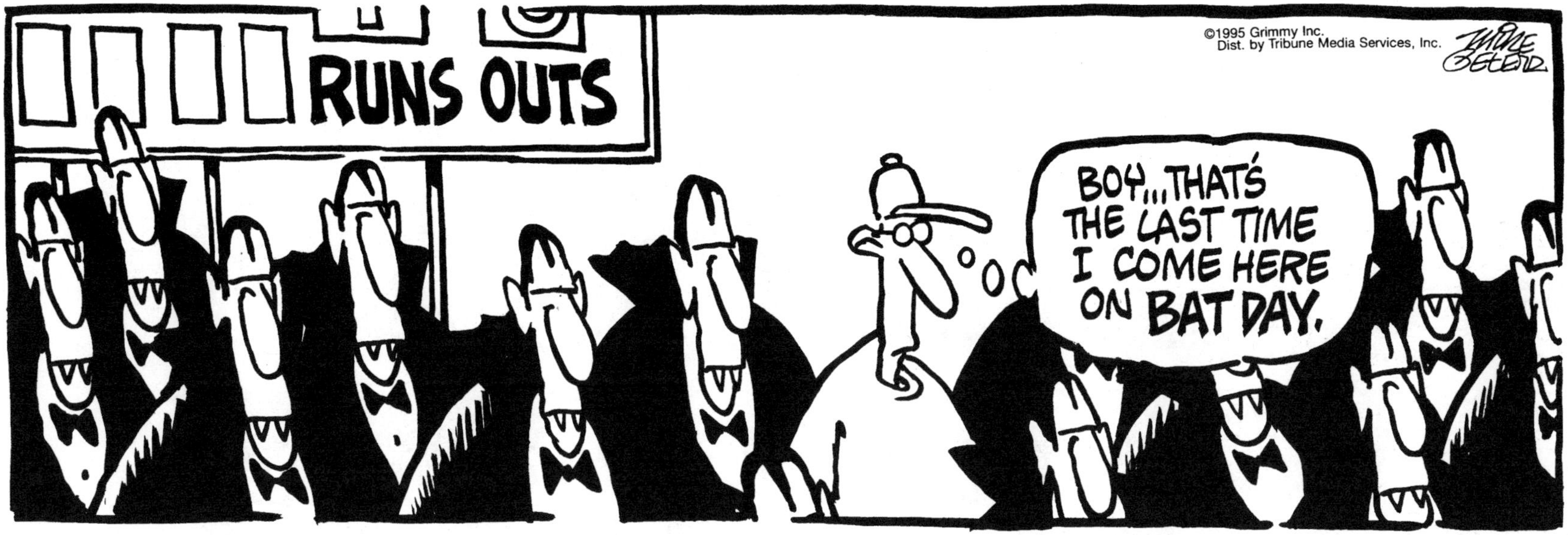
RUNS OUTS
©1995 Grimmy Inc.
Dist. by Tribune Media Services, Inc.
BOY,,,THAT'S THE LAST TIME I COME HERE ON BAT DAY.

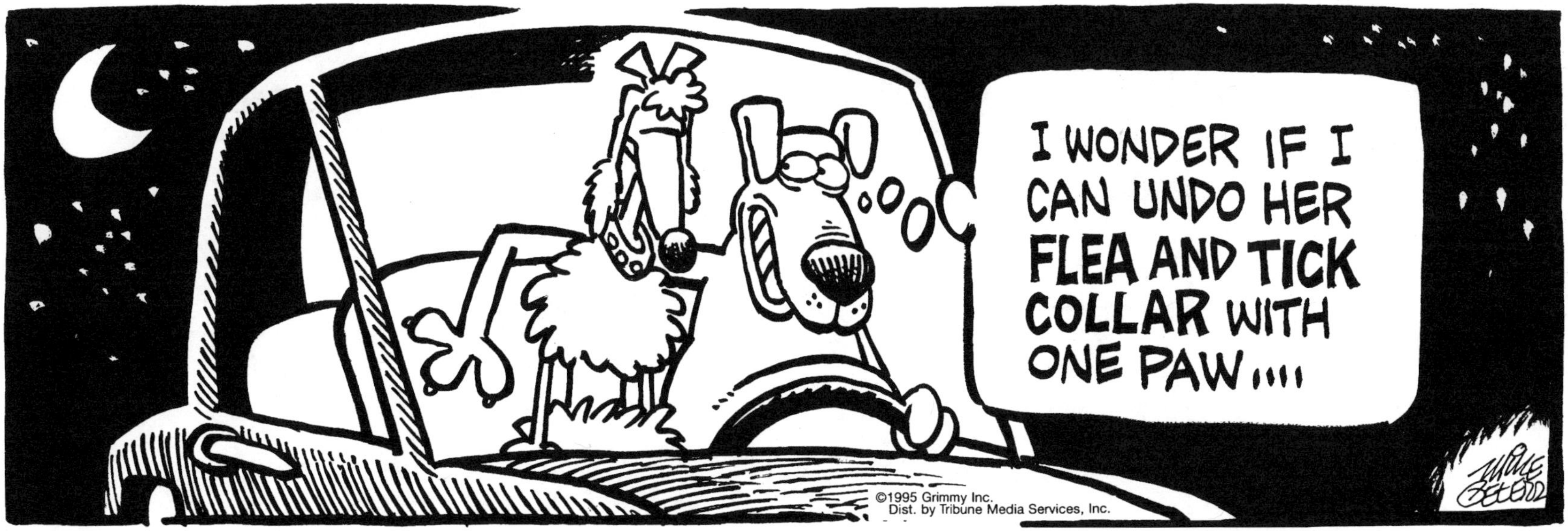
I WONDER IF I CAN UNDO HER FLEA AND TICK COLLAR WITH ONE PAW....
©1995 Grimmy Inc.
Dist. by Tribune Media Services, Inc.

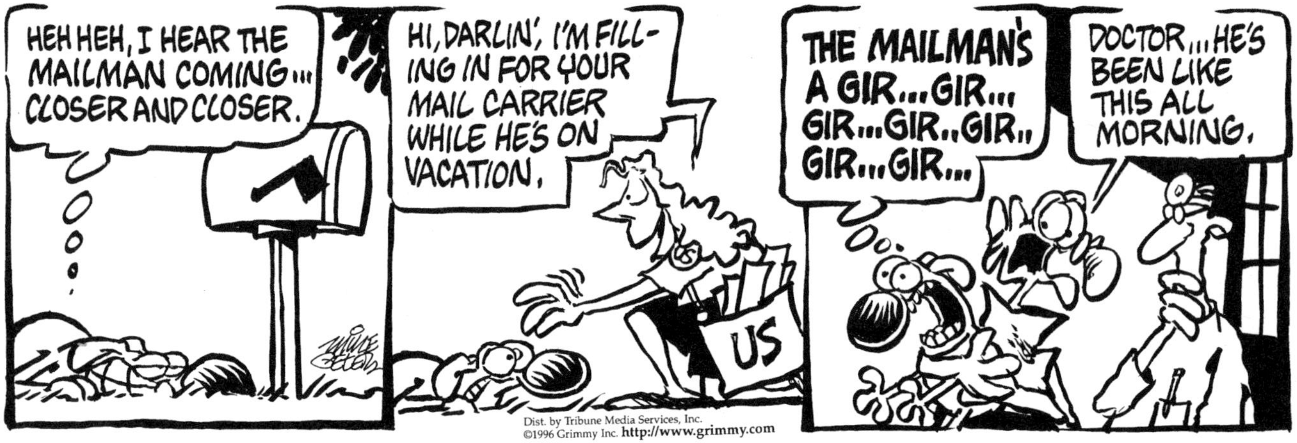
HEH HEH, I HEAR THE MAILMAN COMING... CLOSER AND CLOSER.
HI, DARLIN', I'M FILL-ING IN FOR YOUR MAIL CARRIER WHILE HE'S ON VACATION.
US
Dist. by Tribune Media Services, Inc. ©1996 Grimmy Inc. http://www.grimmy.com
THE MAILMAN'S A GIR...GIR... GIR...GIR..GIR.. GIR...GIR...
DOCTOR... HE'S BEEN LIKE THIS ALL MORNING.

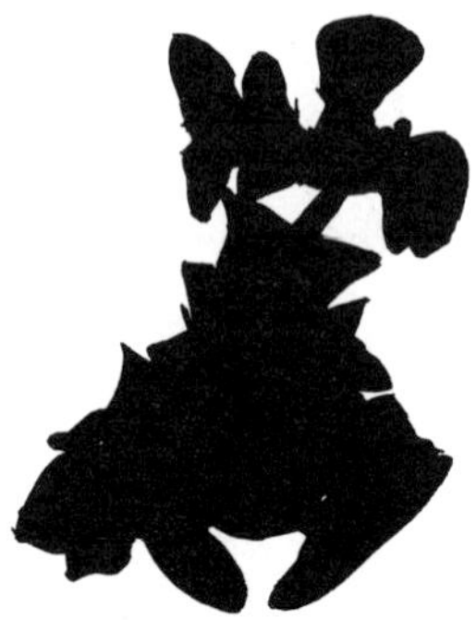

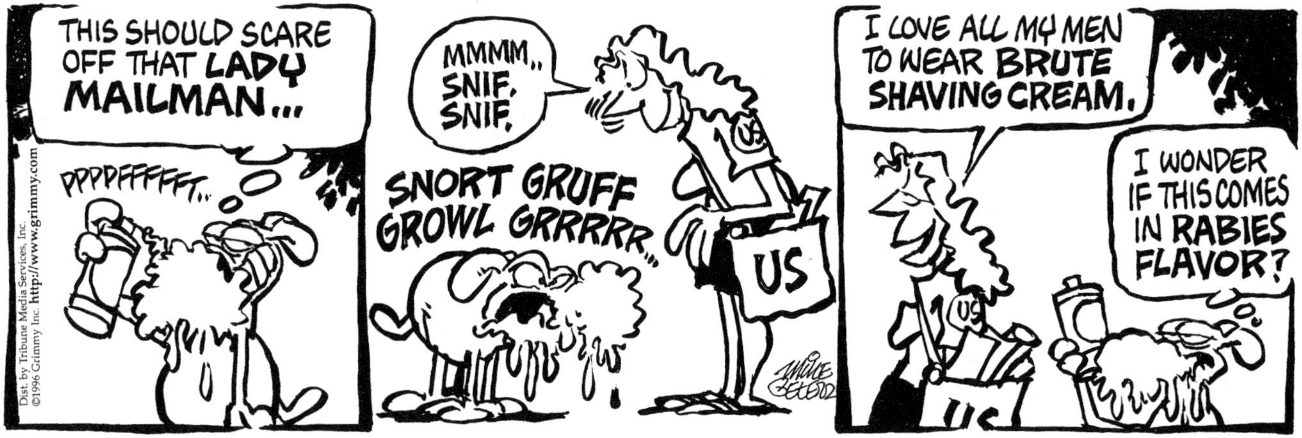
Dist. by Tribune Media Services, Inc. ©1996 Grimmy Inc. http://www.grimmy.com
THIS SHOULD SCARE OFF THAT LADY MAILMAN...
PPPPFFFFFT...
MMMM.. SNIF, SNIF.
SNORT GRUFF GROWL GRRRRR...
US
I LOVE ALL MY MEN TO WEAR BRUTE SHAVING CREAM.
I WONDER IF THIS COMES IN RABIES FLAVOR?

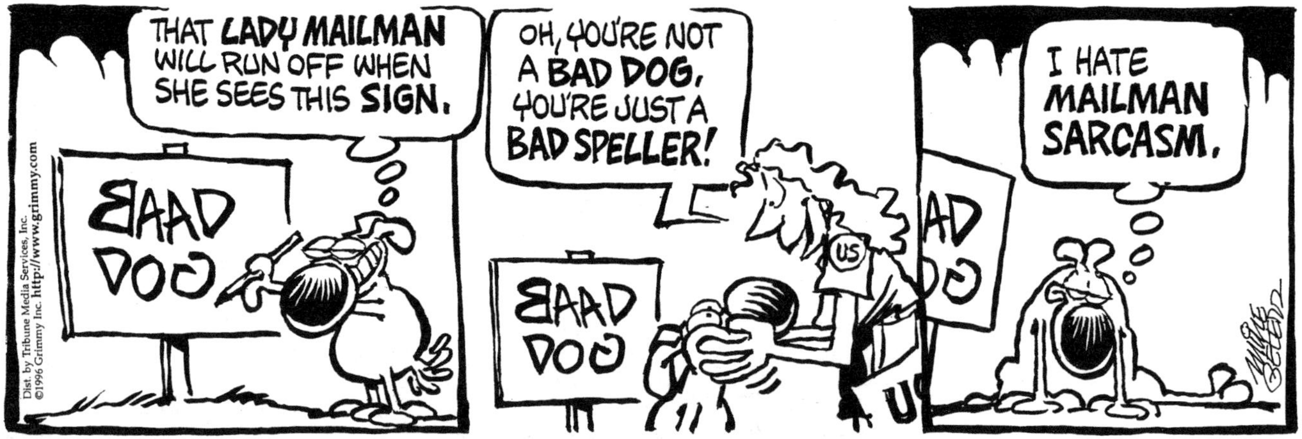
Dist. by Tribune Media Services, Inc. ©1996 Grimmy Inc. http://www.grimmy.com
THAT LADY MAILMAN WILL RUN OFF WHEN SHE SEES THIS SIGN.
BAAD DOG
OH, YOU'RE NOT A BAD DOG, YOU'RE JUST A BAD SPELLER!
BAAD DOG
I HATE MAILMAN SARCASM.

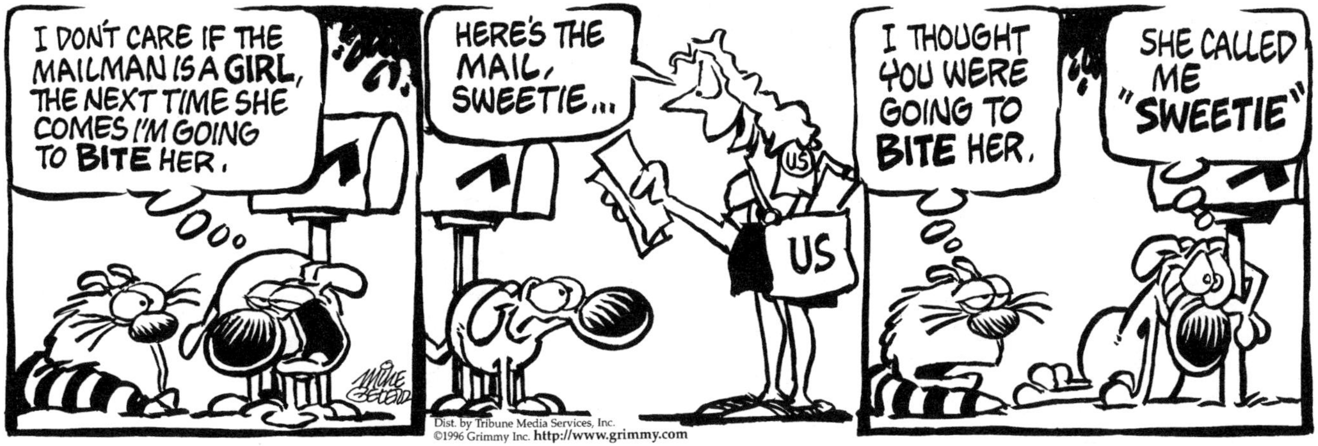
I DON'T CARE IF THE MAILMAN IS A GIRL, THE NEXT TIME SHE COMES I'M GOING TO BITE HER.
HERE'S THE MAIL, SWEETIE...
US
US
I THOUGHT YOU WERE GOING TO BITE HER.
SHE CALLED ME "SWEETIE"
Dist. by Tribune Media Services, Inc.
©1996 Grimmy Inc. http://www.grimmy.com

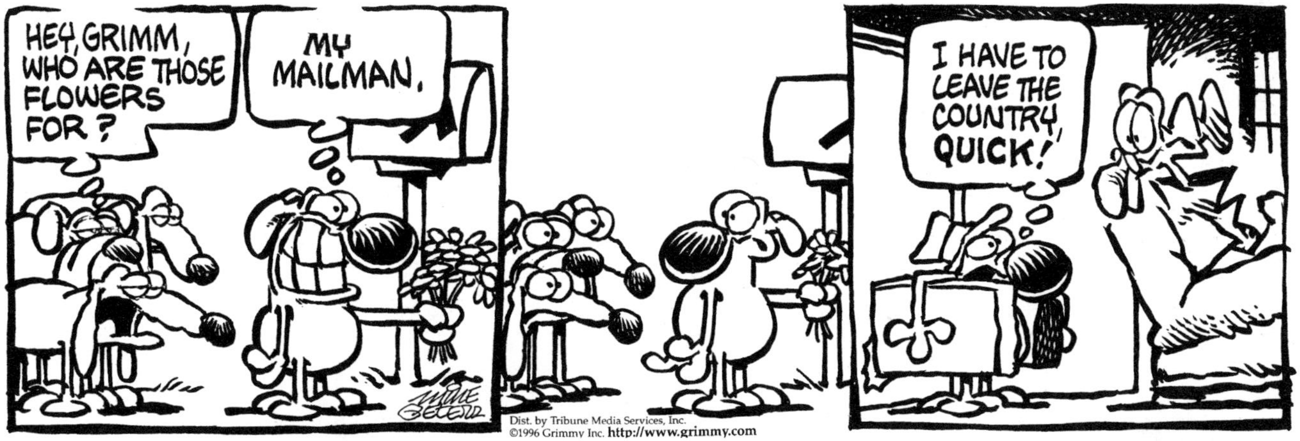
HEY, GRIMM, WHO ARE THOSE FLOWERS FOR?
MY MAILMAN.
I HAVE TO LEAVE THE COUNTRY, QUICK!
Dist. by Tribune Media Services, Inc.
©1996 Grimmy Inc. http://www.grimmy.com

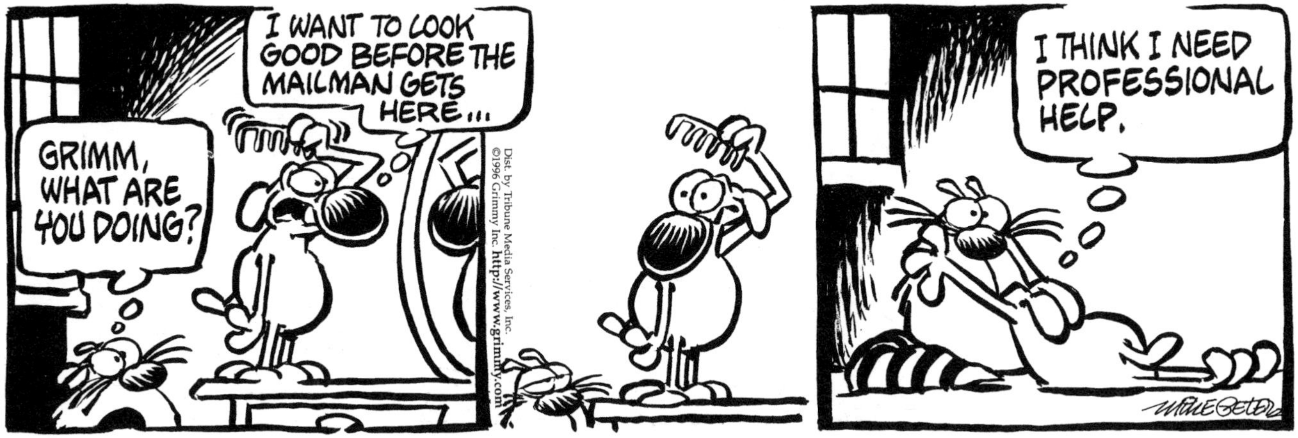
GRIMM, WHAT ARE YOU DOING?
I WANT TO LOOK GOOD BEFORE THE MAILMAN GETS HERE...
I THINK I NEED PROFESSIONAL HELP.
Dist. by Tribune Media Services, Inc.
©1996 Grimmy Inc. http://www.grimmy.com

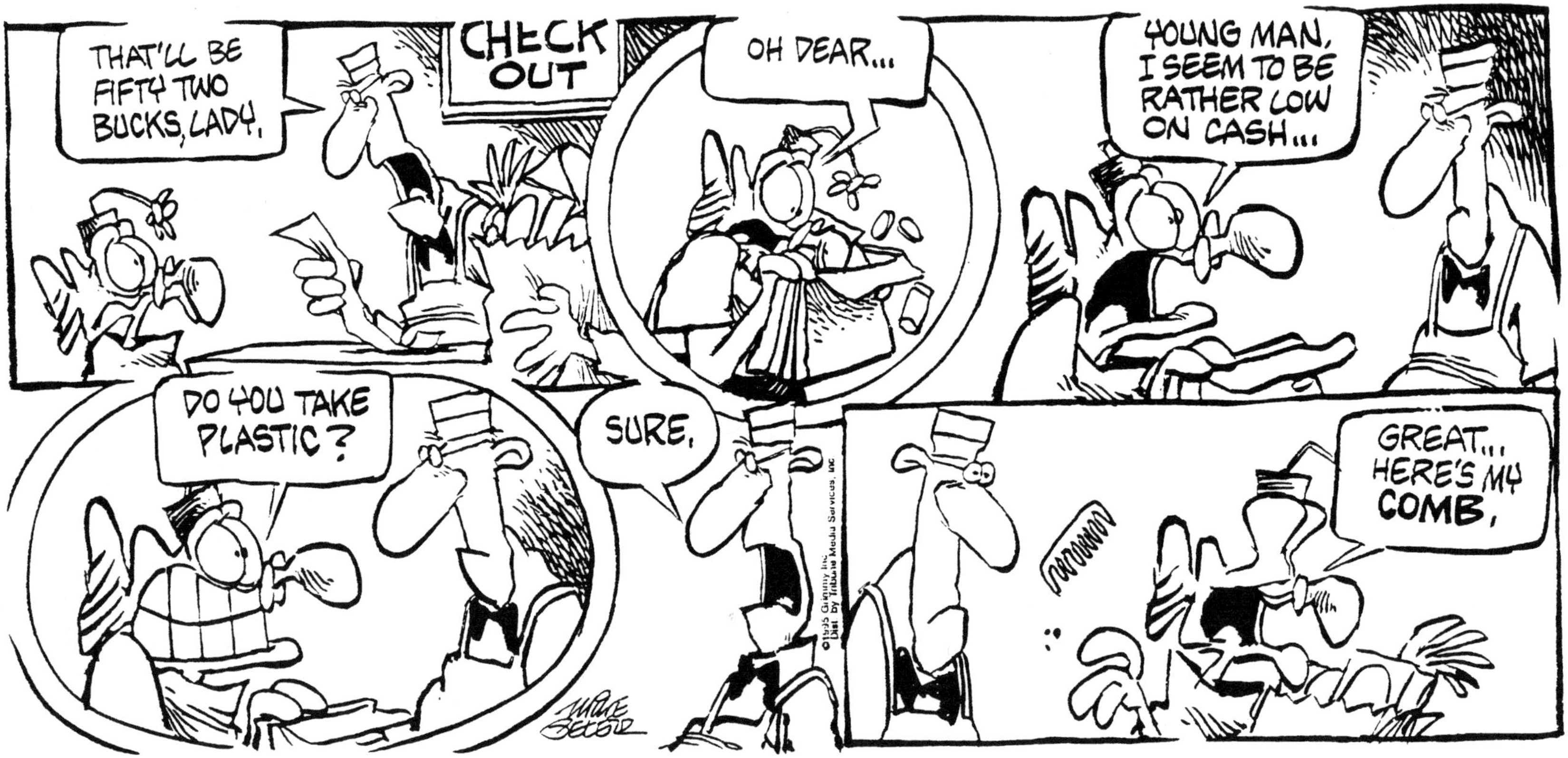
CHECK OUT
THAT'LL BE FIFTY TWO BUCKS, LADY.
OH DEAR...
YOUNG MAN, I SEEM TO BE RATHER LOW ON CASH...
DO YOU TAKE PLASTIC?
SURE.
©1995 Grimmy Inc. Dist by Tribune Media Services, Inc
GREAT... HERE'S MY COMB.

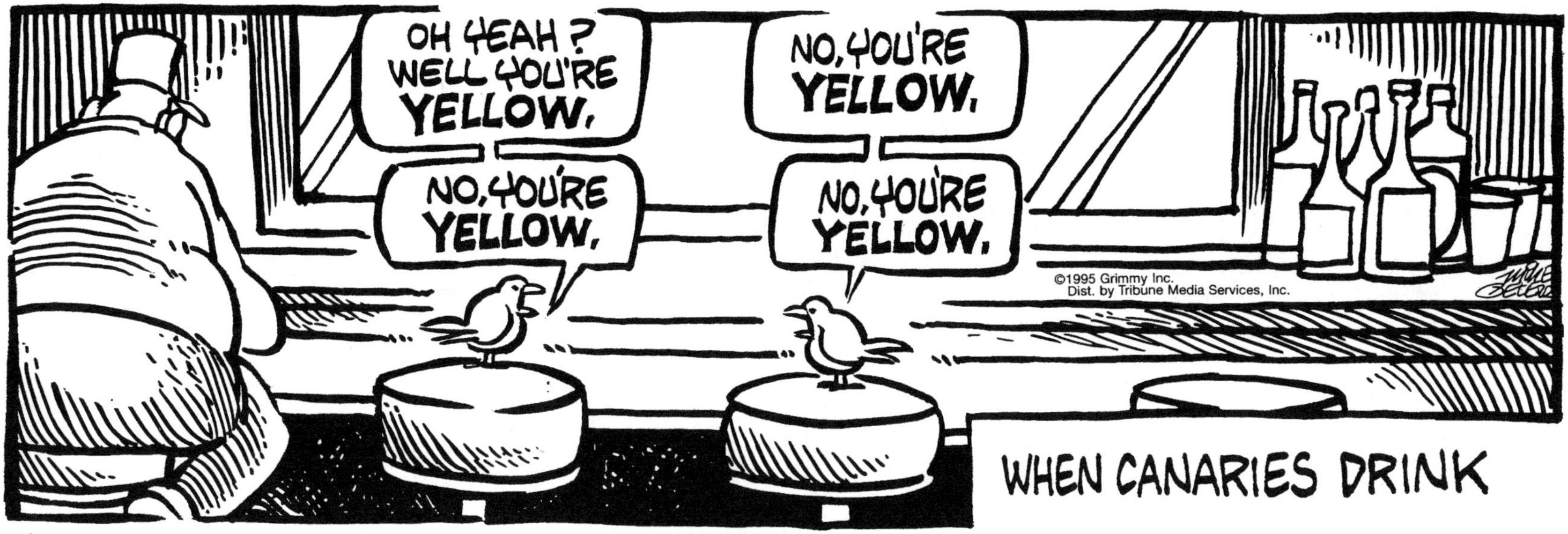
OH YEAH ? WELL YOU'RE YELLOW.
NO, YOU'RE YELLOW.
NO, YOU'RE YELLOW.
NO, YOU'RE YELLOW.
©1995 Grimmy Inc.
Dist. by Tribune Media Services, Inc.

WHEN CANARIES DRINK

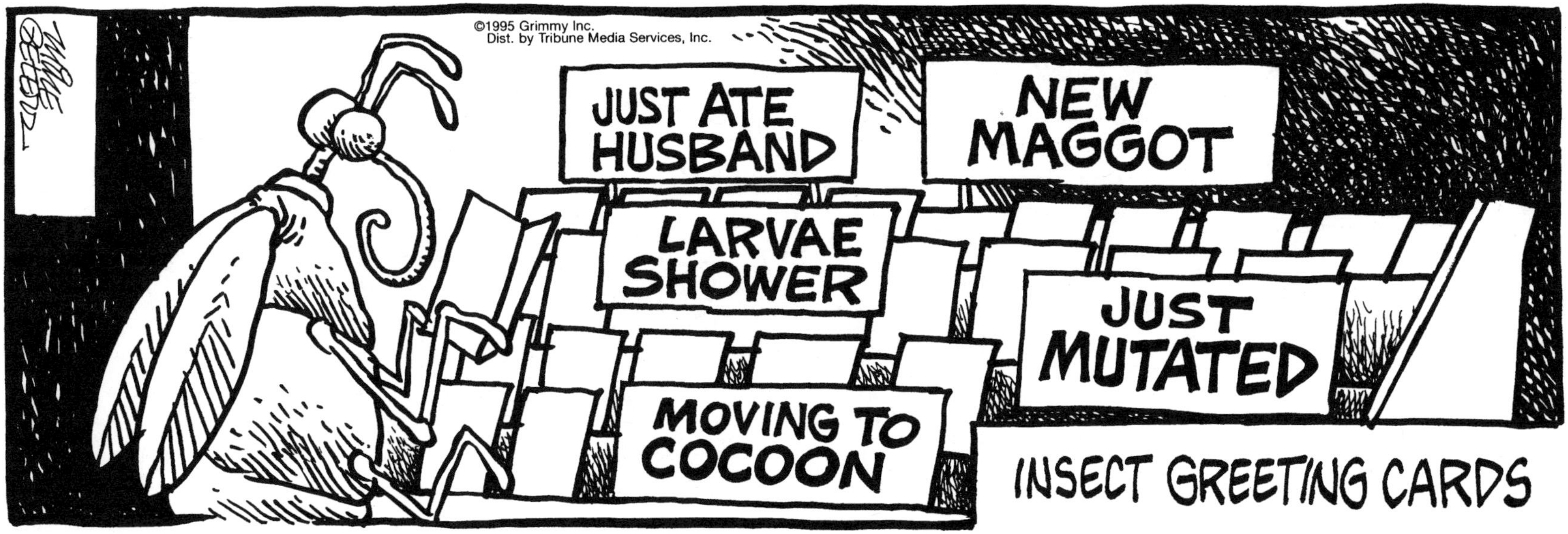
©1995 Grimmy Inc.
Dist. by Tribune Media Services, Inc.
JUST ATE HUSBAND
NEW MAGGOT
LARVAE SHOWER
JUST MUTATED
MOVING TO COCOON

INSECT GREETING CARDS

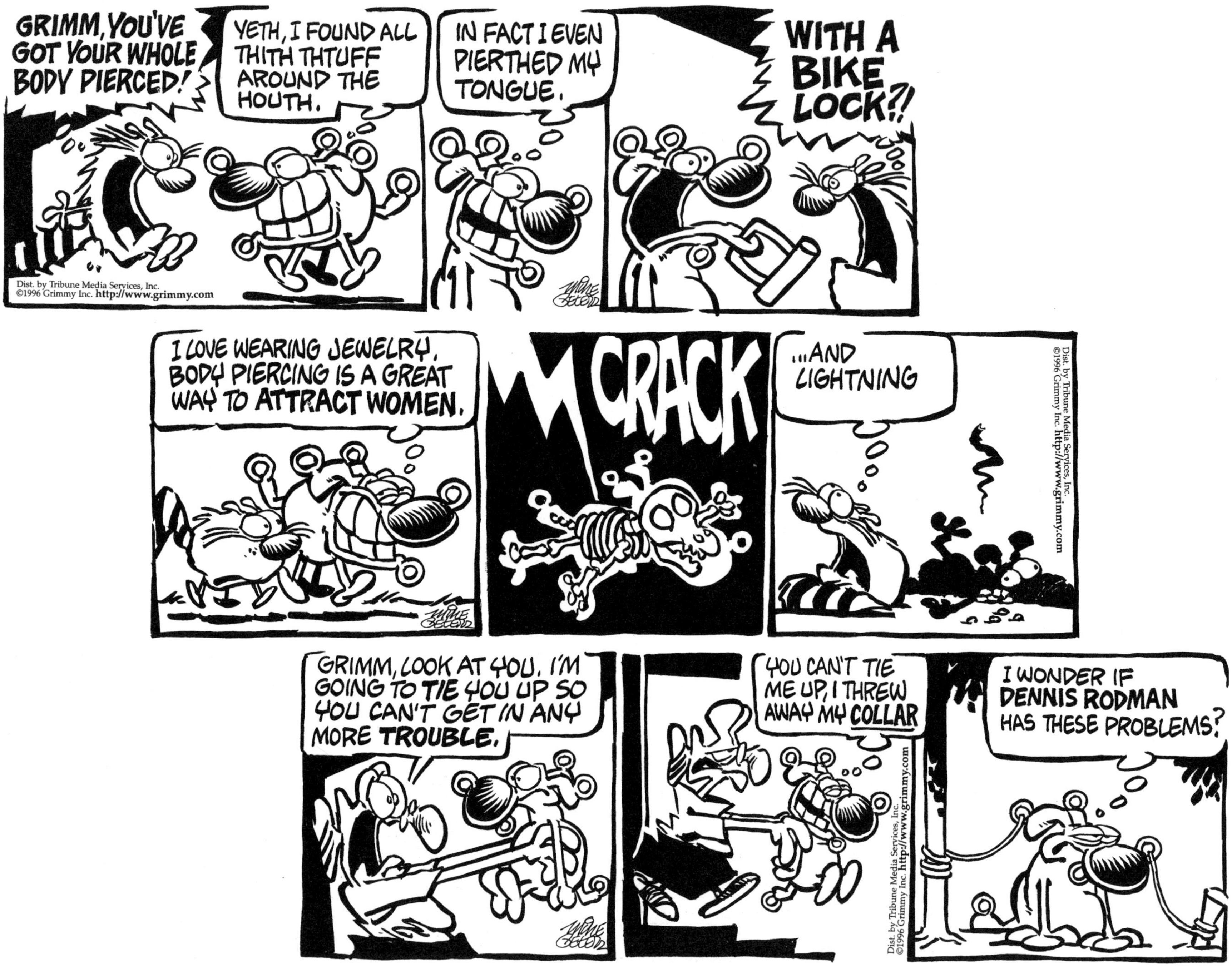
GRIMM, YOU'VE GOT YOUR WHOLE BODY PIERCED!
YETH, I FOUND ALL THITH THTUFF AROUND THE HOUTH.
Dist. by Tribune Media Services, Inc. ©1996 Grimmy Inc. http://www.grimmy.com
IN FACT I EVEN PIERTHED MY TONGUE.
WITH A BIKE LOCK?!
I LOVE WEARING JEWELRY. BODY PIERCING IS A GREAT WAY TO ATTRACT WOMEN.
CRACK
...AND LIGHTNING
Dist. by Tribune Media Services, Inc. ©1996 Grimmy Inc. http://www.grimmy.com
GRIMM, LOOK AT YOU. I'M GOING TO TIE YOU UP SO YOU CAN'T GET IN ANY MORE TROUBLE.
YOU CAN'T TIE ME UP, I THREW AWAY MY COLLAR
Dist. by Tribune Media Services, Inc. ©1996 Grimmy Inc. http://www.grimmy.com
I WONDER IF DENNIS RODMAN HAS THESE PROBLEMS?

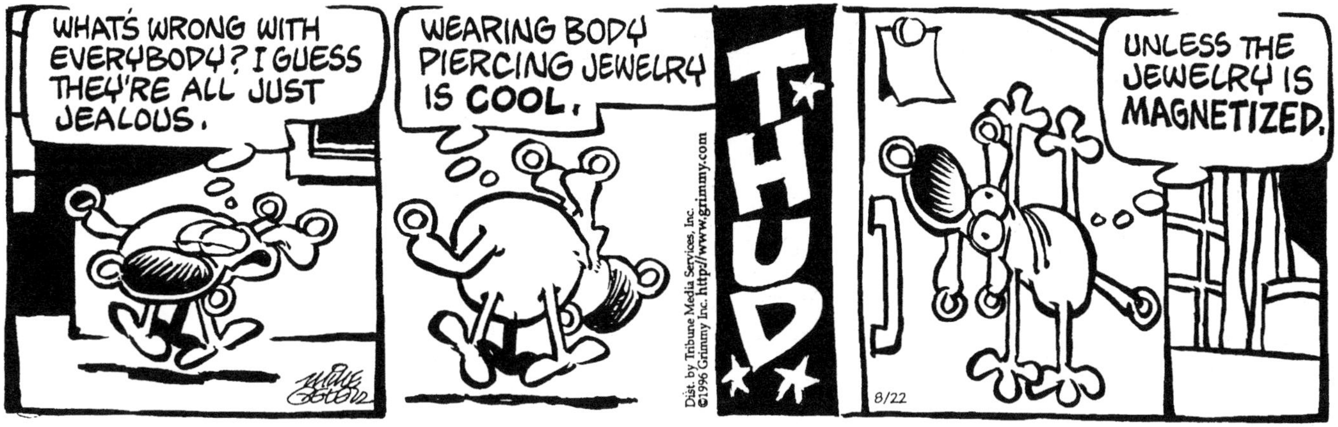
WHAT'S WRONG WITH EVERYBODY? I GUESS THEY'RE ALL JUST JEALOUS.
WEARING BODY PIERCING JEWELRY IS COOL.
Dist. by Tribune Media Services, Inc. ©1996 Grimmy Inc. http://www.grimmy.com
THUD
UNLESS THE JEWELRY IS MAGNETIZED.
8/22

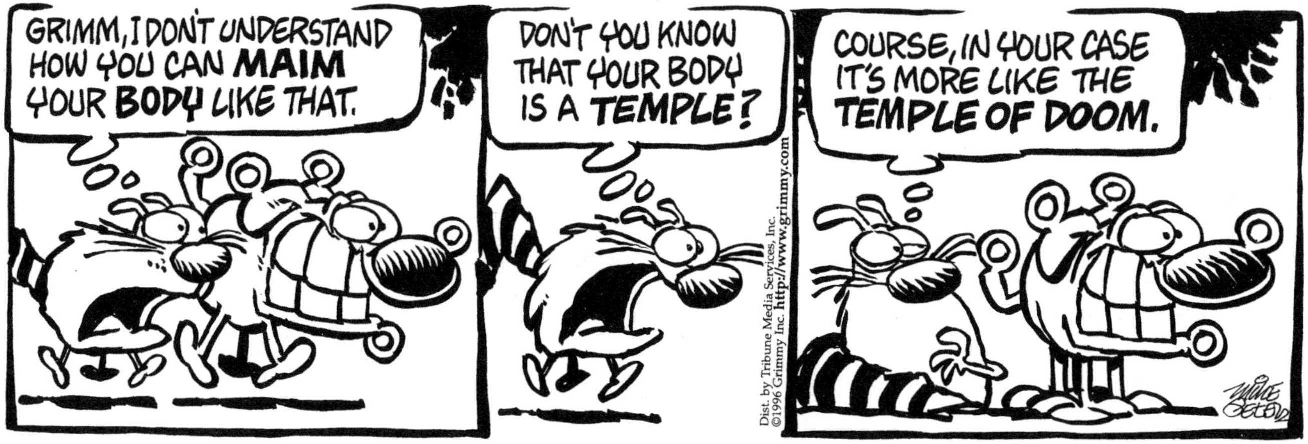
GRIMM, I DON'T UNDERSTAND HOW YOU CAN MAIM YOUR BODY LIKE THAT.
DON'T YOU KNOW THAT YOUR BODY IS A TEMPLE?
Dist. by Tribune Media Services, Inc. ©1996 Grimmy Inc. http://www.grimmy.com
COURSE, IN YOUR CASE IT'S MORE LIKE THE TEMPLE OF DOOM.

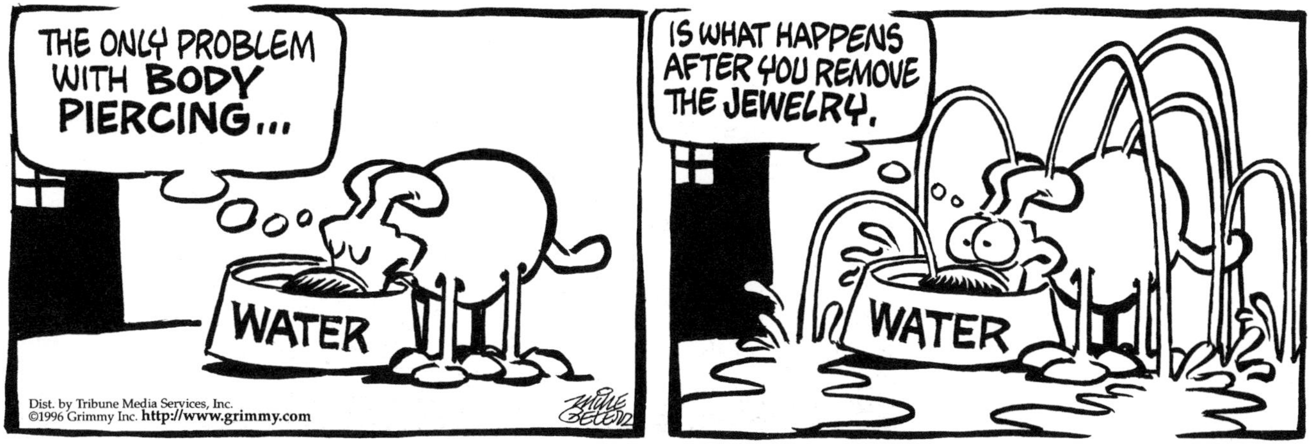
THE ONLY PROBLEM WITH BODY PIERCING...
WATER
Dist. by Tribune Media Services, Inc. ©1996 Grimmy Inc. http://www.grimmy.com
IS WHAT HAPPENS AFTER YOU REMOVE THE JEWELRY.
WATER

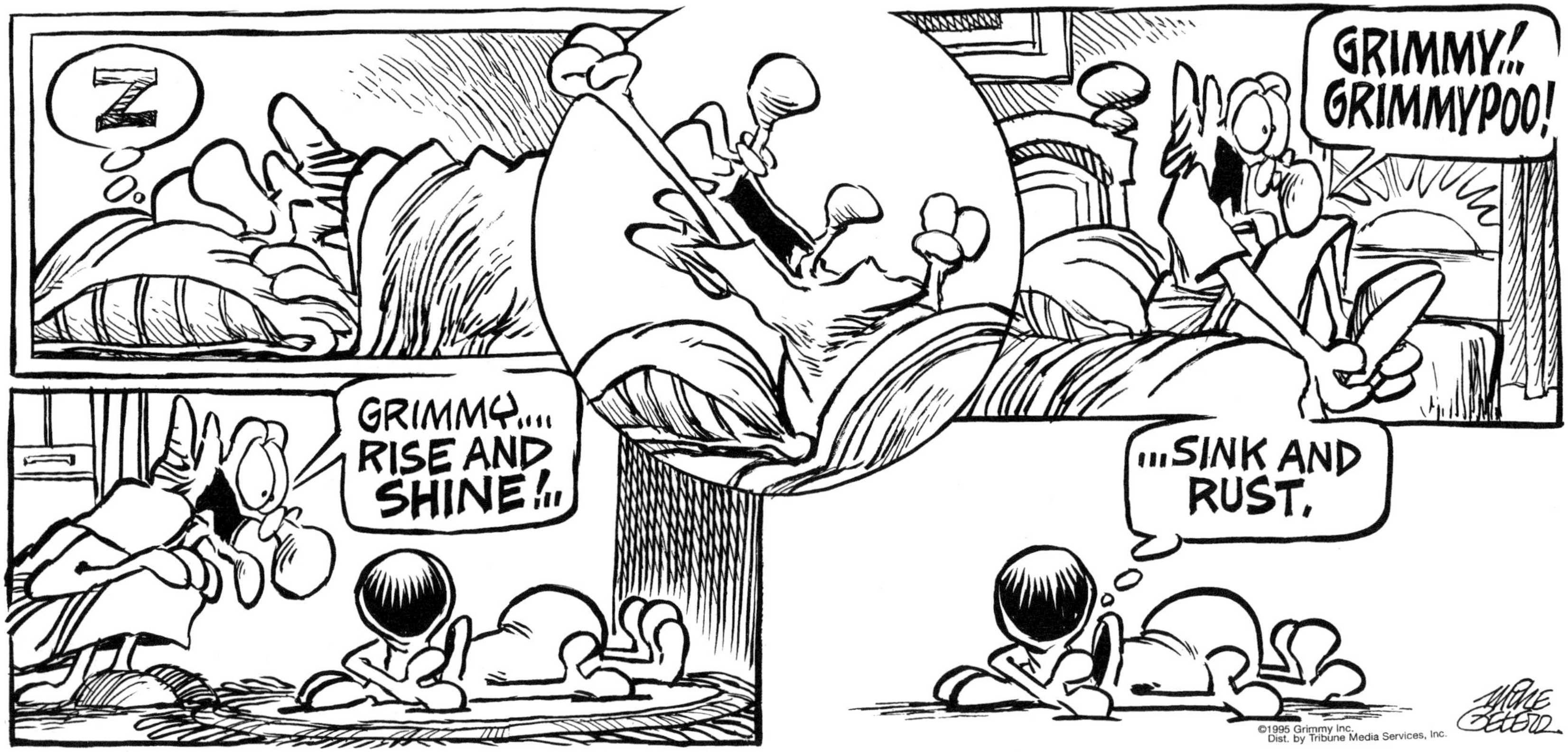
Z
GRIMMY!.. GRIMMYPOO!
GRIMMY.... RISE AND SHINE!..
...SINK AND RUST.
©1995 Grimmy Inc.
Dist. by Tribune Media Services, Inc.

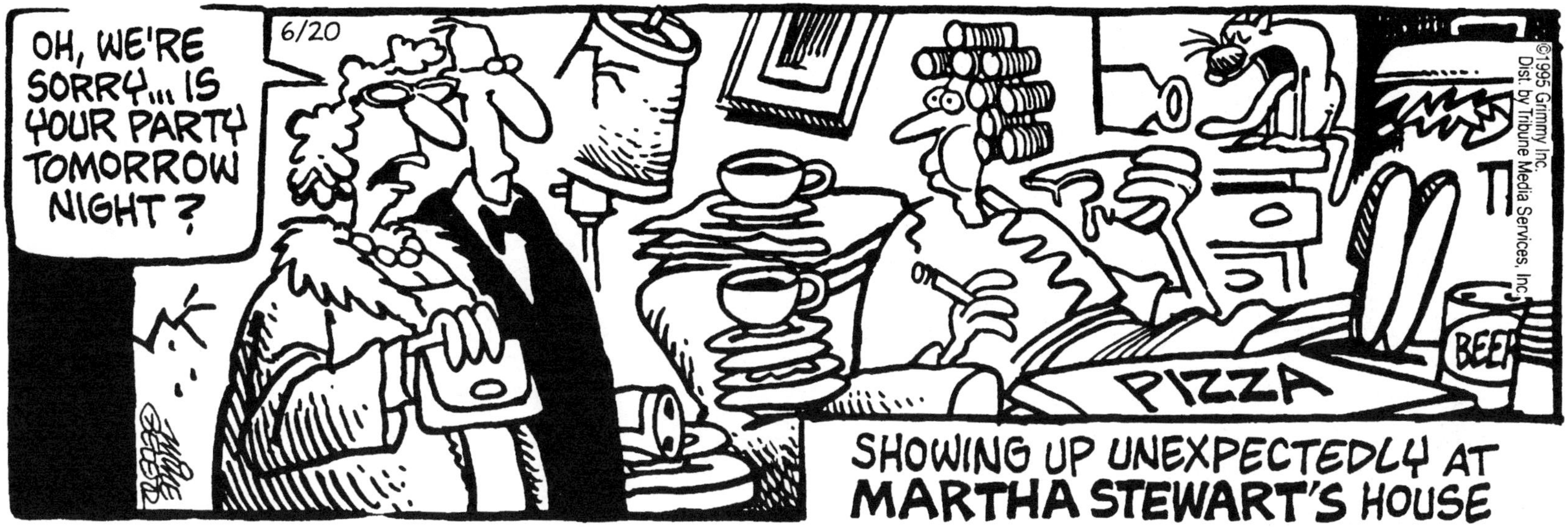
6/20
OH, WE'RE SORRY... IS YOUR PARTY TOMORROW NIGHT?
PIZZA
BEER
SHOWING UP UNEXPECTEDLY AT MARTHA STEWART'S HOUSE
©1995 Grimmy Inc. Dist. by Tribune Media Services, Inc.

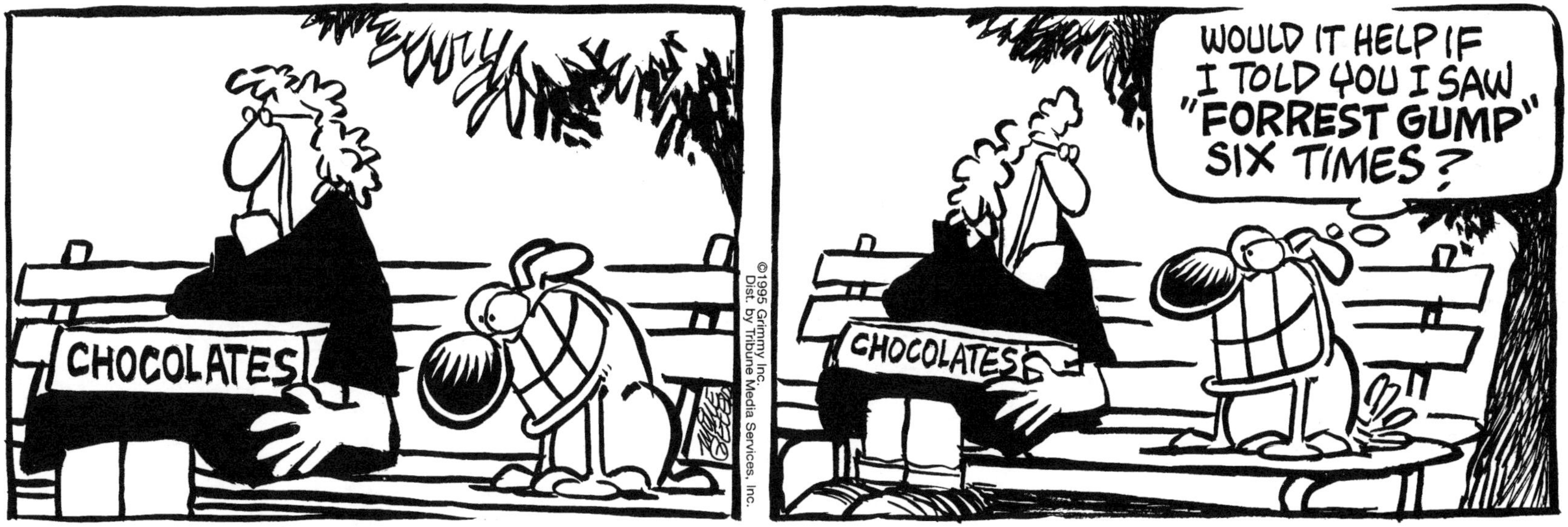
CHOCOLATES
©1995 Grimmy Inc. Dist. by Tribune Media Services, Inc.
WOULD IT HELP IF I TOLD YOU I SAW "FORREST GUMP" SIX TIMES?
CHOCOLATES

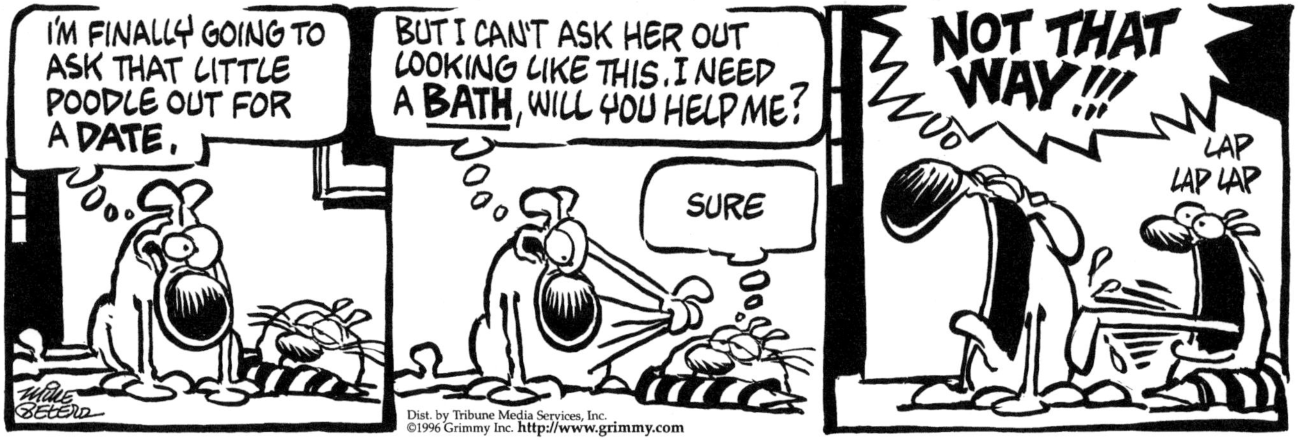
I'M FINALLY GOING TO ASK THAT LITTLE POODLE OUT FOR A DATE.
BUT I CAN'T ASK HER OUT LOOKING LIKE THIS. I NEED A BATH, WILL YOU HELP ME?
SURE
NOT THAT WAY!!!
LAP LAP LAP
Dist. by Tribune Media Services, Inc.
©1996 Grimmy Inc. http://www.grimmy.com

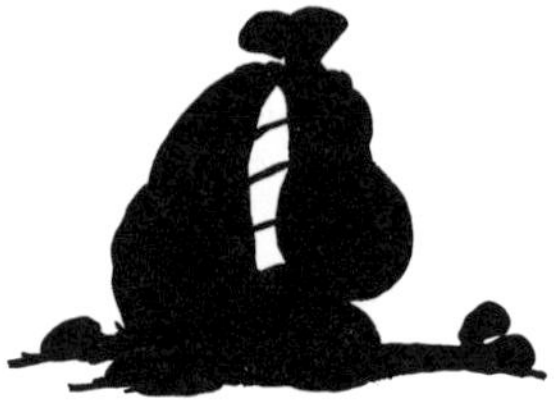

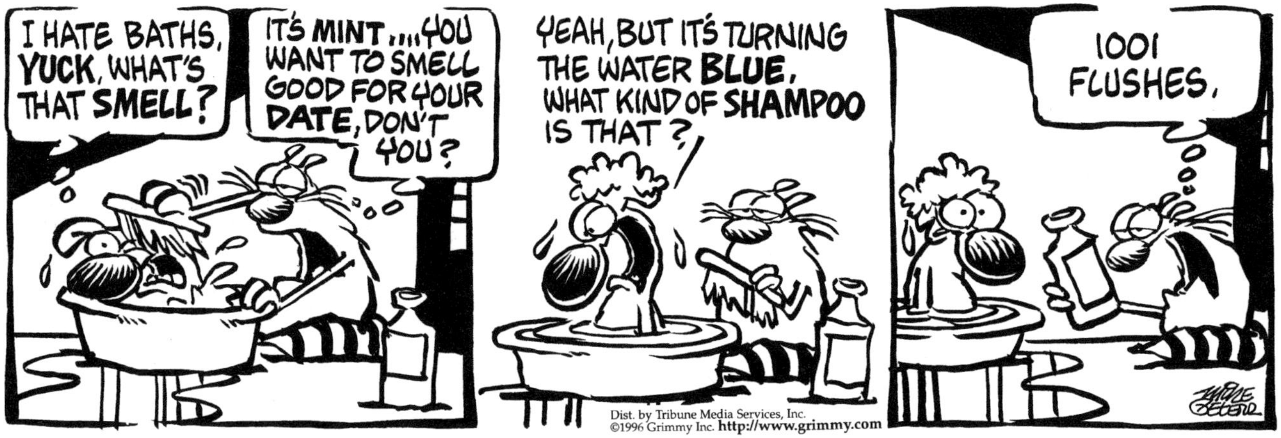
I HATE BATHS, YUCK, WHAT'S THAT SMELL?
IT'S MINT....YOU WANT TO SMELL GOOD FOR YOUR DATE, DON'T YOU?
YEAH, BUT IT'S TURNING THE WATER BLUE, WHAT KIND OF SHAMPOO IS THAT?
1001 FLUSHES.
Dist. by Tribune Media Services, Inc.
©1996 Grimmy Inc. http://www.grimmy.com

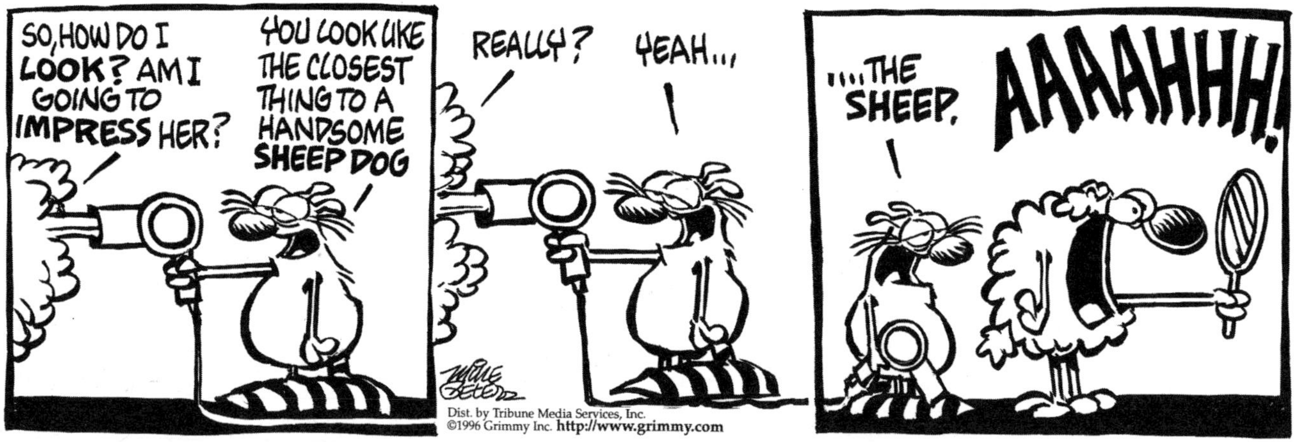
SO, HOW DO I LOOK? AM I GOING TO IMPRESS HER?
YOU LOOK LIKE THE CLOSEST THING TO A HANDSOME SHEEP DOG
REALLY?
YEAH...
....THE SHEEP.
AAAAHHH!
Dist. by Tribune Media Services, Inc.
©1996 Grimmy Inc. http://www.grimmy.com

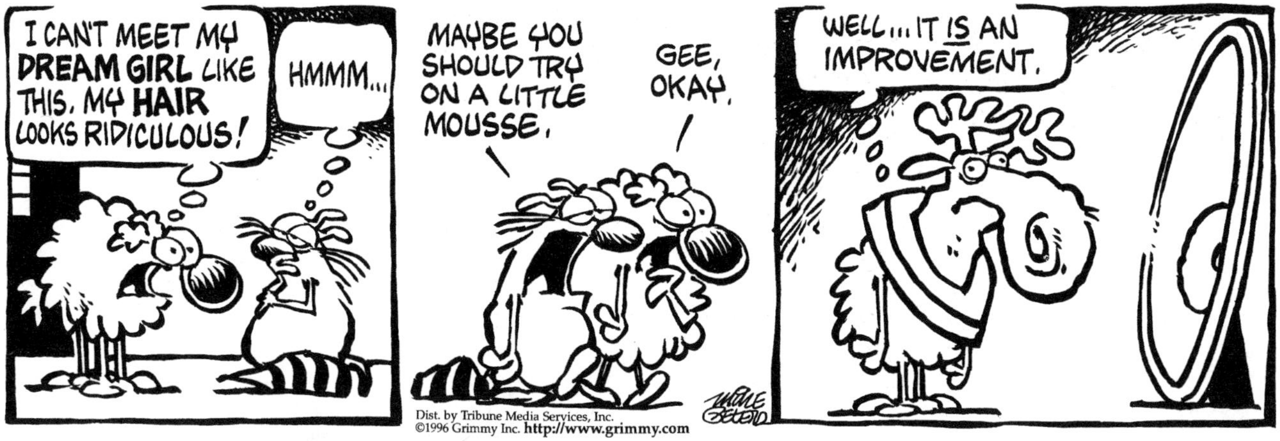
I CAN'T MEET MY DREAM GIRL LIKE THIS. MY HAIR LOOKS RIDICULOUS!
HMMM...
MAYBE YOU SHOULD TRY ON A LITTLE MOUSSE.
GEE, OKAY.
WELL... IT IS AN IMPROVEMENT.
Dist. by Tribune Media Services, Inc.
©1996 Grimmy Inc. http://www.grimmy.com

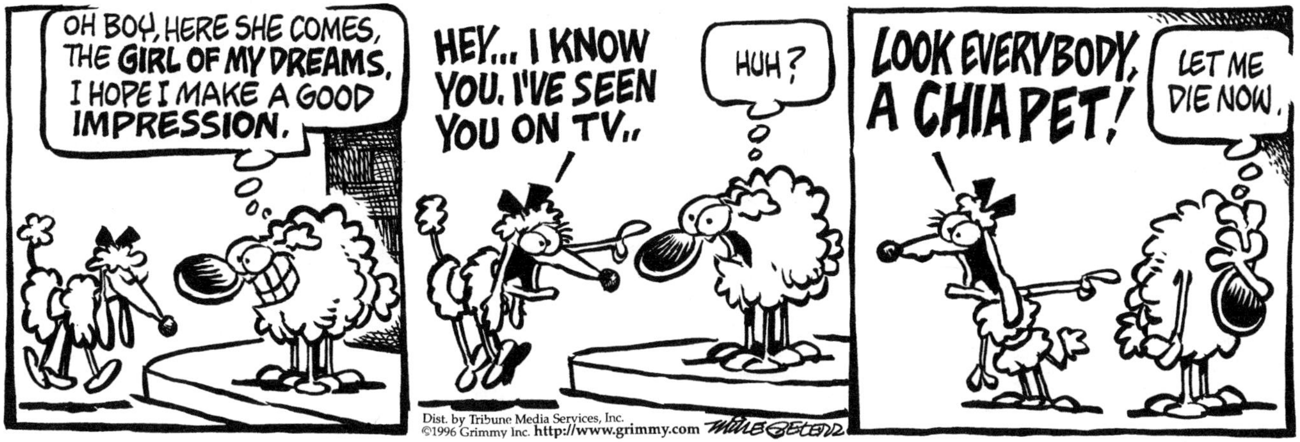
OH BOY, HERE SHE COMES, THE GIRL OF MY DREAMS. I HOPE I MAKE A GOOD IMPRESSION.
HEY... I KNOW YOU. I'VE SEEN YOU ON TV..
HUH?
LOOK EVERYBODY, A CHIA PET!
LET ME DIE NOW.
Dist. by Tribune Media Services, Inc.
©1996 Grimmy Inc. http://www.grimmy.com

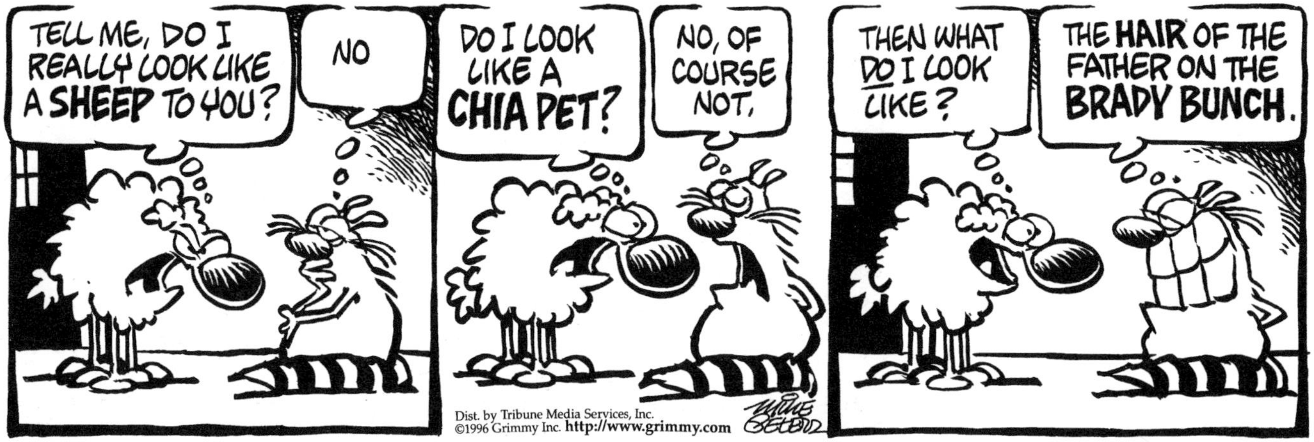
TELL ME, DO I REALLY LOOK LIKE A SHEEP TO YOU?
NO
DO I LOOK LIKE A CHIA PET?
NO, OF COURSE NOT.
THEN WHAT DO I LOOK LIKE?
THE HAIR OF THE FATHER ON THE BRADY BUNCH.
Dist. by Tribune Media Services, Inc.
©1996 Grimmy Inc. http://www.grimmy.com

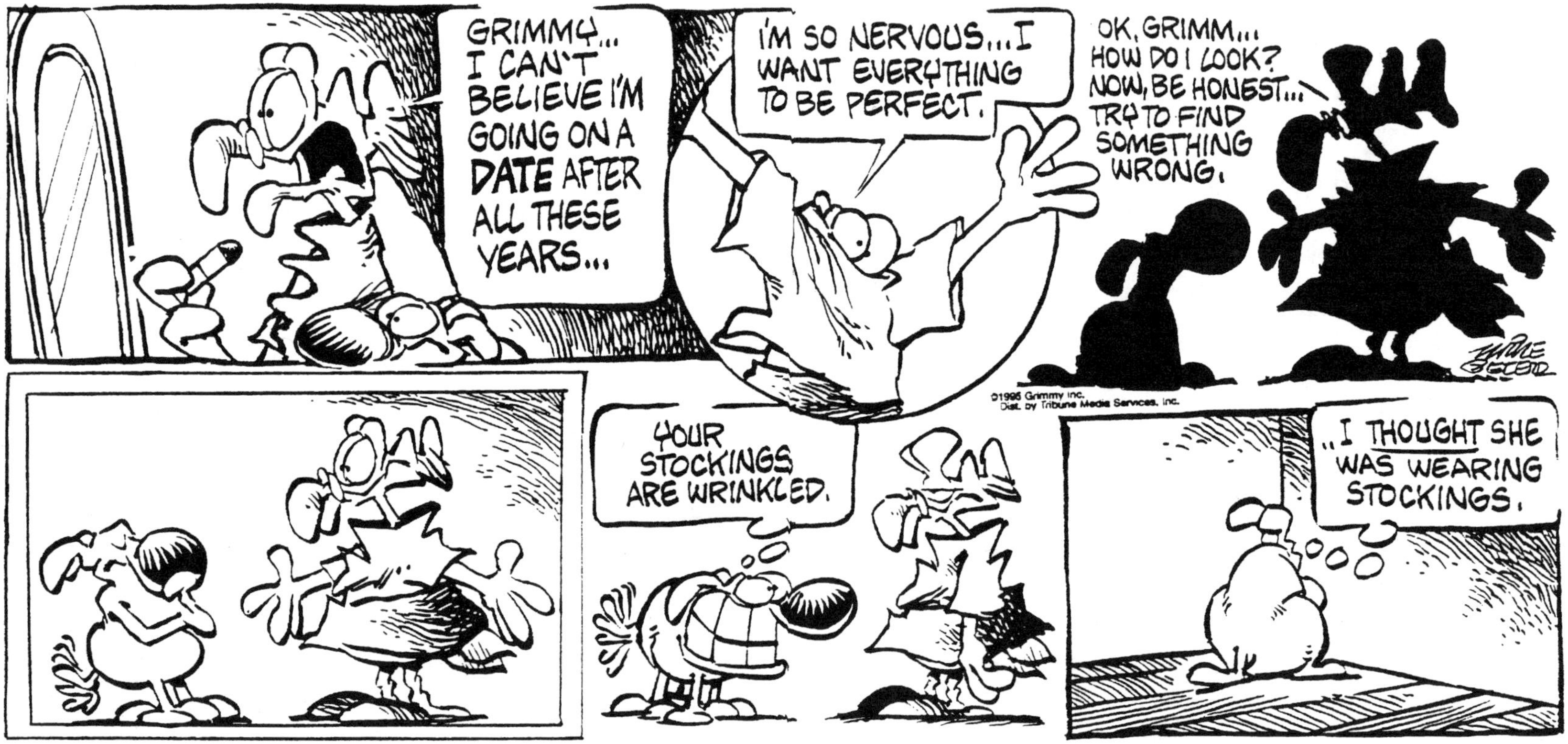
GRIMMY... I CAN'T BELIEVE I'M GOING ON A DATE AFTER ALL THESE YEARS...
I'M SO NERVOUS... I WANT EVERYTHING TO BE PERFECT.
OK, GRIMM... HOW DO I LOOK? NOW, BE HONEST... TRY TO FIND SOMETHING WRONG.
©1995 Grimmy Inc. Dist. by Tribune Media Services, Inc.
YOUR STOCKINGS ARE WRINKLED.
..I THOUGHT SHE WAS WEARING STOCKINGS.

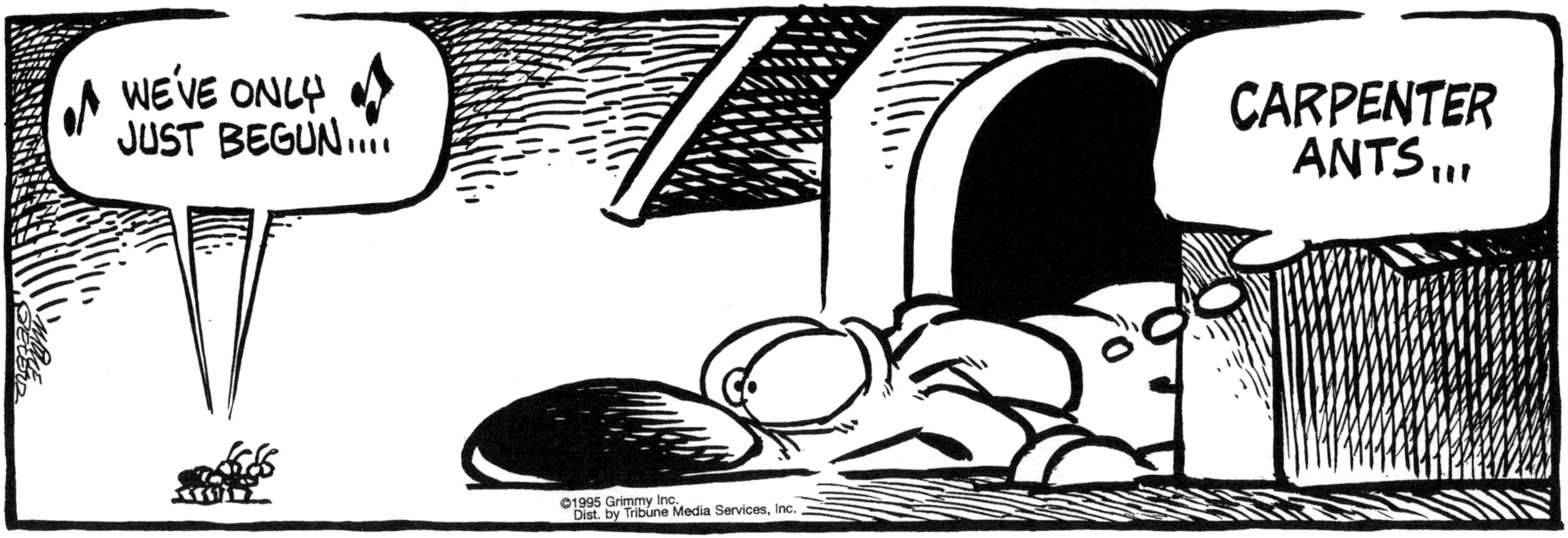
♪ WE'VE ONLY ♪ JUST BEGUN....
CARPENTER ANTS...
©1995 Grimmy Inc. Dist. by Tribune Media Services, Inc.

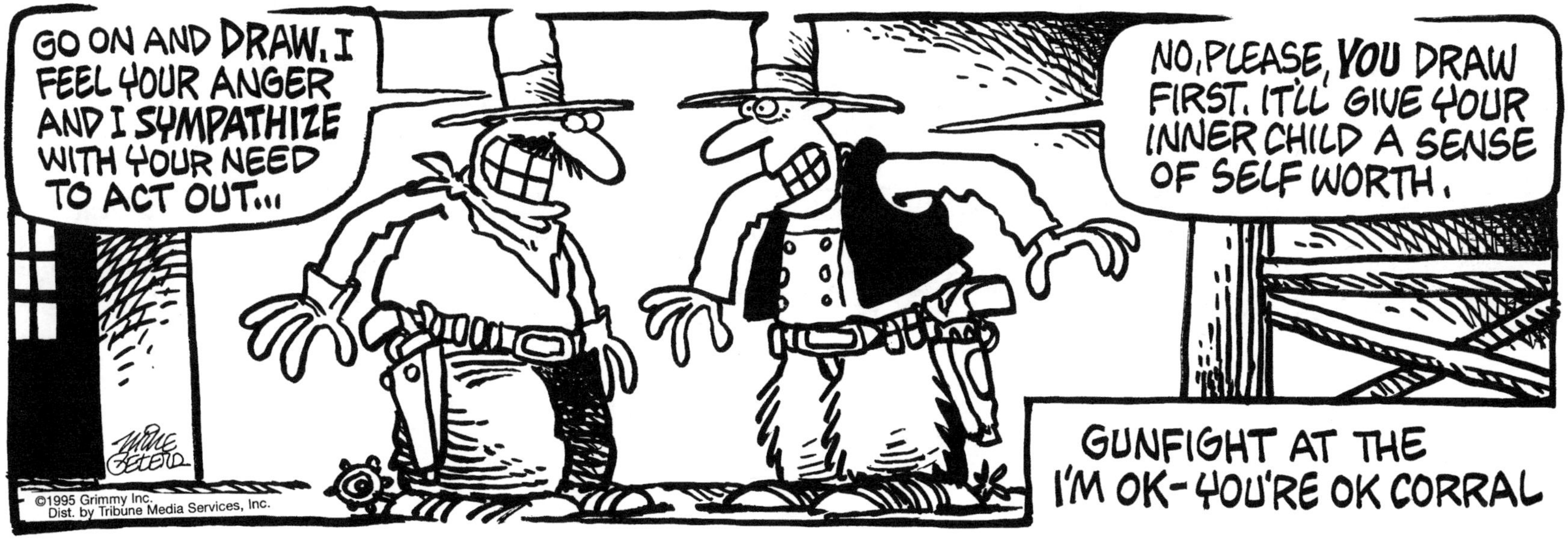
GO ON AND DRAW. I FEEL YOUR ANGER AND I SYMPATHIZE WITH YOUR NEED TO ACT OUT...
NO, PLEASE, YOU DRAW FIRST. IT'LL GIVE YOUR INNER CHILD A SENSE OF SELF WORTH.
GUNFIGHT AT THE I'M OK-YOU'RE OK CORRAL
©1995 Grimmy Inc. Dist. by Tribune Media Services, Inc.

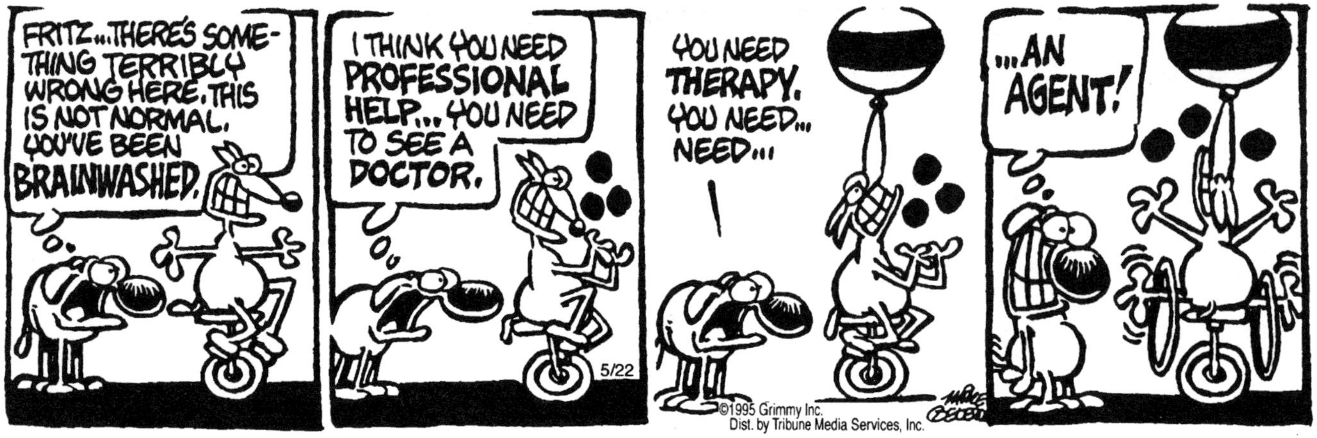
FRITZ...THERE'S SOMETHING TERRIBLY WRONG HERE. THIS IS NOT NORMAL. YOU'VE BEEN BRAINWASHED.
I THINK YOU NEED PROFESSIONAL HELP... YOU NEED TO SEE A DOCTOR.
5/22
YOU NEED THERAPY. YOU NEED... NEED...
!
©1995 Grimmy Inc.
Dist. by Tribune Media Services, Inc.
...AN AGENT!

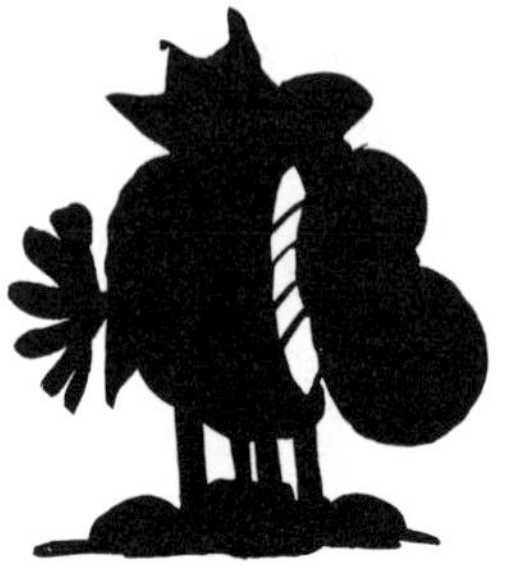

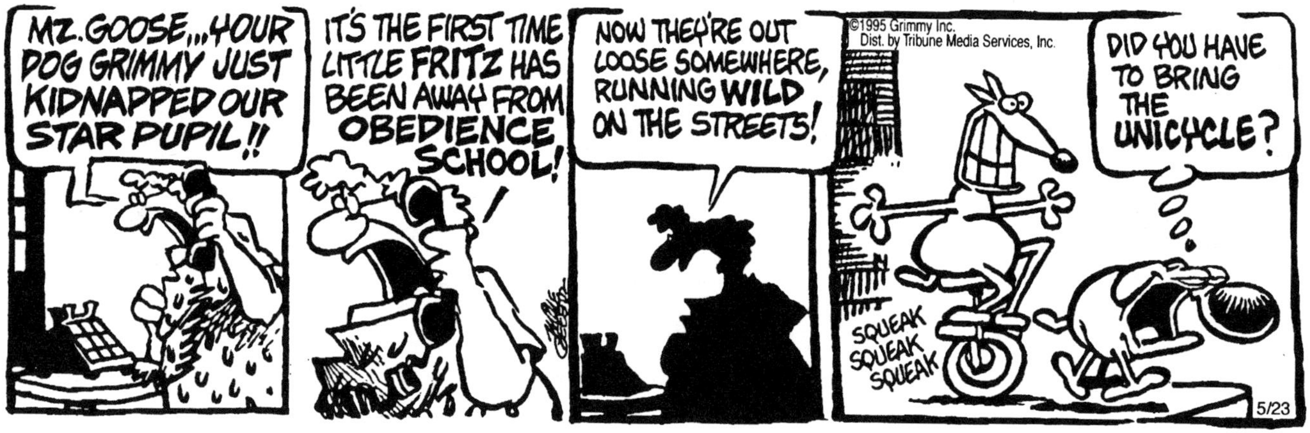
MZ. GOOSE... YOUR DOG GRIMMY JUST KIDNAPPED OUR STAR PUPIL!!
IT'S THE FIRST TIME LITTLE FRITZ HAS BEEN AWAY FROM OBEDIENCE SCHOOL!
NOW THEY'RE OUT LOOSE SOMEWHERE, RUNNING WILD ON THE STREETS!
©1995 Grimmy Inc.
Dist. by Tribune Media Services, Inc.
DID YOU HAVE TO BRING THE UNICYCLE?
SQUEAK
SQUEAK
SQUEAK
5/23

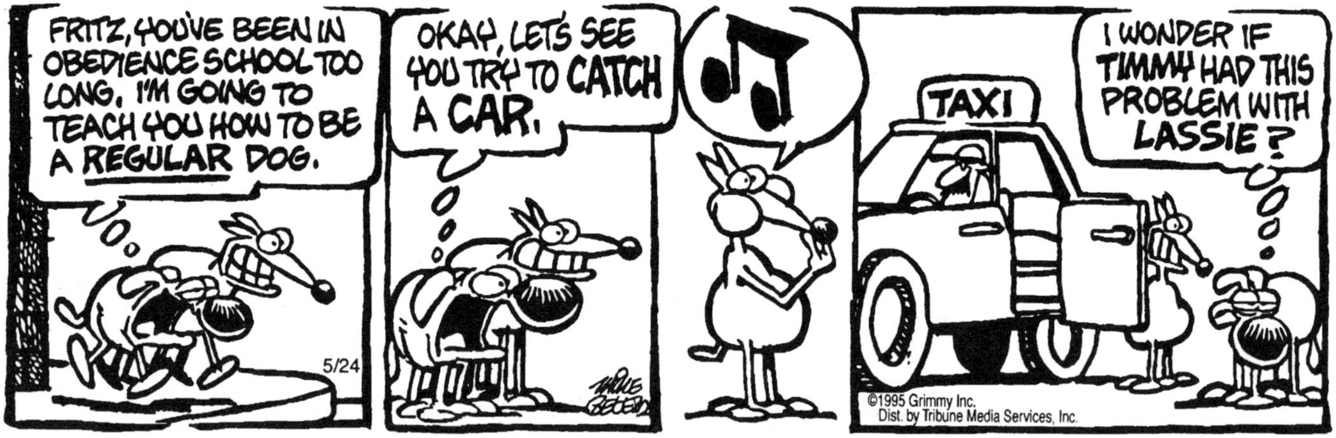
FRITZ, YOU'VE BEEN IN OBEDIENCE SCHOOL TOO LONG. I'M GOING TO TEACH YOU HOW TO BE A REGULAR DOG.
5/24
OKAY, LET'S SEE YOU TRY TO CATCH A CAR.
TAXI
I WONDER IF TIMMY HAD THIS PROBLEM WITH LASSIE?
©1995 Grimmy Inc.
Dist. by Tribune Media Services, Inc.

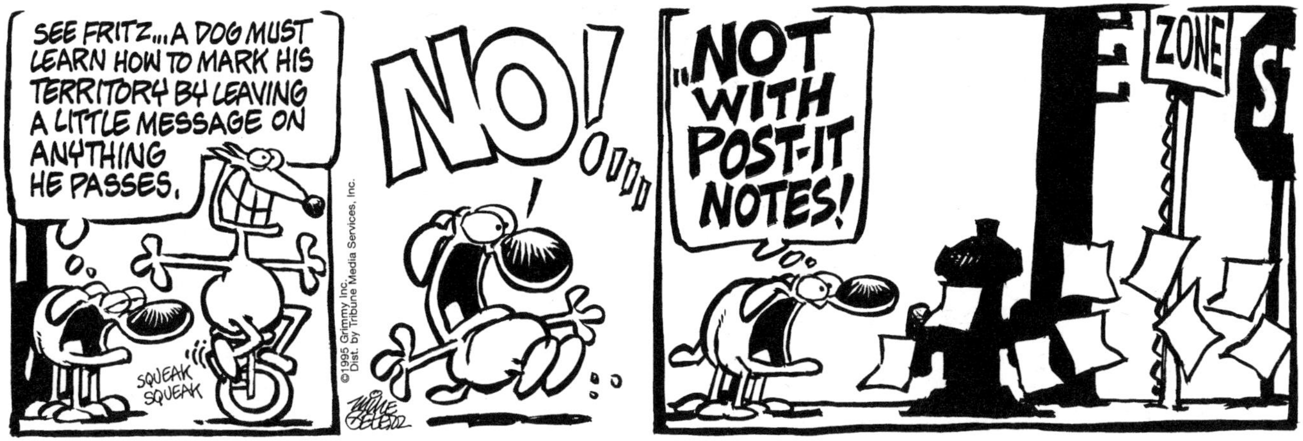
SEE FRITZ... A DOG MUST LEARN HOW TO MARK HIS TERRITORY BY LEAVING A LITTLE MESSAGE ON ANYTHING HE PASSES.
SQUEAK SQUEAK
©1995 Grimmy Inc. Dist. by Tribune Media Services, Inc.
NO! OIII
..NOT WITH POST-IT NOTES!
ZONE

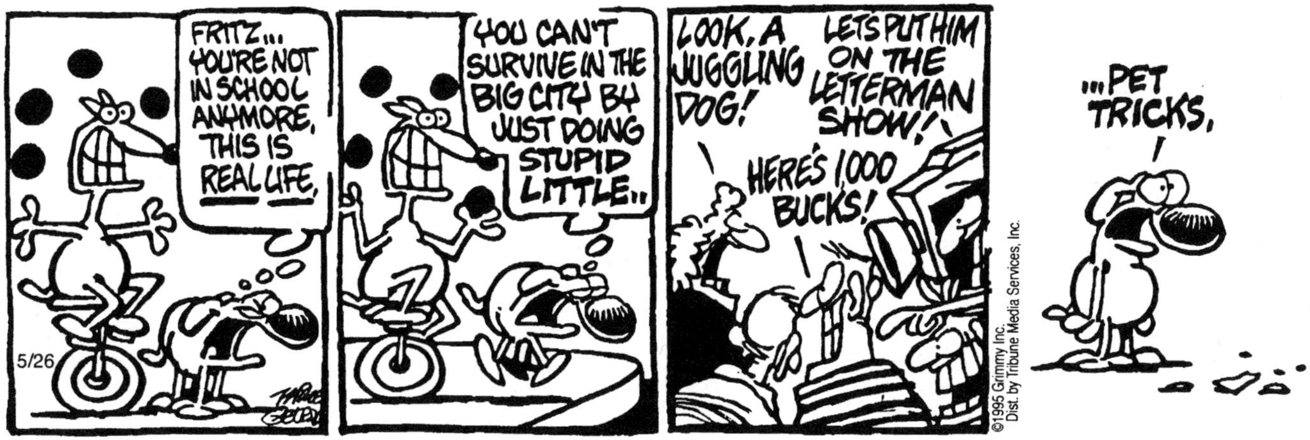
FRITZ... YOU'RE NOT IN SCHOOL ANYMORE. THIS IS REAL LIFE.
5/26
YOU CAN'T SURVIVE IN THE BIG CITY BY JUST DOING STUPID LITTLE..
LOOK, A JUGGLING DOG!
LETS PUT HIM ON THE LETTERMAN SHOW!
HERE'S 1000 BUCKS!
©1995 Grimmy Inc. Dist. by Tribune Media Services, Inc.
...PET TRICKS.

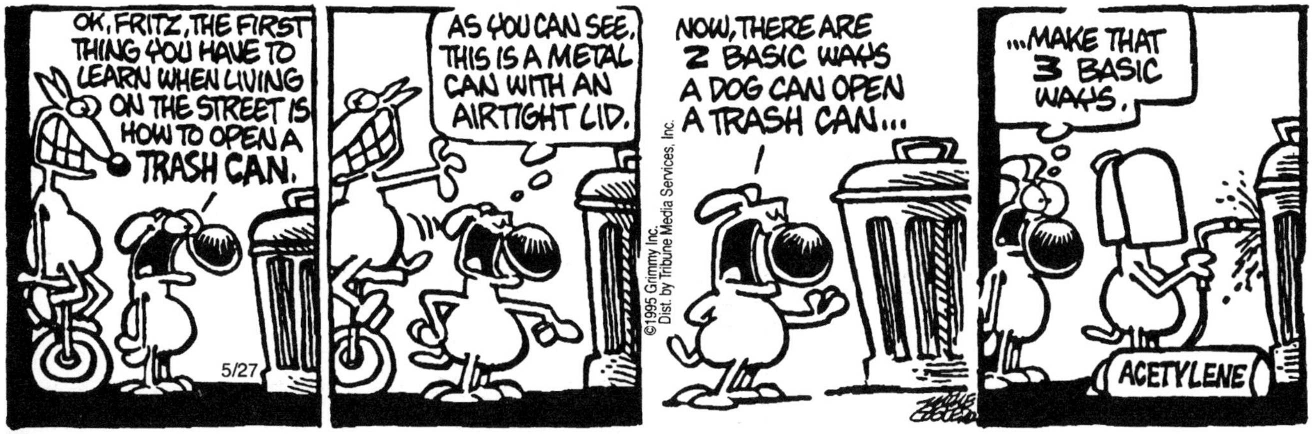
OK, FRITZ, THE FIRST THING YOU HAVE TO LEARN WHEN LIVING ON THE STREET IS HOW TO OPEN A TRASH CAN.
5/27
AS YOU CAN SEE, THIS IS A METAL CAN WITH AN AIRTIGHT LID.
©1995 Grimmy Inc. Dist. by Tribune Media Services, Inc.
NOW, THERE ARE 2 BASIC WAYS A DOG CAN OPEN A TRASH CAN...
...MAKE THAT 3 BASIC WAYS.
ACETYLENE

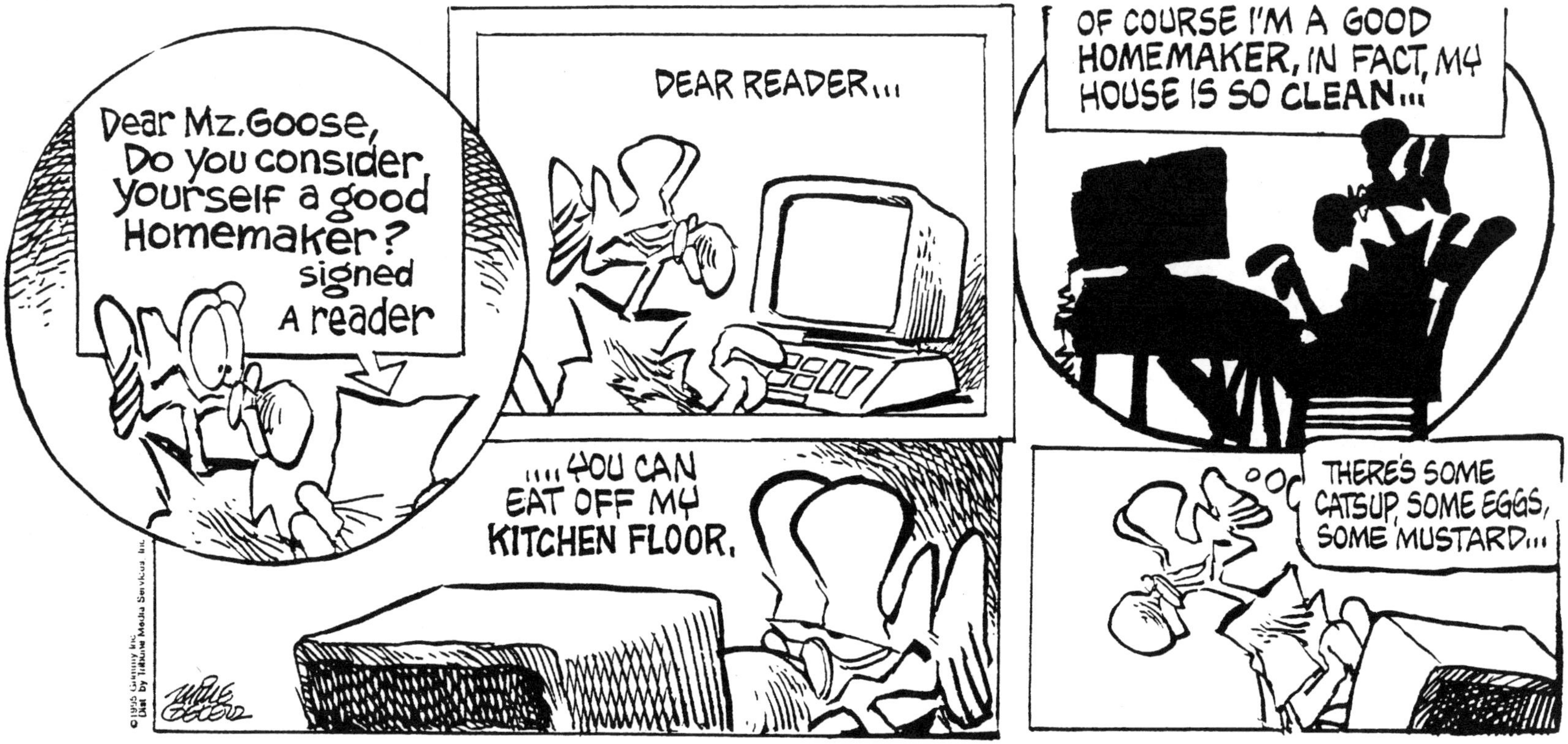

Dear Mz. Goose, Do you consider yourself a good Homemaker? signed A reader
DEAR READER...
OF COURSE I'M A GOOD HOMEMAKER, IN FACT, MY HOUSE IS SO CLEAN...
....YOU CAN EAT OFF MY KITCHEN FLOOR.
THERE'S SOME CATSUP, SOME EGGS, SOME MUSTARD...
© 1995 Grimmy Inc. Dist by Tribune Media Services Inc.

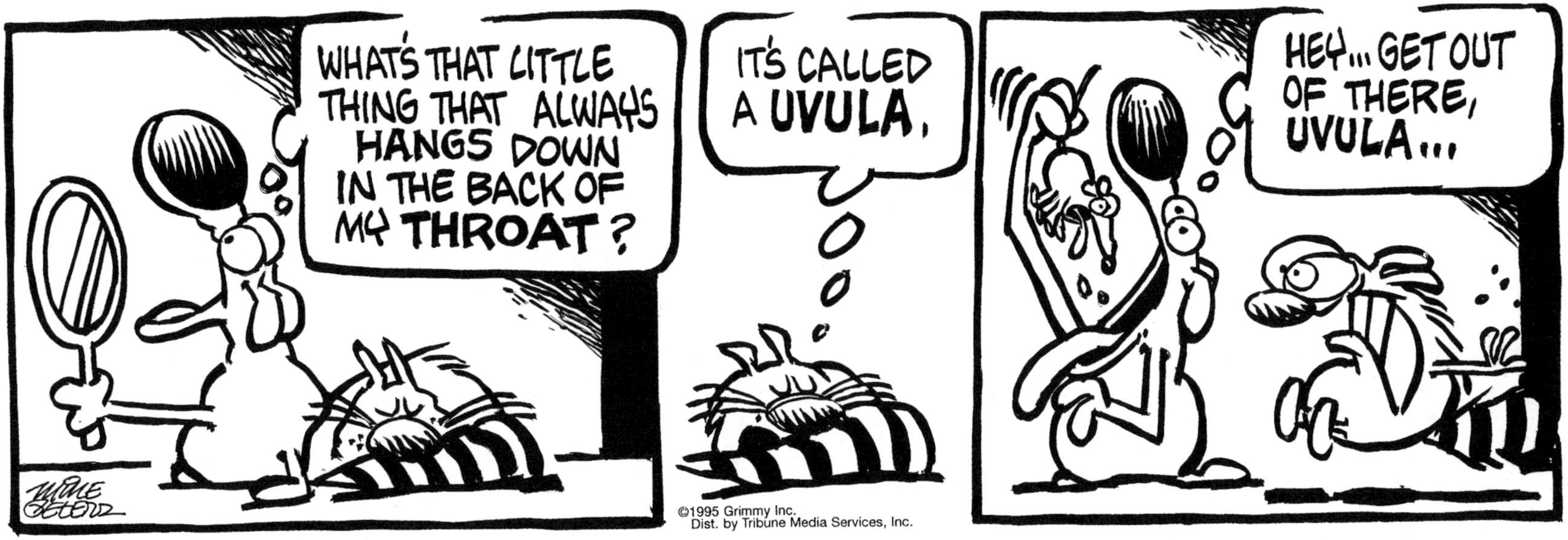
WHAT'S THAT LITTLE THING THAT ALWAYS HANGS DOWN IN THE BACK OF MY THROAT?
IT'S CALLED A UVULA.
HEY... GET OUT OF THERE, UVULA...
©1995 Grimmy Inc. Dist. by Tribune Media Services, Inc.

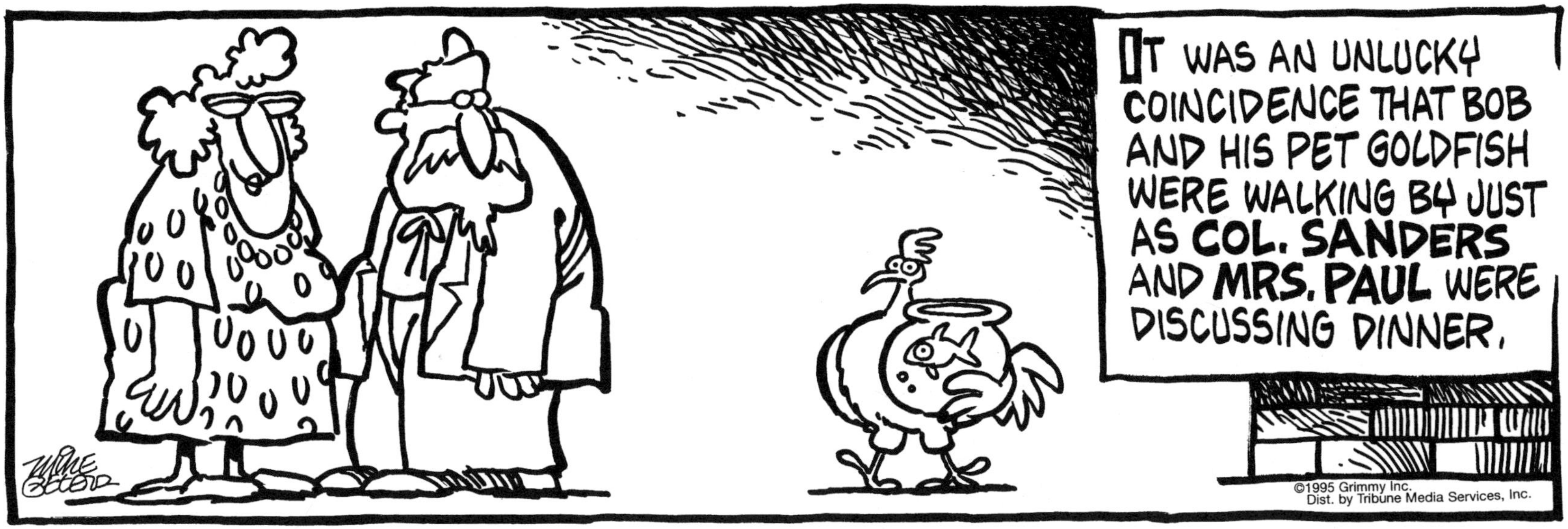
IT WAS AN UNLUCKY COINCIDENCE THAT BOB AND HIS PET GOLDFISH WERE WALKING BY JUST AS COL. SANDERS AND MRS. PAUL WERE DISCUSSING DINNER.
©1995 Grimmy Inc. Dist. by Tribune Media Services, Inc.

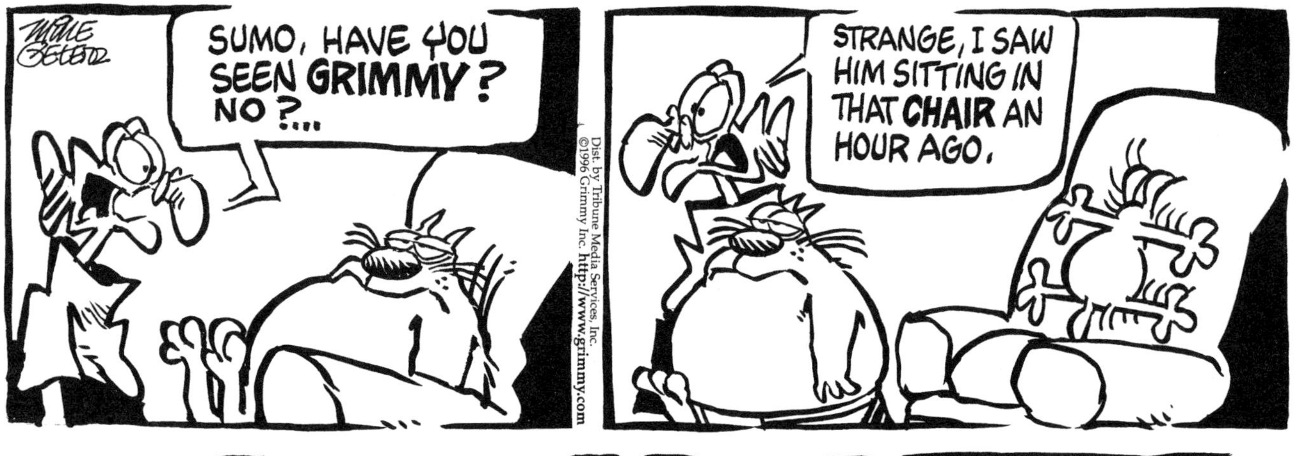
SUMO, HAVE YOU SEEN GRIMMY? NO?...
STRANGE, I SAW HIM SITTING IN THAT CHAIR AN HOUR AGO.
Dist. by Tribune Media Services, Inc. ©1996 Grimmy Inc. http://www.grimmy.com

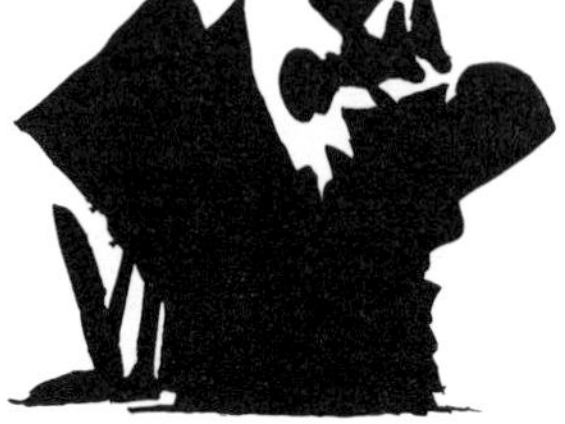

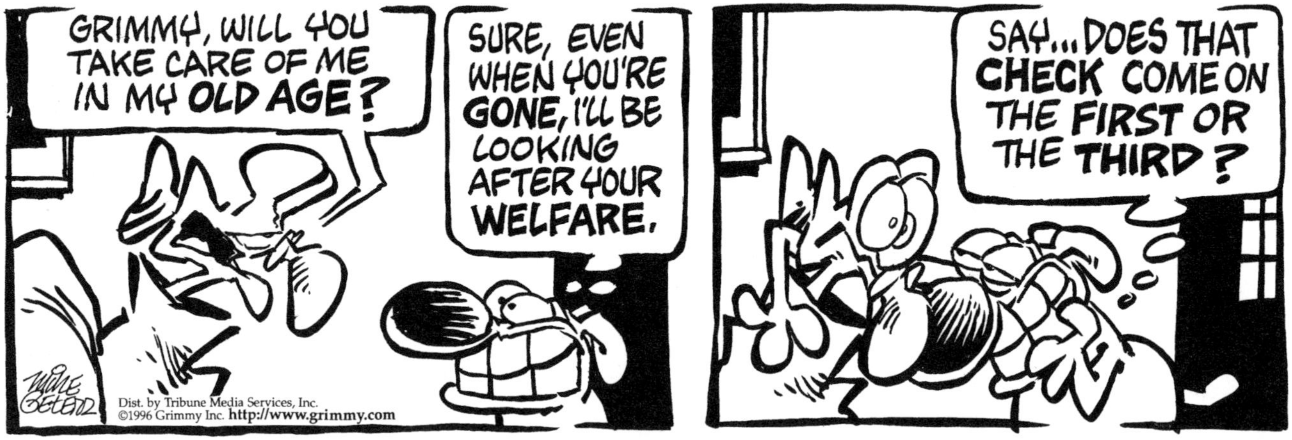
GRIMMY, WILL YOU TAKE CARE OF ME IN MY OLD AGE?
SURE, EVEN WHEN YOU'RE GONE, I'LL BE LOOKING AFTER YOUR WELFARE.
SAY... DOES THAT CHECK COME ON THE FIRST OR THE THIRD?
Dist. by Tribune Media Services, Inc. ©1996 Grimmy Inc. http://www.grimmy.com

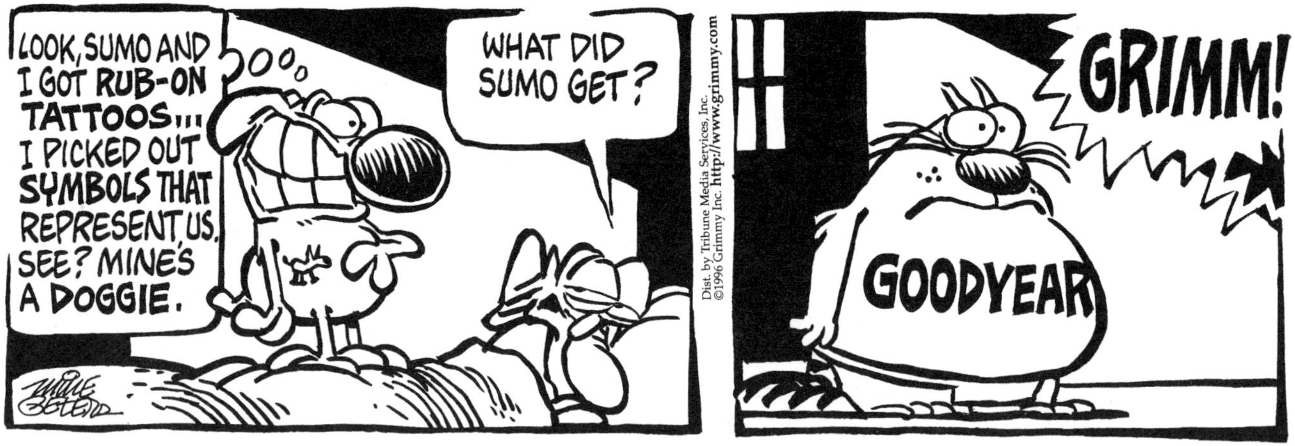
LOOK, SUMO AND I GOT RUB-ON TATTOOS... I PICKED OUT SYMBOLS THAT REPRESENT US, SEE? MINE'S A DOGGIE.
WHAT DID SUMO GET?
GOODYEAR
GRIMM!
Dist. by Tribune Media Services, Inc. ©1996 Grimmy Inc. http://www.grimmy.com

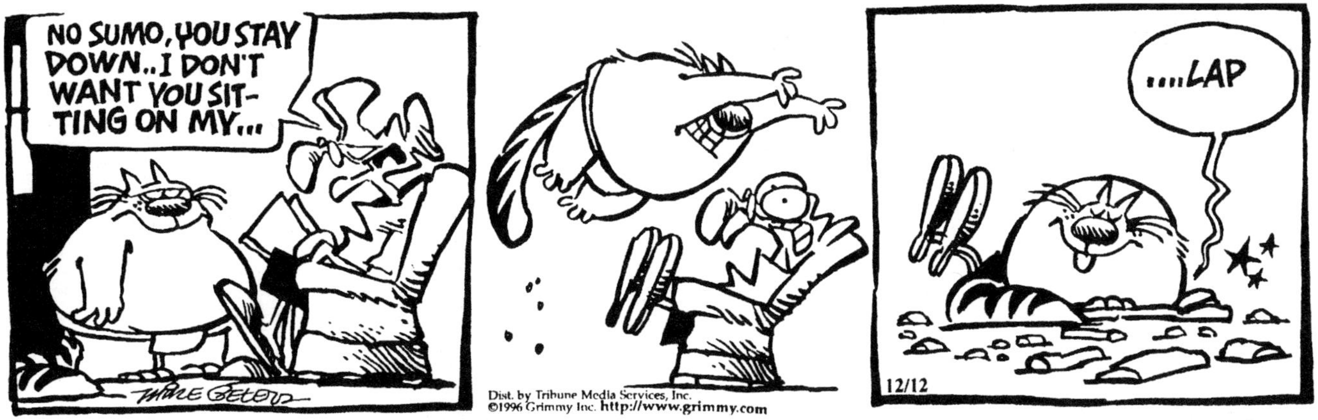
NO SUMO, YOU STAY DOWN.. I DON'T WANT YOU SITTING ON MY...
....LAP
MIKE PETERS
Dist. by Tribune Media Services, Inc. ©1996 Grimmy Inc. http://www.grimmy.com
12/12

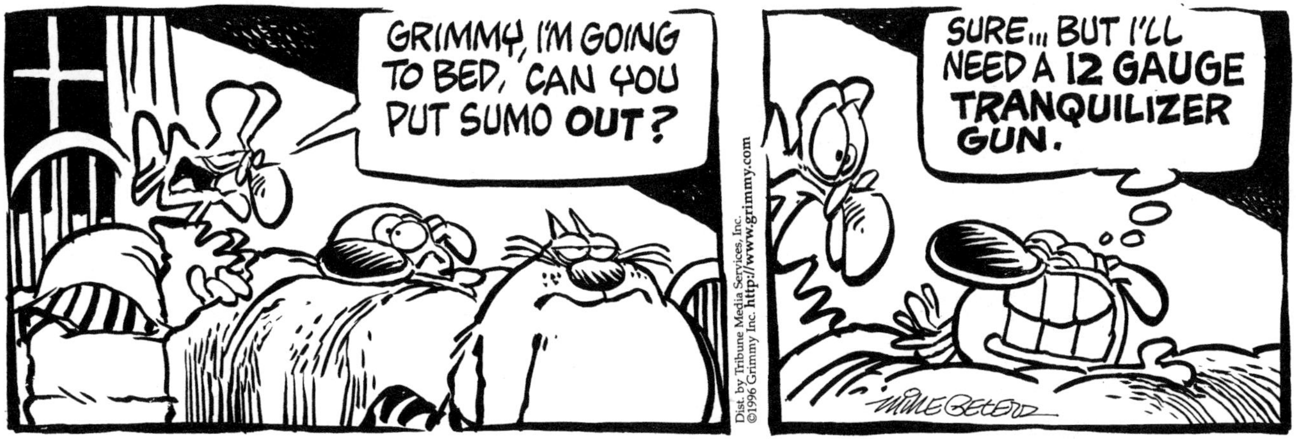
GRIMMY, I'M GOING TO BED, CAN YOU PUT SUMO OUT?
SURE... BUT I'LL NEED A 12 GAUGE TRANQUILIZER GUN.
Dist. by Tribune Media Services, Inc. ©1996 Grimmy Inc. http://www.grimmy.com
MIKE PETERS

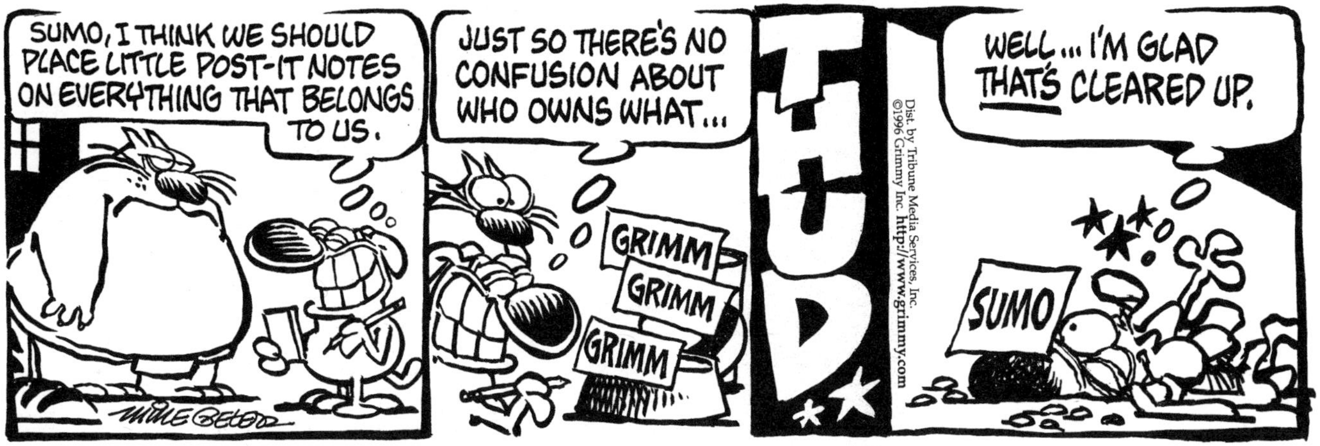
SUMO, I THINK WE SHOULD PLACE LITTLE POST-IT NOTES ON EVERYTHING THAT BELONGS TO US.
JUST SO THERE'S NO CONFUSION ABOUT WHO OWNS WHAT...
GRIMM
GRIMM
GRIMM
THUD
WELL... I'M GLAD THAT'S CLEARED UP.
SUMO
MIKE PETERS
Dist. by Tribune Media Services, Inc. ©1996 Grimmy Inc. http://www.grimmy.com

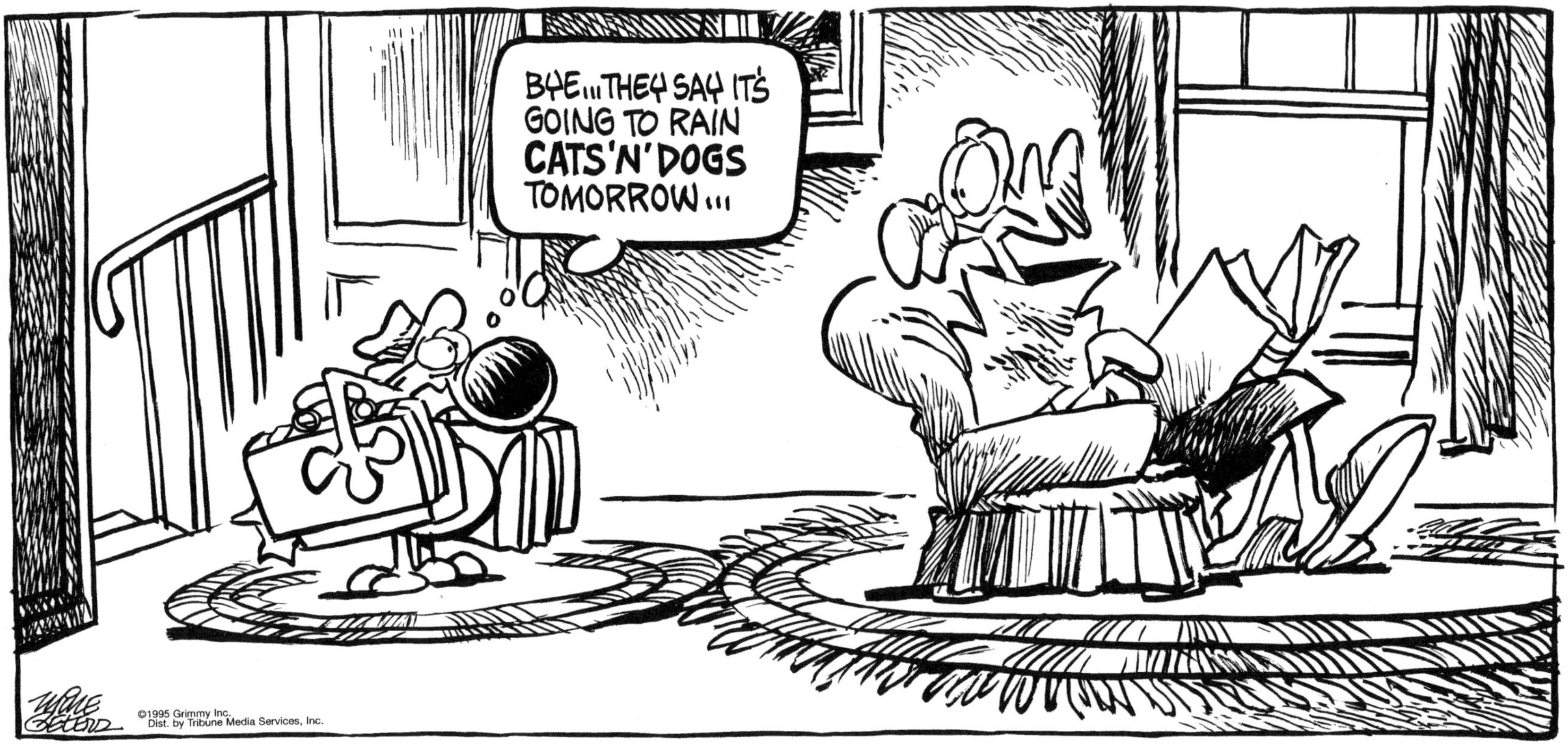
BYE... THEY SAY IT'S GOING TO RAIN CATS'N'DOGS TOMORROW...
©1995 Grimmy Inc.
Dist. by Tribune Media Services, Inc.

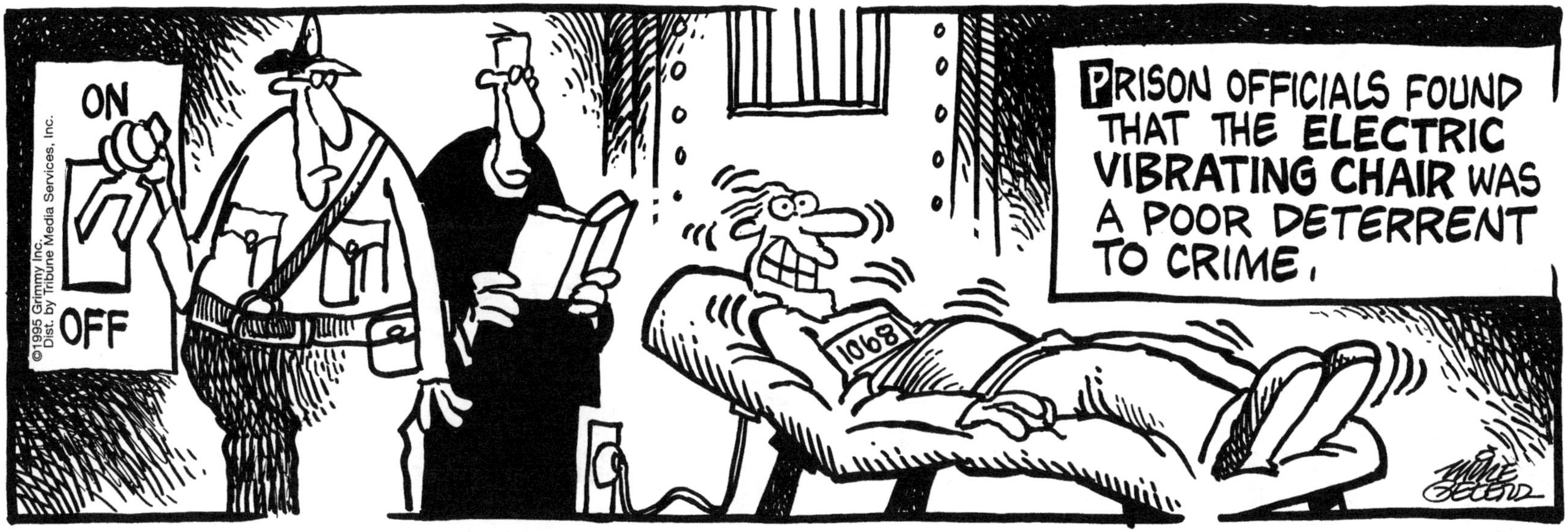
ON
OFF
©1995 Grimmy Inc.
Dist. by Tribune Media Services, Inc.
PRISON OFFICIALS FOUND THAT THE **ELECTRIC VIBRATING CHAIR** WAS A POOR DETERRENT TO CRIME.
1068

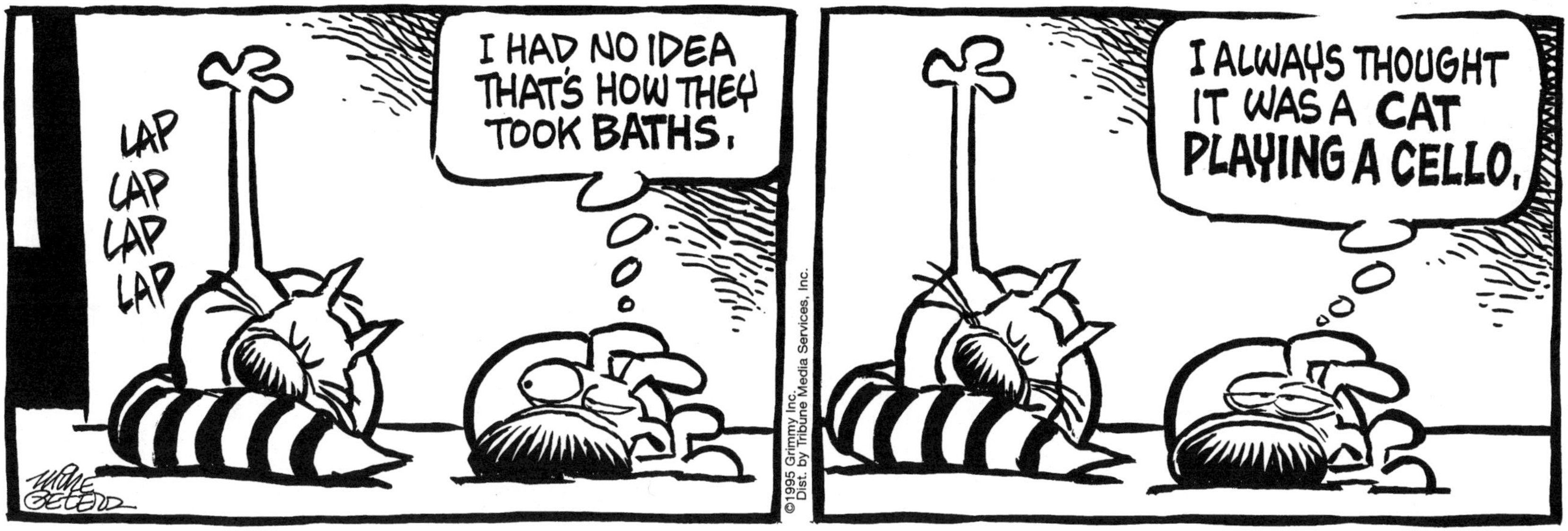
LAP
LAP
LAP
LAP
I HAD NO IDEA THAT'S HOW THEY TOOK **BATHS**.
©1995 Grimmy Inc.
Dist. by Tribune Media Services, Inc.
I ALWAYS THOUGHT IT WAS A **CAT PLAYING A CELLO**.

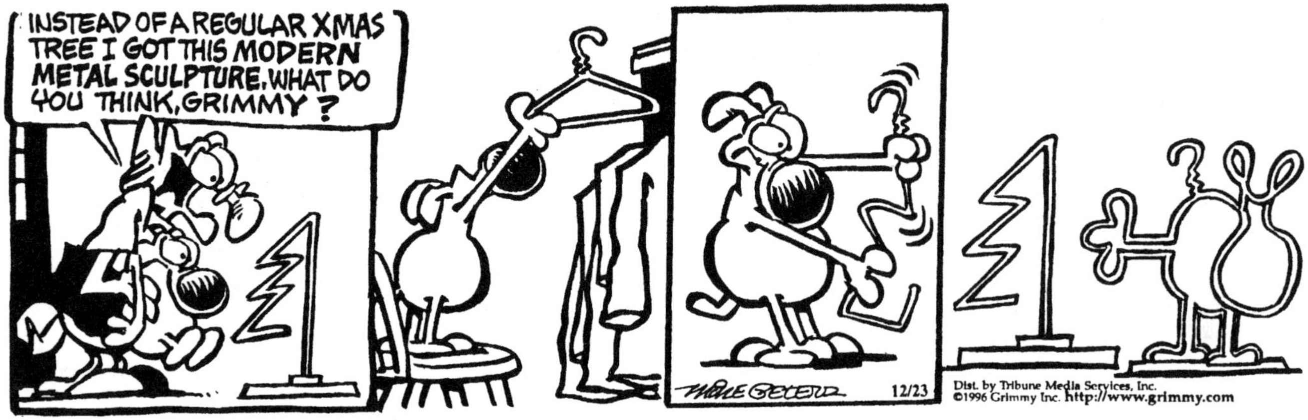
INSTEAD OF A REGULAR XMAS TREE I GOT THIS MODERN METAL SCULPTURE. WHAT DO YOU THINK, GRIMMY?
12/23
Dist. by Tribune Media Services, Inc.
©1996 Grimmy Inc. http://www.grimmy.com

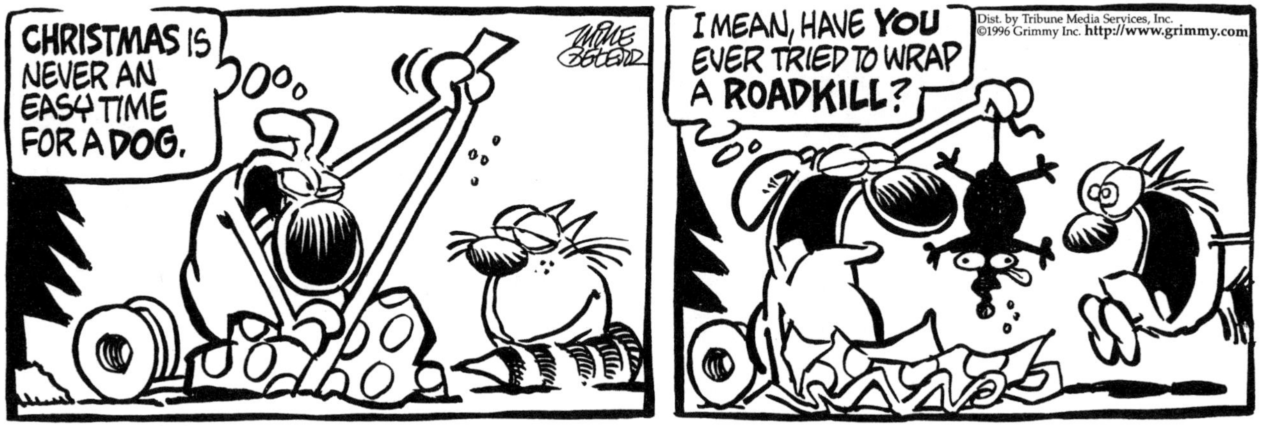
CHRISTMAS IS NEVER AN EASY TIME FOR A DOG.
I MEAN, HAVE YOU EVER TRIED TO WRAP A ROADKILL?
Dist. by Tribune Media Services, Inc.
©1996 Grimmy Inc. http://www.grimmy.com

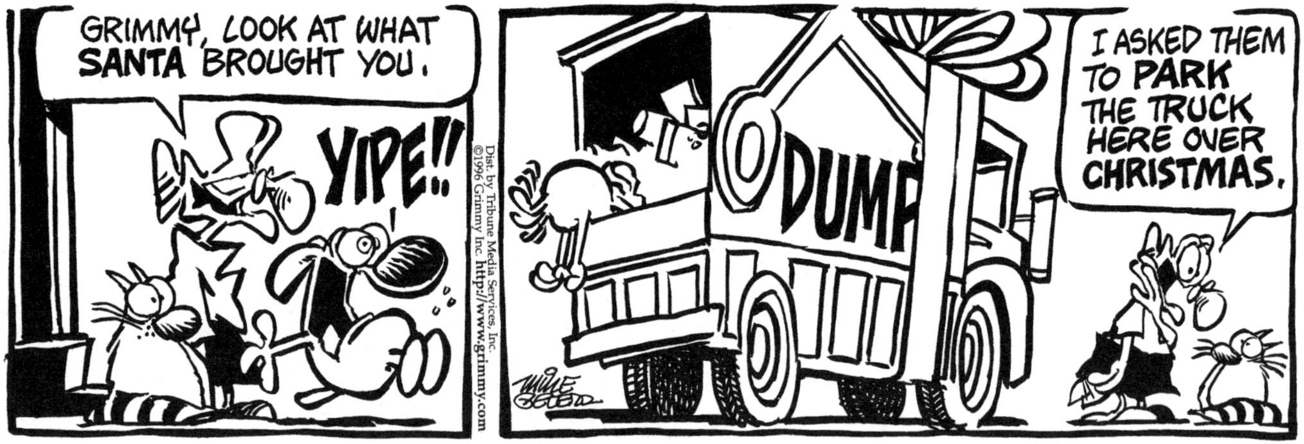
GRIMMY, LOOK AT WHAT SANTA BROUGHT YOU.
YIPE!!
Dist. by Tribune Media Services, Inc.
©1996 Grimmy Inc. http://www.grimmy.com
DUMP
I ASKED THEM TO PARK THE TRUCK HERE OVER CHRISTMAS.

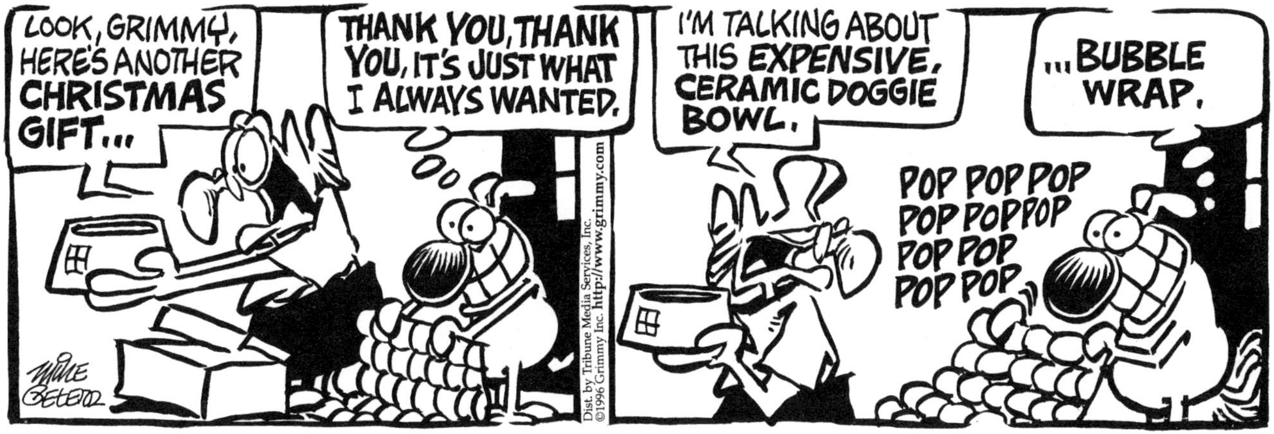
LOOK, GRIMMY, HERE'S ANOTHER CHRISTMAS GIFT...
THANK YOU, THANK YOU, IT'S JUST WHAT I ALWAYS WANTED.
Dist. by Tribune Media Services, Inc. ©1996 Grimmy Inc. http://www.grimmy.com
I'M TALKING ABOUT THIS EXPENSIVE, CERAMIC DOGGIE BOWL.
...BUBBLE WRAP.
POP POP POP POP POP POP POP POP POP POP

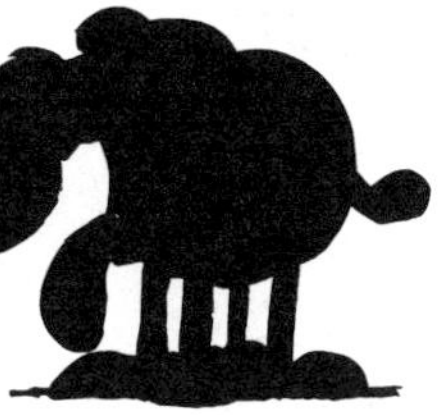

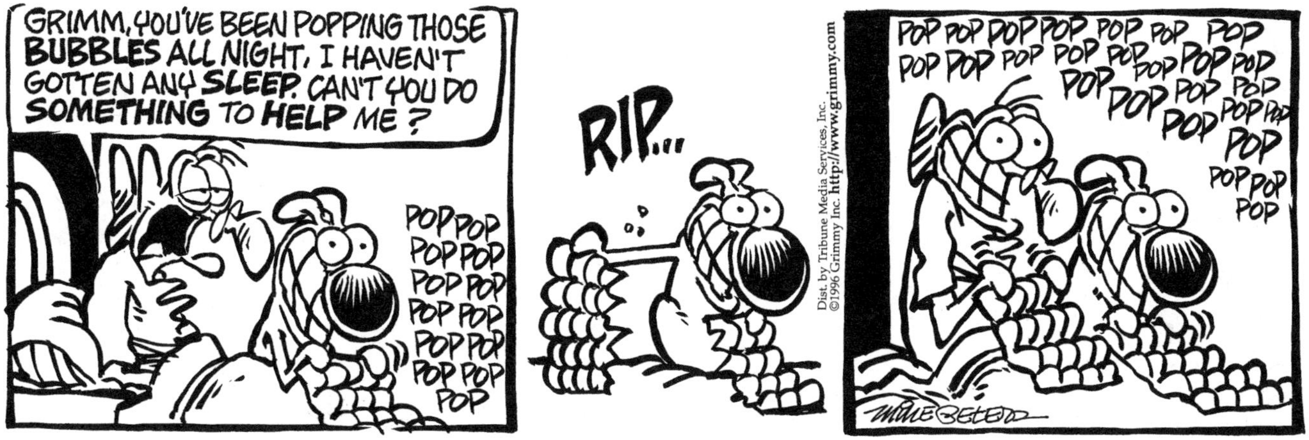
GRIMM, YOU'VE BEEN POPPING THOSE BUBBLES ALL NIGHT. I HAVEN'T GOTTEN ANY SLEEP. CAN'T YOU DO SOMETHING TO HELP ME?
POP POP POP POP POP POP POP POP POP POP POP POP POP
RIP...
Dist. by Tribune Media Services, Inc. ©1996 Grimmy Inc. http://www.grimmy.com
POP POP POP POP POP POP POP POP POP POP POP POP POP POP POP POP POP POP POP POP POP POP POP POP POP POP

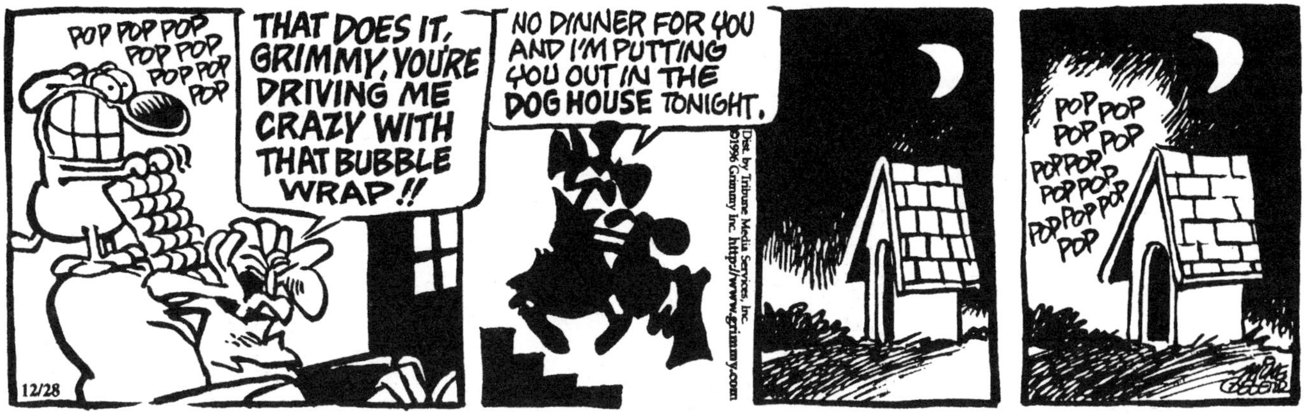
POP POP POP POP POP POP POP POP
THAT DOES IT, GRIMMY, YOU'RE DRIVING ME CRAZY WITH THAT BUBBLE WRAP!!
12/28
NO DINNER FOR YOU AND I'M PUTTING YOU OUT IN THE DOG HOUSE TONIGHT.
Dist. by Tribune Media Services, Inc. ©1996 Grimmy Inc. http://www.grimmy.com
POP POP POP POP POP POP POP POP POP POP POP POP

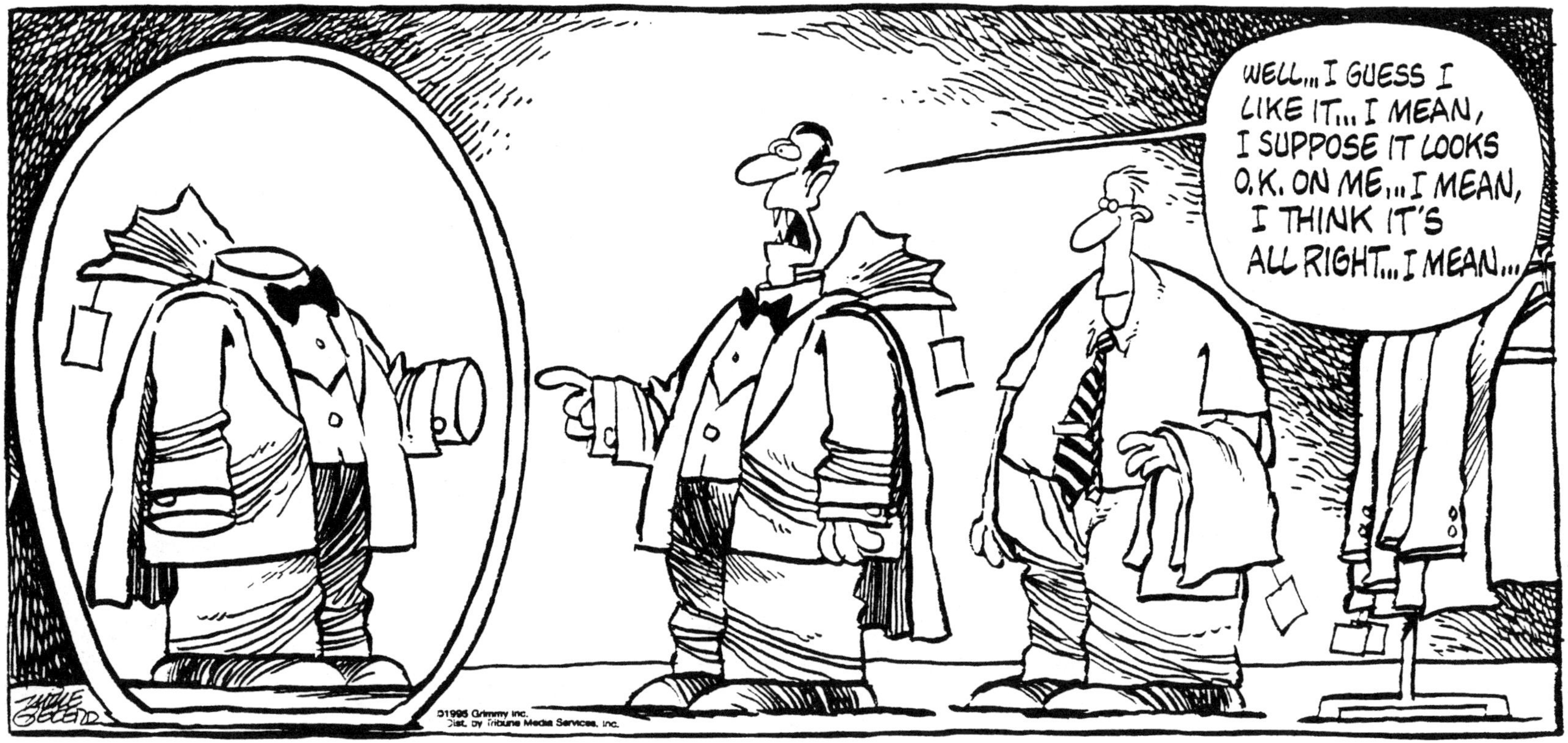
WELL... I GUESS I LIKE IT... I MEAN, I SUPPOSE IT LOOKS O.K. ON ME... I MEAN, I THINK IT'S ALL RIGHT... I MEAN...
©1996 Grimmy Inc.
Dist. by Tribune Media Services, Inc.

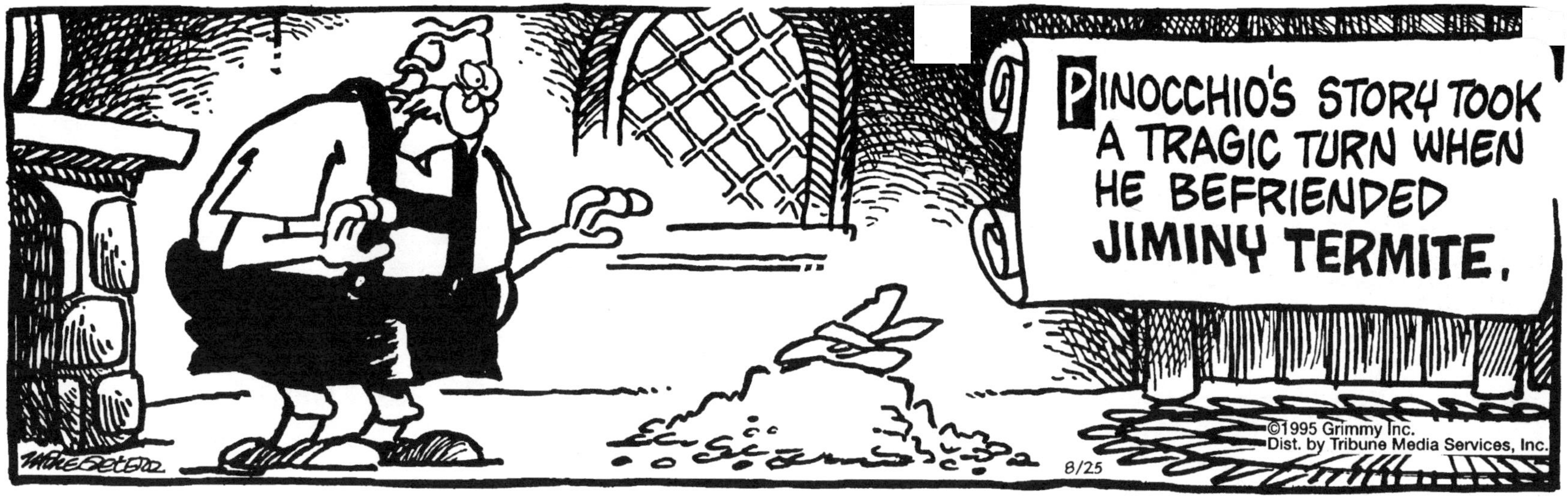
PINOCCHIO'S STORY TOOK A TRAGIC TURN WHEN HE BEFRIENDED JIMINY TERMITE.
©1995 Grimmy Inc.
Dist. by Tribune Media Services, Inc.
8/25

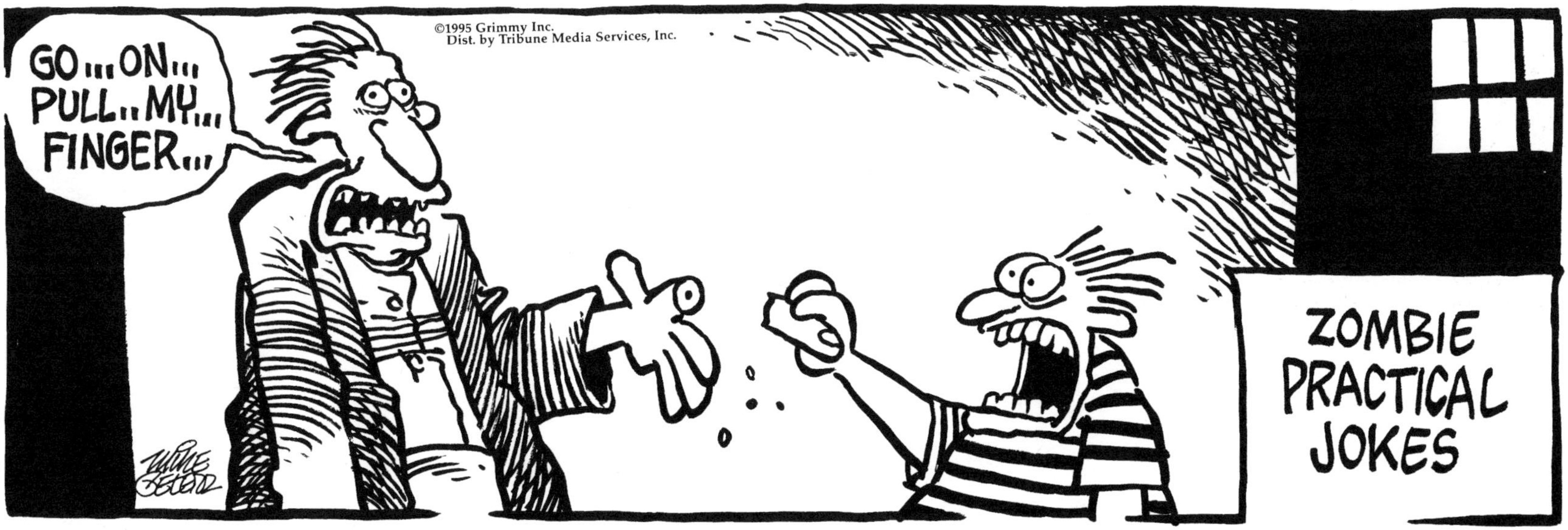
©1995 Grimmy Inc.
Dist. by Tribune Media Services, Inc.
GO... ON... PULL.. MY... FINGER...
ZOMBIE PRACTICAL JOKES

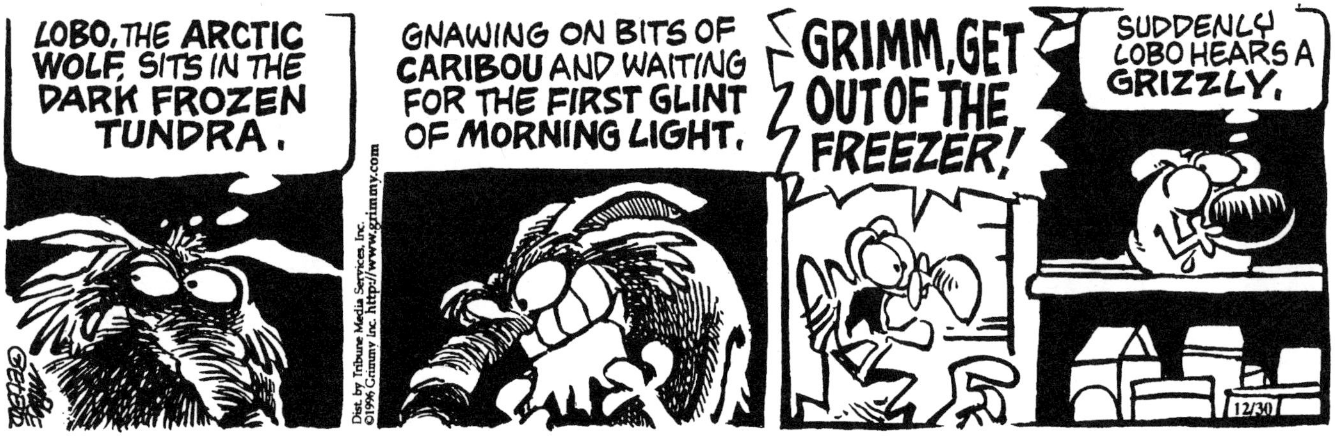
LOBO, THE ARCTIC WOLF, SITS IN THE DARK FROZEN TUNDRA.
Dist. by Tribune Media Services, Inc. ©1996 Grimmy Inc. http://www.grimmy.com
GNAWING ON BITS OF CARIBOU AND WAITING FOR THE FIRST GLINT OF MORNING LIGHT.
GRIMM, GET OUT OF THE FREEZER!
SUDDENLY LOBO HEARS A GRIZZLY.
12/30

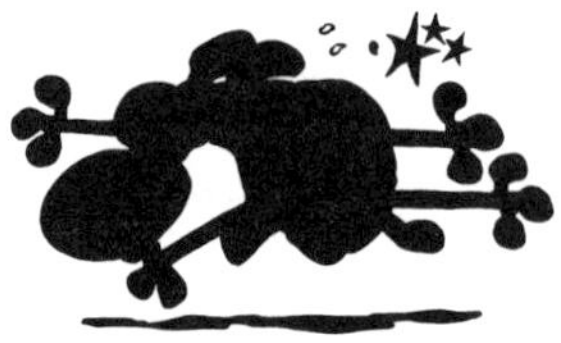

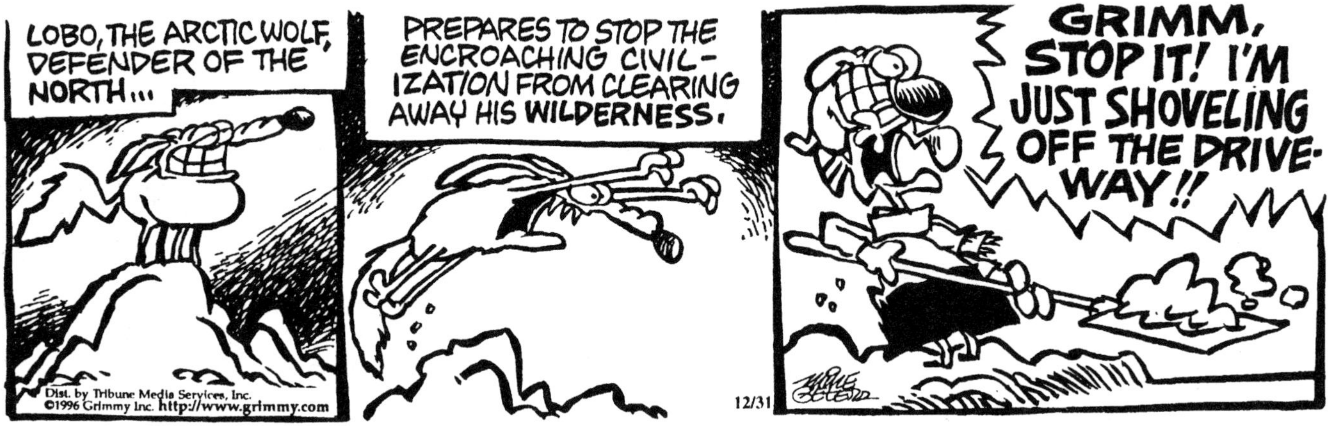
LOBO, THE ARCTIC WOLF, DEFENDER OF THE NORTH...
Dist. by Tribune Media Services, Inc. ©1996 Grimmy Inc. http://www.grimmy.com
PREPARES TO STOP THE ENCROACHING CIVIL-IZATION FROM CLEARING AWAY HIS WILDERNESS.
12/31
GRIMM, STOP IT! I'M JUST SHOVELING OFF THE DRIVE-WAY!!

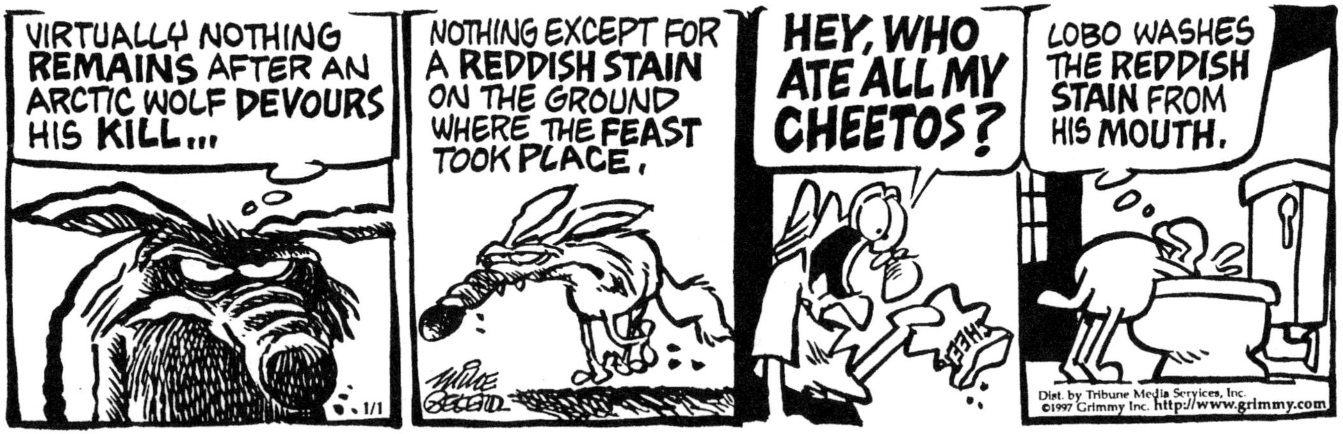
VIRTUALLY NOTHING REMAINS AFTER AN ARCTIC WOLF DEVOURS HIS KILL...
1/1
NOTHING EXCEPT FOR A REDDISH STAIN ON THE GROUND WHERE THE FEAST TOOK PLACE.
HEY, WHO ATE ALL MY CHEETOS?
LOBO WASHES THE REDDISH STAIN FROM HIS MOUTH.
Dist. by Tribune Media Services, Inc. ©1997 Grimmy Inc. http://www.grimmy.com

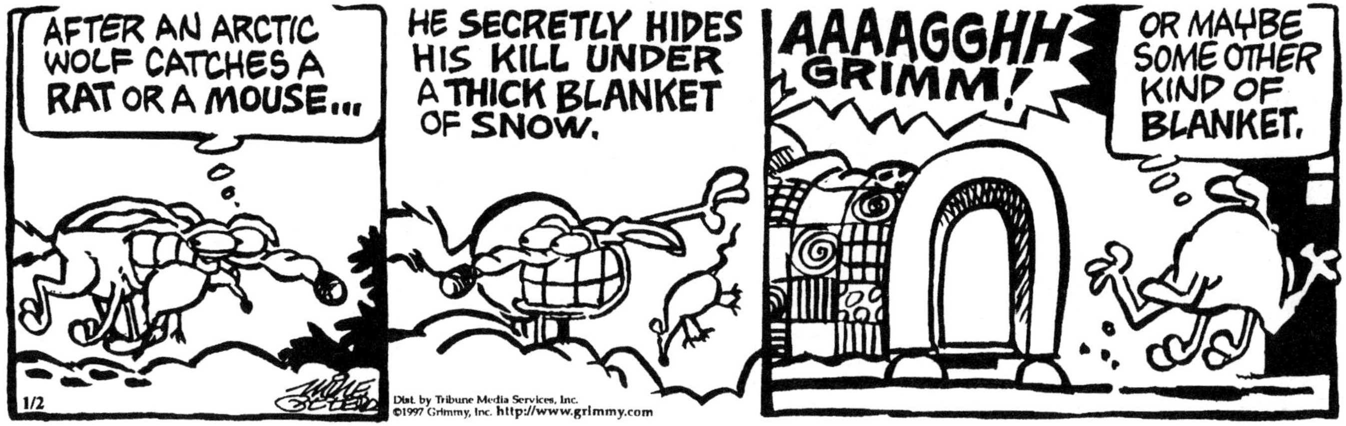
AFTER AN ARCTIC WOLF CATCHES A RAT OR A MOUSE...
HE SECRETLY HIDES HIS KILL UNDER A THICK BLANKET OF SNOW.
AAAAGGHH GRIMM!
OR MAYBE SOME OTHER KIND OF BLANKET.
1/2
Dist. by Tribune Media Services, Inc. ©1997 Grimmy, Inc. http://www.grimmy.com

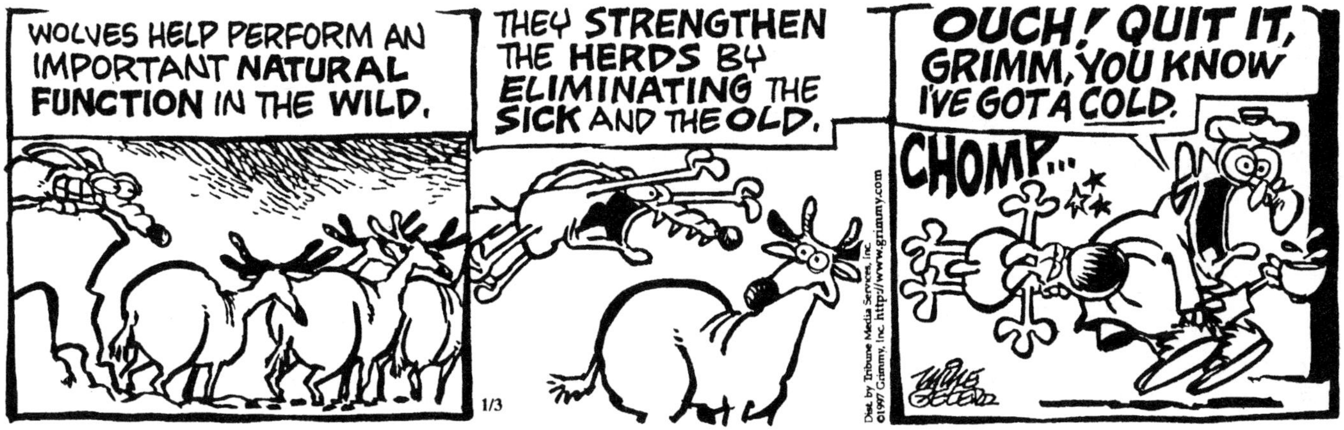
WOLVES HELP PERFORM AN IMPORTANT NATURAL FUNCTION IN THE WILD.
THEY STRENGTHEN THE HERDS BY ELIMINATING THE SICK AND THE OLD.
OUCH! QUIT IT, GRIMM, YOU KNOW I'VE GOT A COLD.
CHOMP...
1/3
Dist. by Tribune Media Services, Inc. ©1997 Grimmy, Inc. http://www.grimmy.com

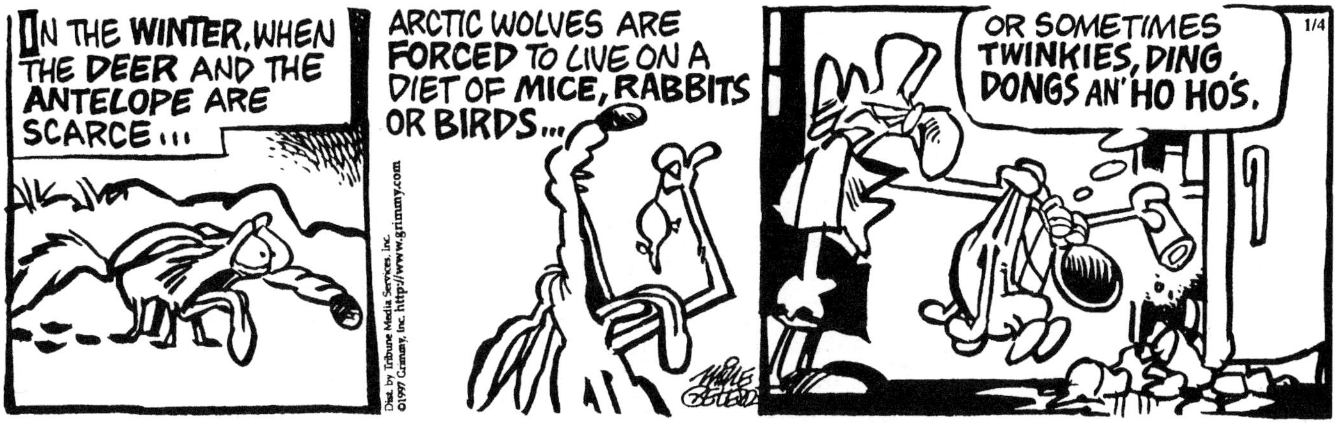
IN THE WINTER, WHEN THE DEER AND THE ANTELOPE ARE SCARCE...
ARCTIC WOLVES ARE FORCED TO LIVE ON A DIET OF MICE, RABBITS OR BIRDS...
OR SOMETIMES TWINKIES, DING DONGS AN' HO HO'S.
1/4
Dist. by Tribune Media Services, Inc. ©1997 Grimmy, Inc. http://www.grimmy.com

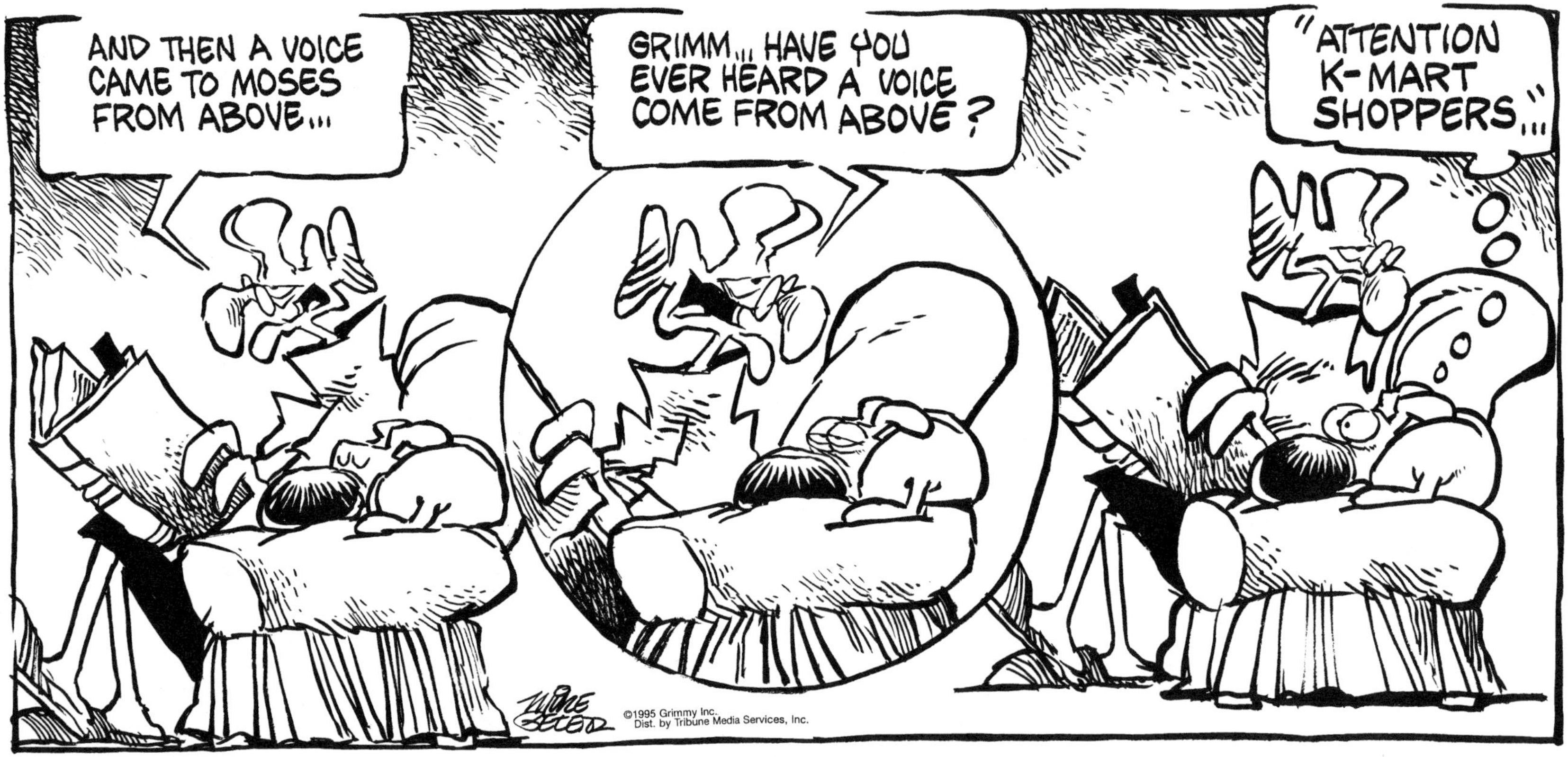
AND THEN A VOICE CAME TO MOSES FROM ABOVE...
GRIMM... HAVE YOU EVER HEARD A VOICE COME FROM ABOVE?
"ATTENTION K-MART SHOPPERS,"...
MIKE PETERS
©1995 Grimmy Inc.
Dist. by Tribune Media Services, Inc.

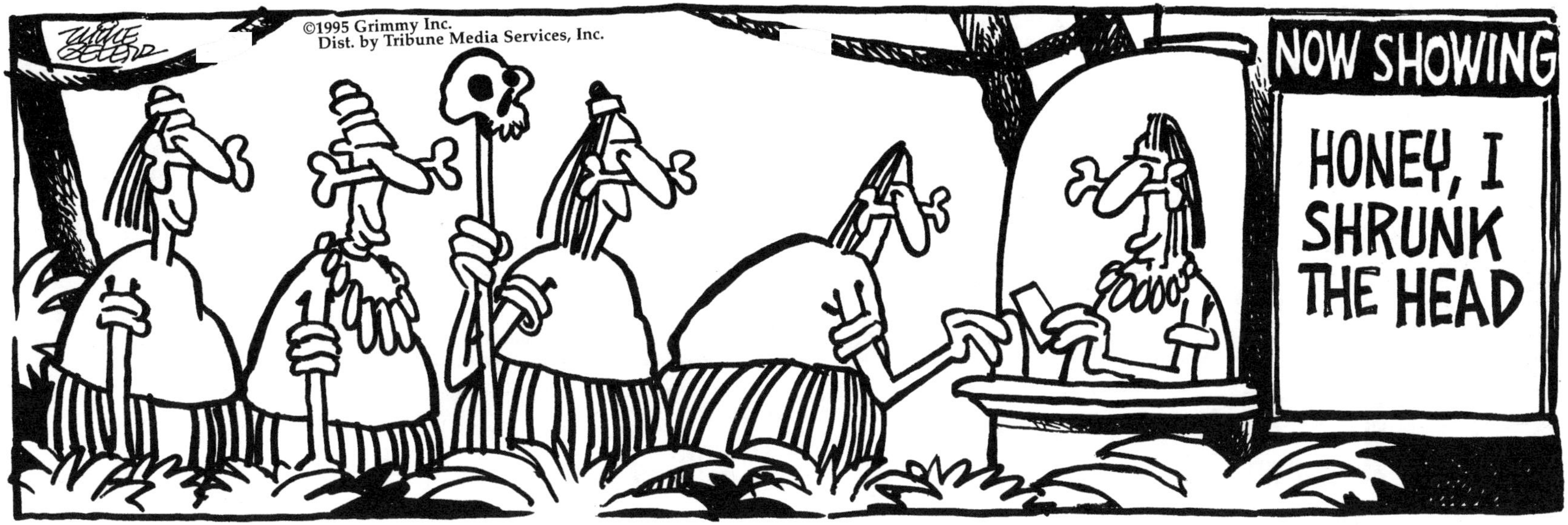
©1995 Grimmy Inc.
Dist. by Tribune Media Services, Inc.
NOW SHOWING
HONEY, I SHRUNK THE HEAD

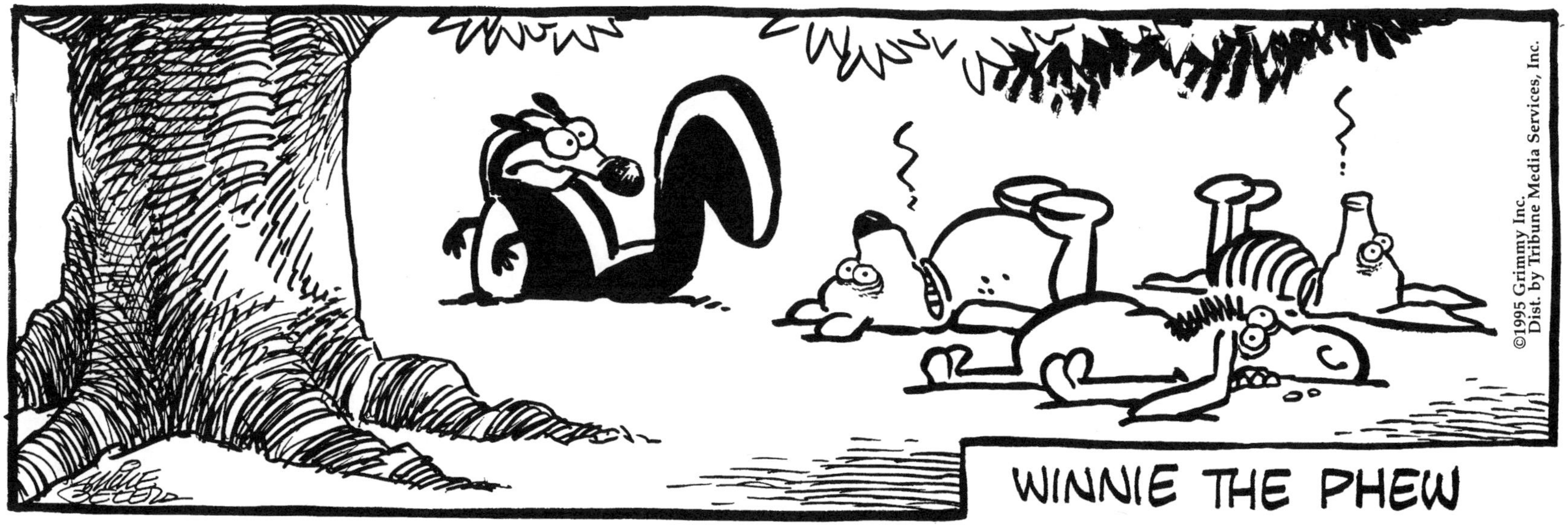
©1995 Grimmy Inc.
Dist. by Tribune Media Services, Inc.

WINNIE THE PHEW

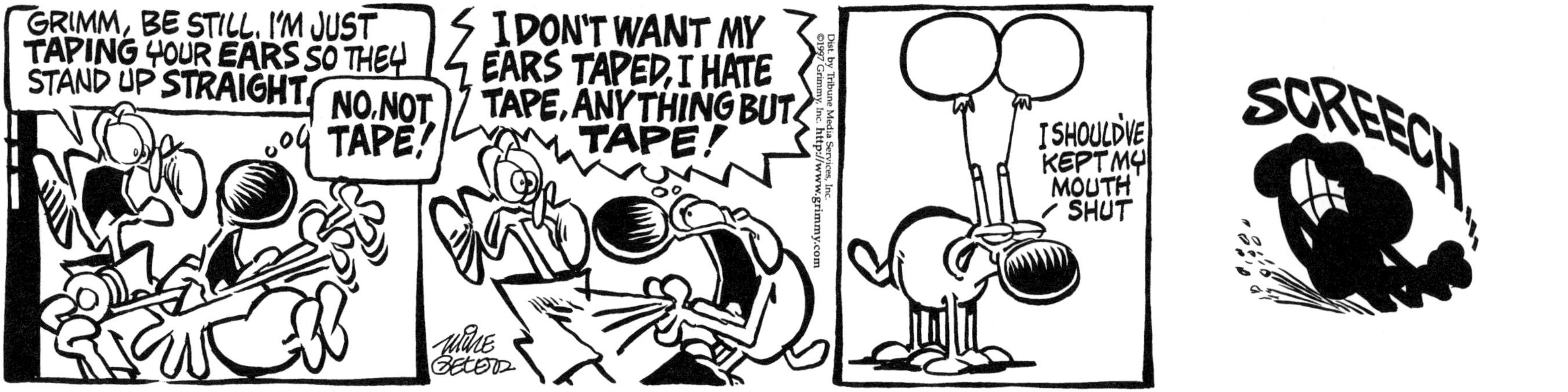
GRIMM, BE STILL. I'M JUST TAPING YOUR EARS SO THEY STAND UP STRAIGHT.
NO, NOT TAPE!
I DON'T WANT MY EARS TAPED, I HATE TAPE, ANYTHING BUT TAPE!
Dist. by Tribune Media Services, Inc. ©1997 Grimmy, Inc. http://www.grimmy.com
I SHOULD'VE KEPT MY MOUTH SHUT
SCREECH!!!

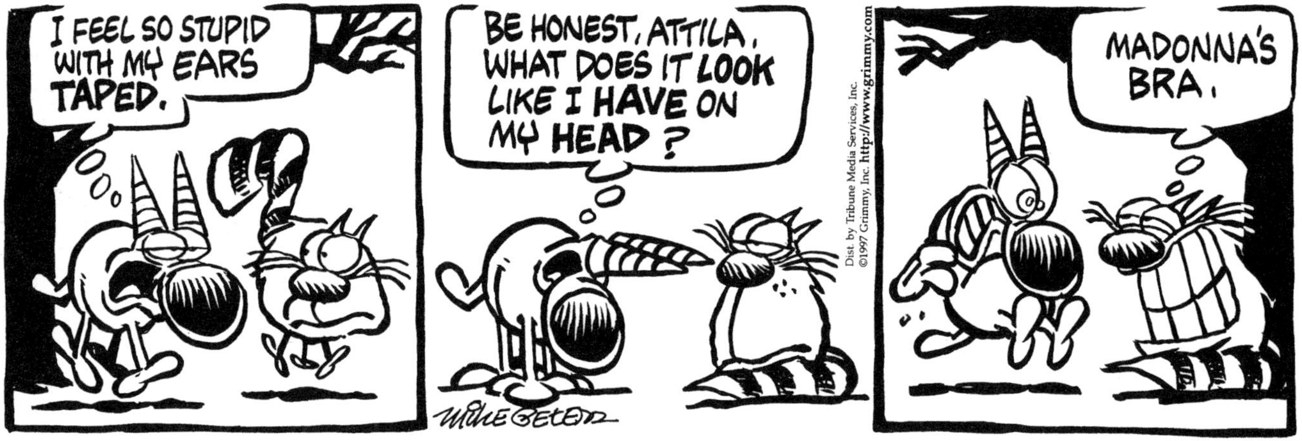
I FEEL SO STUPID WITH MY EARS TAPED.
BE HONEST, ATTILA. WHAT DOES IT LOOK LIKE I HAVE ON MY HEAD?
Dist. by Tribune Media Services, Inc. ©1997 Grimmy, Inc. http://www.grimmy.com
MADONNA'S BRA.

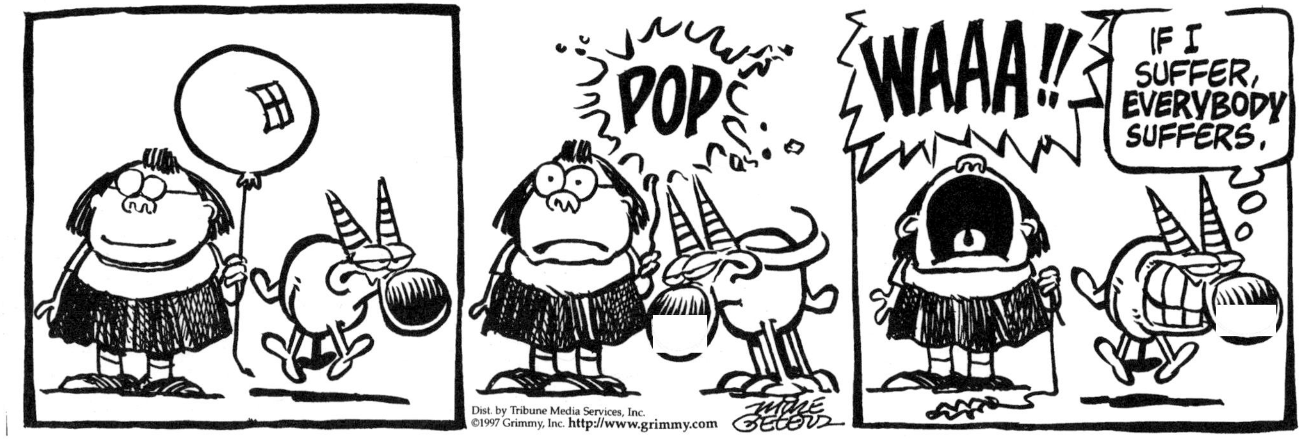
POP
Dist. by Tribune Media Services, Inc. ©1997 Grimmy, Inc. http://www.grimmy.com
WAAA!!
IF I SUFFER, EVERYBODY SUFFERS.

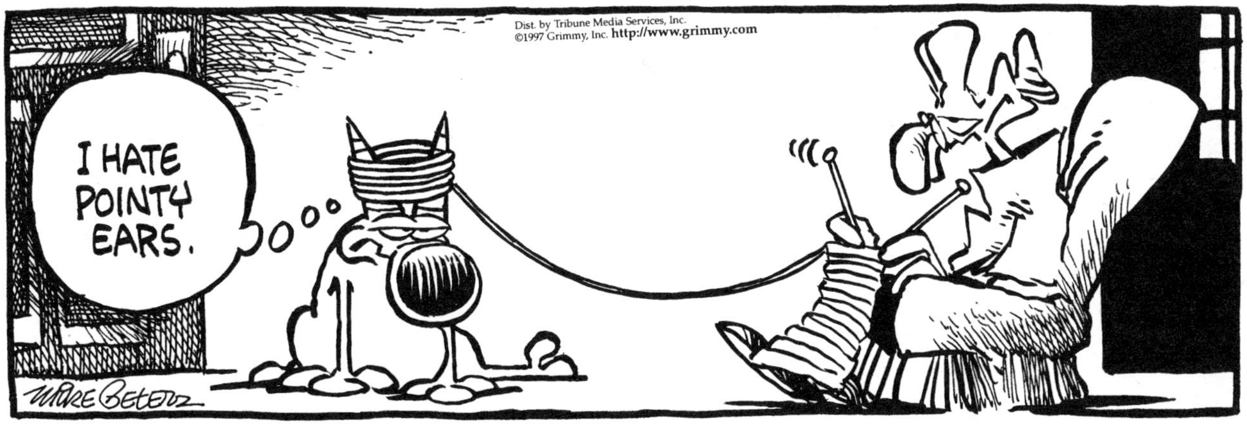
Dist. by Tribune Media Services, Inc.
©1997 Grimmy, Inc. http://www.grimmy.com
I HATE POINTY EARS.

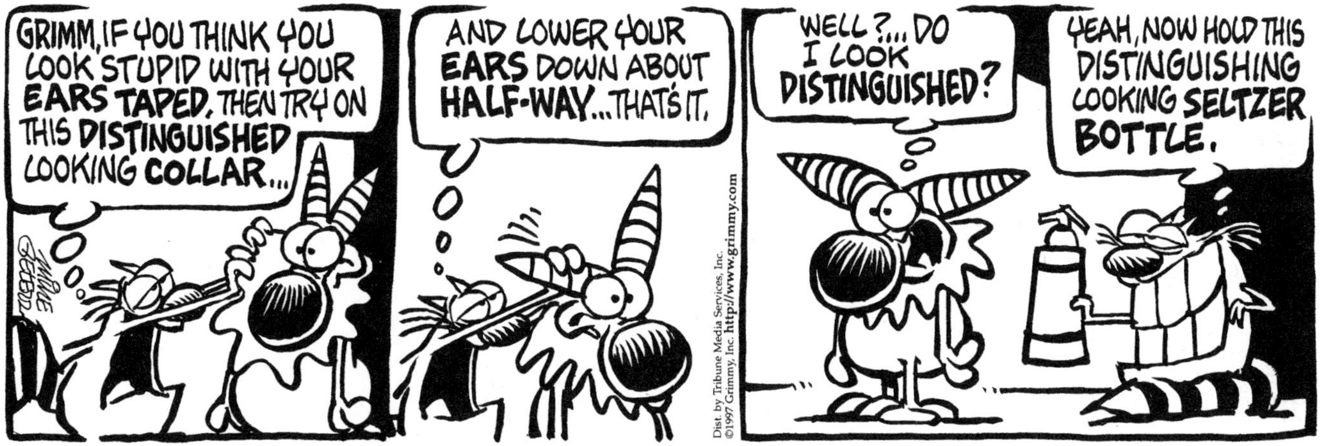
GRIMM, IF YOU THINK YOU LOOK STUPID WITH YOUR EARS TAPED, THEN TRY ON THIS DISTINGUISHED LOOKING COLLAR...
AND LOWER YOUR EARS DOWN ABOUT HALF-WAY...THAT'S IT.
Dist. by Tribune Media Services, Inc.
©1997 Grimmy, Inc. http://www.grimmy.com
WELL?... DO I LOOK DISTINGUISHED?
YEAH, NOW HOLD THIS DISTINGUISHING LOOKING SELTZER BOTTLE.

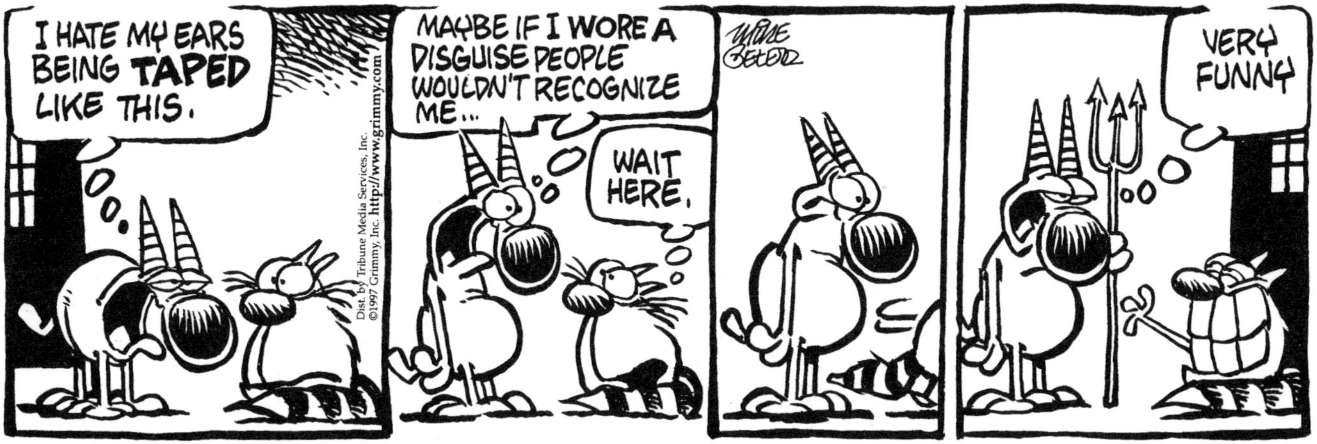
I HATE MY EARS BEING TAPED LIKE THIS.
Dist. by Tribune Media Services, Inc.
©1997 Grimmy, Inc. http://www.grimmy.com
MAYBE IF I WORE A DISGUISE PEOPLE WOULDN'T RECOGNIZE ME...
WAIT HERE.
VERY FUNNY

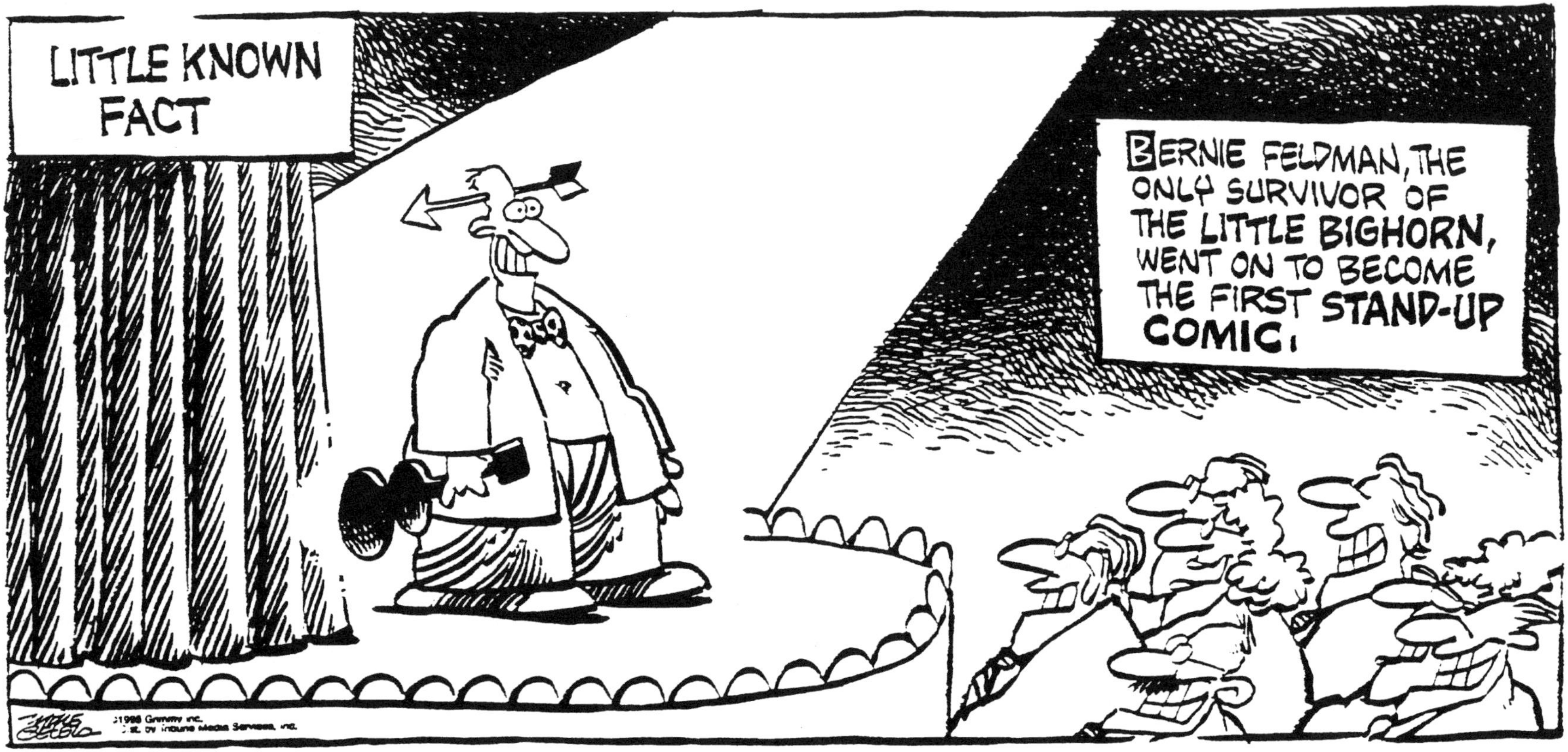

LITTLE KNOWN FACT
BERNIE FELDMAN, THE ONLY SURVIVOR OF THE LITTLE BIGHORN, WENT ON TO BECOME THE FIRST STAND-UP COMIC.

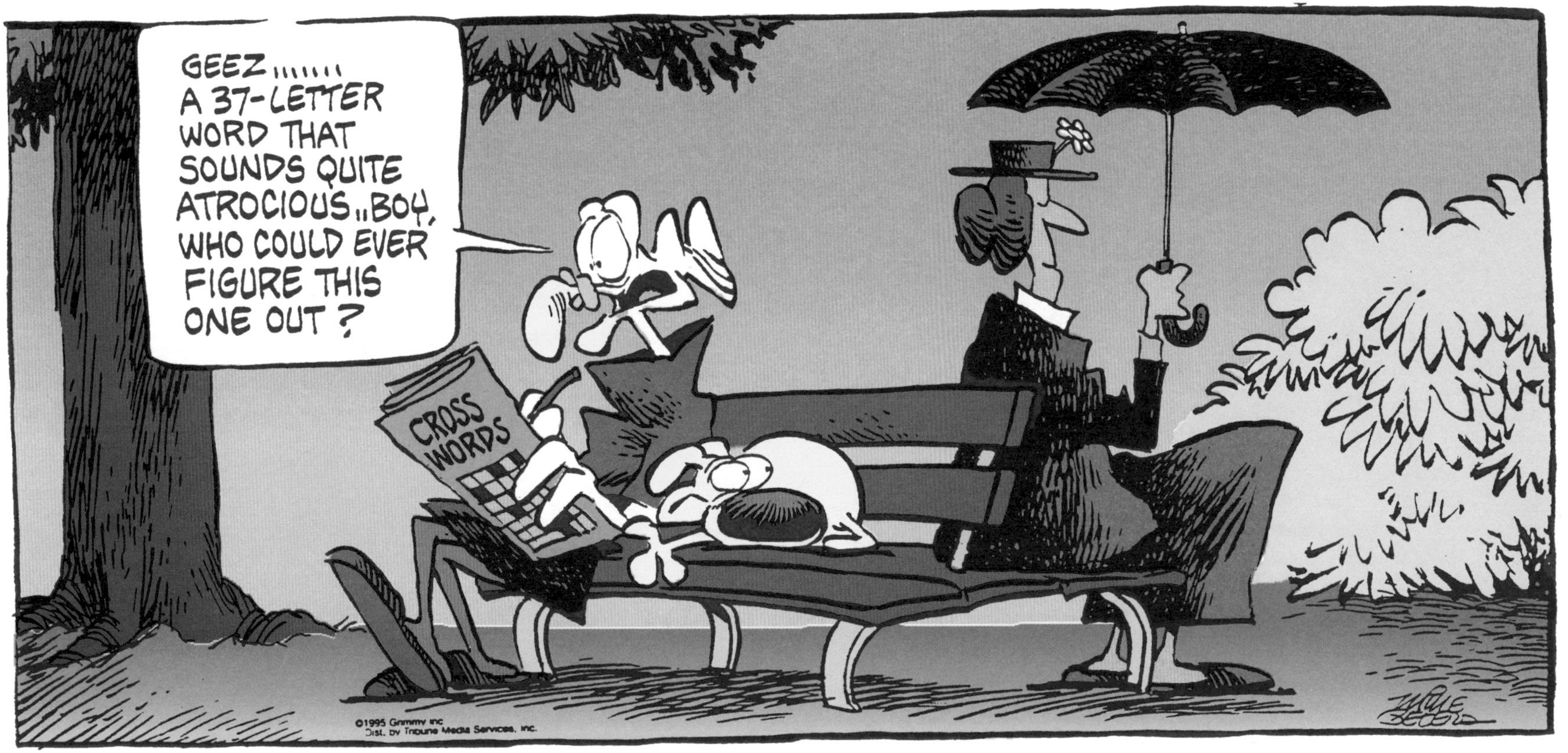
GEEZ....... A 37-LETTER WORD THAT SOUNDS QUITE ATROCIOUS..BOY, WHO COULD EVER FIGURE THIS ONE OUT ?
CROSS WORDS
©1995 Grimmy inc
Dist. by Tribune Media Services, Inc.

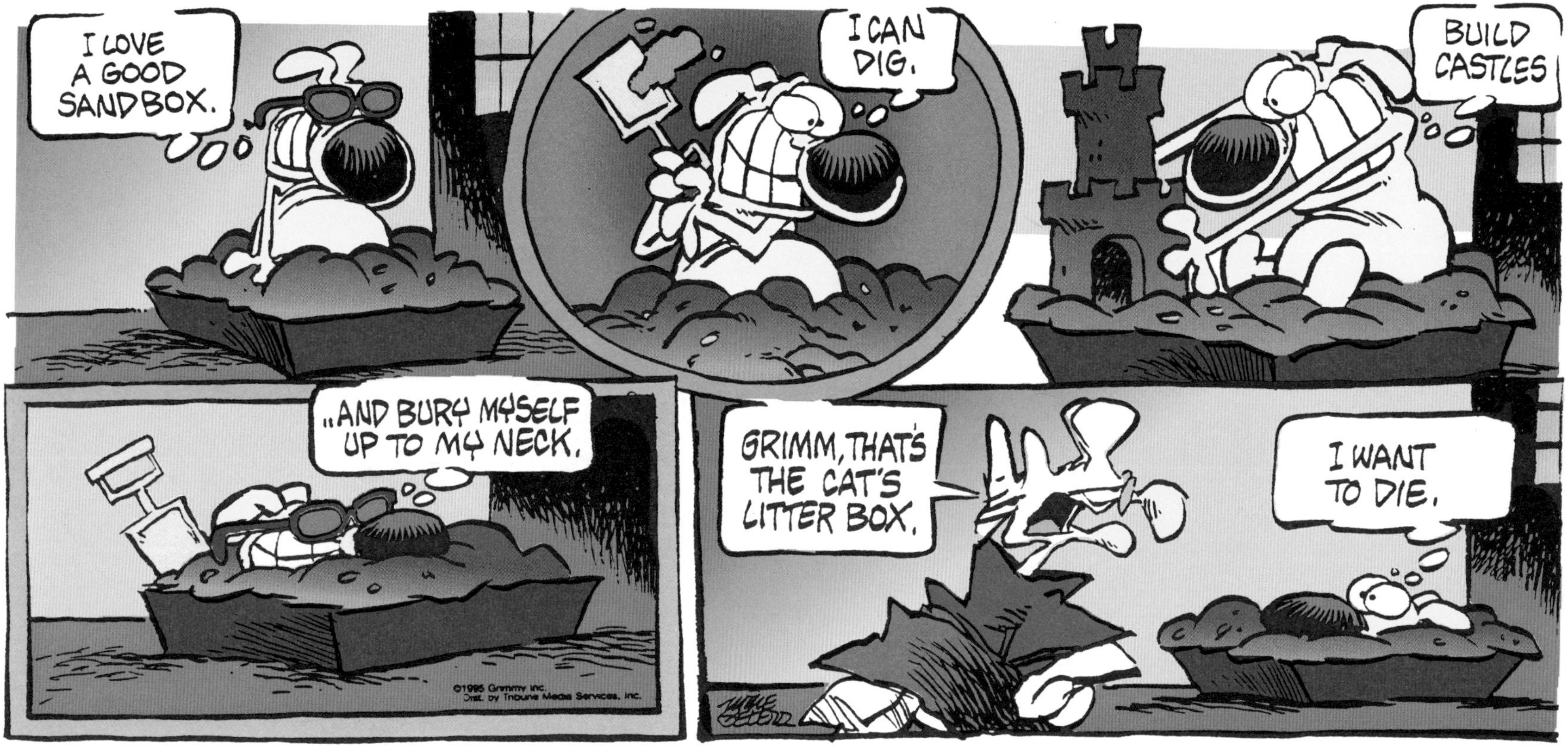
I LOVE A GOOD SANDBOX.
I CAN DIG.
BUILD CASTLES
...AND BURY MYSELF UP TO MY NECK.
©1995 Grimmy Inc.
Dist. by Tribune Media Services, Inc.
GRIMM, THAT'S THE CAT'S LITTER BOX.
I WANT TO DIE.

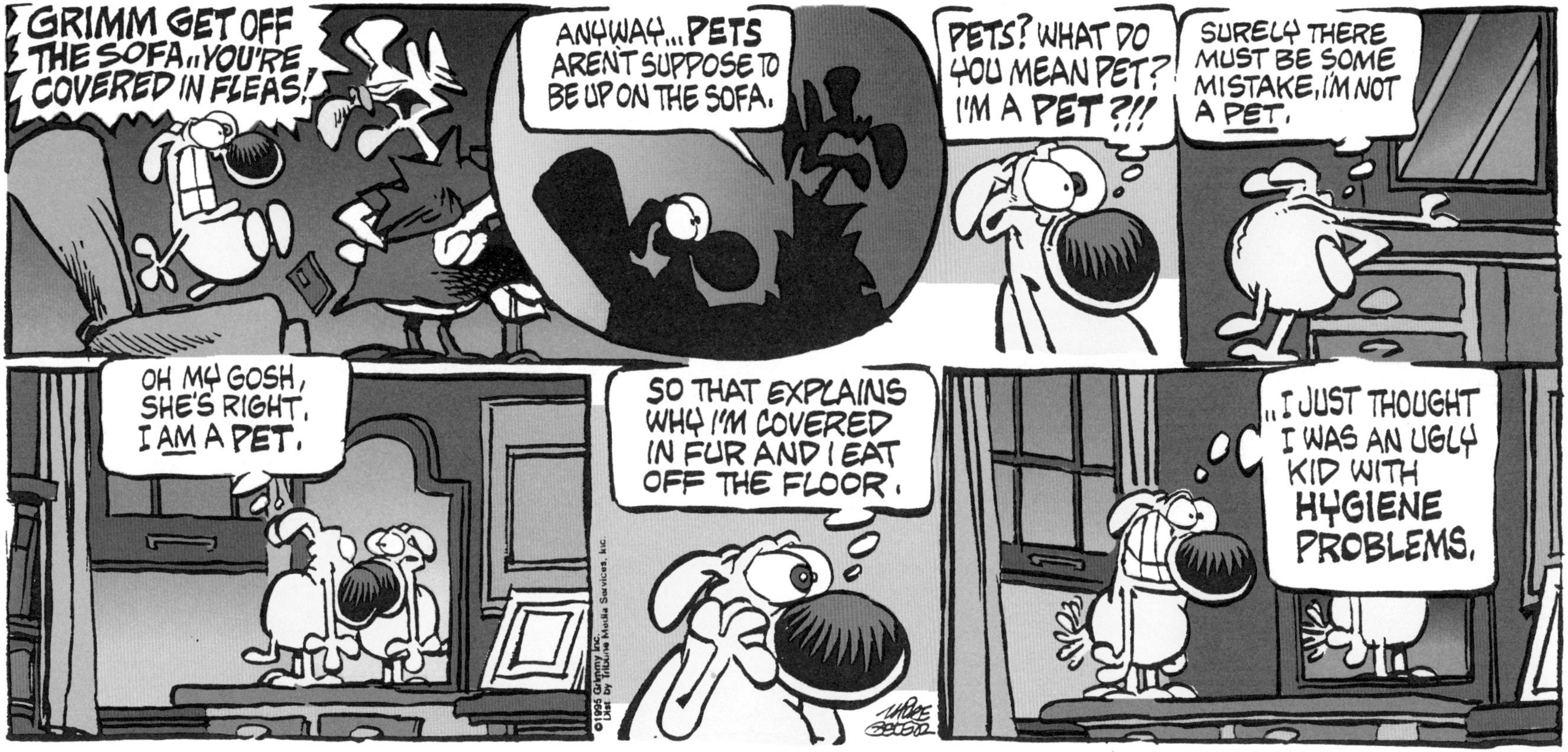
GRIMM GET OFF THE SOFA.. YOU'RE COVERED IN FLEAS!
ANYWAY... PETS AREN'T SUPPOSE TO BE UP ON THE SOFA.
PETS? WHAT DO YOU MEAN PET? I'M A PET ?!!
SURELY THERE MUST BE SOME MISTAKE, I'M NOT A PET.
OH MY GOSH, SHE'S RIGHT. I AM A PET.
©1995 Grimmy Inc. Dist by Tribune Media Services, Inc.
SO THAT EXPLAINS WHY I'M COVERED IN FUR AND I EAT OFF THE FLOOR.
..I JUST THOUGHT I WAS AN UGLY KID WITH HYGIENE PROBLEMS.

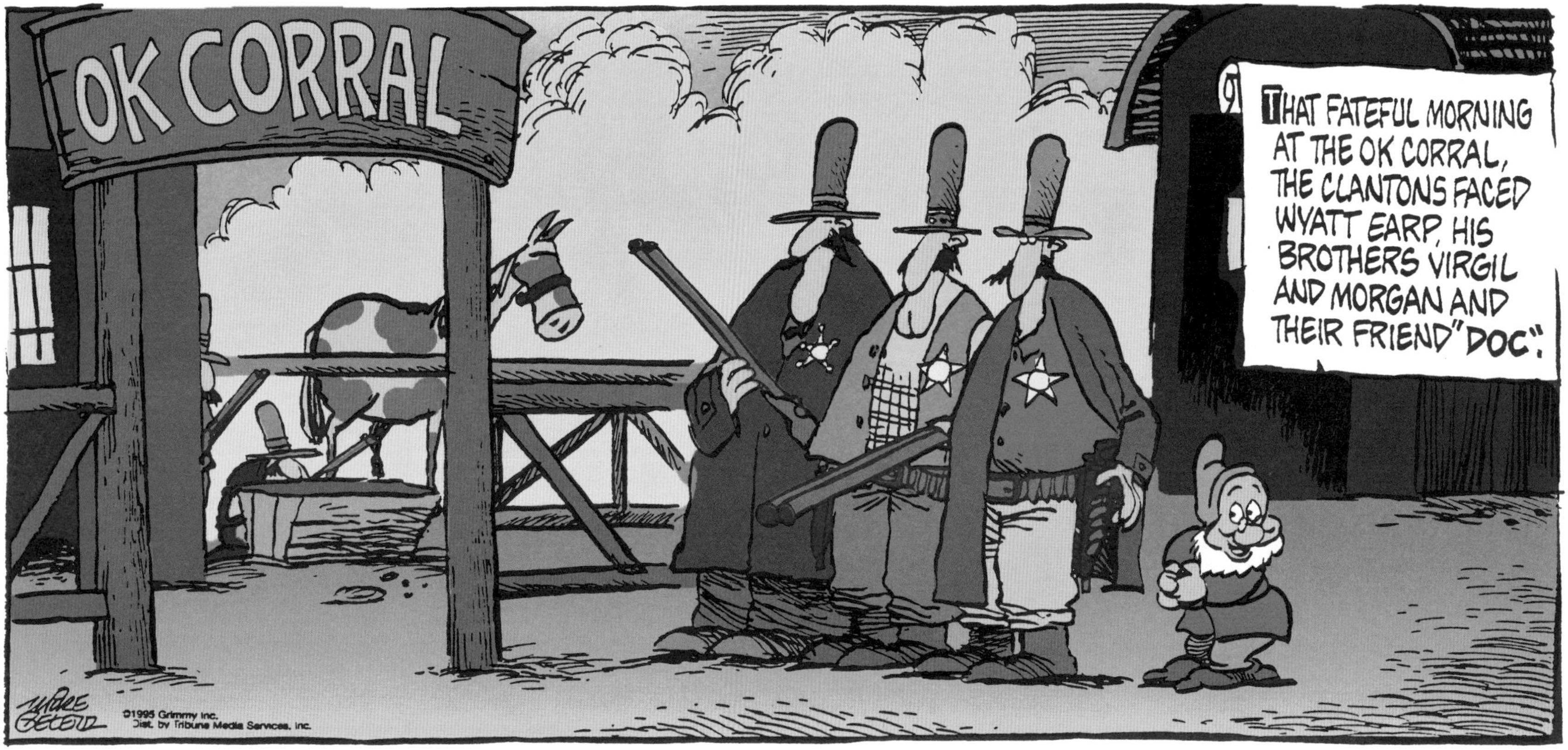
OK CORRAL
THAT FATEFUL MORNING AT THE OK CORRAL, THE CLANTONS FACED WYATT EARP, HIS BROTHERS VIRGIL AND MORGAN AND THEIR FRIEND "DOC".
©1995 Grimmy Inc.
Dist. by Tribune Media Services, Inc.

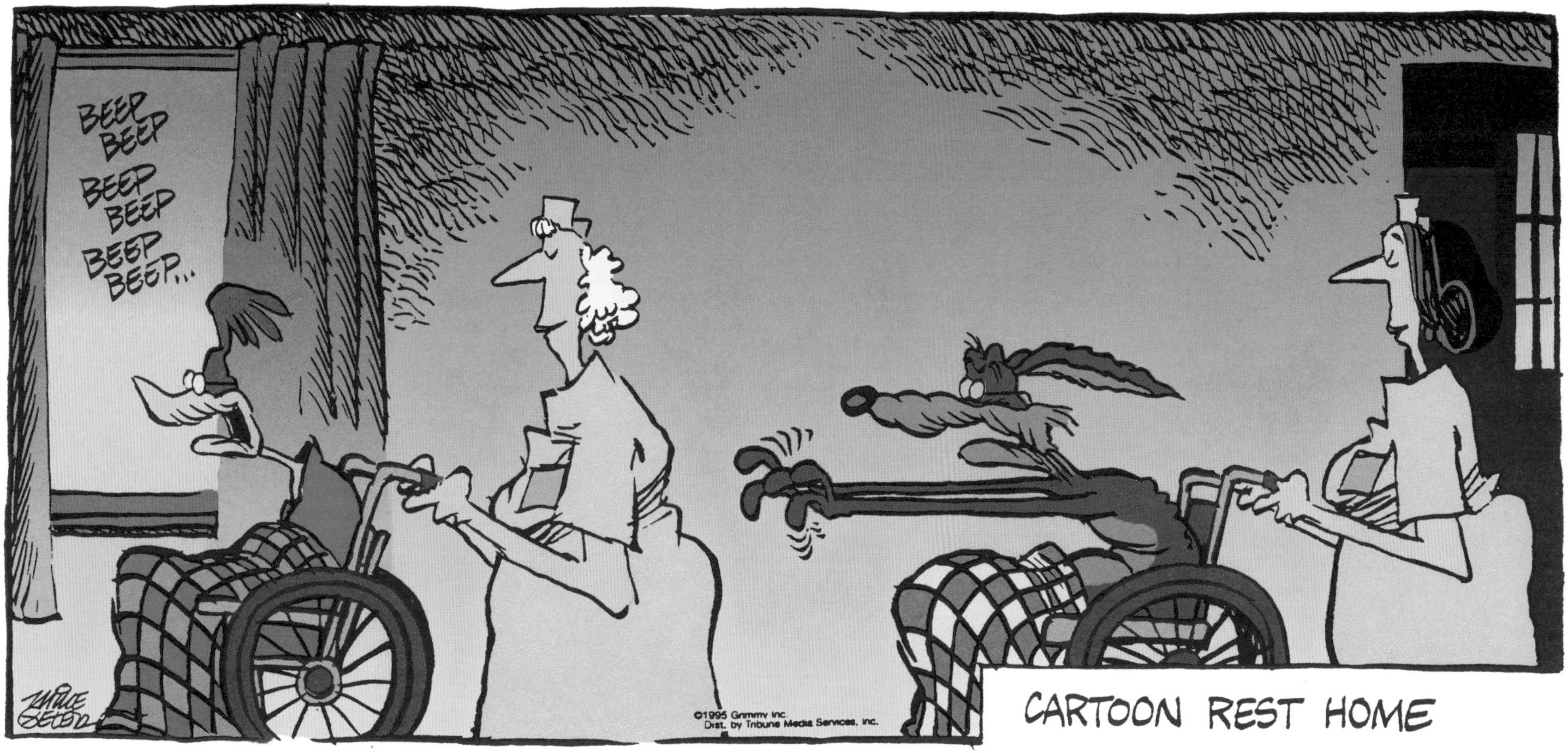
BEEP BEEP
BEEP BEEP
BEEP BEEP...
©1995 Grimmy Inc.
Dist. by Tribune Media Services, Inc.

CARTOON REST HOME

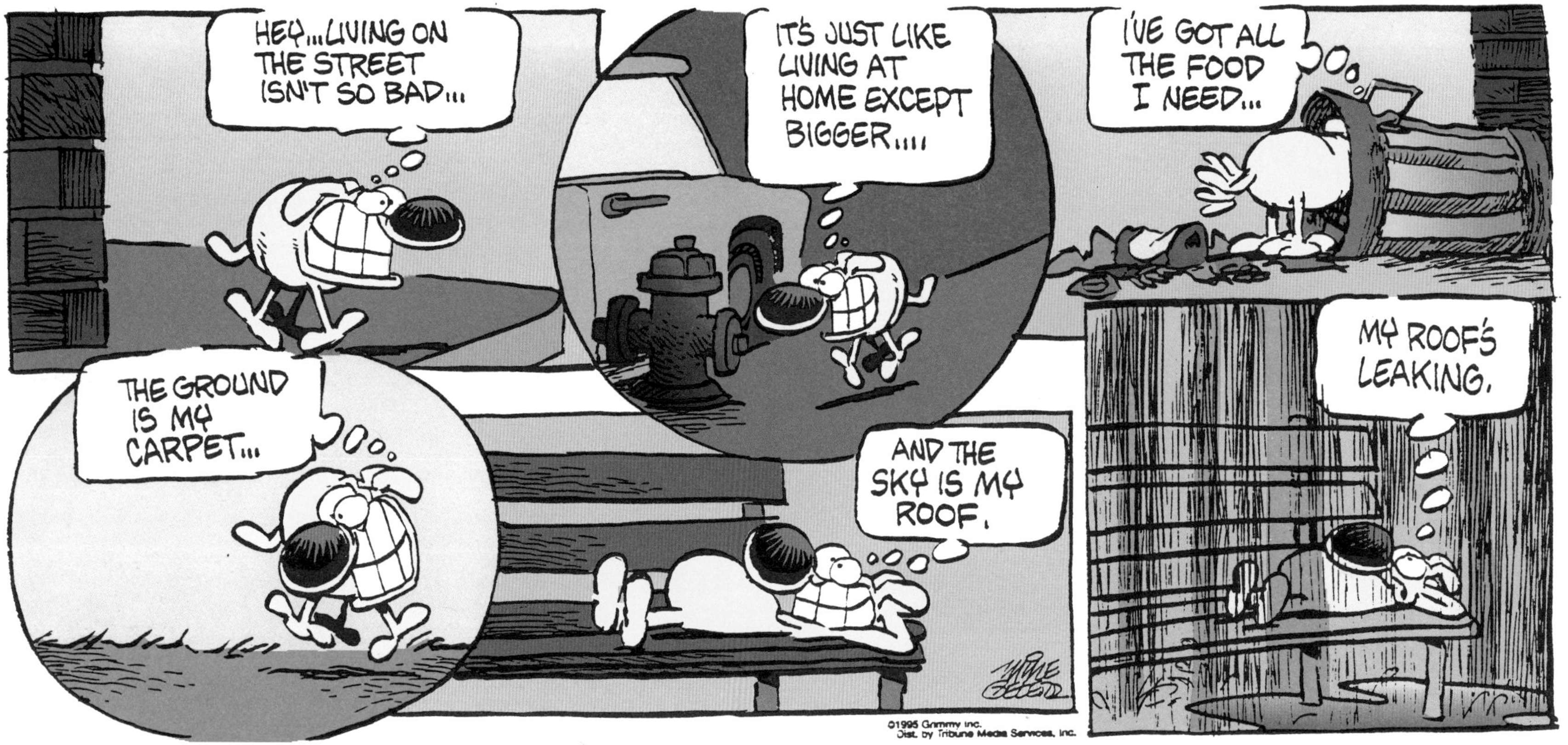
HEY...LIVING ON THE STREET ISN'T SO BAD...
IT'S JUST LIKE LIVING AT HOME EXCEPT BIGGER....
I'VE GOT ALL THE FOOD I NEED...
THE GROUND IS MY CARPET...
AND THE SKY IS MY ROOF.
MY ROOF'S LEAKING.
©1995 Grimmy Inc.
Dist. by Tribune Media Services, Inc.

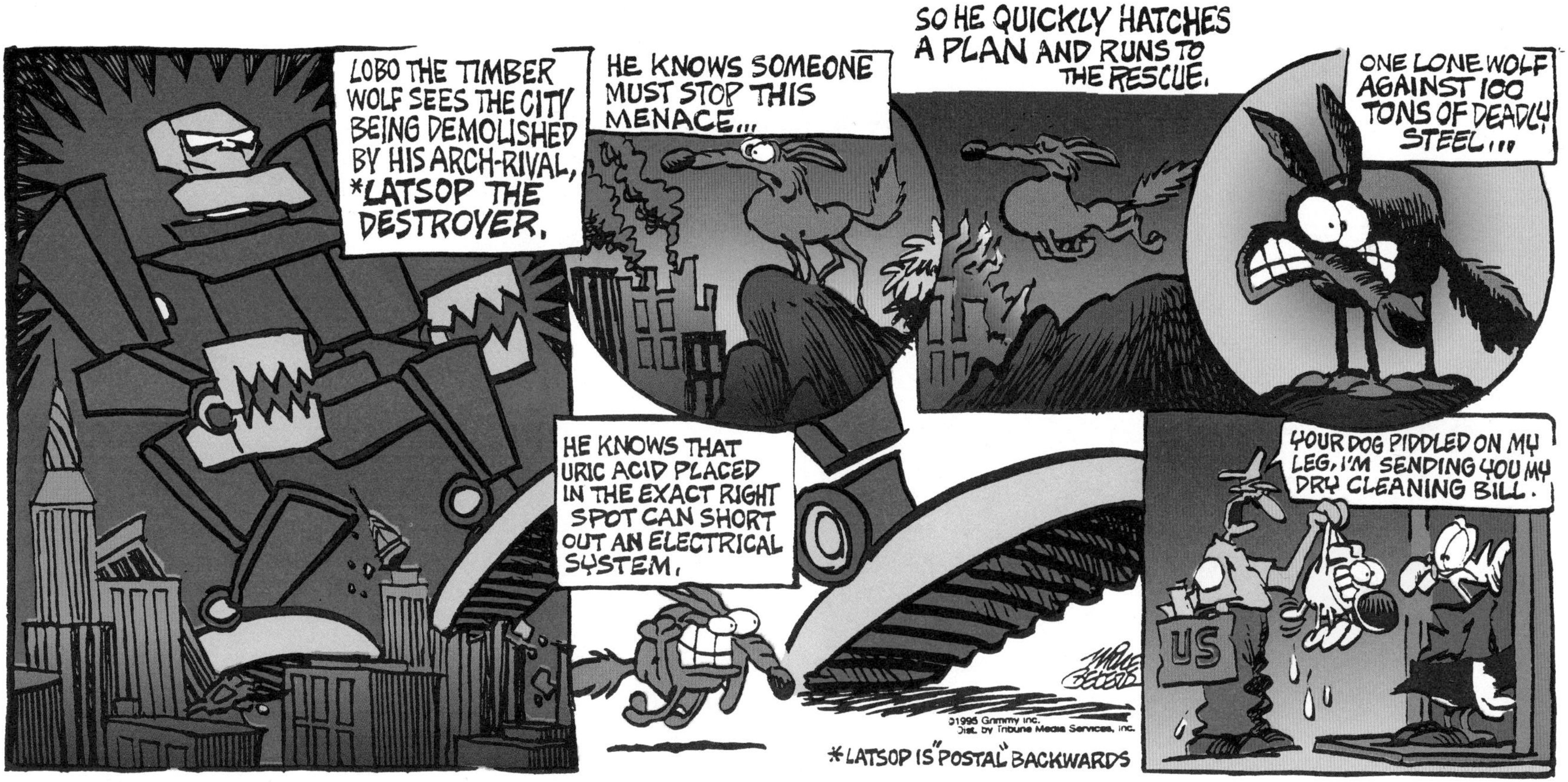
LOBO THE TIMBER WOLF SEES THE CITY BEING DEMOLISHED BY HIS ARCH-RIVAL, *LATSOP THE DESTROYER.
HE KNOWS SOMEONE MUST STOP THIS MENACE...
SO HE QUICKLY HATCHES A PLAN AND RUNS TO THE RESCUE.
ONE LONE WOLF AGAINST 100 TONS OF DEADLY STEEL...
HE KNOWS THAT URIC ACID PLACED IN THE EXACT RIGHT SPOT CAN SHORT OUT AN ELECTRICAL SYSTEM.
YOUR DOG PIDDLED ON MY LEG, I'M SENDING YOU MY DRY CLEANING BILL.
US
©1995 Grimmy Inc. Dist. by Tribune Media Services, Inc.
*LATSOP IS "POSTAL" BACKWARDS

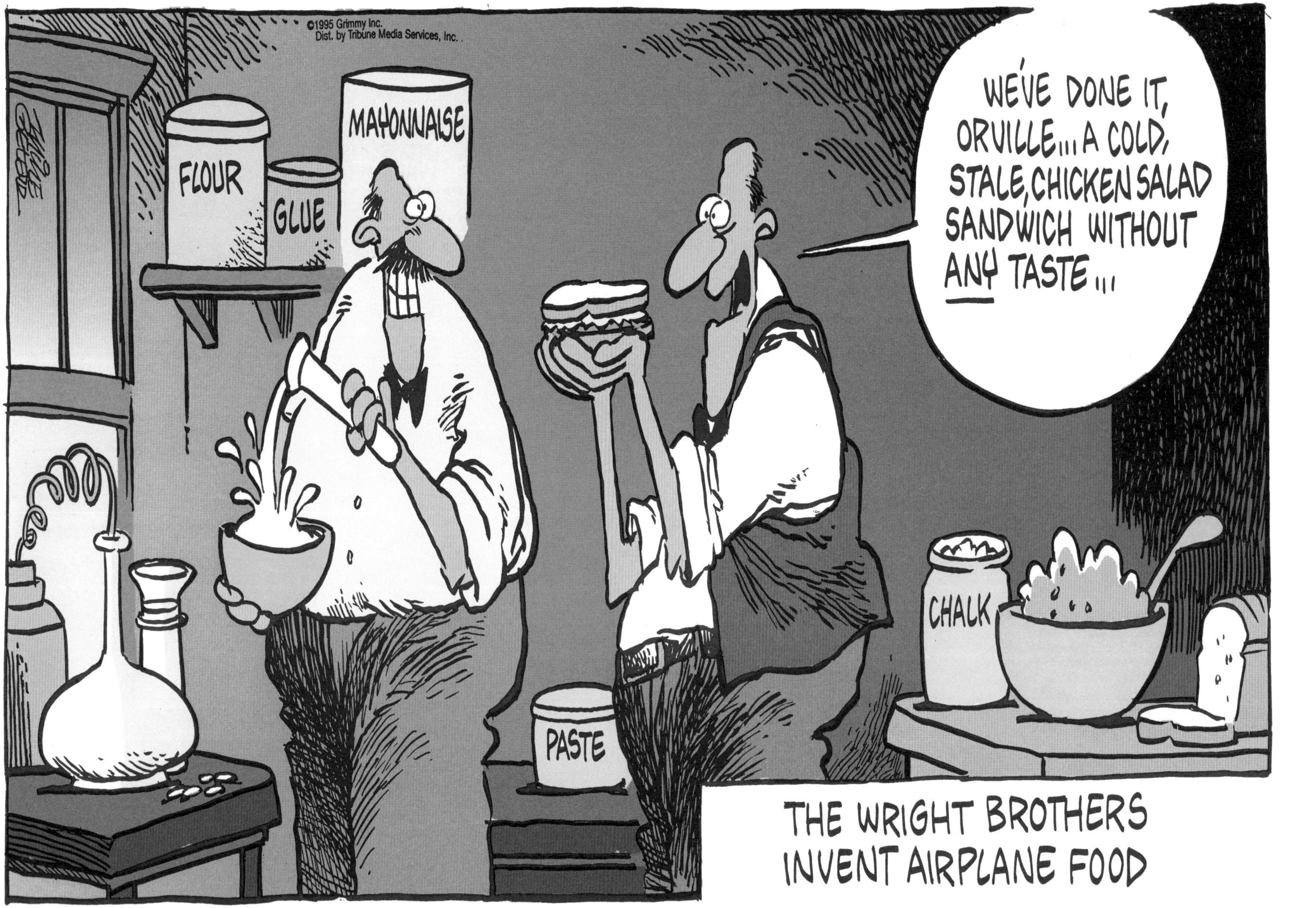
©1995 Grimmy Inc.
Dist. by Tribune Media Services, Inc.
FLOUR
GLUE
MAYONNAISE
WE'VE DONE IT, ORVILLE... A COLD, STALE, CHICKEN SALAD SANDWICH WITHOUT ANY TASTE...
CHALK
PASTE

THE WRIGHT BROTHERS INVENT AIRPLANE FOOD

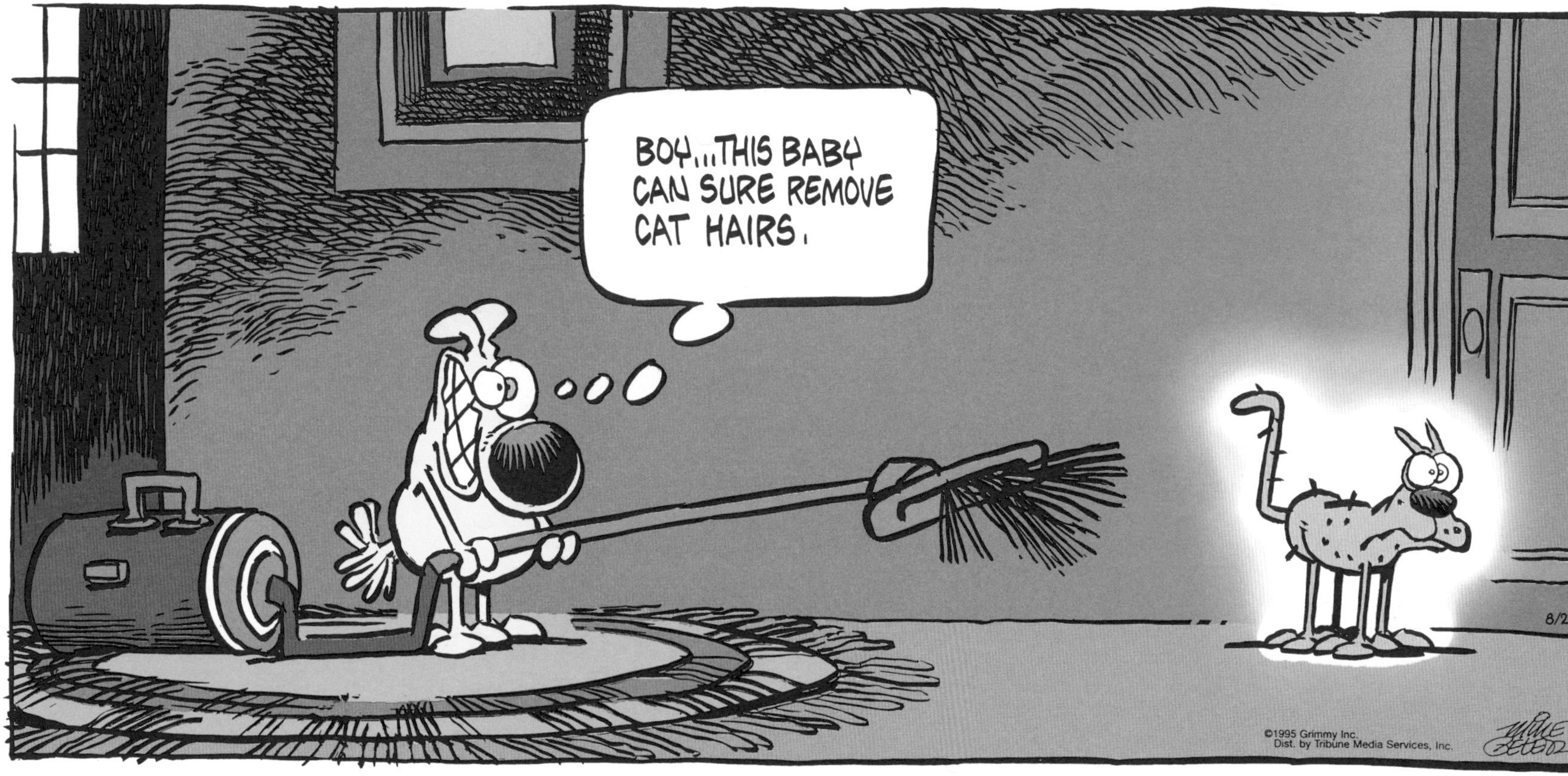
BOY...THIS BABY CAN SURE REMOVE CAT HAIRS.
8/27
©1995 Grimmy Inc.
Dist. by Tribune Media Services, Inc.

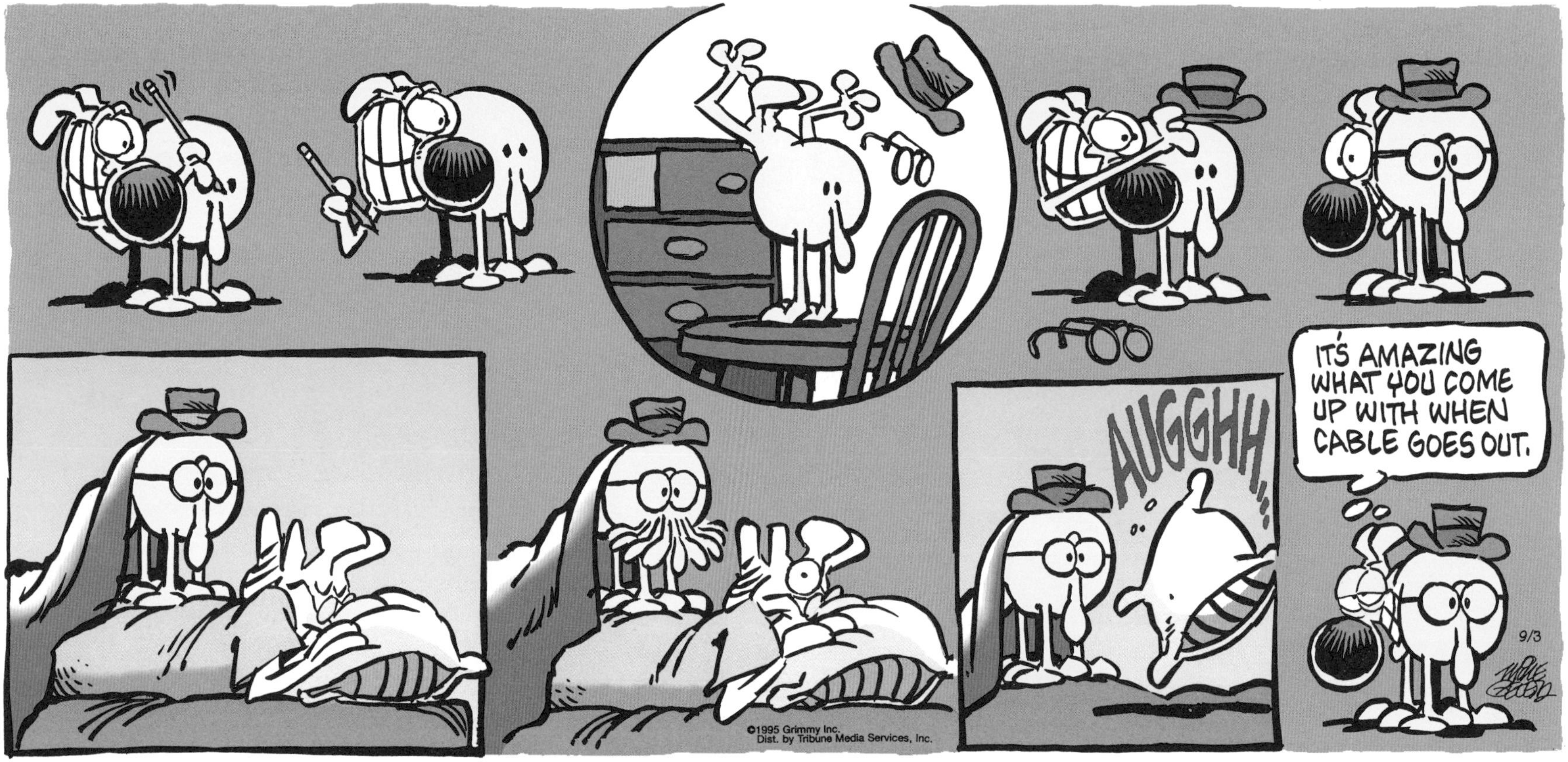
AUGGHH...
IT'S AMAZING WHAT YOU COME UP WITH WHEN CABLE GOES OUT.
9/3
©1995 Grimmy Inc.
Dist. by Tribune Media Services, Inc.

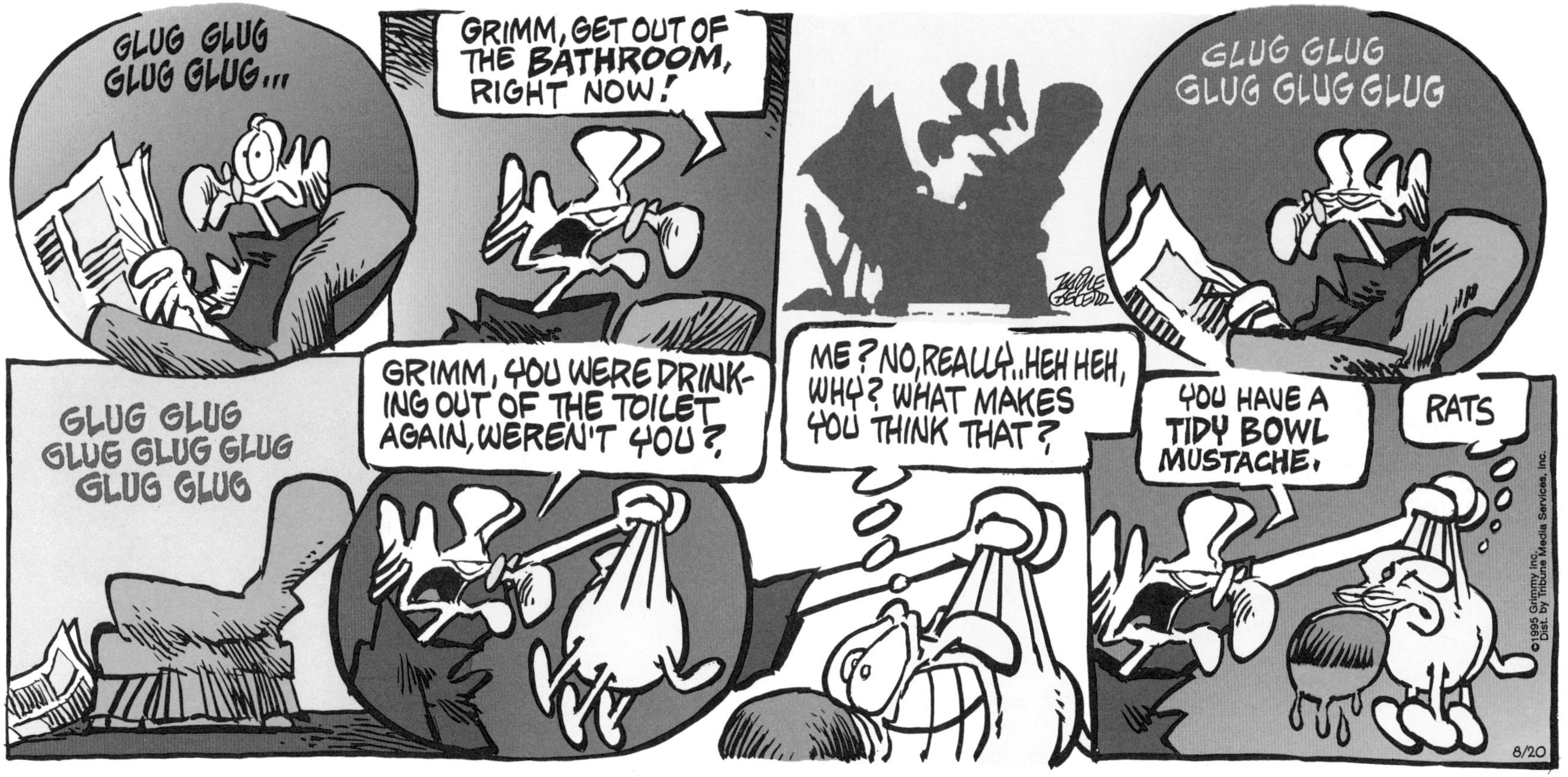
GLUG GLUG GLUG GLUG...
GRIMM, GET OUT OF THE BATHROOM, RIGHT NOW!
GLUG GLUG GLUG GLUG GLUG
GLUG GLUG GLUG GLUG GLUG GLUG GLUG
GRIMM, YOU WERE DRINKING OUT OF THE TOILET AGAIN, WEREN'T YOU?
ME? NO, REALLY..HEH HEH, WHY? WHAT MAKES YOU THINK THAT?
YOU HAVE A TIDY BOWL MUSTACHE.
RATS
©1995 Grimmy Inc. Dist. by Tribune Media Services, Inc.
8/20

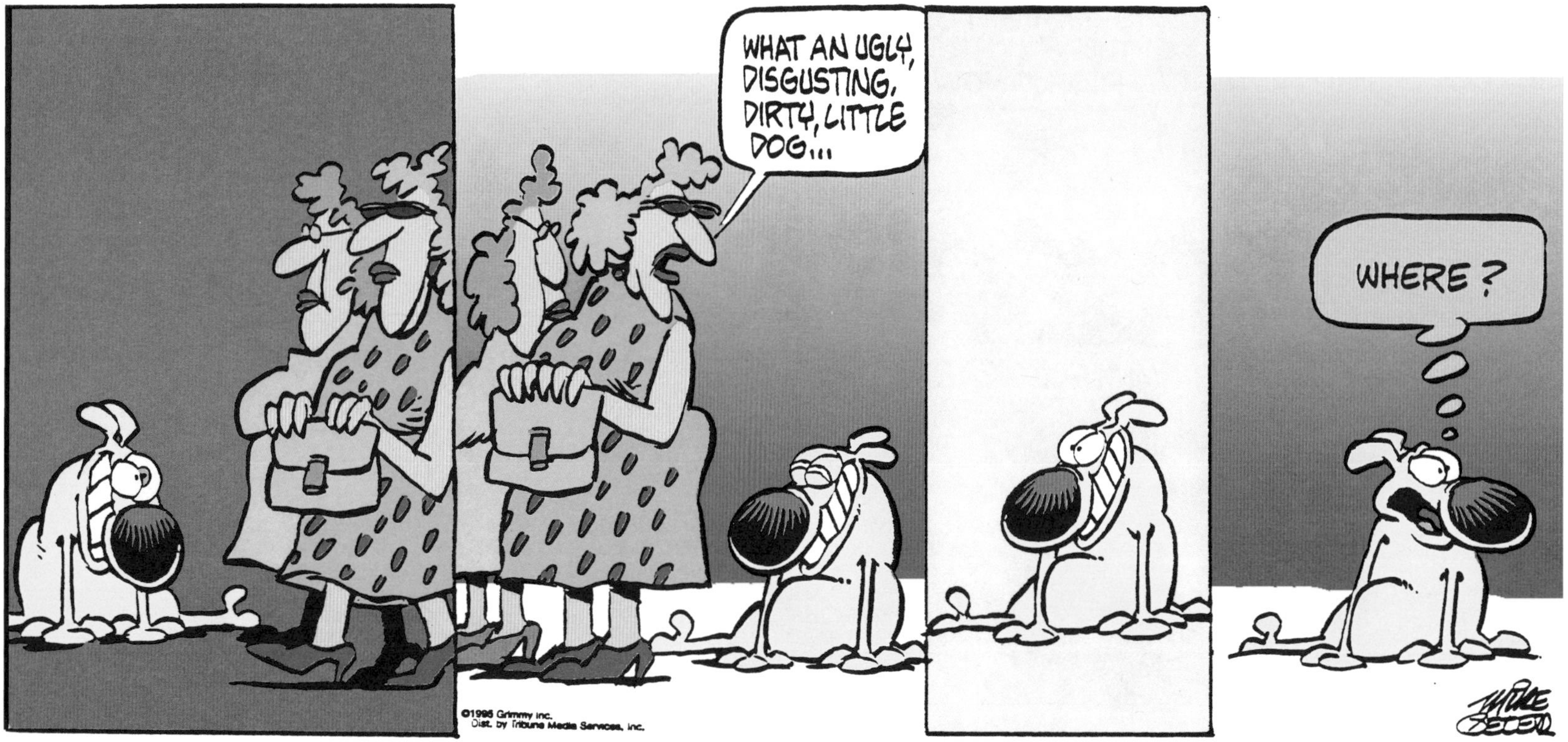
WHAT AN UGLY, DISGUSTING, DIRTY, LITTLE DOG...
WHERE?
©1996 Grimmy Inc.
Dist. by Tribune Media Services, Inc.

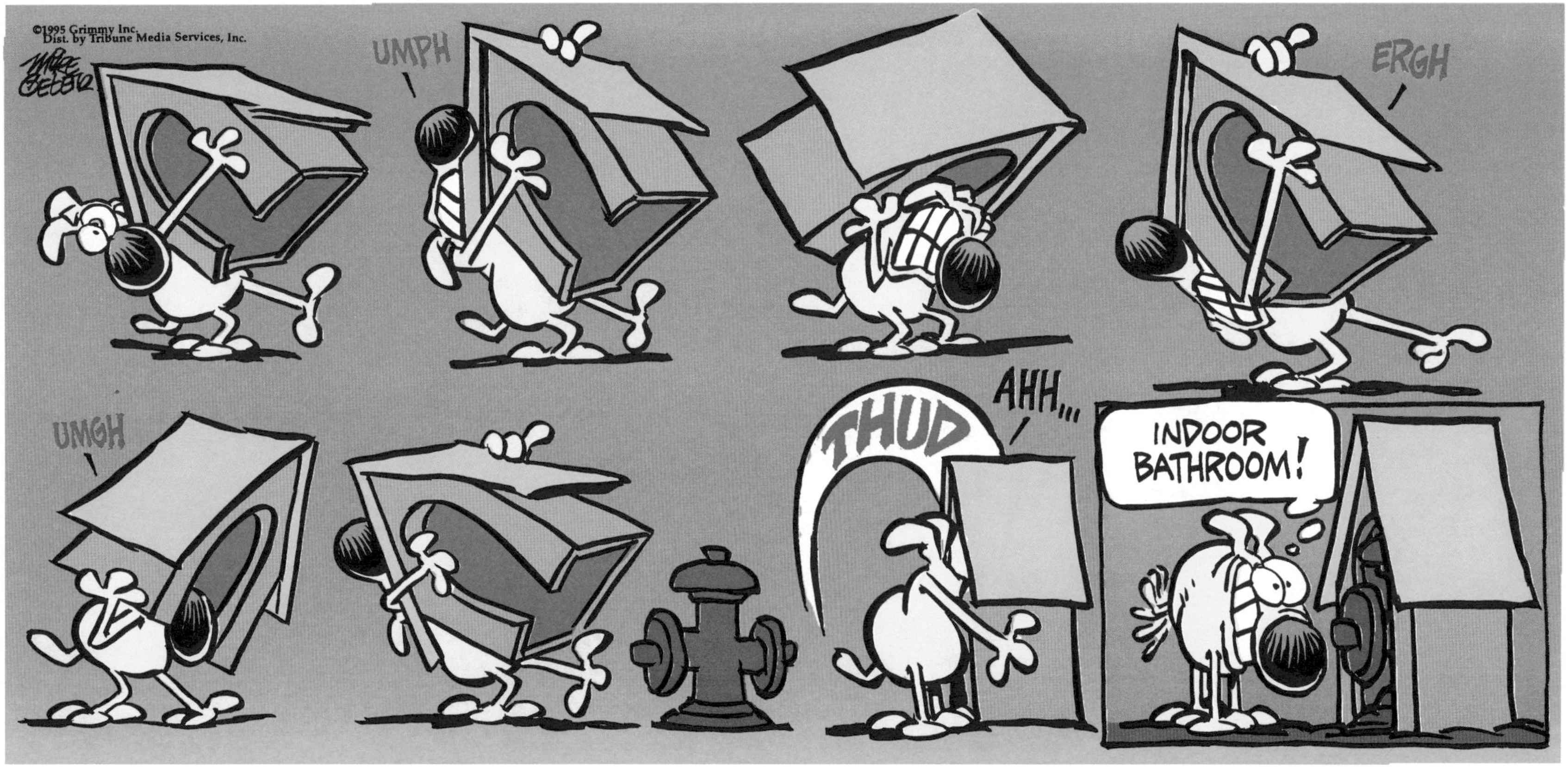
©1995 Grimmy Inc.
Dist. by Tribune Media Services, Inc.
UMPH
ERGH
UMGH
THUD
AHH...
INDOOR BATHROOM!

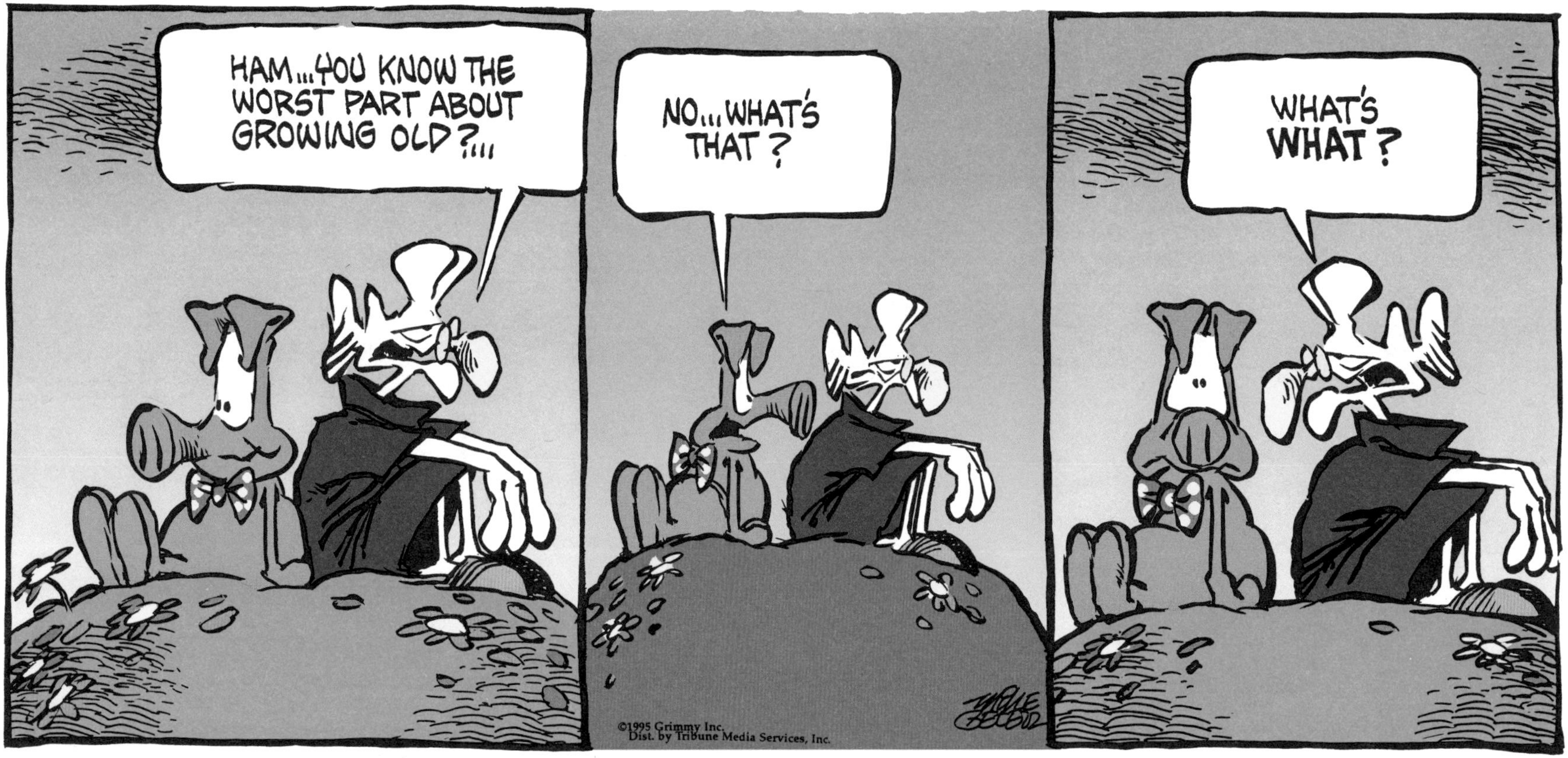
HAM...YOU KNOW THE WORST PART ABOUT GROWING OLD?...
NO... WHAT'S THAT?
WHAT'S **WHAT**?
©1995 Grimmy Inc. Dist. by Tribune Media Services, Inc.

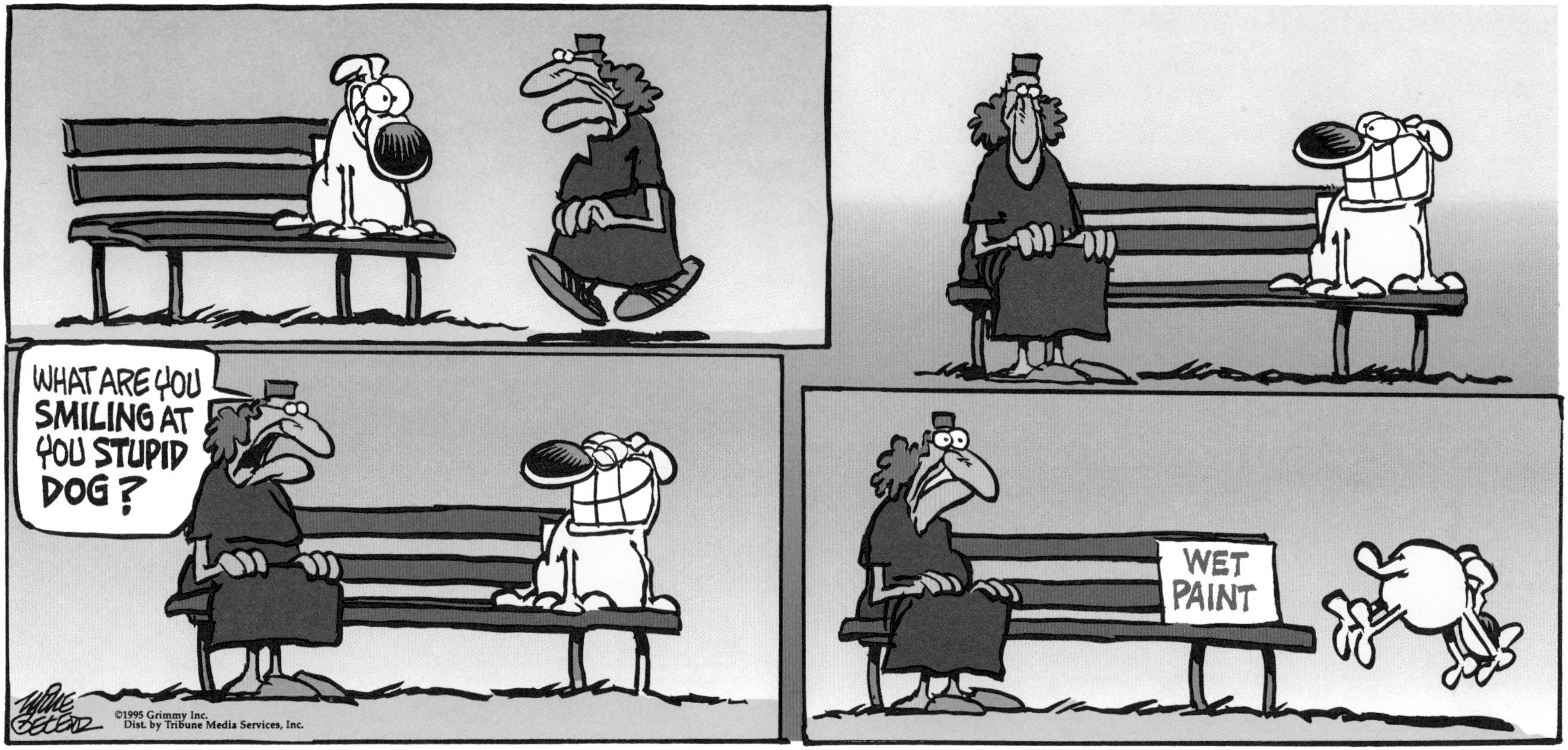
WHAT ARE YOU SMILING AT YOU STUPID DOG ?
©1995 Grimmy Inc.
Dist. by Tribune Media Services, Inc.
WET PAINT

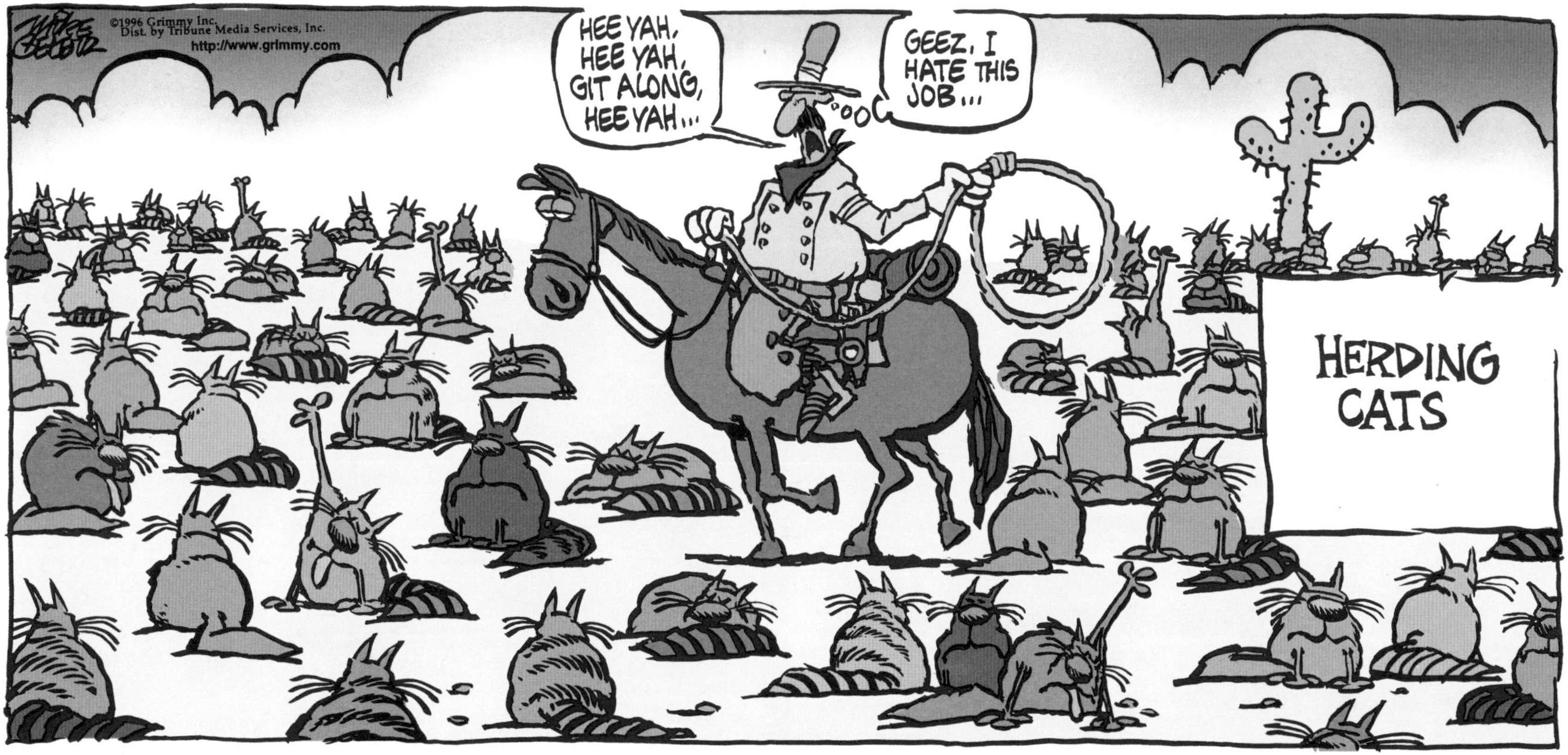
©1996 Grimmy Inc.
Dist. by Tribune Media Services, Inc.
http://www.grimmy.com
HEE YAH, HEE YAH, GIT ALONG, HEE YAH...
GEEZ, I HATE THIS JOB...
HERDING CATS

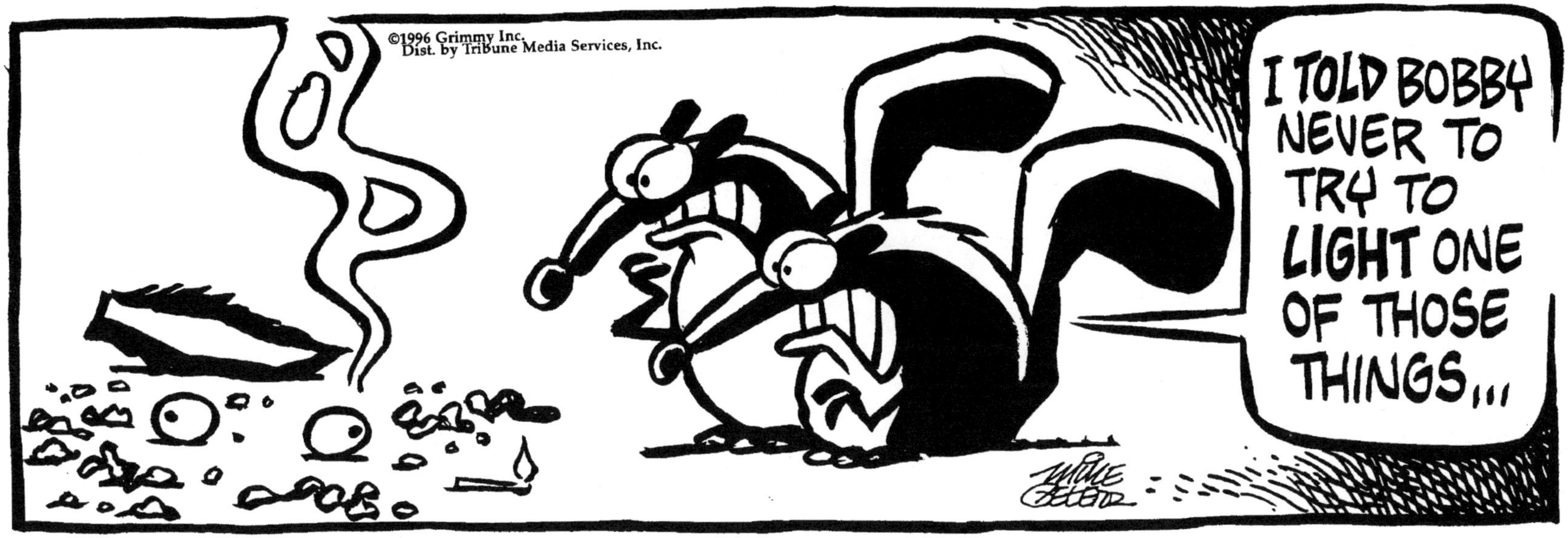
©1996 Grimmy Inc.
Dist. by Tribune Media Services, Inc.
I TOLD BOBBY NEVER TO TRY TO LIGHT ONE OF THOSE THINGS...

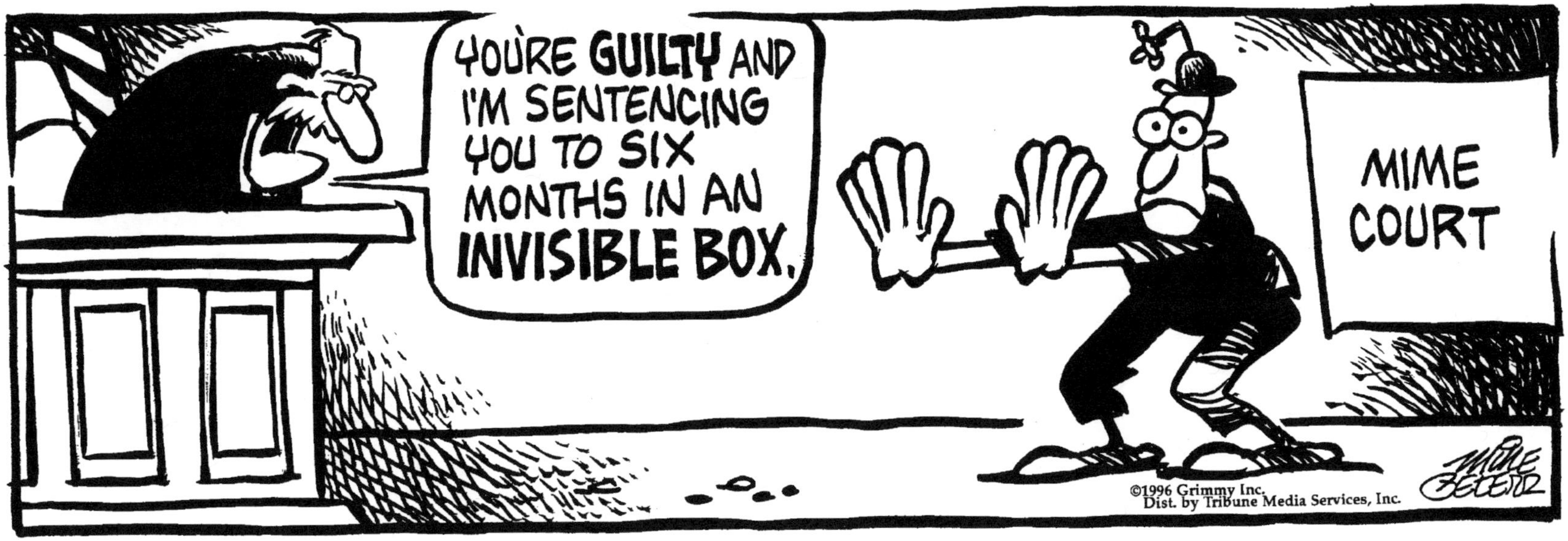
YOU'RE GUILTY AND I'M SENTENCING YOU TO SIX MONTHS IN AN INVISIBLE BOX.
MIME COURT
©1996 Grimmy Inc.
Dist. by Tribune Media Services, Inc.

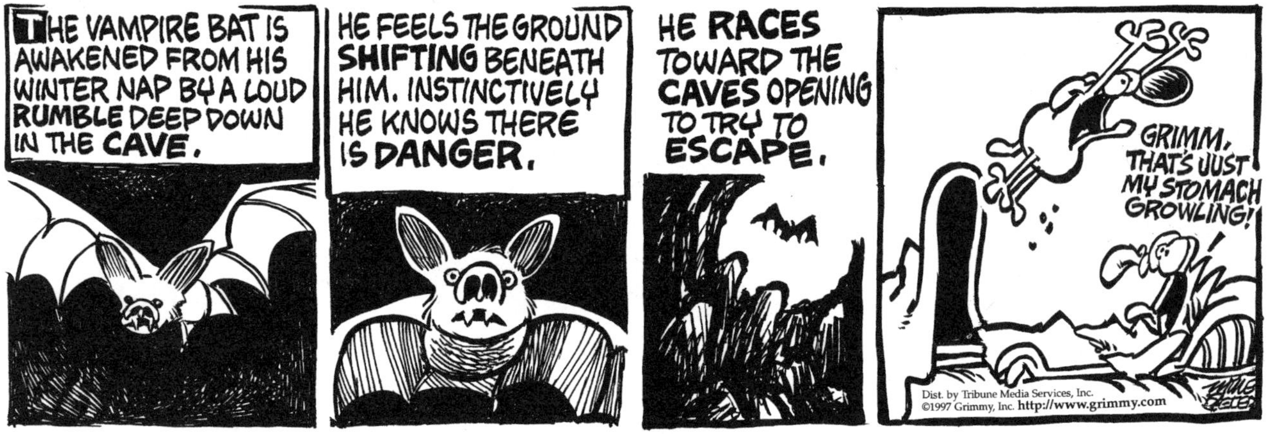
THE VAMPIRE BAT IS AWAKENED FROM HIS WINTER NAP BY A LOUD RUMBLE DEEP DOWN IN THE CAVE.
HE FEELS THE GROUND SHIFTING BENEATH HIM. INSTINCTIVELY HE KNOWS THERE IS DANGER.
HE RACES TOWARD THE CAVES OPENING TO TRY TO ESCAPE.
GRIMM, THAT'S JUST MY STOMACH GROWLING!
Dist. by Tribune Media Services, Inc.
©1997 Grimmy, Inc. http://www.grimmy.com

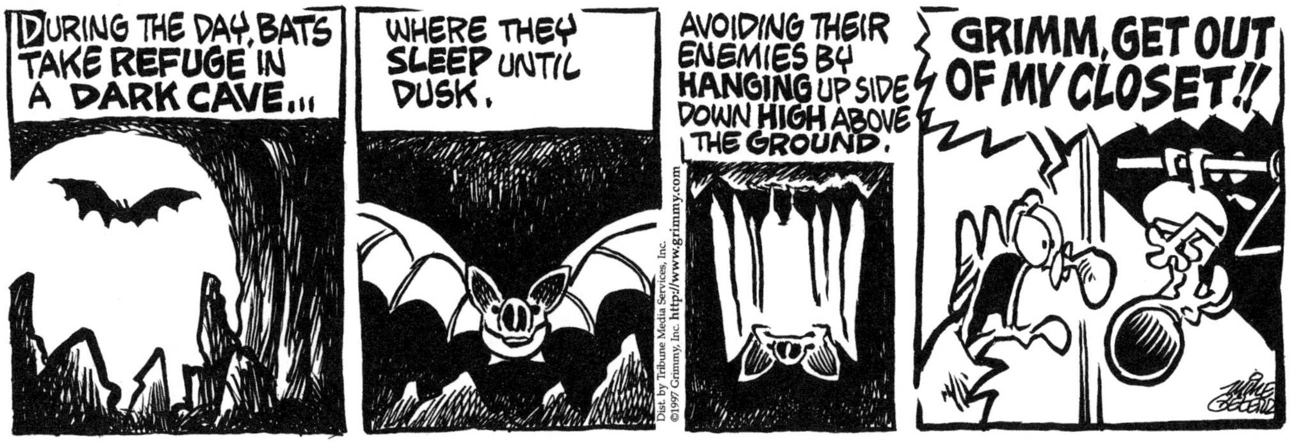
DURING THE DAY, BATS TAKE REFUGE IN A DARK CAVE...
WHERE THEY SLEEP UNTIL DUSK.
Dist. by Tribune Media Services, Inc.
©1997 Grimmy, Inc. http://www.grimmy.com
AVOIDING THEIR ENEMIES BY HANGING UP SIDE DOWN HIGH ABOVE THE GROUND.
GRIMM, GET OUT OF MY CLOSET!!

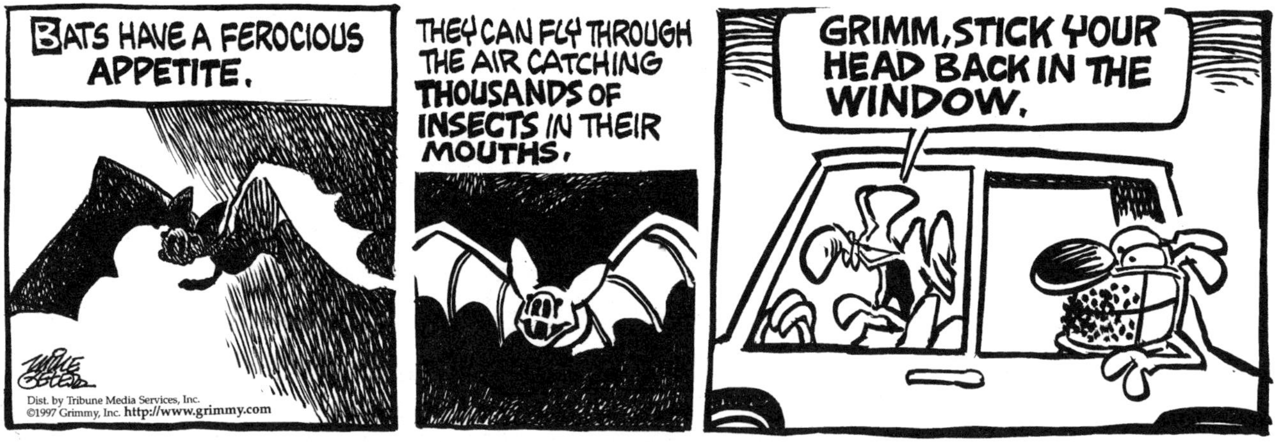
BATS HAVE A FEROCIOUS APPETITE.
Dist. by Tribune Media Services, Inc.
©1997 Grimmy, Inc. http://www.grimmy.com
THEY CAN FLY THROUGH THE AIR CATCHING THOUSANDS OF INSECTS IN THEIR MOUTHS.
GRIMM, STICK YOUR HEAD BACK IN THE WINDOW.

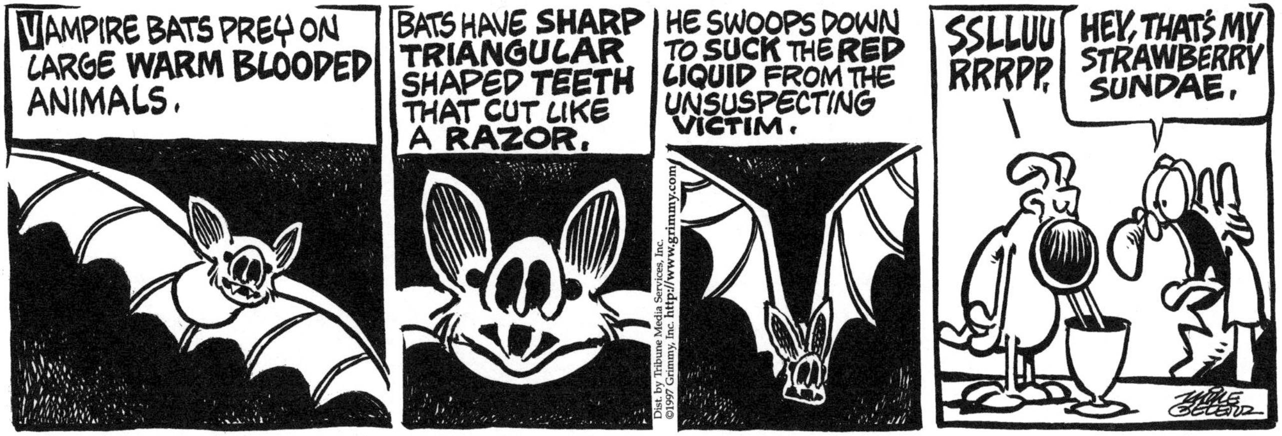
VAMPIRE BATS PREY ON LARGE WARM BLOODED ANIMALS.
BATS HAVE SHARP TRIANGULAR SHAPED TEETH THAT CUT LIKE A RAZOR.
HE SWOOPS DOWN TO SUCK THE RED LIQUID FROM THE UNSUSPECTING VICTIM.
SSLLUU RRRPP.
HEY, THAT'S MY STRAWBERRY SUNDAE.
Dist. by Tribune Media Services, Inc.
©1997 Grimmy, Inc. http://www.grimmy.com

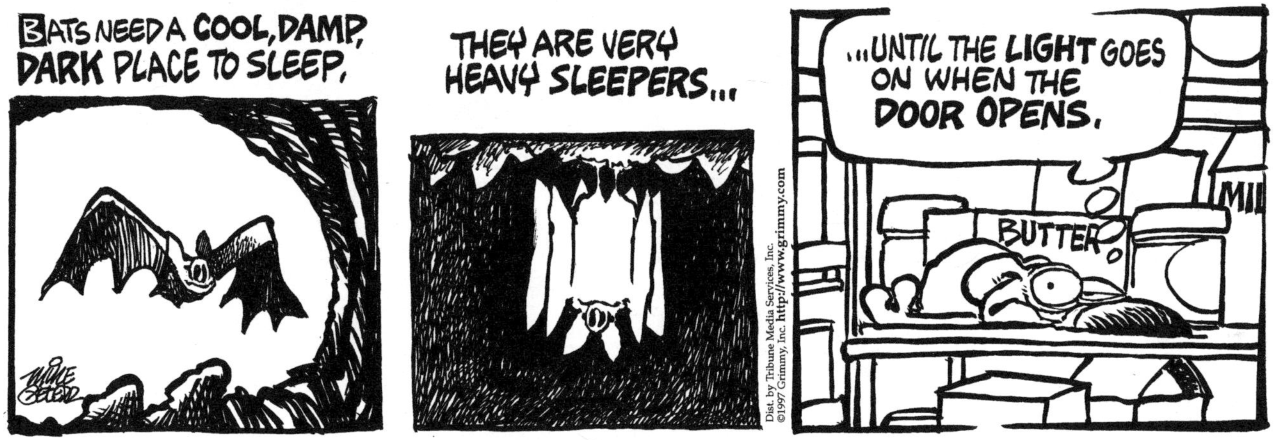
BATS NEED A COOL, DAMP, DARK PLACE TO SLEEP.
THEY ARE VERY HEAVY SLEEPERS...
...UNTIL THE LIGHT GOES ON WHEN THE DOOR OPENS.
BUTTER
Dist. by Tribune Media Services, Inc.
©1997 Grimmy, Inc. http://www.grimmy.com

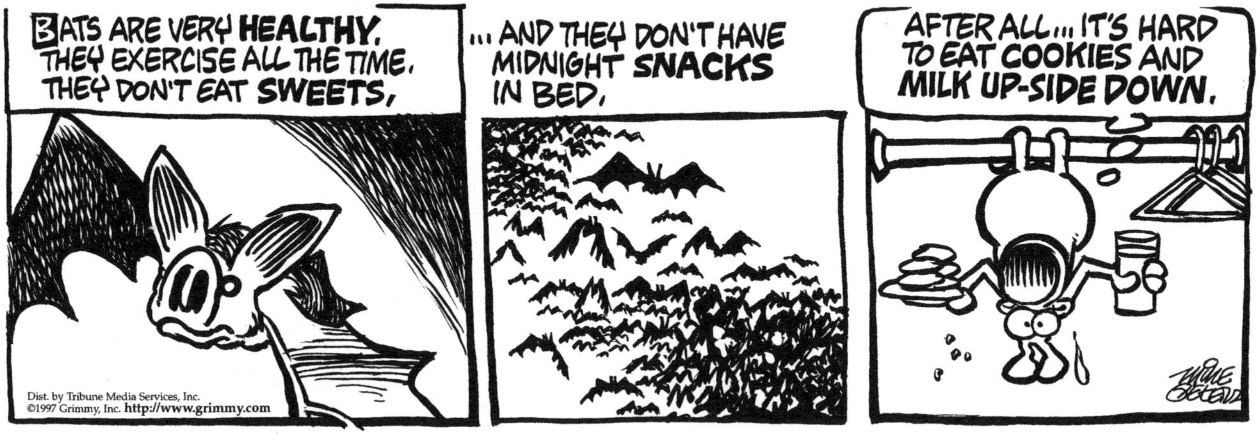
BATS ARE VERY HEALTHY. THEY EXERCISE ALL THE TIME. THEY DON'T EAT SWEETS,
...AND THEY DON'T HAVE MIDNIGHT SNACKS IN BED.
AFTER ALL... IT'S HARD TO EAT COOKIES AND MILK UP-SIDE DOWN.
Dist. by Tribune Media Services, Inc.
©1997 Grimmy, Inc. http://www.grimmy.com

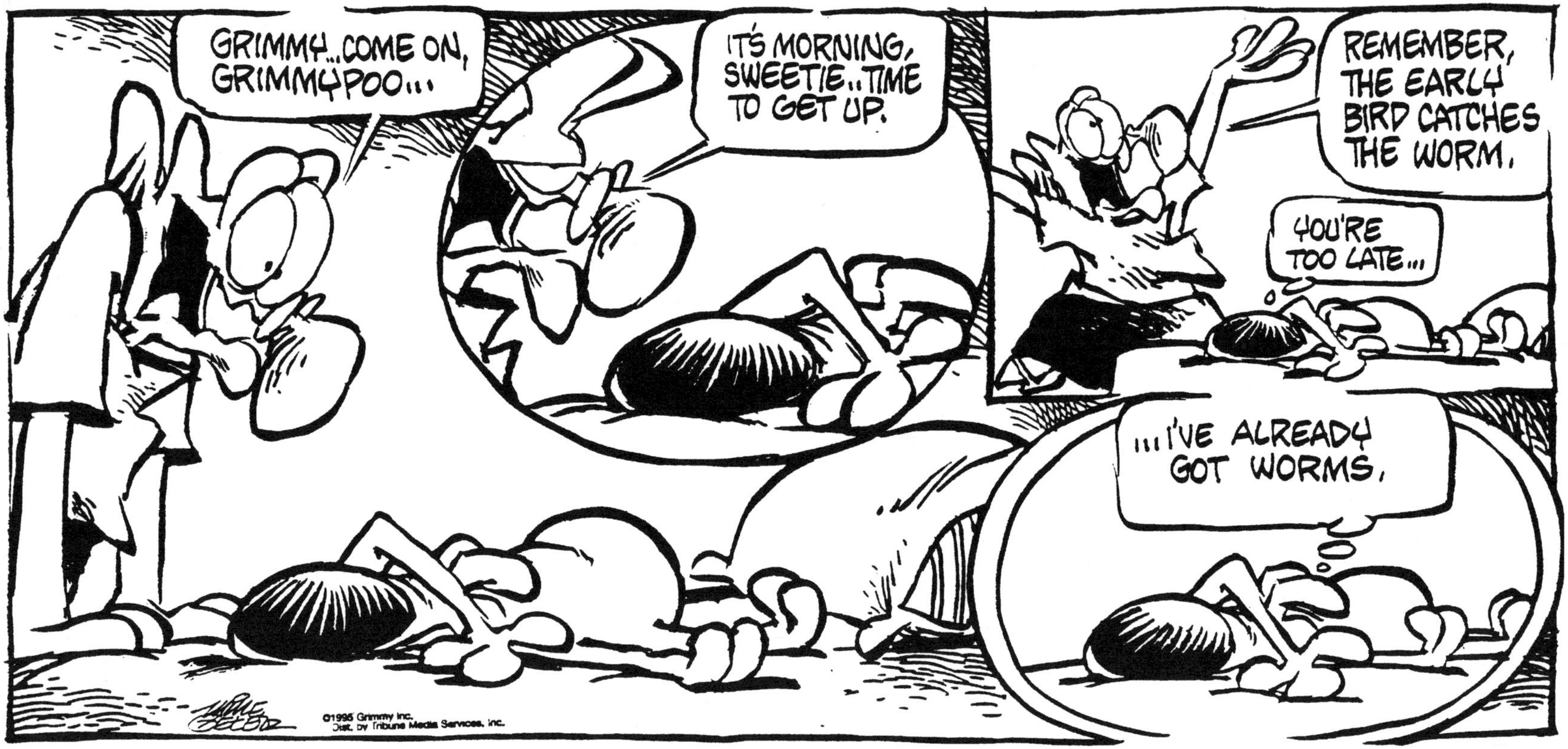

GRIMMY...COME ON, GRIMMYPOO...
IT'S MORNING, SWEETIE...TIME TO GET UP.
REMEMBER, THE EARLY BIRD CATCHES THE WORM.
YOU'RE TOO LATE...
...I'VE ALREADY GOT WORMS.
©1996 Grimmy Inc.
Dist. by Tribune Media Services, Inc.

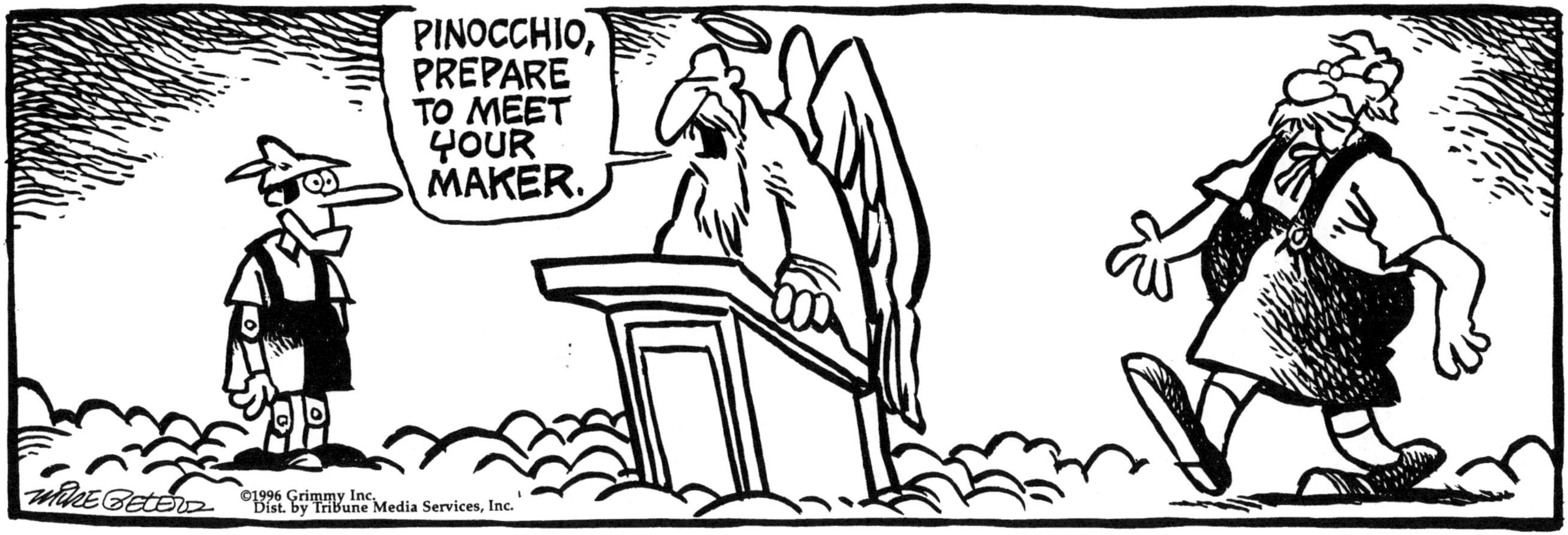
PINOCCHIO, PREPARE TO MEET YOUR MAKER.
©1996 Grimmy Inc.
Dist. by Tribune Media Services, Inc.

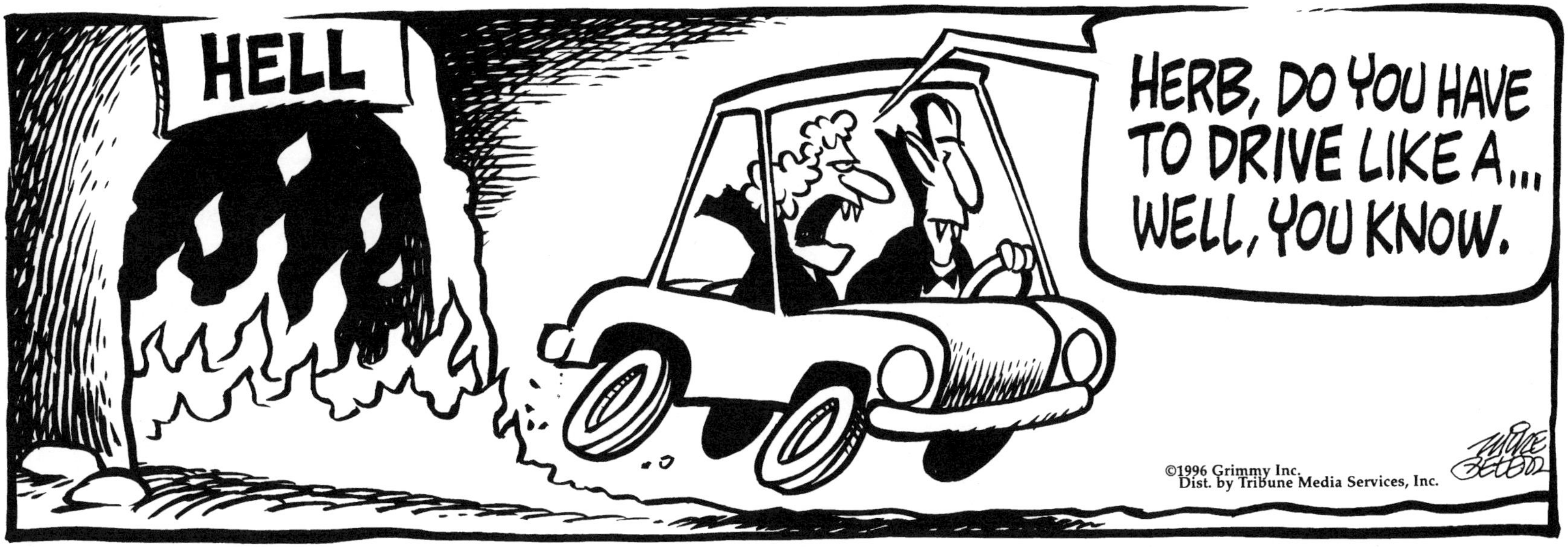
HELL
HERB, DO YOU HAVE TO DRIVE LIKE A... WELL, YOU KNOW.
©1996 Grimmy Inc.
Dist. by Tribune Media Services, Inc.

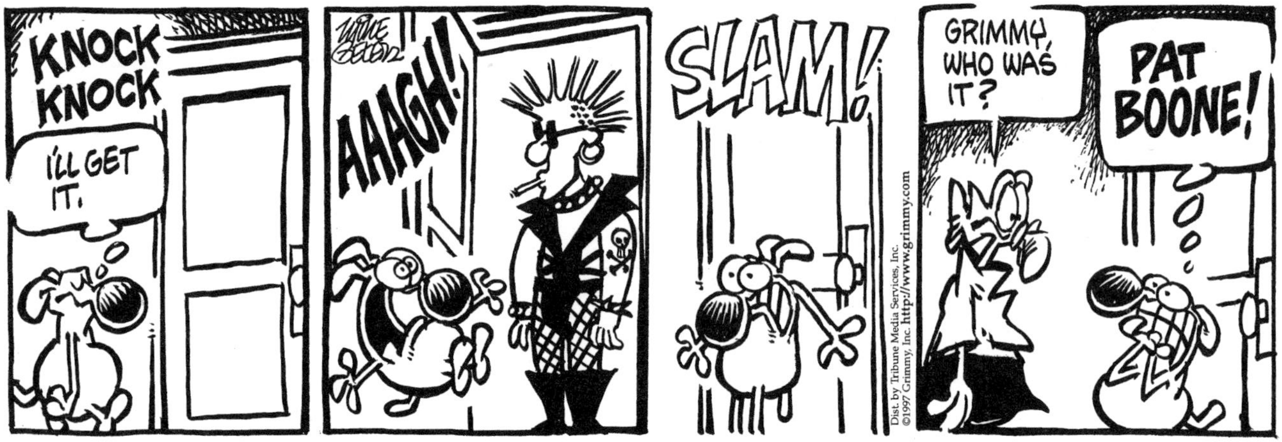
KNOCK KNOCK
I'LL GET IT.
AAAGH!
SLAM!
GRIMMY, WHO WAS IT?
PAT BOONE!
Dist. by Tribune Media Services, Inc. ©1997 Grimmy, Inc. http://www.grimmy.com

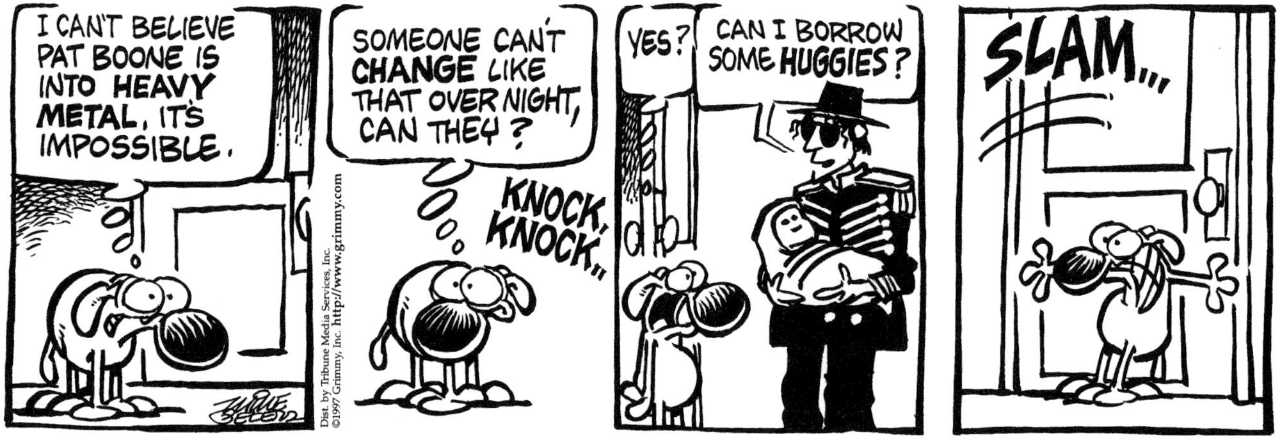
I CAN'T BELIEVE PAT BOONE IS INTO HEAVY METAL, IT'S IMPOSSIBLE.
SOMEONE CAN'T CHANGE LIKE THAT OVER NIGHT, CAN THEY?
KNOCK, KNOCK..
YES?
CAN I BORROW SOME HUGGIES?
SLAM...
Dist. by Tribune Media Services, Inc. ©1997 Grimmy, Inc. http://www.grimmy.com

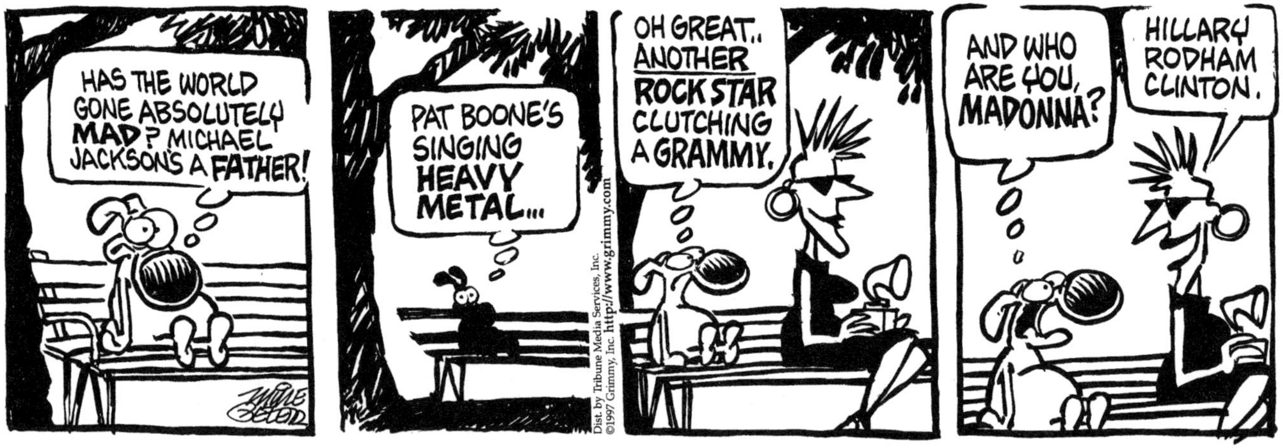
HAS THE WORLD GONE ABSOLUTELY MAD? MICHAEL JACKSON'S A FATHER!
PAT BOONE'S SINGING HEAVY METAL...
OH GREAT.. ANOTHER ROCK STAR CLUTCHING A GRAMMY.
AND WHO ARE YOU, MADONNA?
HILLARY RODHAM CLINTON.
Dist. by Tribune Media Services, Inc. ©1997 Grimmy, Inc. http://www.grimmy.com

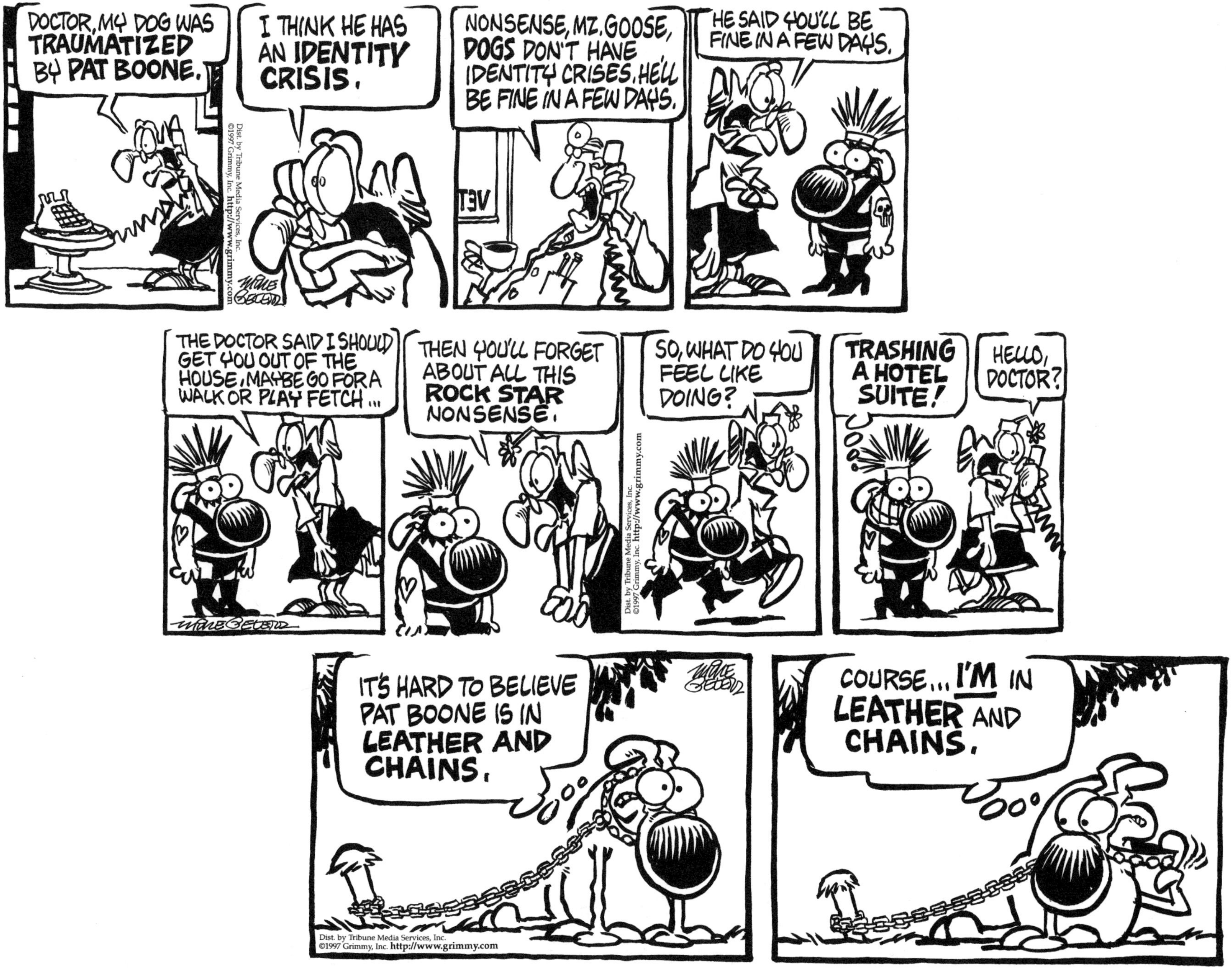
DOCTOR, MY DOG WAS TRAUMATIZED BY PAT BOONE.
Dist. by Tribune Media Services, Inc. ©1997 Grimmy, Inc. http://www.grimmy.com
I THINK HE HAS AN IDENTITY CRISIS.
NONSENSE, MZ. GOOSE, DOGS DON'T HAVE IDENTITY CRISES. HE'LL BE FINE IN A FEW DAYS.
VET
HE SAID YOU'LL BE FINE IN A FEW DAYS.
THE DOCTOR SAID I SHOULD GET YOU OUT OF THE HOUSE, MAYBE GO FOR A WALK OR PLAY FETCH...
THEN YOU'LL FORGET ABOUT ALL THIS ROCK STAR NONSENSE.
Dist. by Tribune Media Services, Inc. ©1997 Grimmy, Inc. http://www.grimmy.com
SO, WHAT DO YOU FEEL LIKE DOING?
TRASHING A HOTEL SUITE!
HELLO, DOCTOR?
IT'S HARD TO BELIEVE PAT BOONE IS IN LEATHER AND CHAINS.
Dist. by Tribune Media Services, Inc. ©1997 Grimmy, Inc. http://www.grimmy.com
COURSE... I'M IN LEATHER AND CHAINS.

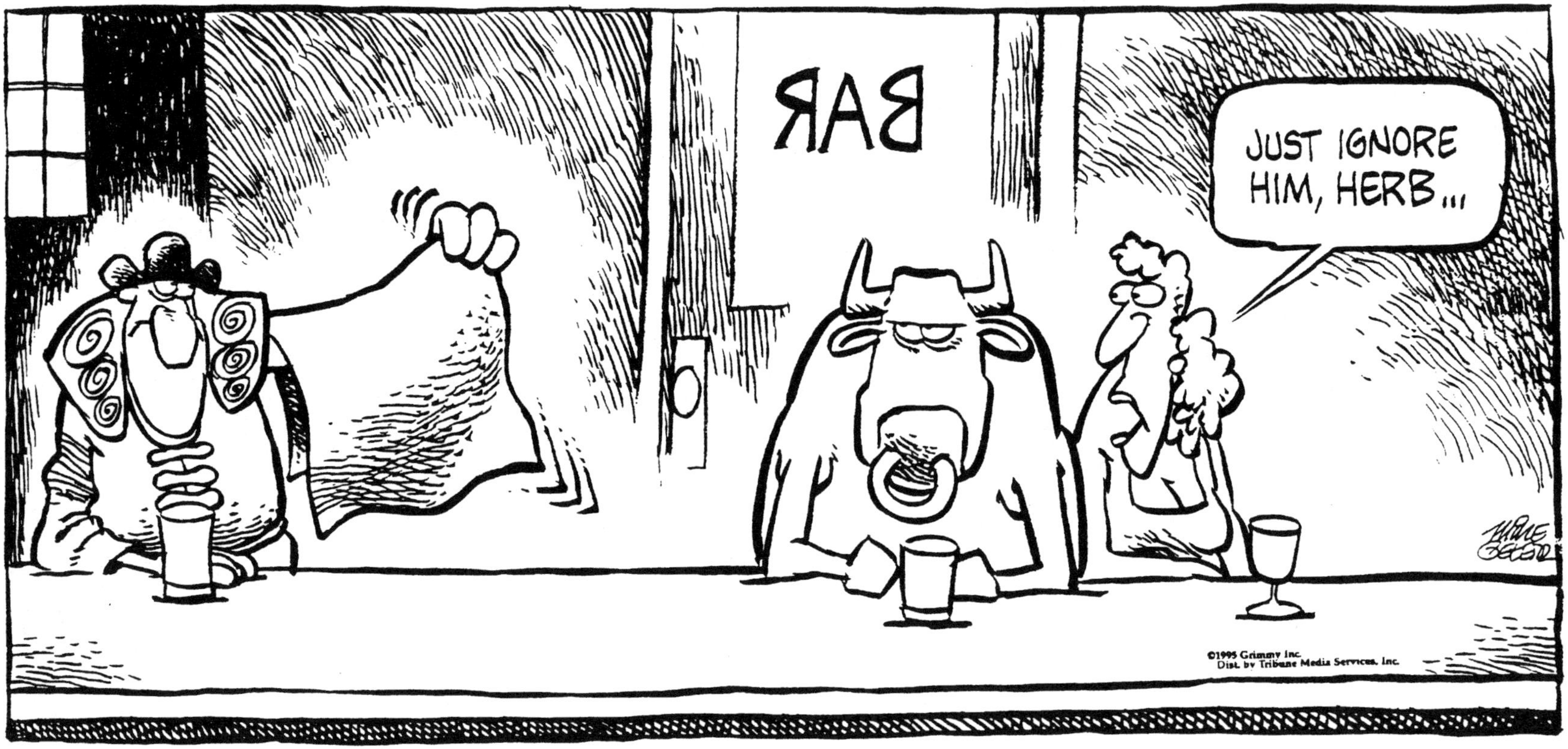
JUST IGNORE HIM, HERB...
©1995 Grimmy Inc. Dist. by Tribune Media Services, Inc.

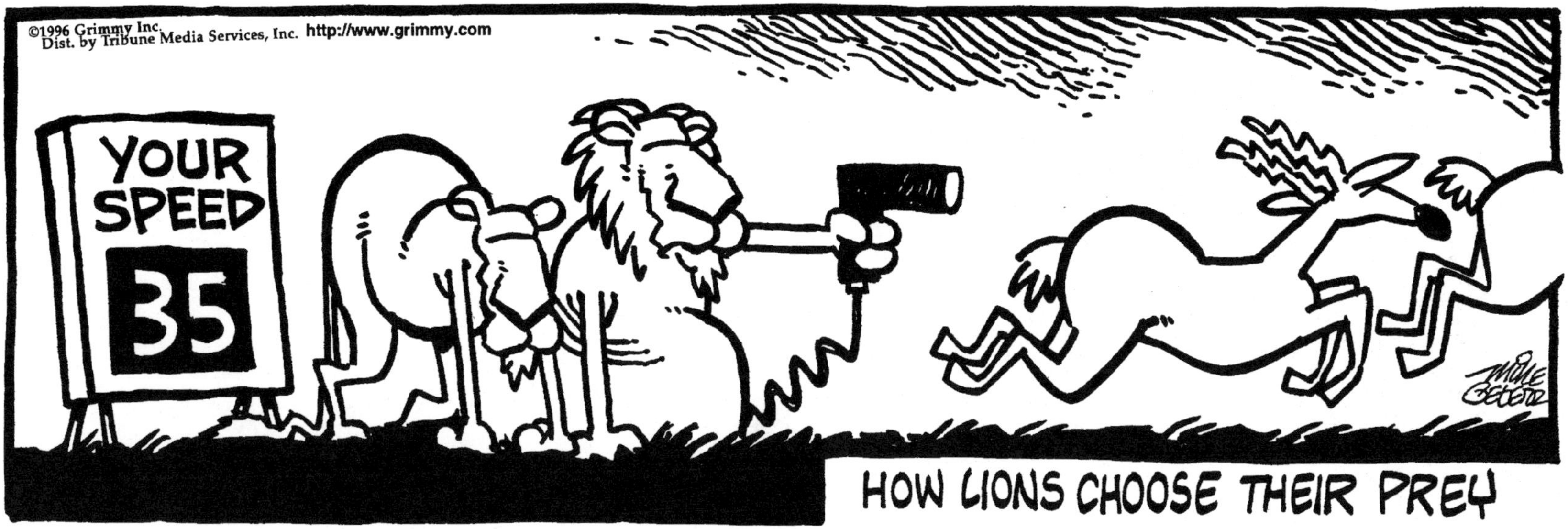
©1996 Grimmy Inc.
Dist. by Tribune Media Services, Inc. http://www.grimmy.com
YOUR SPEED
35
HOW LIONS CHOOSE THEIR PREY

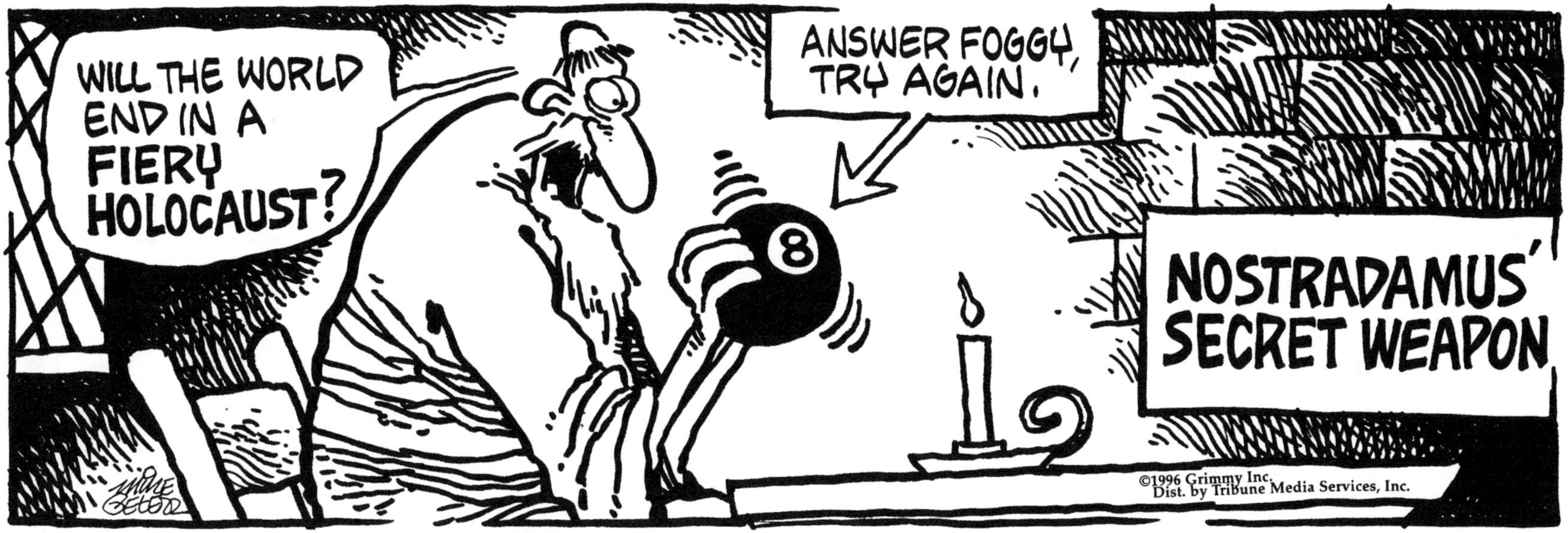
WILL THE WORLD END IN A FIERY HOLOCAUST?
ANSWER FOGGY, TRY AGAIN.
8
NOSTRADAMUS' SECRET WEAPON
©1996 Grimmy Inc.
Dist. by Tribune Media Services, Inc.

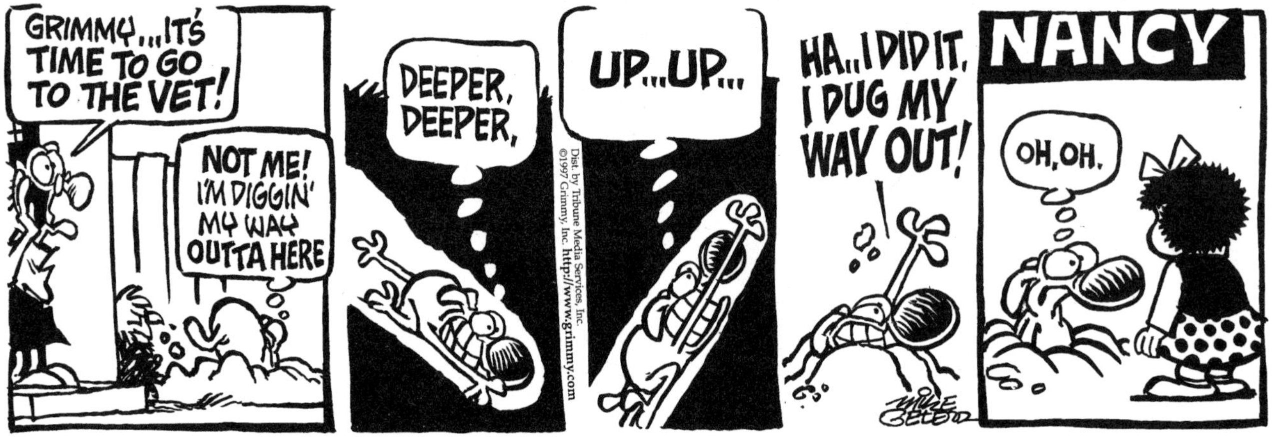
NANCY
GRIMMY...IT'S TIME TO GO TO THE VET!
NOT ME! I'M DIGGIN' MY WAY OUTTA HERE
DEEPER, DEEPER,
Dist. by Tribune Media Services, Inc. ©1997 Grimmy, Inc. http://www.grimmy.com
UP...UP...
HA..I DID IT, I DUG MY WAY OUT!
OH,OH.

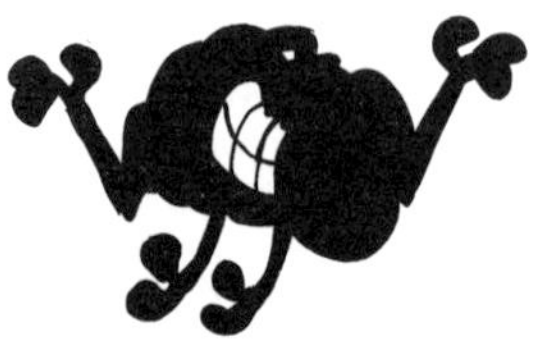

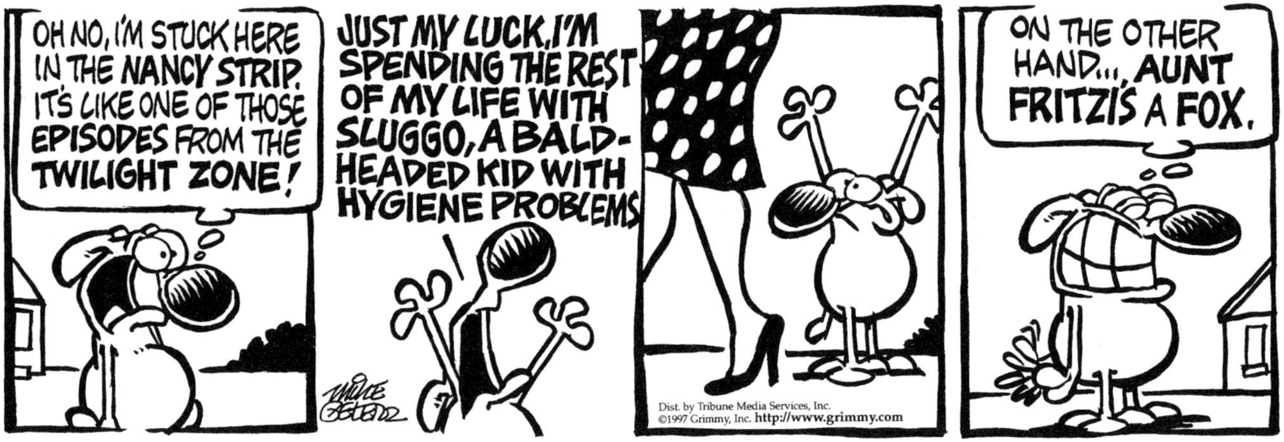
OH NO, I'M STUCK HERE IN THE NANCY STRIP. IT'S LIKE ONE OF THOSE EPISODES FROM THE TWILIGHT ZONE!
JUST MY LUCK, I'M SPENDING THE REST OF MY LIFE WITH SLUGGO, A BALD-HEADED KID WITH HYGIENE PROBLEMS
Dist. by Tribune Media Services, Inc. ©1997 Grimmy, Inc. http://www.grimmy.com
ON THE OTHER HAND..., AUNT FRITZI'S A FOX.

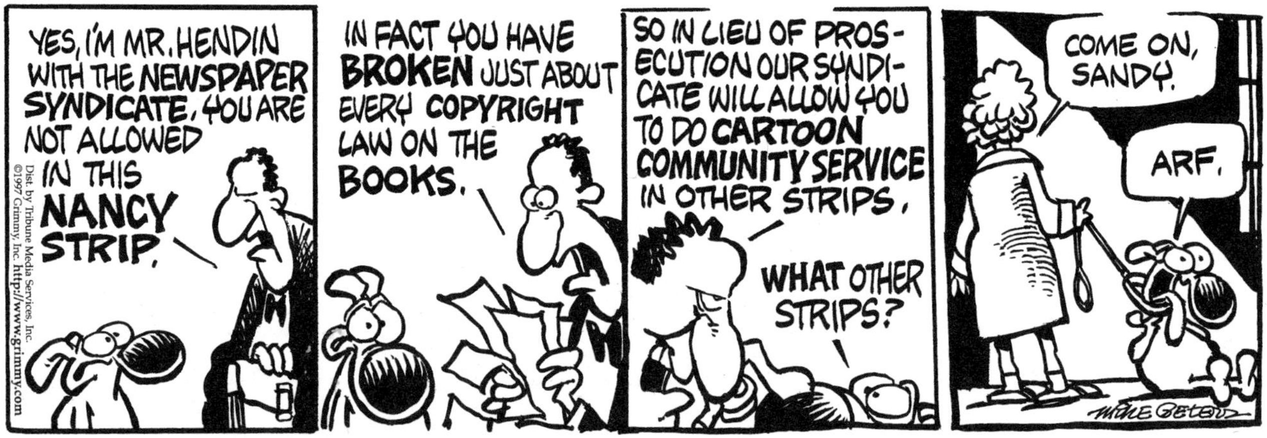
YES, I'M MR. HENDIN WITH THE NEWSPAPER SYNDICATE. YOU ARE NOT ALLOWED IN THIS NANCY STRIP.
Dist. by Tribune Media Services, Inc. ©1997 Grimmy, Inc. http://www.grimmy.com
IN FACT YOU HAVE BROKEN JUST ABOUT EVERY COPYRIGHT LAW ON THE BOOKS.
SO IN LIEU OF PROSECUTION OUR SYNDICATE WILL ALLOW YOU TO DO CARTOON COMMUNITY SERVICE IN OTHER STRIPS.
WHAT OTHER STRIPS?
COME ON, SANDY.
ARF.

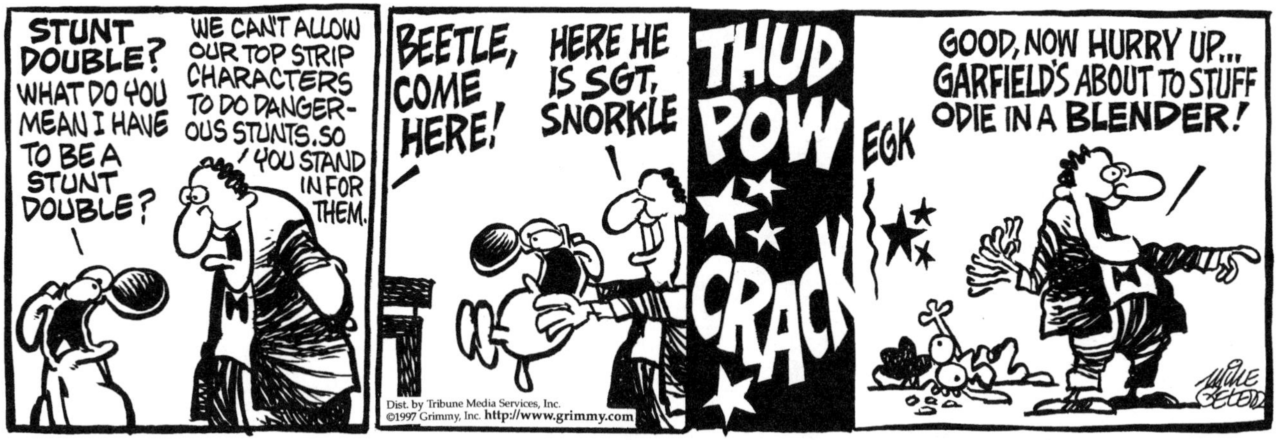
STUNT DOUBLE? WHAT DO YOU MEAN I HAVE TO BE A STUNT DOUBLE?
WE CAN'T ALLOW OUR TOP STRIP CHARACTERS TO DO DANGER-OUS STUNTS. SO YOU STAND IN FOR THEM.
BEETLE, COME HERE!
HERE HE IS SGT. SNORKLE
Dist. by Tribune Media Services, Inc. ©1997 Grimmy, Inc. http://www.grimmy.com
THUD
POW
CRACK
EGK
GOOD, NOW HURRY UP... GARFIELD'S ABOUT TO STUFF ODIE IN A BLENDER!

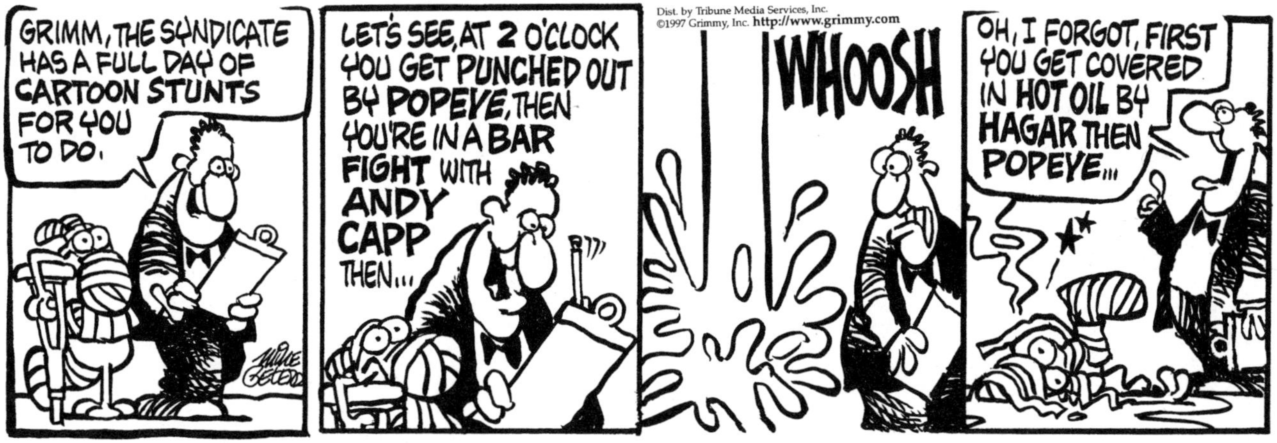
GRIMM, THE SYNDICATE HAS A FULL DAY OF CARTOON STUNTS FOR YOU TO DO.
LET'S SEE, AT 2 O'CLOCK YOU GET PUNCHED OUT BY POPEYE, THEN YOU'RE IN A BAR FIGHT WITH ANDY CAPP THEN...
Dist. by Tribune Media Services, Inc. ©1997 Grimmy, Inc. http://www.grimmy.com
WHOOSH
OH, I FORGOT, FIRST YOU GET COVERED IN HOT OIL BY HAGAR THEN POPEYE...

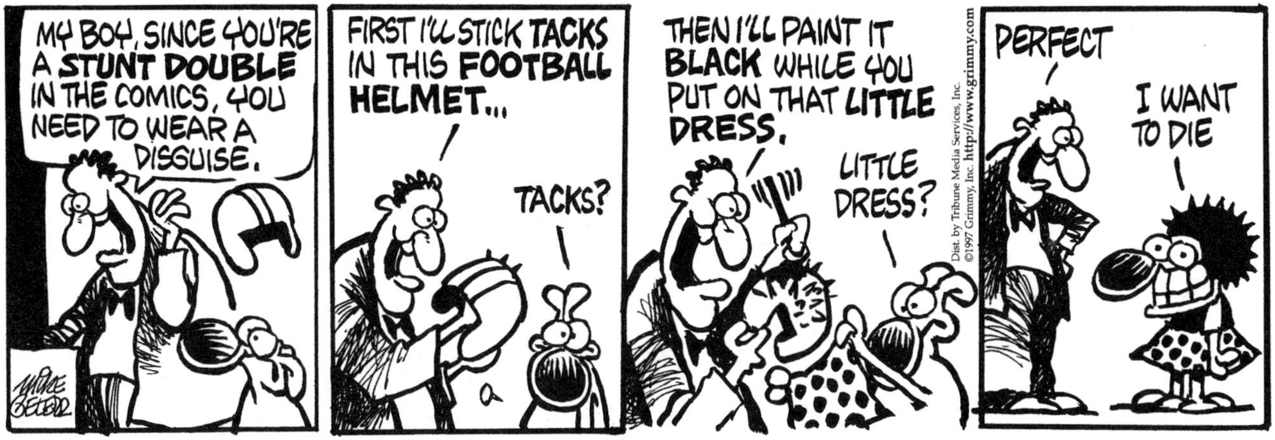
MY BOY, SINCE YOU'RE A STUNT DOUBLE IN THE COMICS, YOU NEED TO WEAR A DISGUISE.
FIRST I'LL STICK TACKS IN THIS FOOTBALL HELMET...
TACKS?
THEN I'LL PAINT IT BLACK WHILE YOU PUT ON THAT LITTLE DRESS.
LITTLE DRESS?
Dist. by Tribune Media Services, Inc. ©1997 Grimmy, Inc. http://www.grimmy.com
PERFECT
I WANT TO DIE

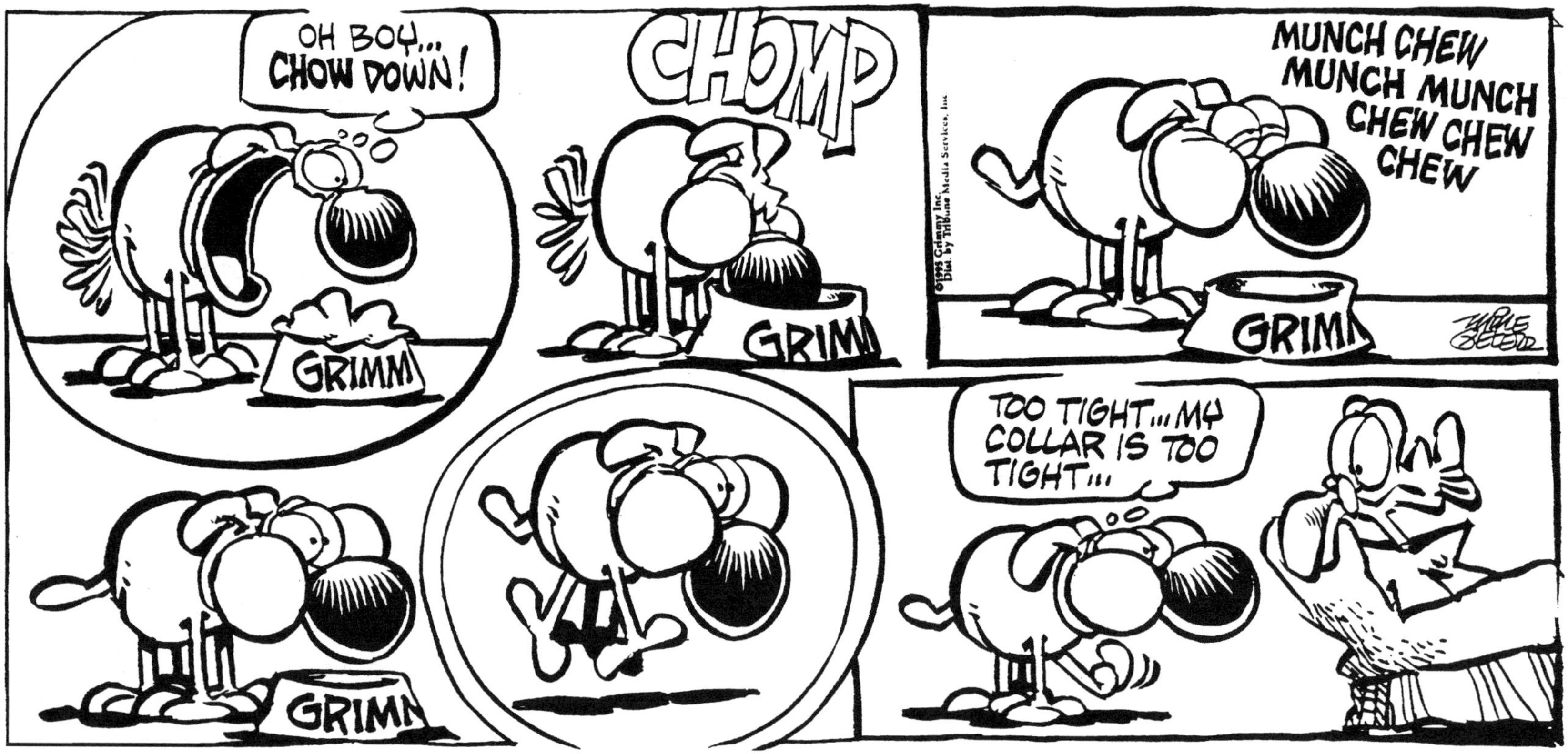
OH BOY... CHOW DOWN!
GRIMM
CHOMP
GRIM
MUNCH CHEW MUNCH MUNCH CHEW CHEW CHEW
GRIM
©1995 Grimmy Inc. Dist. by Tribune Media Services, Inc
GRIMM
TOO TIGHT... MY COLLAR IS TOO TIGHT...

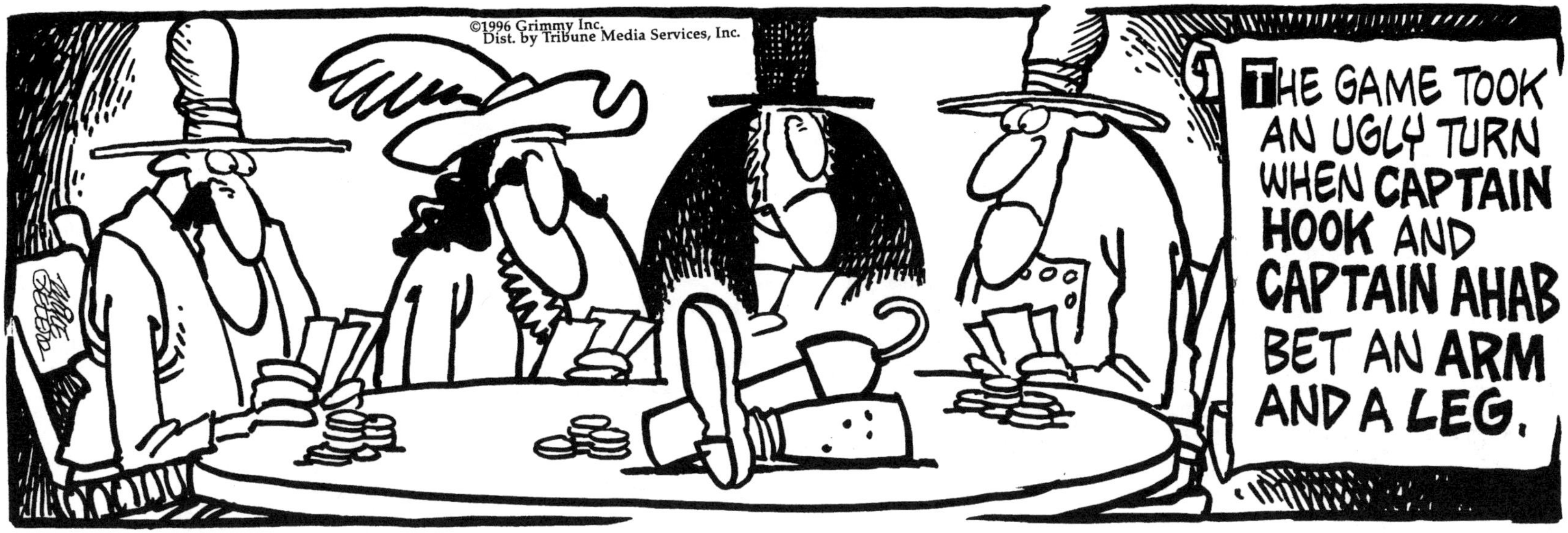
©1996 Grimmy Inc.
Dist. by Tribune Media Services, Inc.
THE GAME TOOK AN UGLY TURN WHEN CAPTAIN HOOK AND CAPTAIN AHAB BET AN ARM AND A LEG.

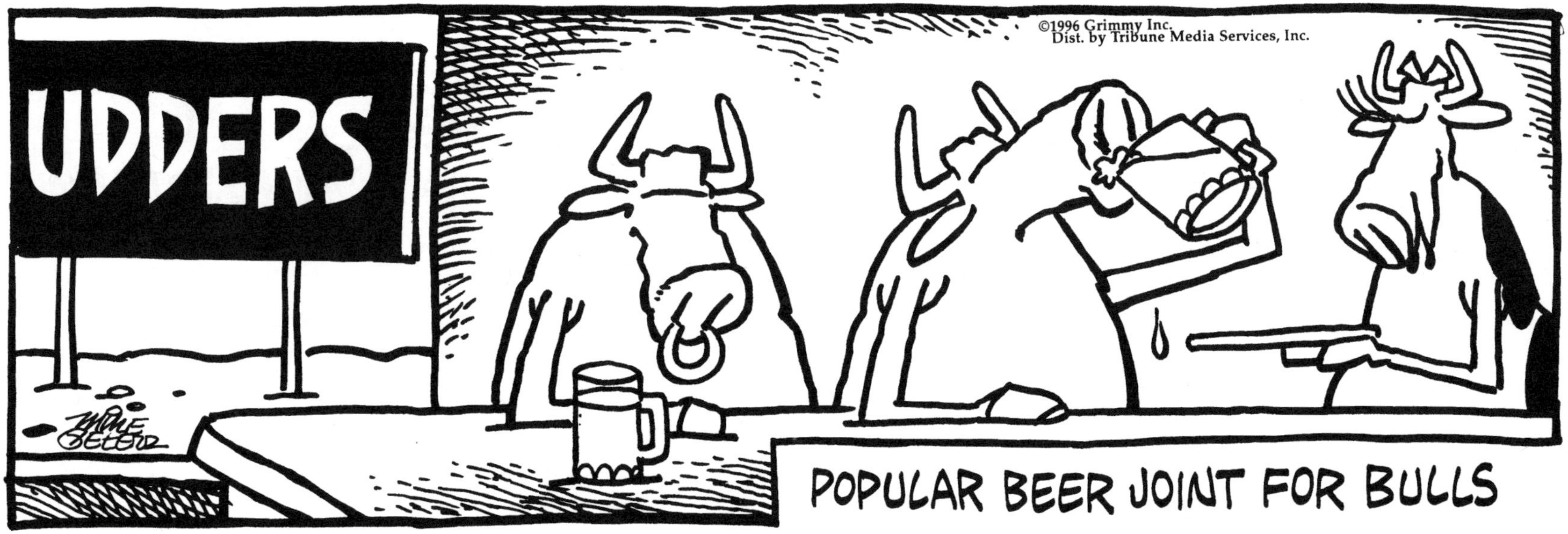
UDDERS
©1996 Grimmy Inc.
Dist. by Tribune Media Services, Inc.
POPULAR BEER JOINT FOR BULLS

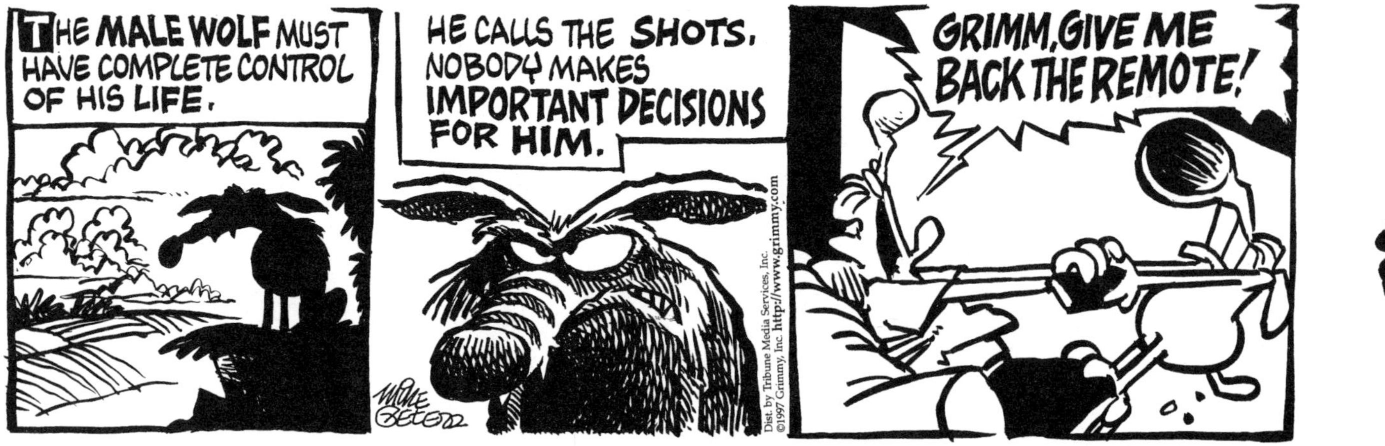
THE MALE WOLF MUST HAVE COMPLETE CONTROL OF HIS LIFE.
HE CALLS THE SHOTS. NOBODY MAKES IMPORTANT DECISIONS FOR HIM.
Dist. by Tribune Media Services, Inc. ©1997 Grimmy, Inc. http://www.grimmy.com
GRIMM, GIVE ME BACK THE REMOTE!

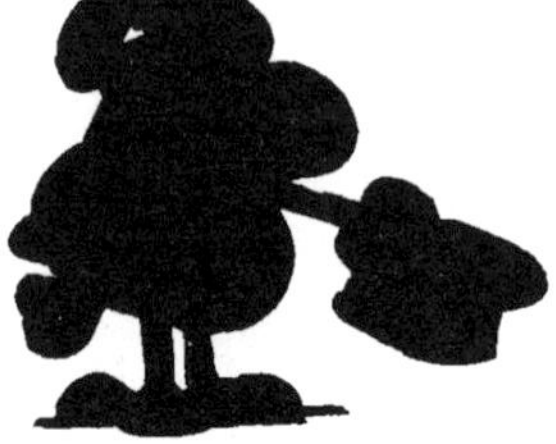

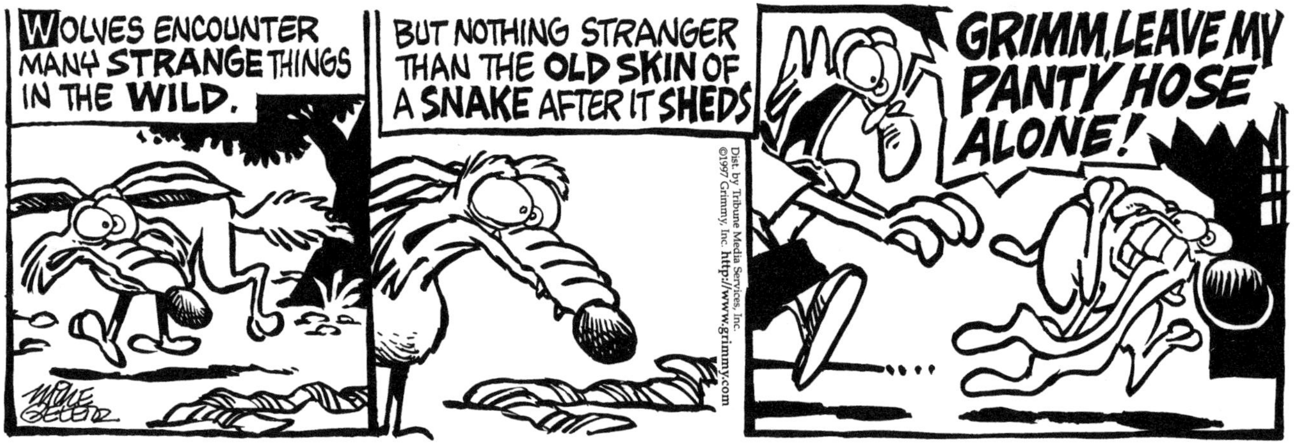
WOLVES ENCOUNTER MANY STRANGE THINGS IN THE WILD.
BUT NOTHING STRANGER THAN THE OLD SKIN OF A SNAKE AFTER IT SHEDS
Dist. by Tribune Media Services, Inc. ©1997 Grimmy, Inc. http://www.grimmy.com
GRIMM, LEAVE MY PANTY HOSE ALONE!

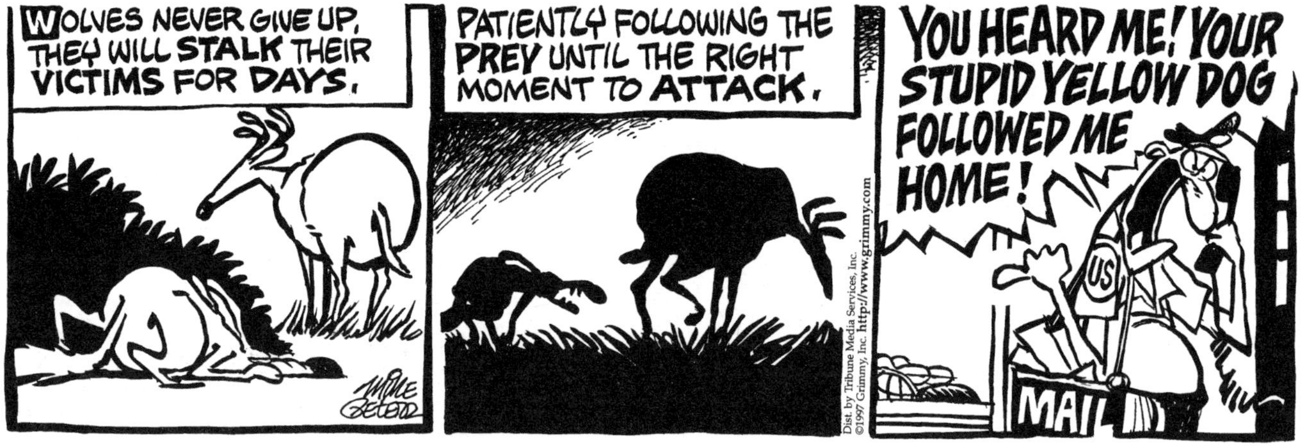
WOLVES NEVER GIVE UP, THEY WILL STALK THEIR VICTIMS FOR DAYS.
PATIENTLY FOLLOWING THE PREY UNTIL THE RIGHT MOMENT TO ATTACK.
Dist. by Tribune Media Services, Inc. ©1997 Grimmy, Inc. http://www.grimmy.com
YOU HEARD ME! YOUR STUPID YELLOW DOG FOLLOWED ME HOME!
US
MAI

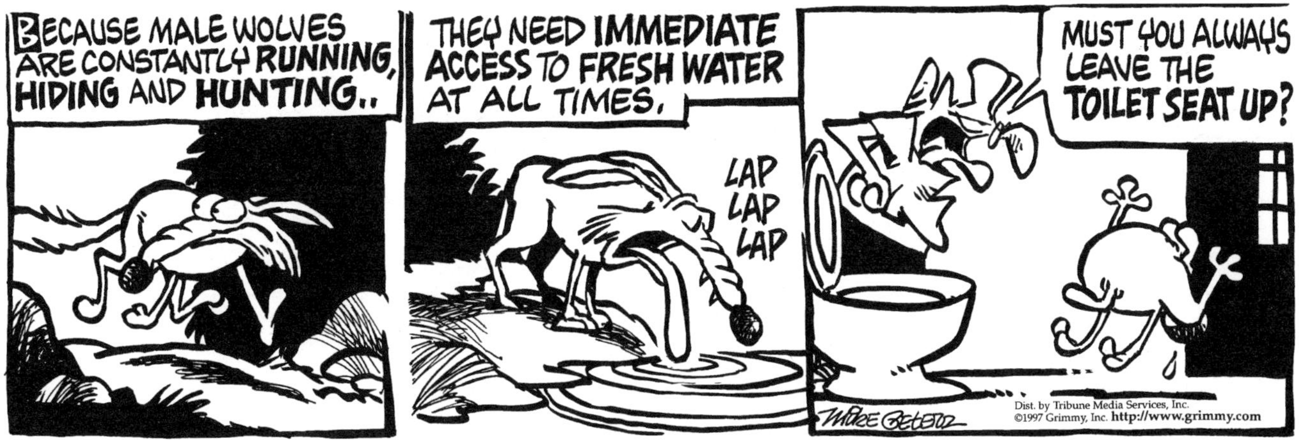
BECAUSE MALE WOLVES ARE CONSTANTLY RUNNING, HIDING AND HUNTING..
THEY NEED IMMEDIATE ACCESS TO FRESH WATER AT ALL TIMES.
LAP LAP LAP
MUST YOU ALWAYS LEAVE THE TOILET SEAT UP?
Dist. by Tribune Media Services, Inc.
©1997 Grimmy, Inc. http://www.grimmy.com

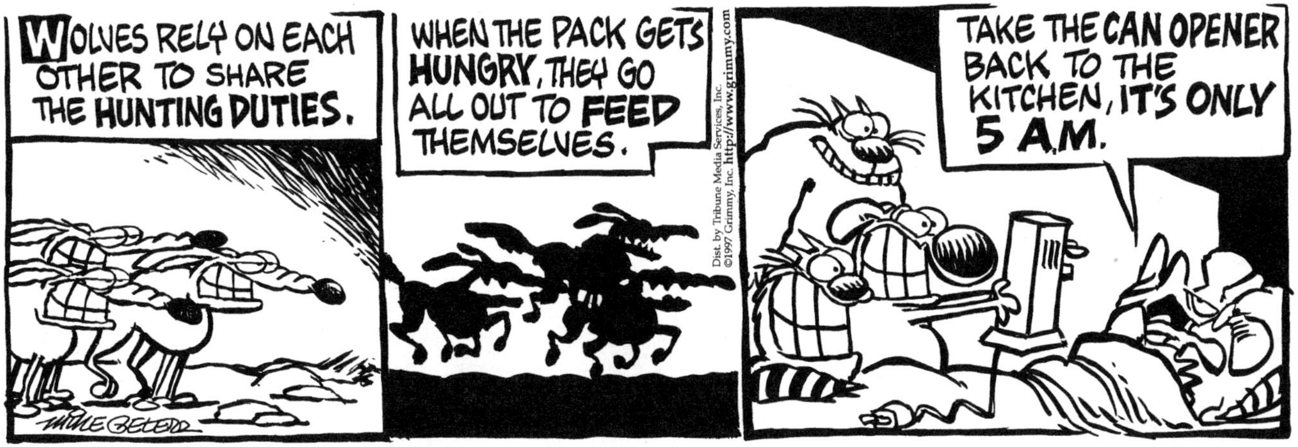
WOLVES RELY ON EACH OTHER TO SHARE THE HUNTING DUTIES.
WHEN THE PACK GETS HUNGRY, THEY GO ALL OUT TO FEED THEMSELVES.
Dist. by Tribune Media Services, Inc.
©1997 Grimmy, Inc. http://www.grimmy.com
TAKE THE CAN OPENER BACK TO THE KITCHEN, IT'S ONLY 5 A.M.

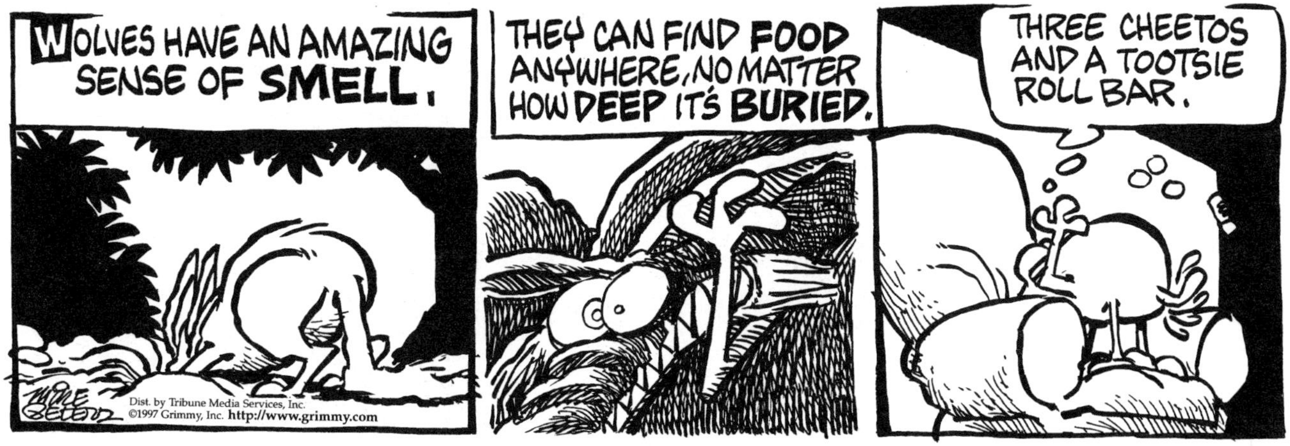
WOLVES HAVE AN AMAZING SENSE OF SMELL.
Dist. by Tribune Media Services, Inc.
©1997 Grimmy, Inc. http://www.grimmy.com
THEY CAN FIND FOOD ANYWHERE, NO MATTER HOW DEEP IT'S BURIED.
THREE CHEETOS AND A TOOTSIE ROLL BAR.

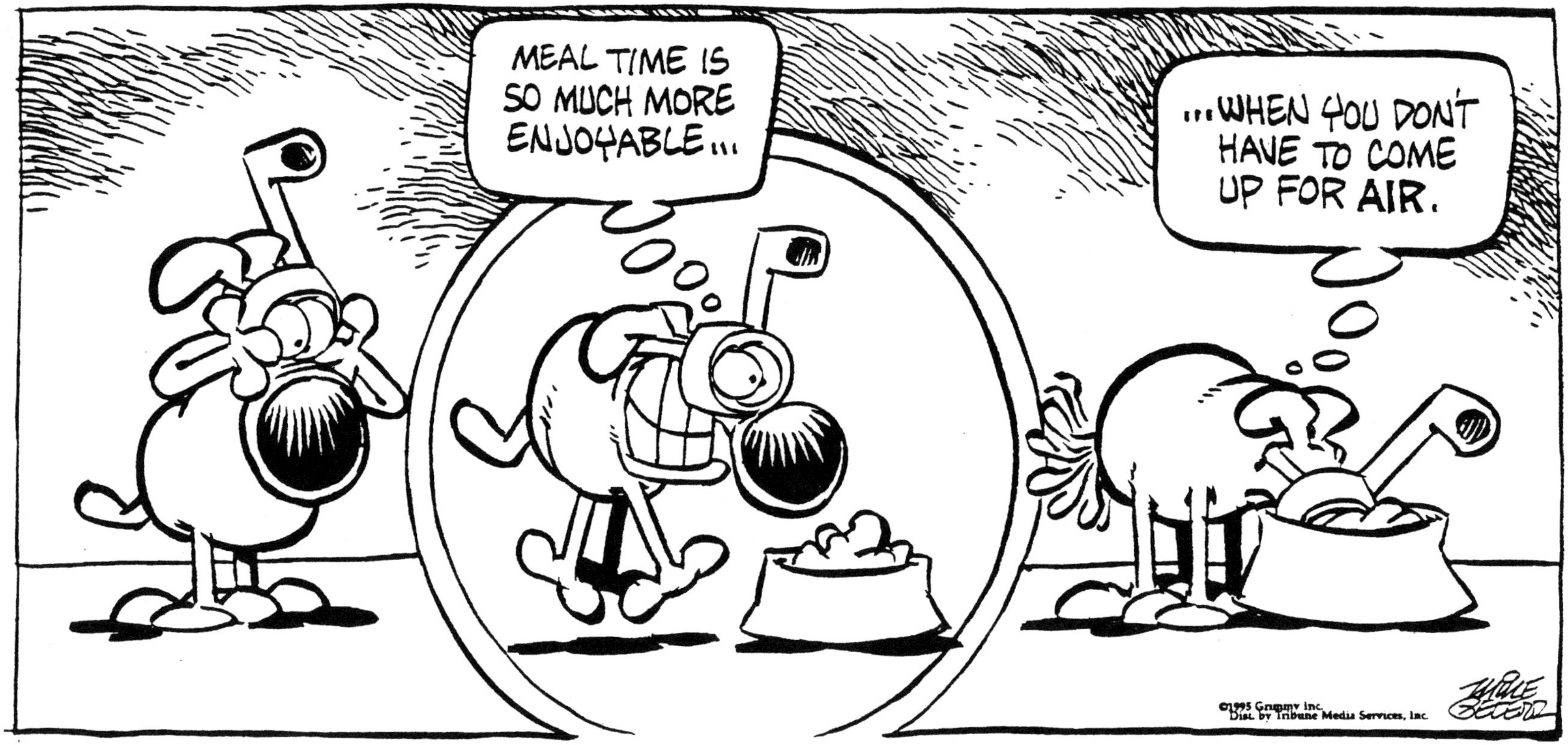
MEAL TIME IS SO MUCH MORE ENJOYABLE...
...WHEN YOU DON'T HAVE TO COME UP FOR AIR.
©1995 Grimmy Inc.
Dist. by Tribune Media Services, Inc.

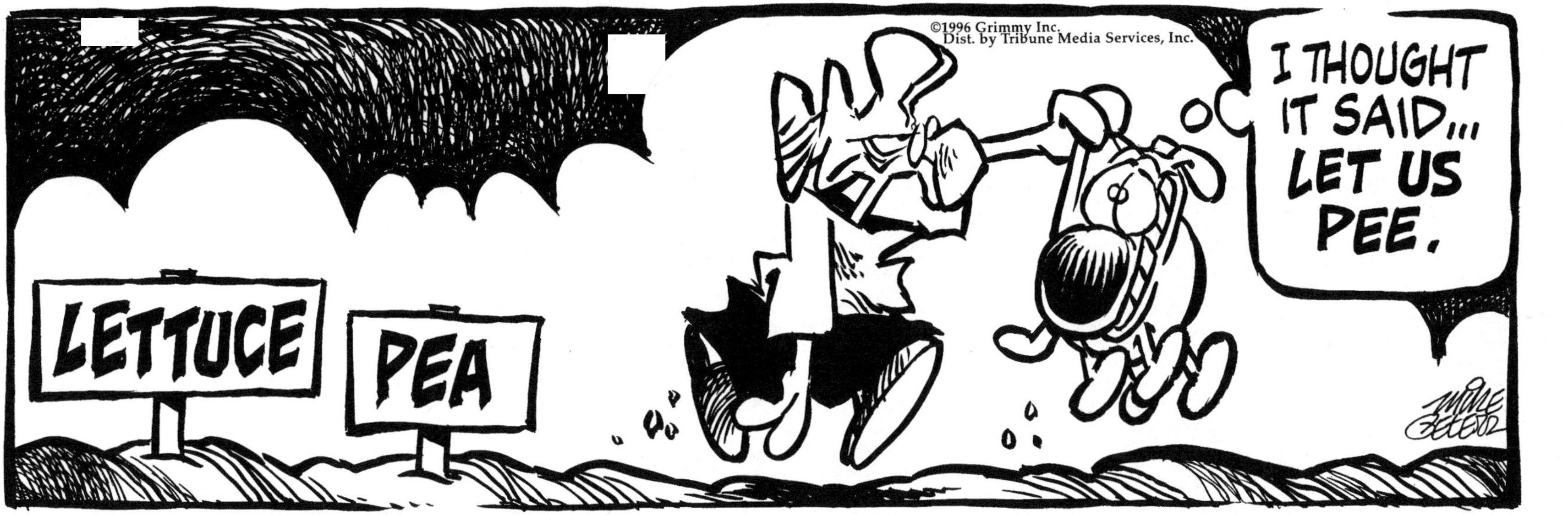
©1996 Grimmy Inc.
Dist. by Tribune Media Services, Inc.
LETTUCE
PEA
I THOUGHT IT SAID... LET US PEE.
MIKE PETERS

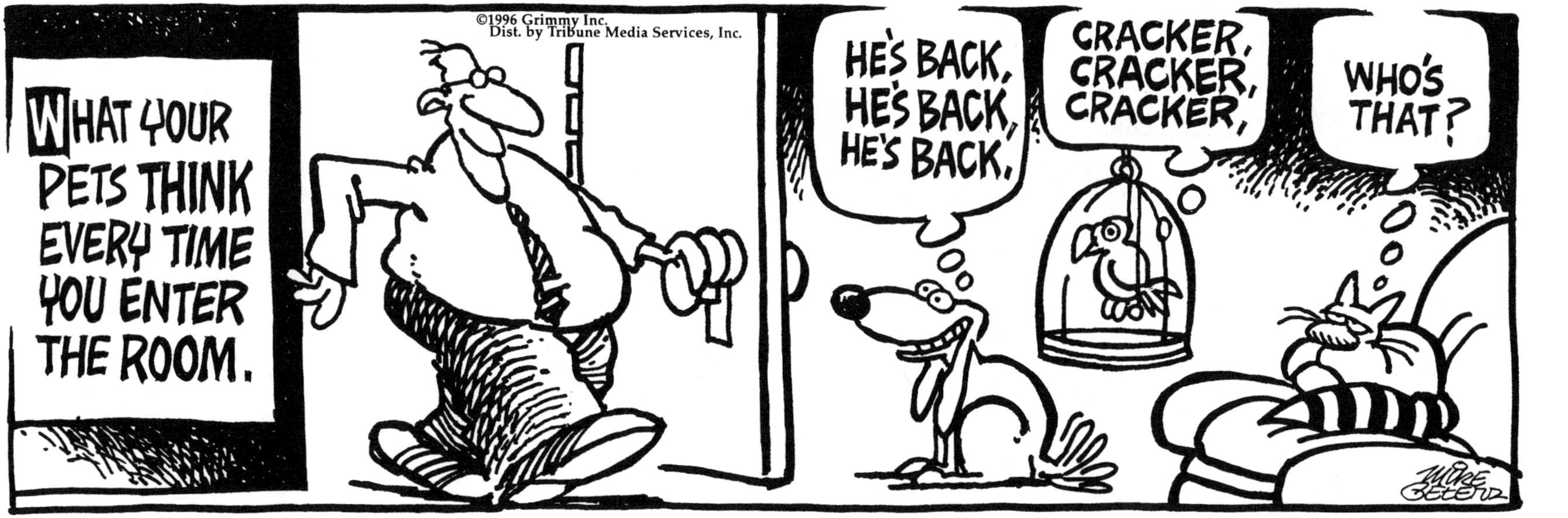
WHAT YOUR PETS THINK EVERY TIME YOU ENTER THE ROOM.
©1996 Grimmy Inc.
Dist. by Tribune Media Services, Inc.
HE'S BACK, HE'S BACK, HE'S BACK,
CRACKER, CRACKER, CRACKER,
WHO'S THAT?
MIKE PETERS

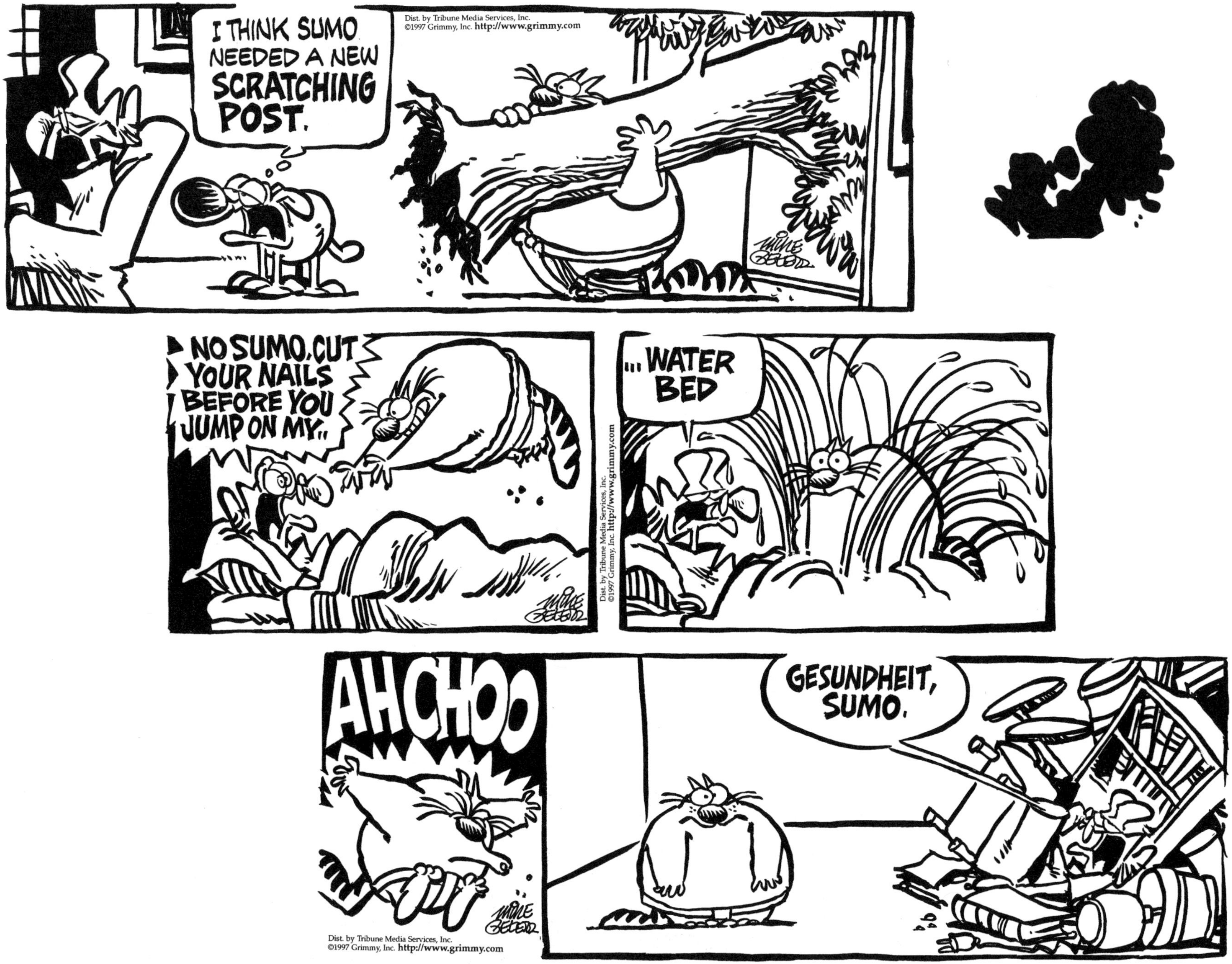
I THINK SUMO NEEDED A NEW SCRATCHING POST.
Dist. by Tribune Media Services, Inc. ©1997 Grimmy, Inc. http://www.grimmy.com
NO SUMO, CUT YOUR NAILS BEFORE YOU JUMP ON MY...
Dist. by Tribune Media Services, Inc. ©1997 Grimmy, Inc. http://www.grimmy.com
...WATER BED
AHCHOO
Dist. by Tribune Media Services, Inc. ©1997 Grimmy, Inc. http://www.grimmy.com
GESUNDHEIT, SUMO.

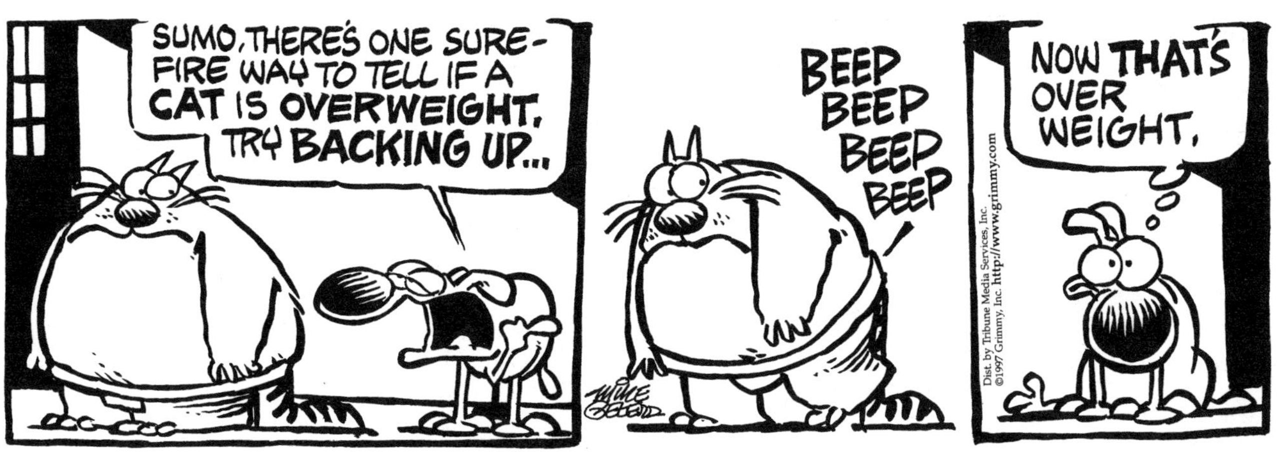
SUMO, THERE'S ONE SURE-FIRE WAY TO TELL IF A **CAT** IS **OVERWEIGHT.** TRY **BACKING UP...**
BEEP BEEP BEEP BEEP
MIKE PETERS
Dist. by Tribune Media Services, Inc. ©1997 Grimmy, Inc. http://www.grimmy.com
NOW **THAT'S** OVER WEIGHT.

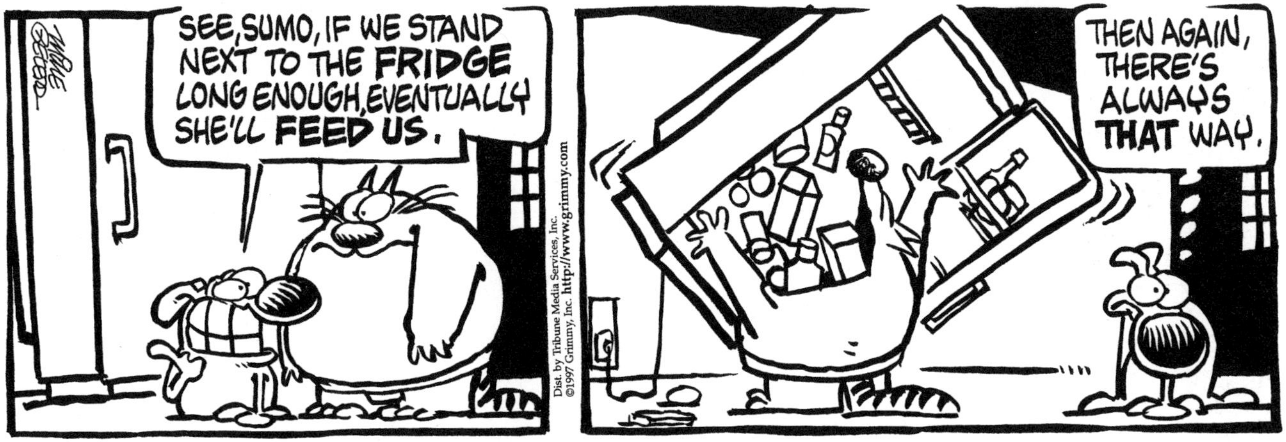
MIKE PETERS
SEE, SUMO, IF WE STAND NEXT TO THE **FRIDGE** LONG ENOUGH, EVENTUALLY SHE'LL **FEED US.**
Dist. by Tribune Media Services, Inc. ©1997 Grimmy, Inc. http://www.grimmy.com
THEN AGAIN, THERE'S ALWAYS **THAT** WAY.

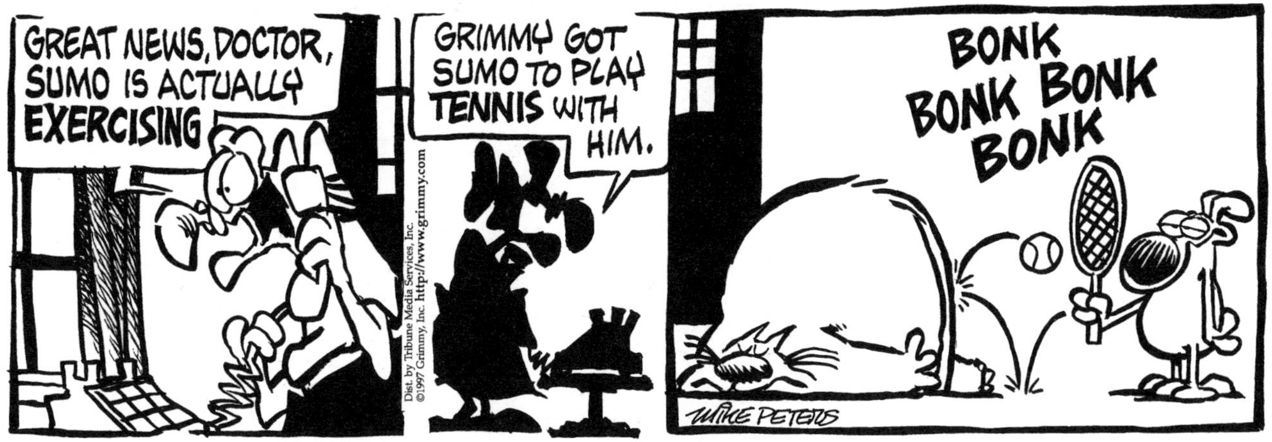
GREAT NEWS, DOCTOR, SUMO IS ACTUALLY **EXERCISING**
Dist. by Tribune Media Services, Inc. ©1997 Grimmy, Inc. http://www.grimmy.com
GRIMMY GOT SUMO TO PLAY **TENNIS** WITH HIM.
BONK BONK BONK BONK
MIKE PETERS

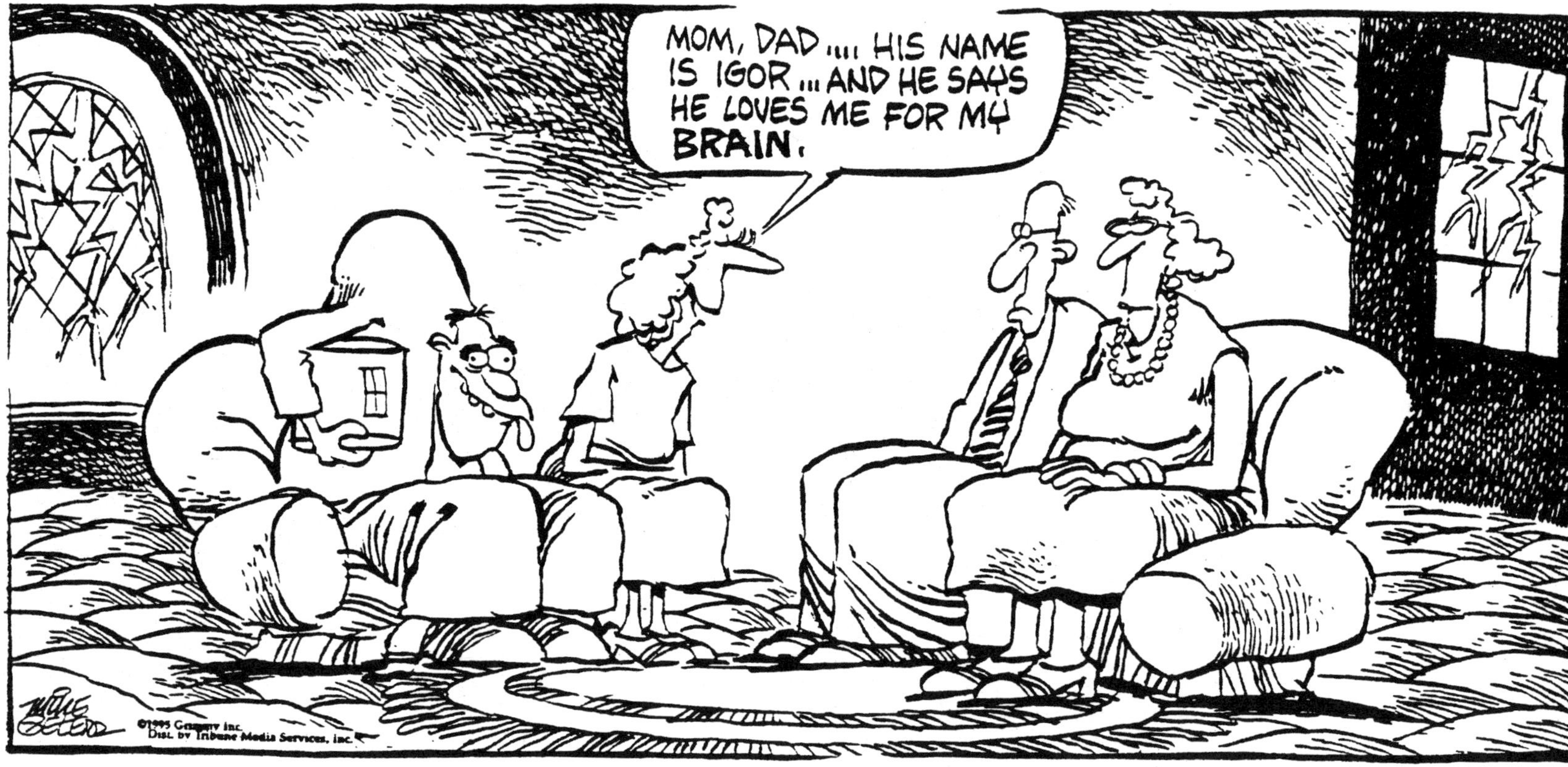
MOM, DAD.... HIS NAME IS IGOR... AND HE SAYS HE LOVES ME FOR MY **BRAIN**.
Dist. by Tribune Media Services, Inc.

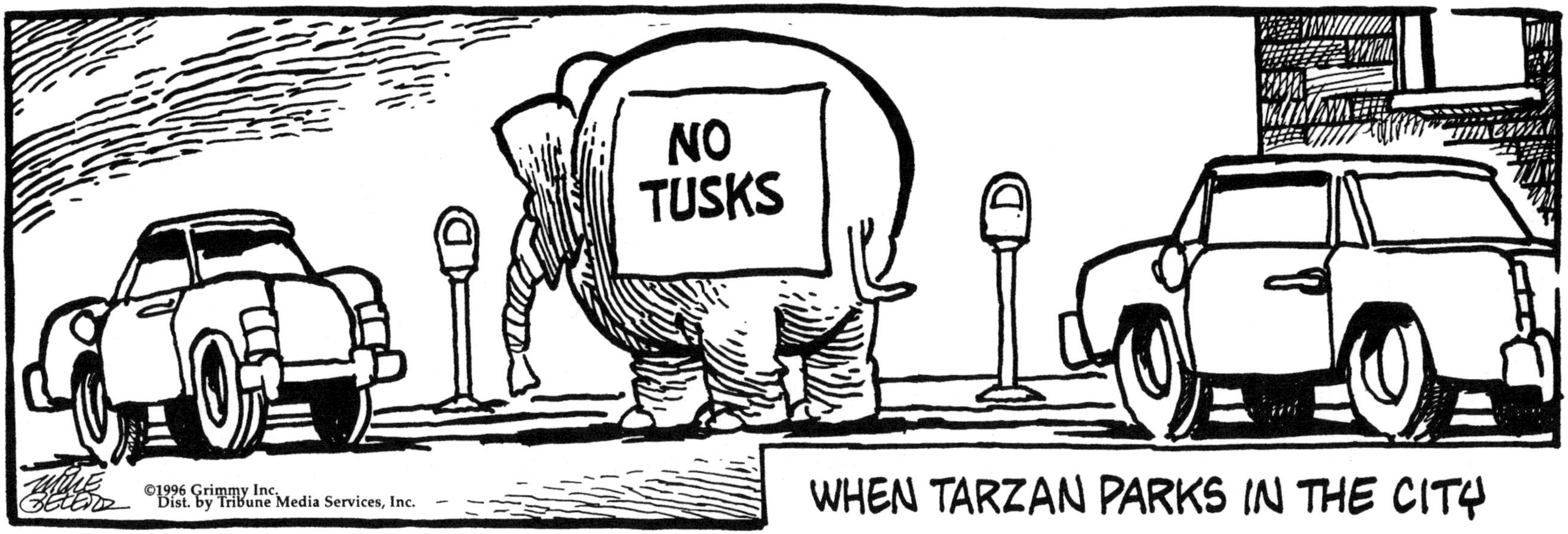
NO TUSKS
©1996 Grimmy Inc. Dist. by Tribune Media Services, Inc.
WHEN TARZAN PARKS IN THE CITY

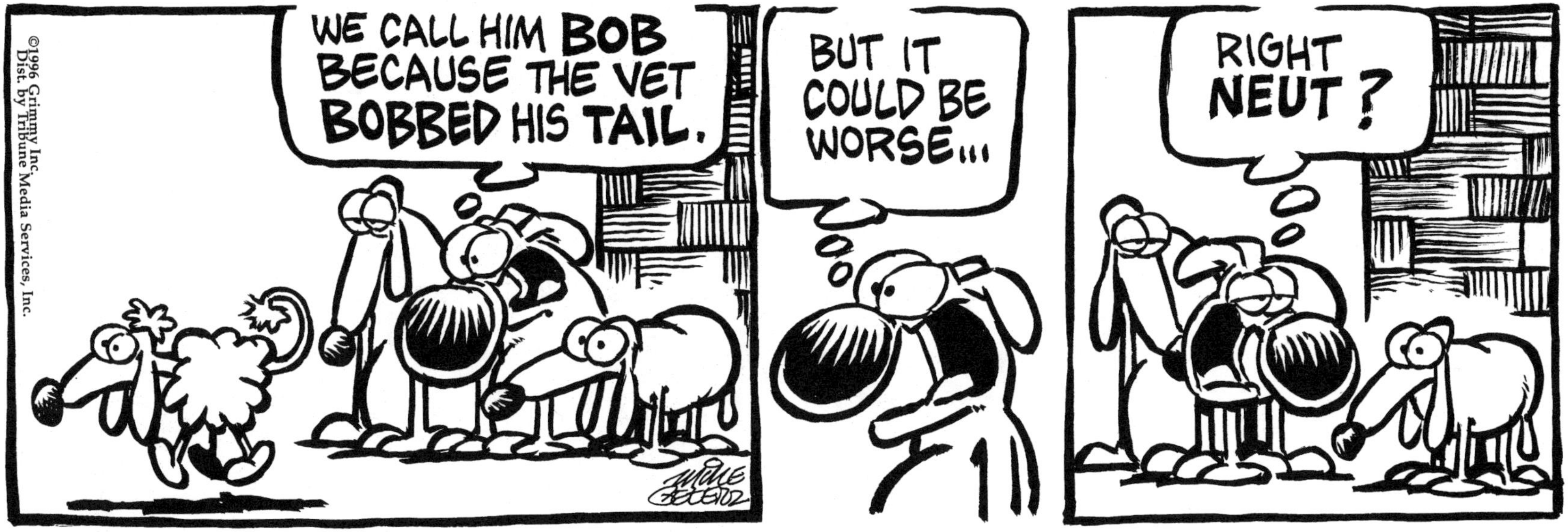
©1996 Grimmy Inc. Dist. by Tribune Media Services, Inc.
WE CALL HIM BOB BECAUSE THE VET BOBBED HIS TAIL.
BUT IT COULD BE WORSE...
RIGHT NEUT ?

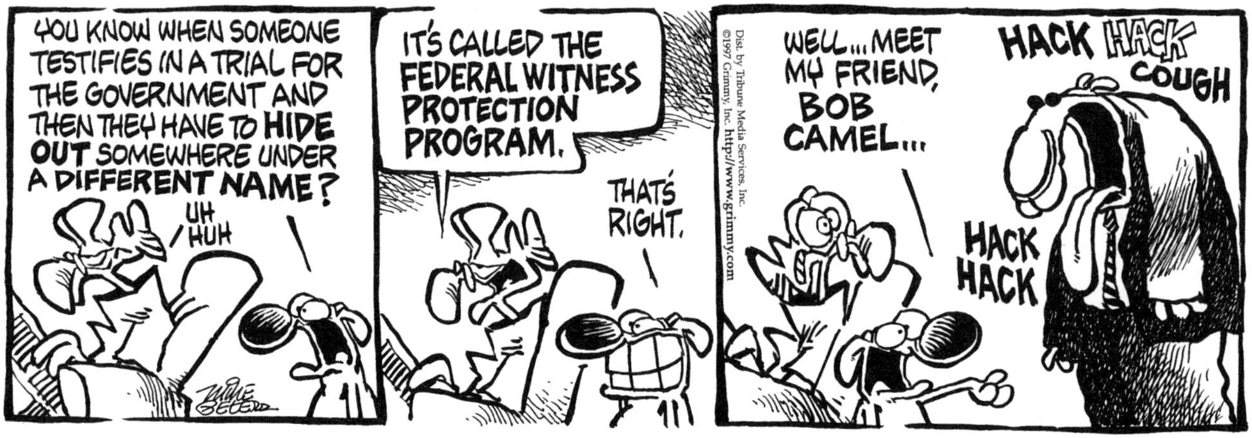
YOU KNOW WHEN SOMEONE TESTIFIES IN A TRIAL FOR THE GOVERNMENT AND THEN THEY HAVE TO HIDE OUT SOMEWHERE UNDER A DIFFERENT NAME?
UH HUH
IT'S CALLED THE FEDERAL WITNESS PROTECTION PROGRAM.
THAT'S RIGHT.
Dist. by Tribune Media Services, Inc. ©1997 Grimmy, Inc. http://www.grimmy.com
WELL... MEET MY FRIEND, BOB CAMEL...
HACK HACK
COUGH
HACK HACK

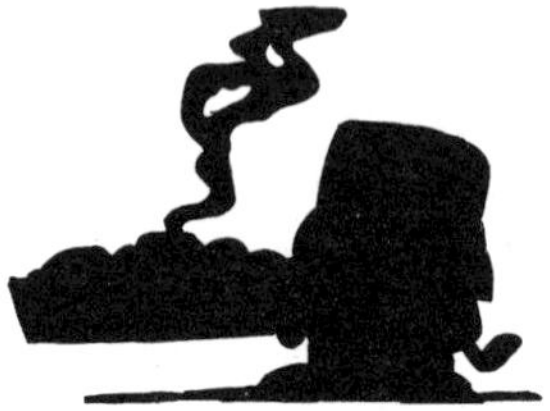

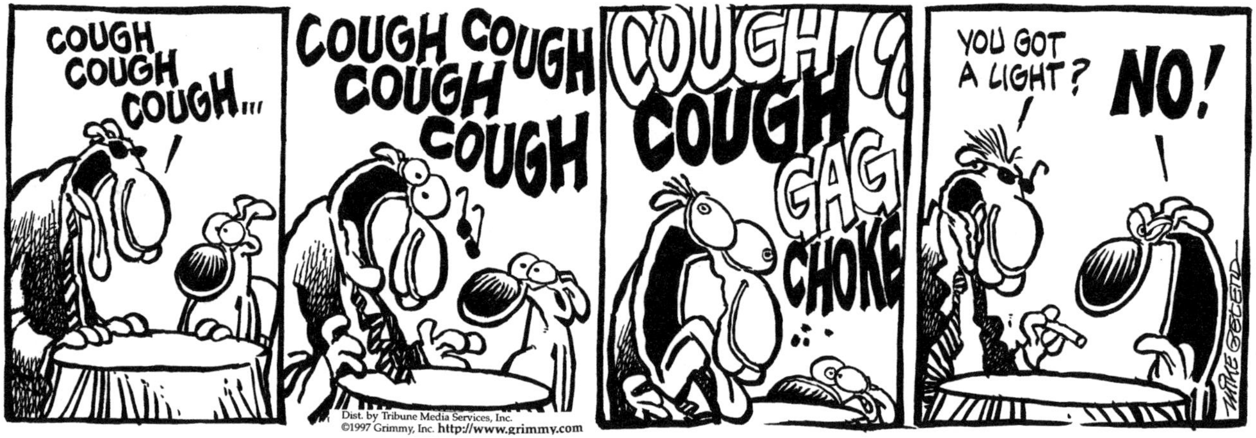
COUGH COUGH COUGH...
COUGH COUGH COUGH COUGH
COUGH COUGH
GAG
CHOKE
YOU GOT A LIGHT?
NO!
Dist. by Tribune Media Services, Inc. ©1997 Grimmy, Inc. http://www.grimmy.com

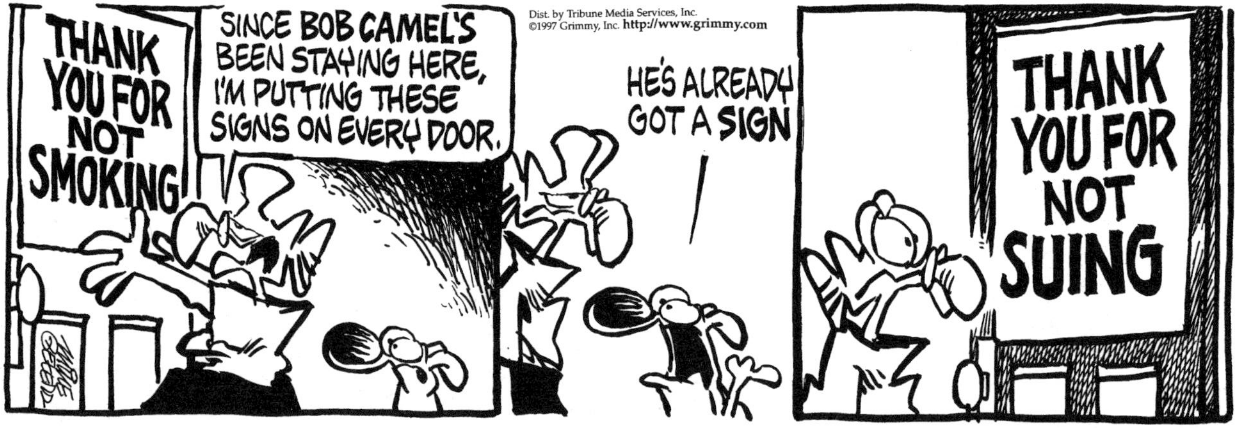
THANK YOU FOR NOT SMOKING
SINCE BOB CAMEL'S BEEN STAYING HERE, I'M PUTTING THESE SIGNS ON EVERY DOOR.
Dist. by Tribune Media Services, Inc. ©1997 Grimmy, Inc. http://www.grimmy.com
HE'S ALREADY GOT A SIGN
THANK YOU FOR NOT SUING

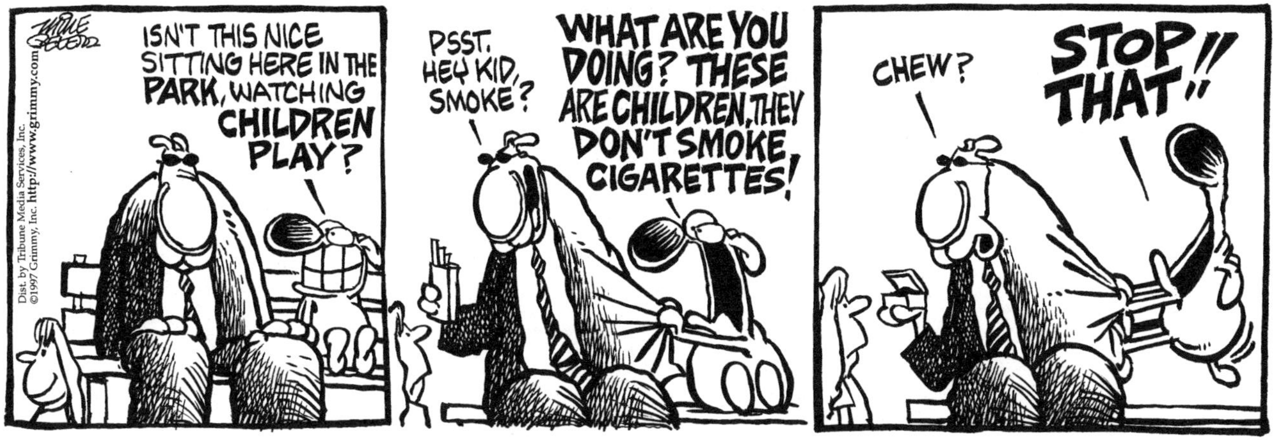
ISN'T THIS NICE SITTING HERE IN THE PARK, WATCHING CHILDREN PLAY?
PSST. HEY KID, SMOKE?
WHAT ARE YOU DOING? THESE ARE CHILDREN, THEY DON'T SMOKE CIGARETTES!
CHEW?
STOP THAT!!
Dist. by Tribune Media Services, Inc.
©1997 Grimmy, Inc. http://www.grimmy.com

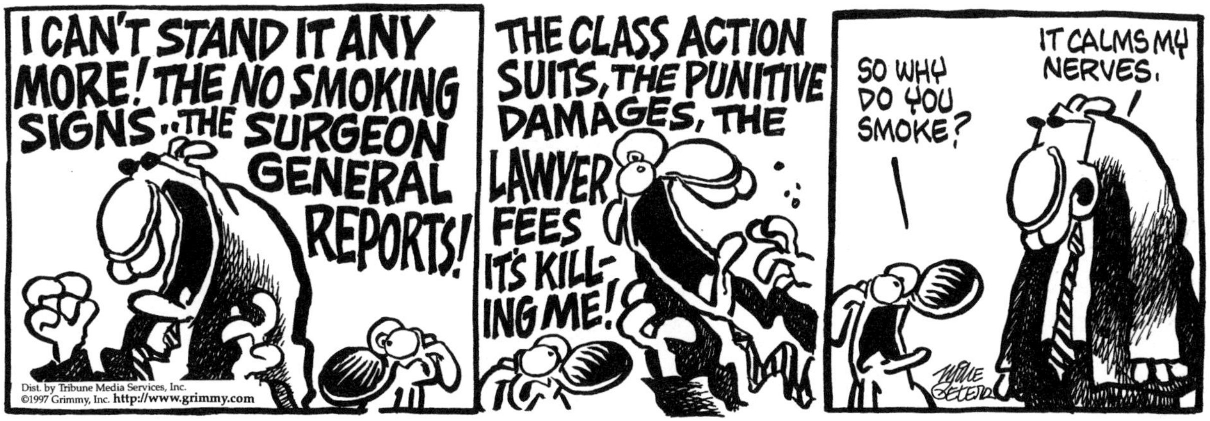
I CAN'T STAND IT ANY MORE! THE NO SMOKING SIGNS..THE SURGEON GENERAL REPORTS!
THE CLASS ACTION SUITS, THE PUNITIVE DAMAGES, THE LAWYER FEES IT'S KILLING ME!
SO WHY DO YOU SMOKE?
IT CALMS MY NERVES.
Dist. by Tribune Media Services, Inc.
©1997 Grimmy, Inc. http://www.grimmy.com

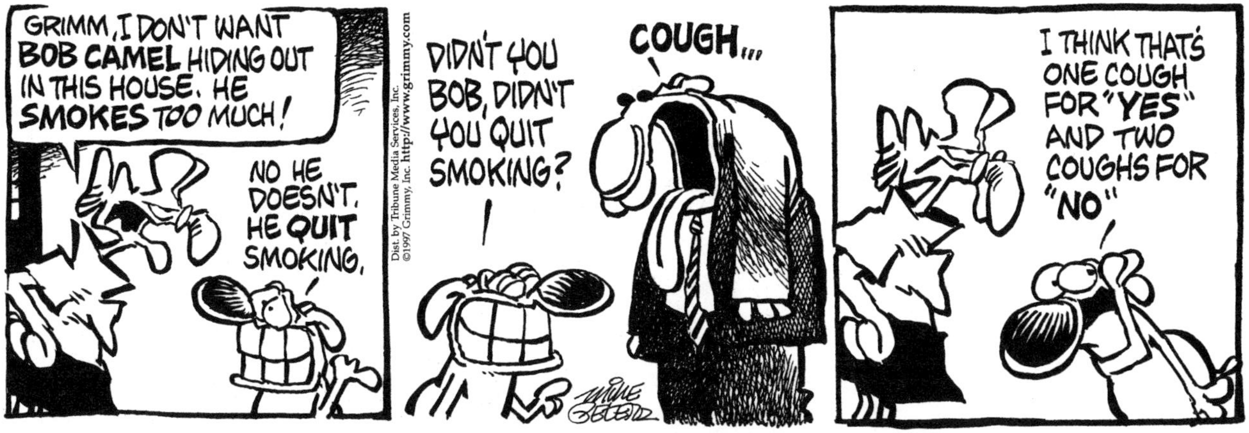
GRIMM, I DON'T WANT BOB CAMEL HIDING OUT IN THIS HOUSE. HE SMOKES TOO MUCH!
NO HE DOESN'T. HE QUIT SMOKING.
DIDN'T YOU BOB, DIDN'T YOU QUIT SMOKING?
COUGH...
I THINK THAT'S ONE COUGH FOR "YES" AND TWO COUGHS FOR "NO"
Dist. by Tribune Media Services, Inc.
©1997 Grimmy, Inc. http://www.grimmy.com

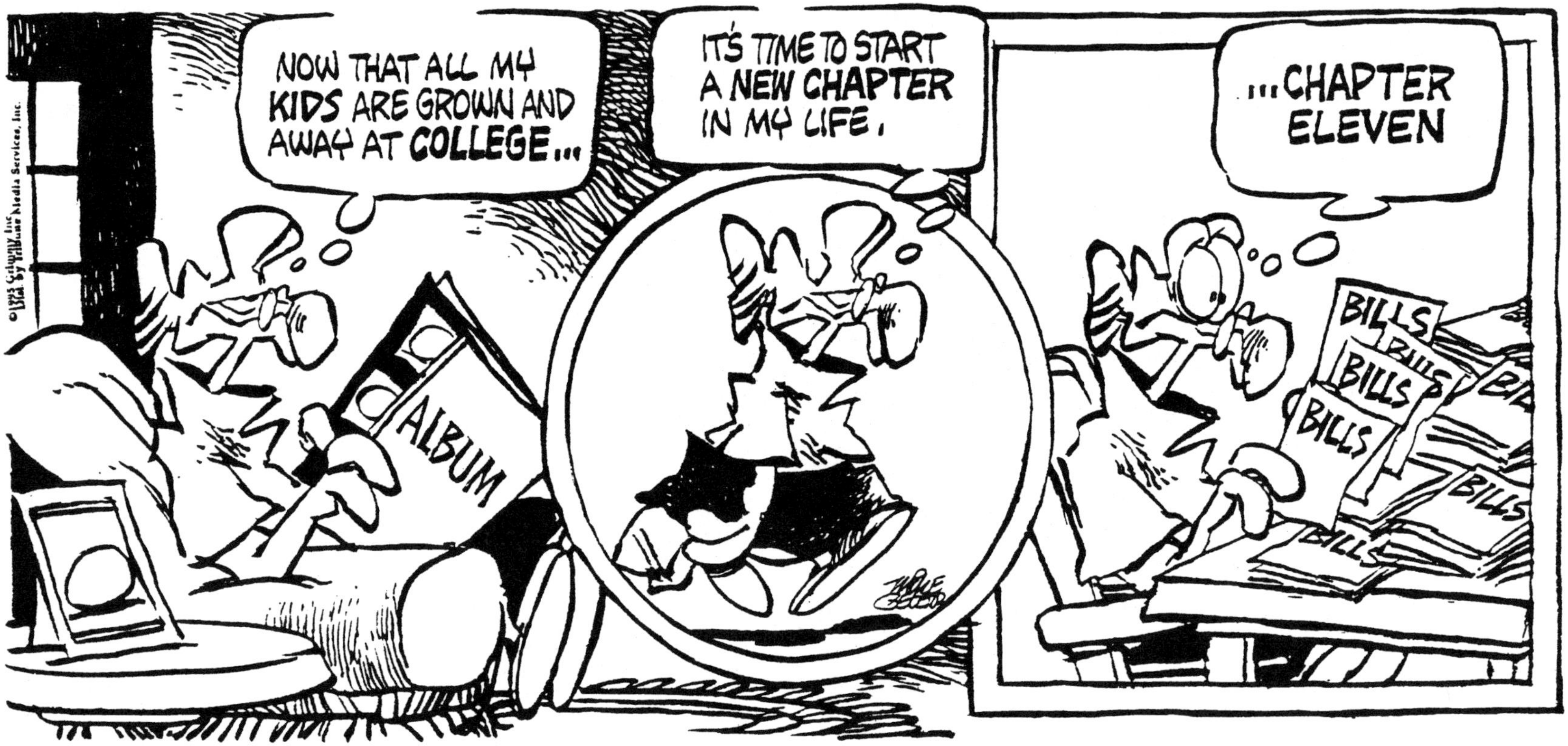
NOW THAT ALL MY KIDS ARE GROWN AND AWAY AT COLLEGE...
ALBUM
IT'S TIME TO START A NEW CHAPTER IN MY LIFE.
...CHAPTER ELEVEN
BILLS

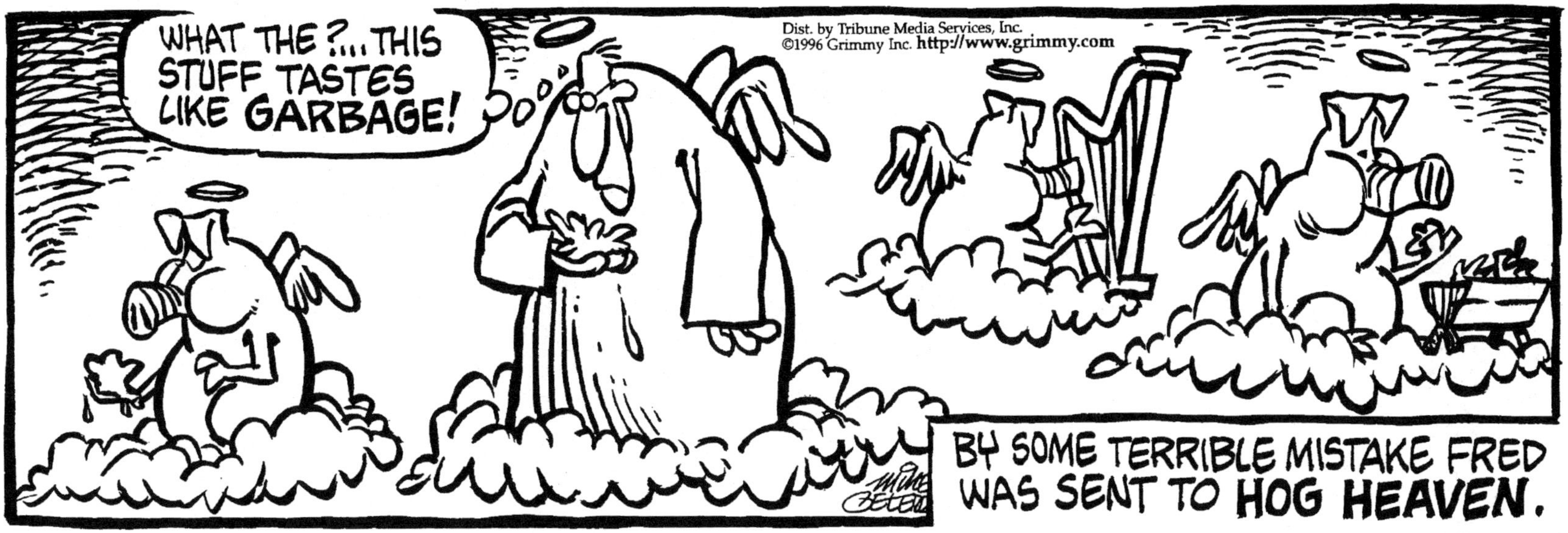

WHAT THE ?....THIS STUFF TASTES LIKE GARBAGE!
BY SOME TERRIBLE MISTAKE FRED WAS SENT TO HOG HEAVEN.
Dist. by Tribune Media Services, Inc.
©1996 Grimmy Inc. http://www.grimmy.com

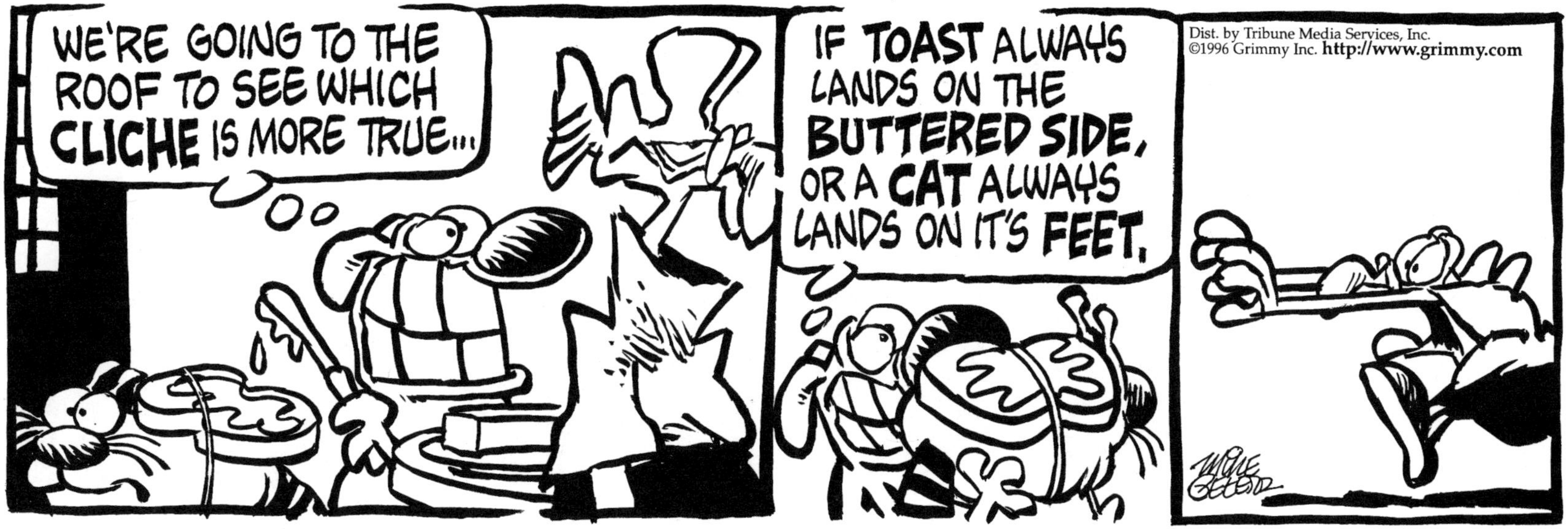

WE'RE GOING TO THE ROOF TO SEE WHICH CLICHE IS MORE TRUE...
IF TOAST ALWAYS LANDS ON THE BUTTERED SIDE, OR A CAT ALWAYS LANDS ON IT'S FEET.
Dist. by Tribune Media Services, Inc.
©1996 Grimmy Inc. http://www.grimmy.com

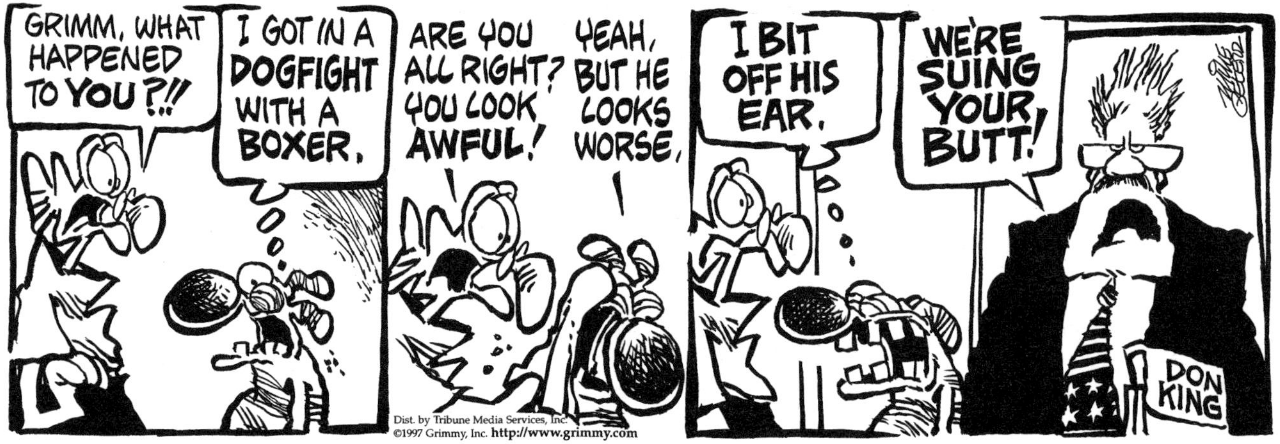
GRIMM, WHAT HAPPENED TO YOU?!!
I GOT IN A DOGFIGHT WITH A BOXER.
ARE YOU ALL RIGHT? YOU LOOK AWFUL!
YEAH, BUT HE LOOKS WORSE.
I BIT OFF HIS EAR.
WE'RE SUING YOUR BUTT!
DON KING
Dist. by Tribune Media Services, Inc.
©1997 Grimmy, Inc. http://www.grimmy.com

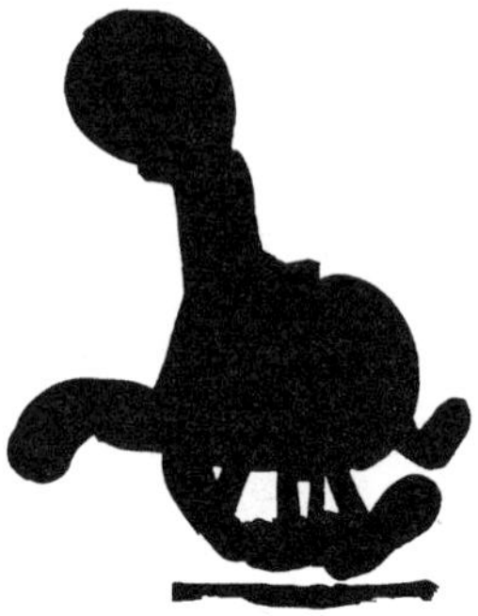

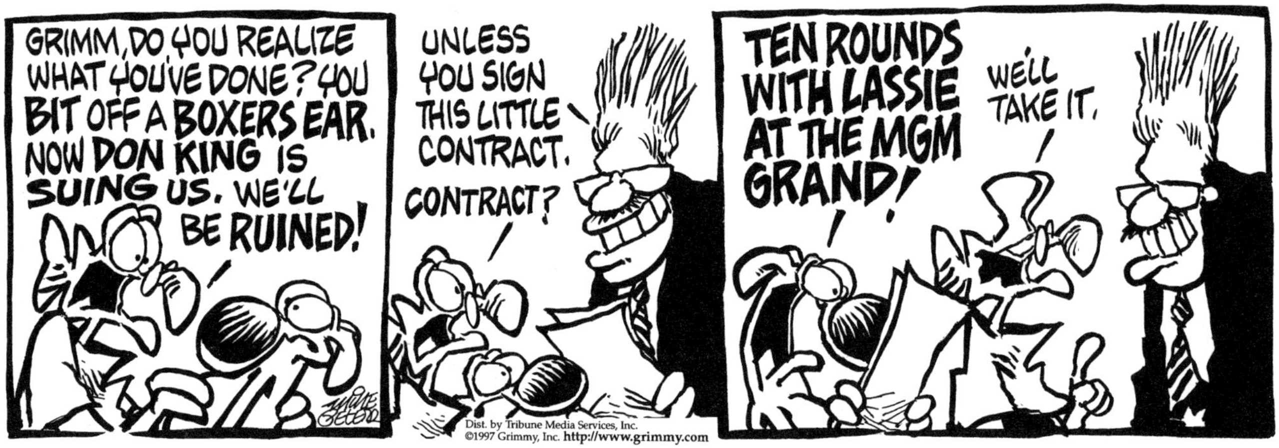
GRIMM, DO YOU REALIZE WHAT YOU'VE DONE? YOU BIT OFF A BOXERS EAR. NOW DON KING IS SUING US. WE'LL BE RUINED!
UNLESS YOU SIGN THIS LITTLE CONTRACT.
CONTRACT?
TEN ROUNDS WITH LASSIE AT THE MGM GRAND!
WE'LL TAKE IT.
Dist. by Tribune Media Services, Inc.
©1997 Grimmy, Inc. http://www.grimmy.com

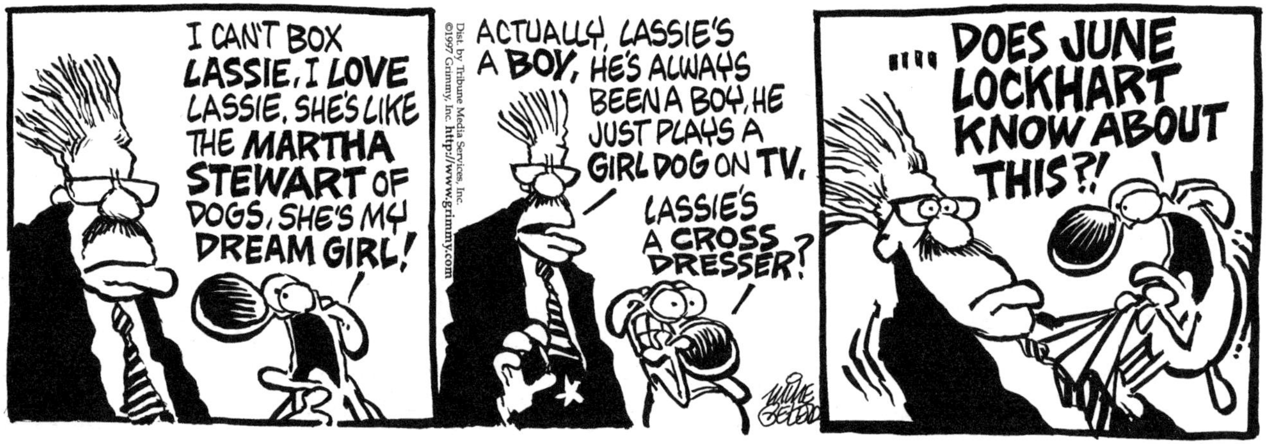
I CAN'T BOX LASSIE. I LOVE LASSIE. SHE'S LIKE THE MARTHA STEWART OF DOGS. SHE'S MY DREAM GIRL!
Dist. by Tribune Media Services, Inc.
©1997 Grimmy, Inc. http://www.grimmy.com
ACTUALLY, LASSIE'S A BOY. HE'S ALWAYS BEEN A BOY. HE JUST PLAYS A GIRL DOG ON TV.
LASSIE'S A CROSS DRESSER?
....DOES JUNE LOCKHART KNOW ABOUT THIS?!

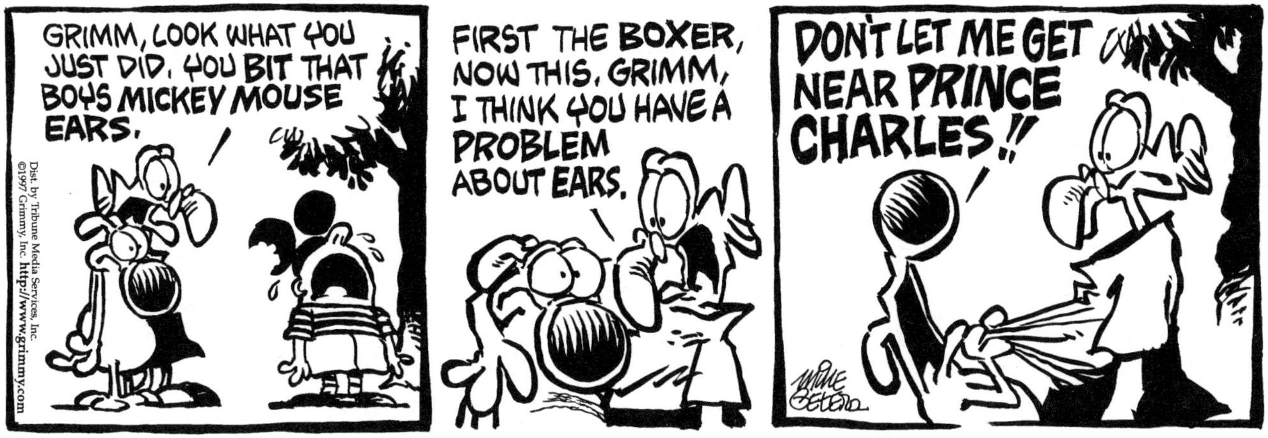
GRIMM, LOOK WHAT YOU JUST DID. YOU BIT THAT BOYS MICKEY MOUSE EARS.
Dist. by Tribune Media Services, Inc. ©1997 Grimmy, Inc. http://www.grimmy.com
FIRST THE BOXER, NOW THIS. GRIMM, I THINK YOU HAVE A PROBLEM ABOUT EARS.
DON'T LET ME GET NEAR PRINCE CHARLES!!

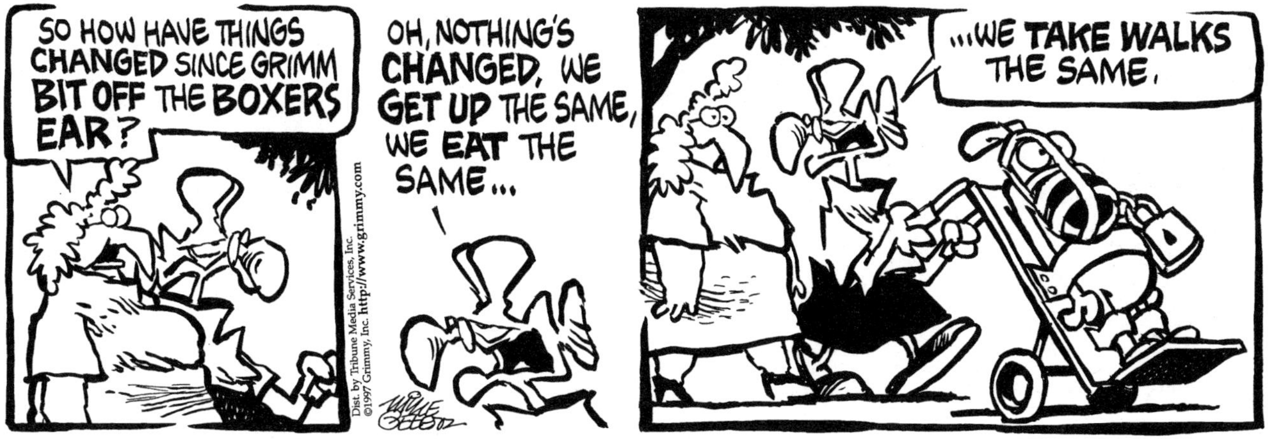
SO HOW HAVE THINGS CHANGED SINCE GRIMM BIT OFF THE BOXERS EAR?
Dist. by Tribune Media Services, Inc. ©1997 Grimmy, Inc. http://www.grimmy.com
OH, NOTHING'S CHANGED. WE GET UP THE SAME, WE EAT THE SAME...
...WE TAKE WALKS THE SAME.

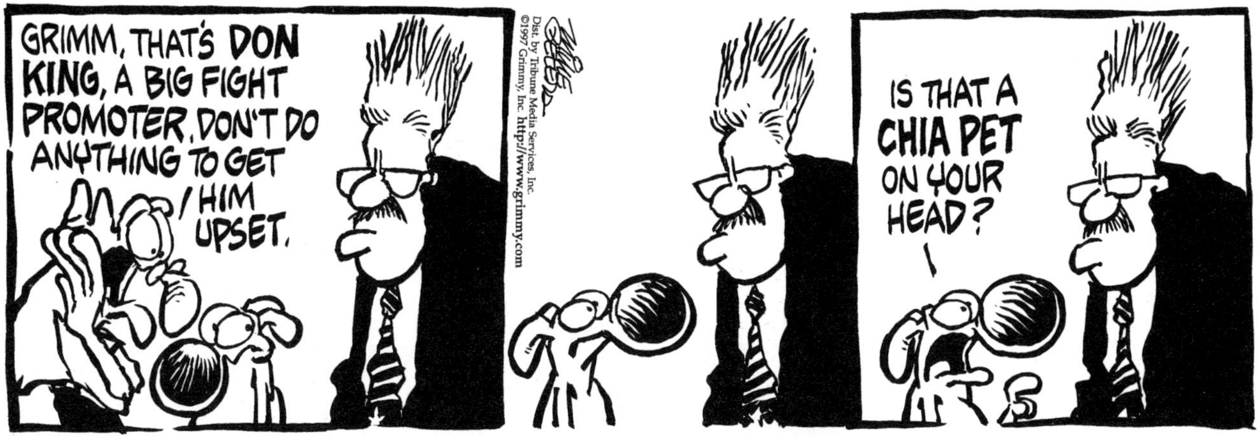
GRIMM, THAT'S DON KING, A BIG FIGHT PROMOTER. DON'T DO ANYTHING TO GET HIM UPSET.
Dist. by Tribune Media Services, Inc. ©1997 Grimmy, Inc. http://www.grimmy.com
IS THAT A CHIA PET ON YOUR HEAD?

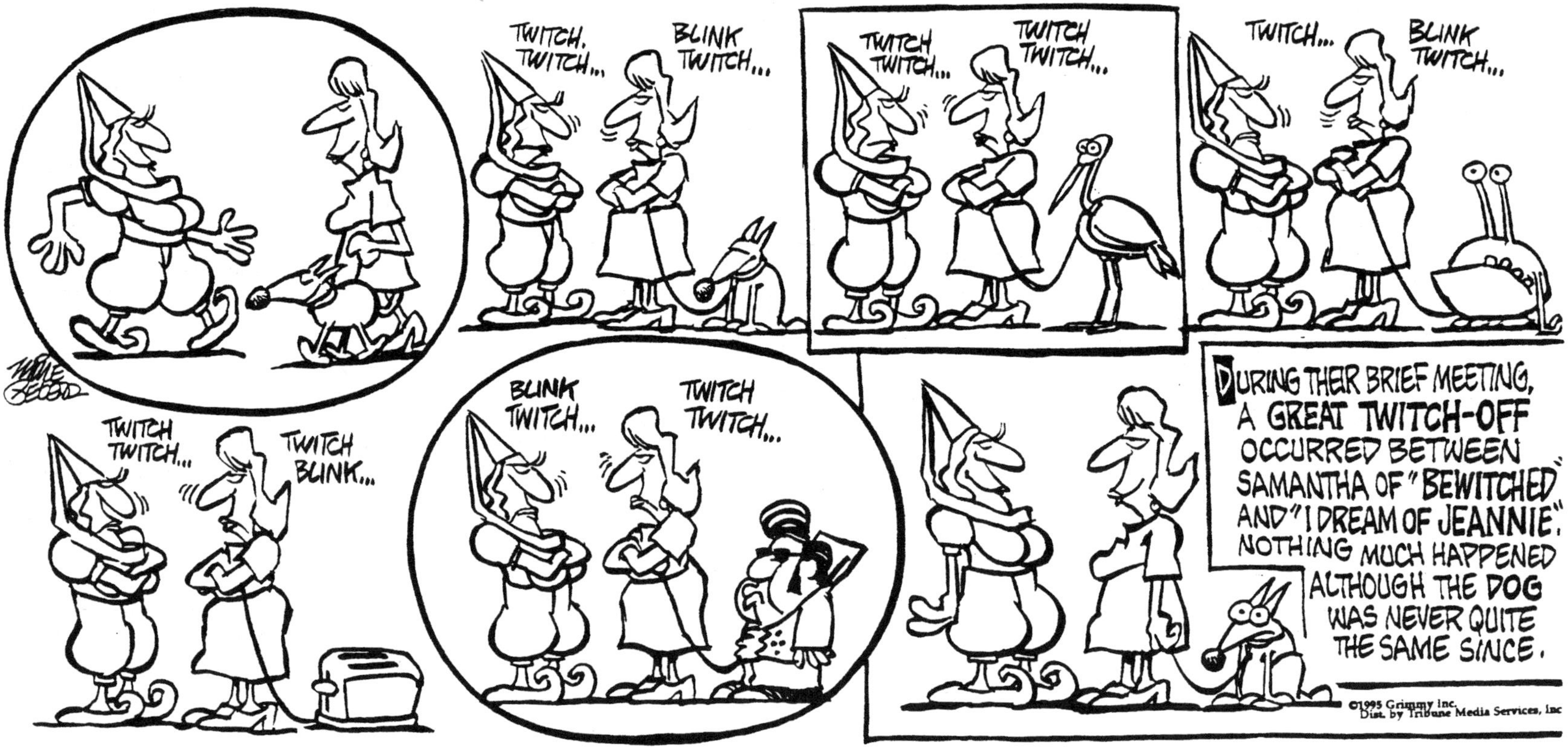
TWITCH, TWITCH...
BLINK TWITCH...
TWITCH TWITCH...
TWITCH TWITCH...
TWITCH...
BLINK TWITCH...
TWITCH TWITCH...
TWITCH BLINK...
BLINK TWITCH...
TWITCH TWITCH...
DURING THEIR BRIEF MEETING, A GREAT TWITCH-OFF OCCURRED BETWEEN SAMANTHA OF "BEWITCHED" AND "I DREAM OF JEANNIE". NOTHING MUCH HAPPENED ALTHOUGH THE DOG WAS NEVER QUITE THE SAME SINCE.
©1995 Grimmy Inc.
Dist. by Tribune Media Services, Inc

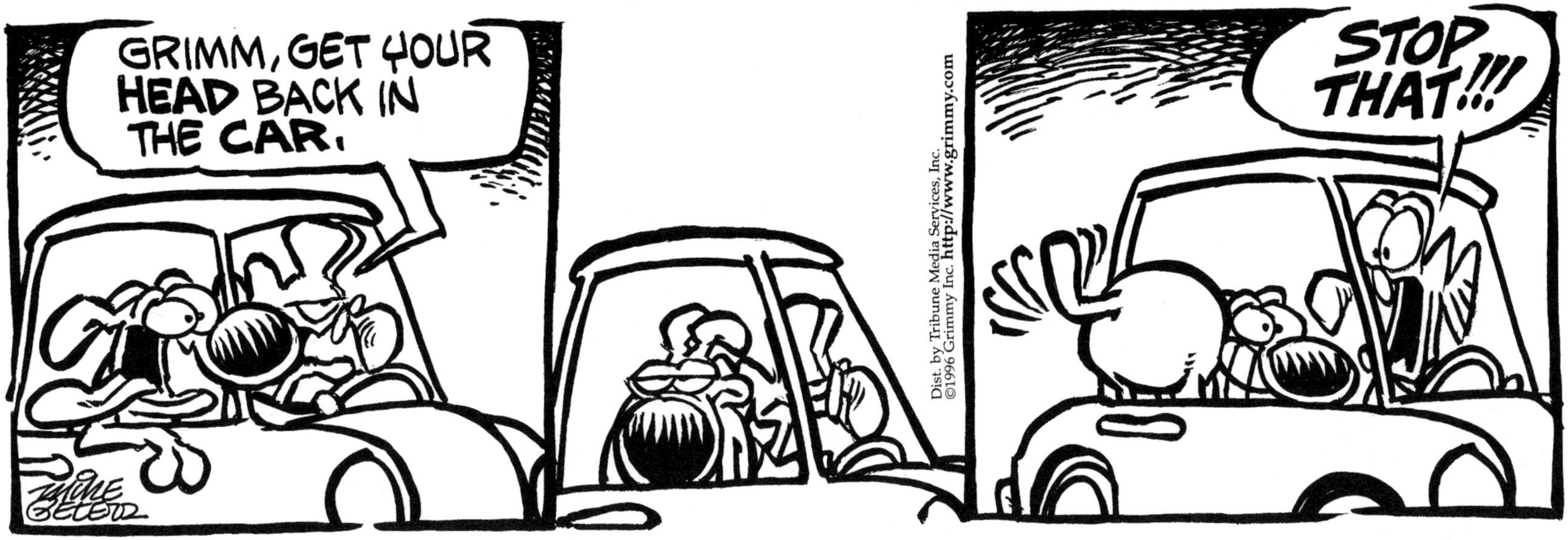
GRIMM, GET YOUR HEAD BACK IN THE CAR.
STOP THAT!!!
Dist. by Tribune Media Services, Inc. ©1996 Grimmy Inc. http://www.grimmy.com

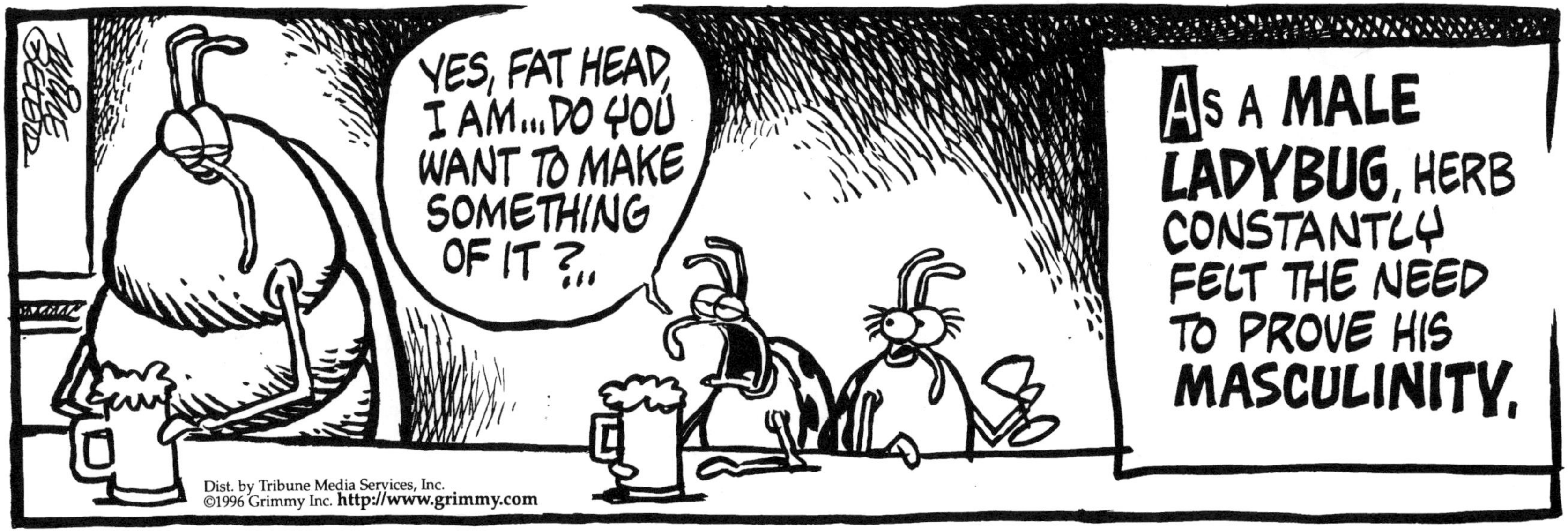
YES, FAT HEAD, I AM... DO YOU WANT TO MAKE SOMETHING OF IT?..
AS A MALE LADYBUG, HERB CONSTANTLY FELT THE NEED TO PROVE HIS MASCULINITY.
Dist. by Tribune Media Services, Inc. ©1996 Grimmy Inc. http://www.grimmy.com

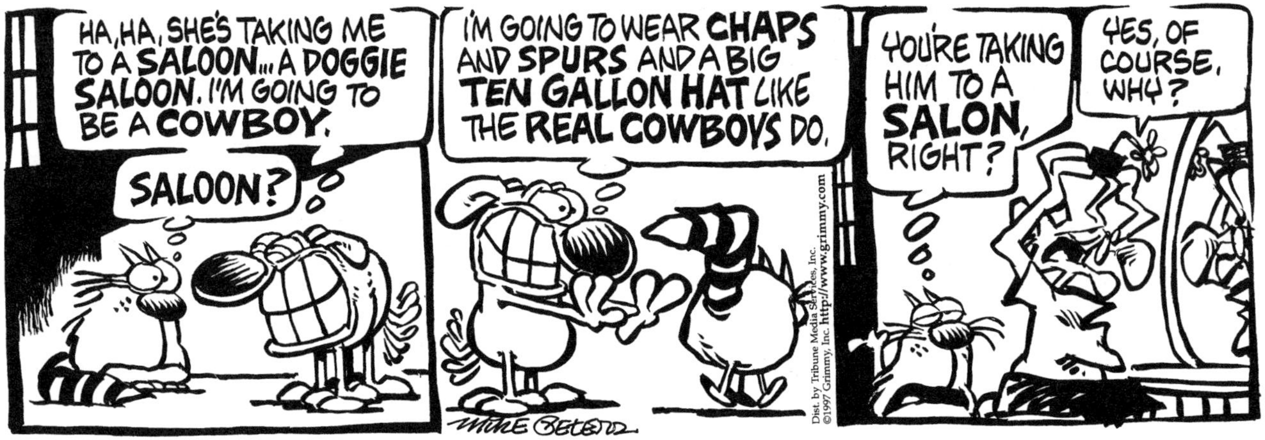
HA, HA, SHE'S TAKING ME TO A SALOON... A DOGGIE SALOON. I'M GOING TO BE A COWBOY.
SALOON?
I'M GOING TO WEAR CHAPS AND SPURS AND A BIG TEN GALLON HAT LIKE THE REAL COWBOYS DO.
MIKE PETERS
Dist. by Tribune Media Services, Inc. ©1997 Grimmy, Inc. http://www.grimmy.com
YOU'RE TAKING HIM TO A SALON, RIGHT?
YES, OF COURSE. WHY?

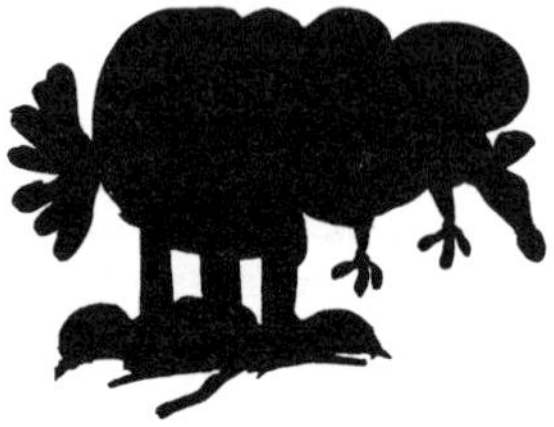

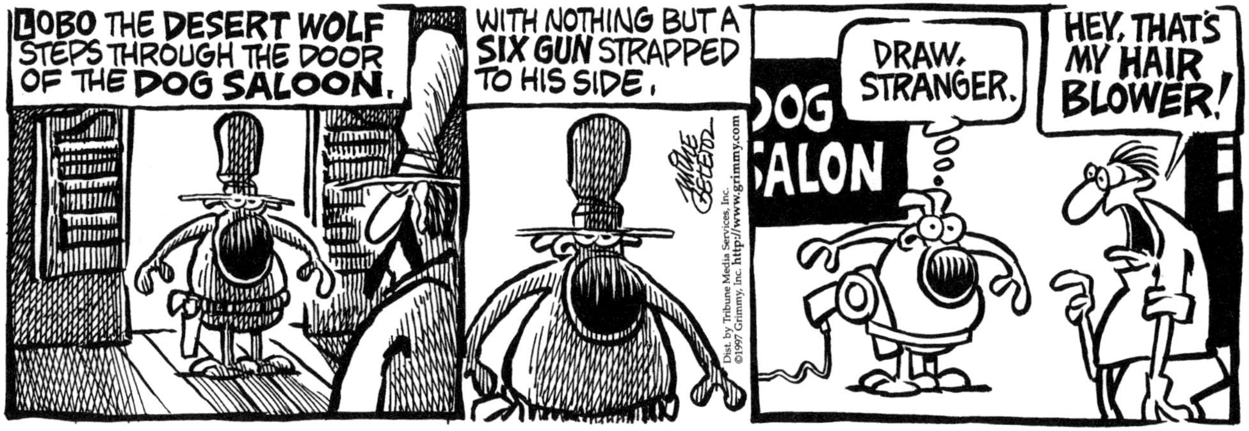
LOBO THE DESERT WOLF STEPS THROUGH THE DOOR OF THE DOG SALOON.
WITH NOTHING BUT A SIX GUN STRAPPED TO HIS SIDE.
MIKE PETERS
Dist. by Tribune Media Services, Inc. ©1997 Grimmy, Inc. http://www.grimmy.com
DOG SALON
DRAW, STRANGER.
HEY, THAT'S MY HAIR BLOWER!

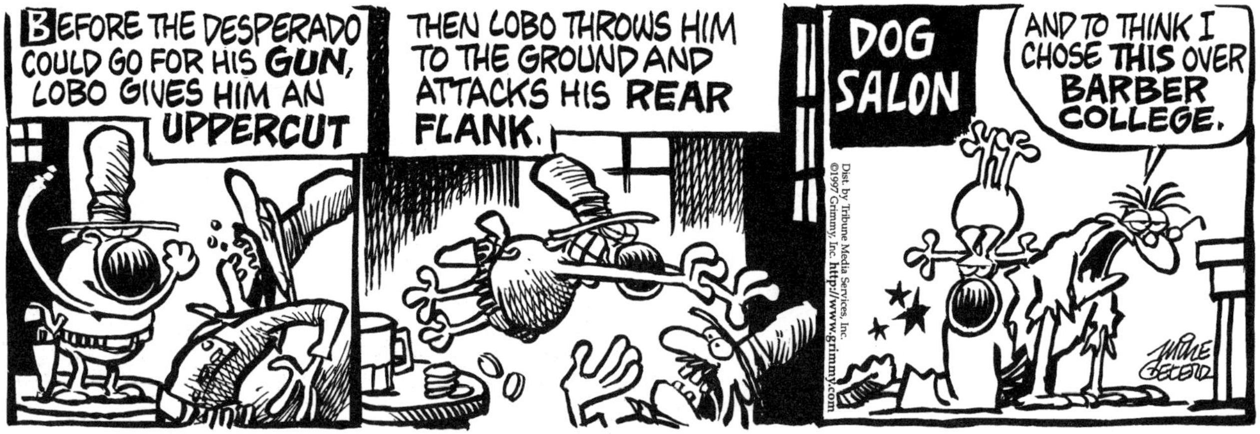
BEFORE THE DESPERADO COULD GO FOR HIS GUN, LOBO GIVES HIM AN UPPERCUT
THEN LOBO THROWS HIM TO THE GROUND AND ATTACKS HIS REAR FLANK.
DOG SALON
Dist. by Tribune Media Services, Inc. ©1997 Grimmy, Inc. http://www.grimmy.com
AND TO THINK I CHOSE THIS OVER BARBER COLLEGE.
MIKE PETERS

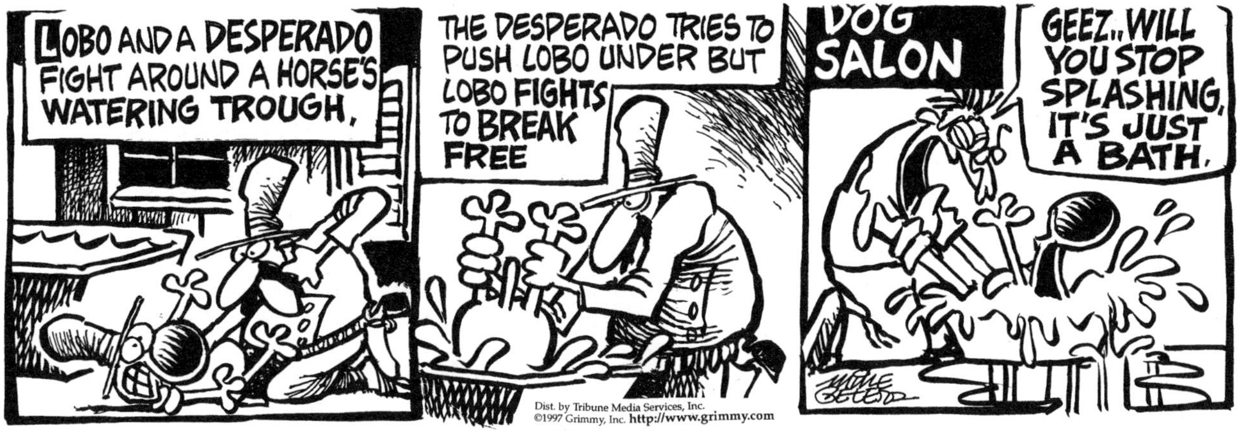
LOBO AND A DESPERADO FIGHT AROUND A HORSE'S WATERING TROUGH.
THE DESPERADO TRIES TO PUSH LOBO UNDER BUT LOBO FIGHTS TO BREAK FREE
DOG SALON
GEEZ.. WILL YOU STOP SPLASHING. IT'S JUST A BATH.
Dist. by Tribune Media Services, Inc. ©1997 Grimmy, Inc. http://www.grimmy.com

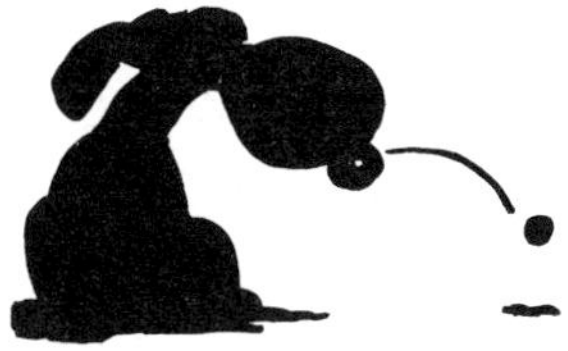

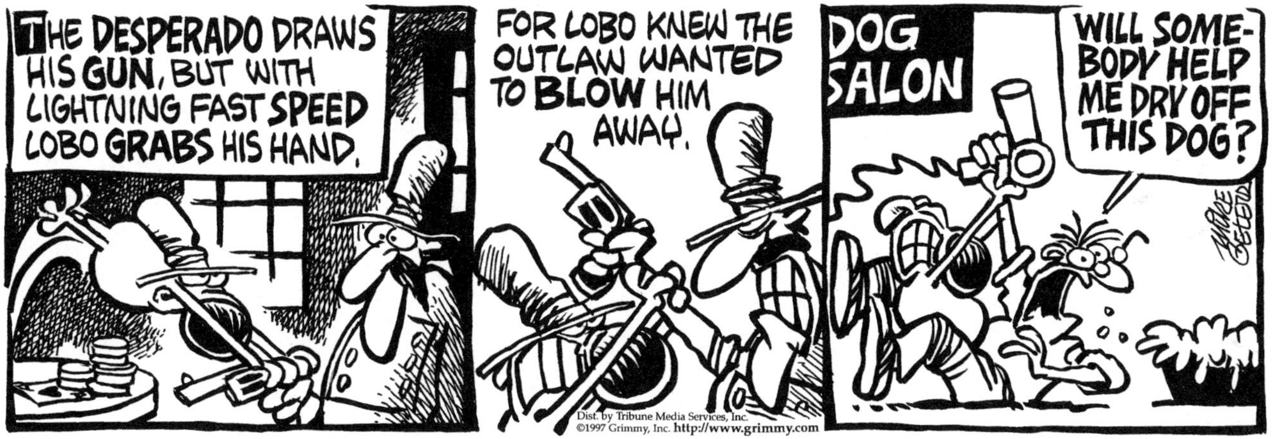
THE DESPERADO DRAWS HIS GUN, BUT WITH LIGHTNING FAST SPEED LOBO GRABS HIS HAND.
FOR LOBO KNEW THE OUTLAW WANTED TO BLOW HIM AWAY.
DOG SALON
WILL SOMEBODY HELP ME DRY OFF THIS DOG?
Dist. by Tribune Media Services, Inc. ©1997 Grimmy, Inc. http://www.grimmy.com

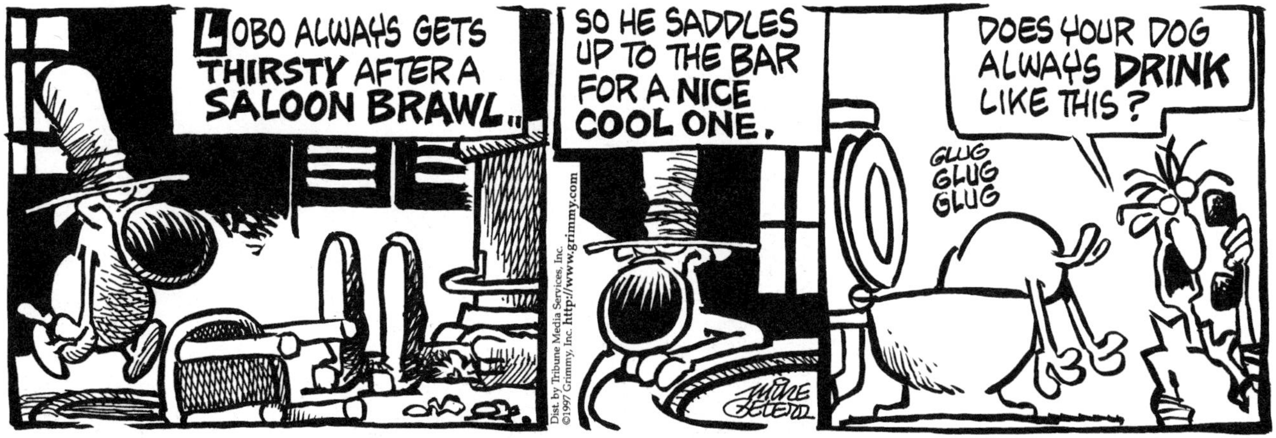
LOBO ALWAYS GETS THIRSTY AFTER A SALOON BRAWL..
SO HE SADDLES UP TO THE BAR FOR A NICE COOL ONE.
Dist. by Tribune Media Services, Inc. ©1997 Grimmy, Inc. http://www.grimmy.com
DOES YOUR DOG ALWAYS DRINK LIKE THIS?
GLUG GLUG GLUG

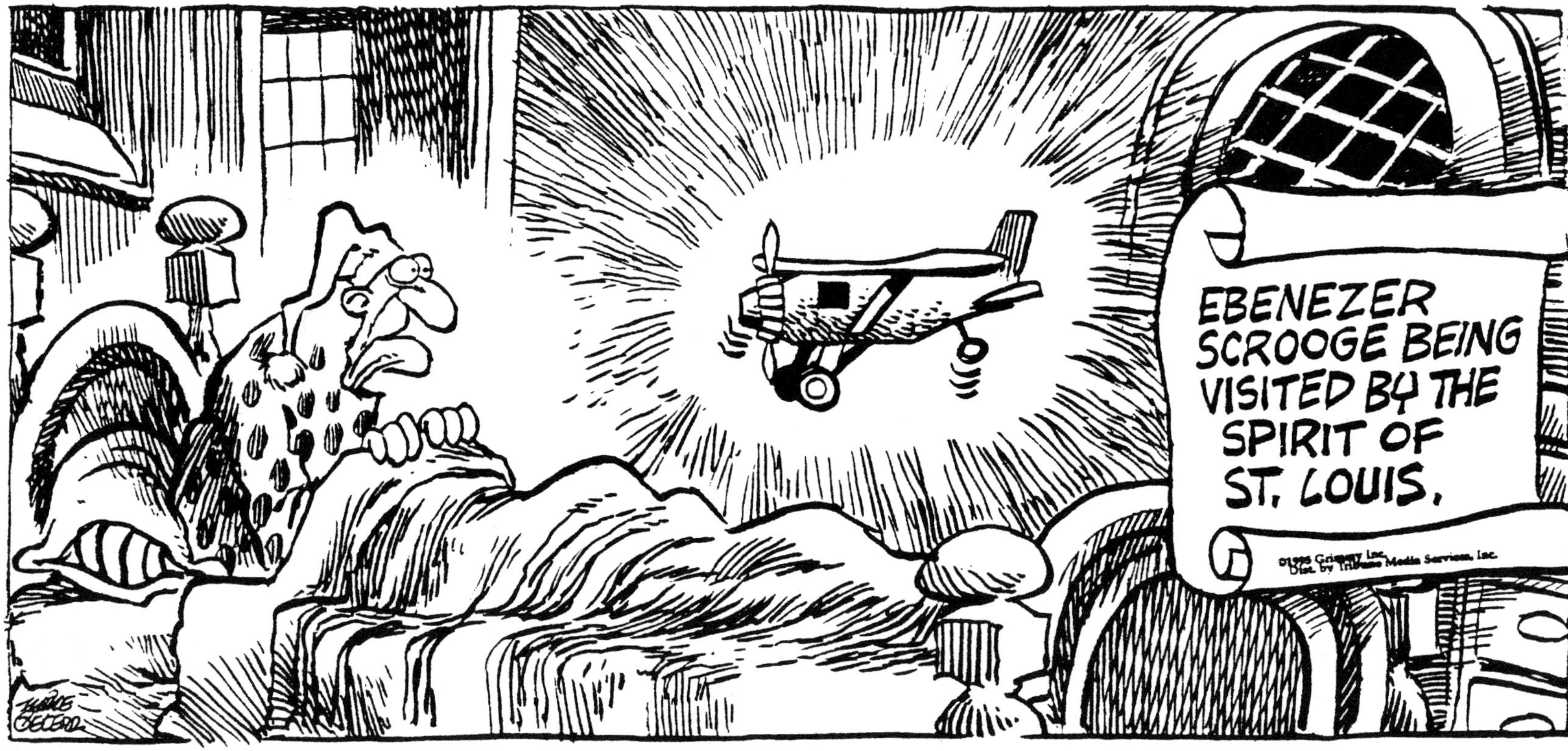
EBENEZER SCROOGE BEING VISITED BY THE SPIRIT OF ST. LOUIS.

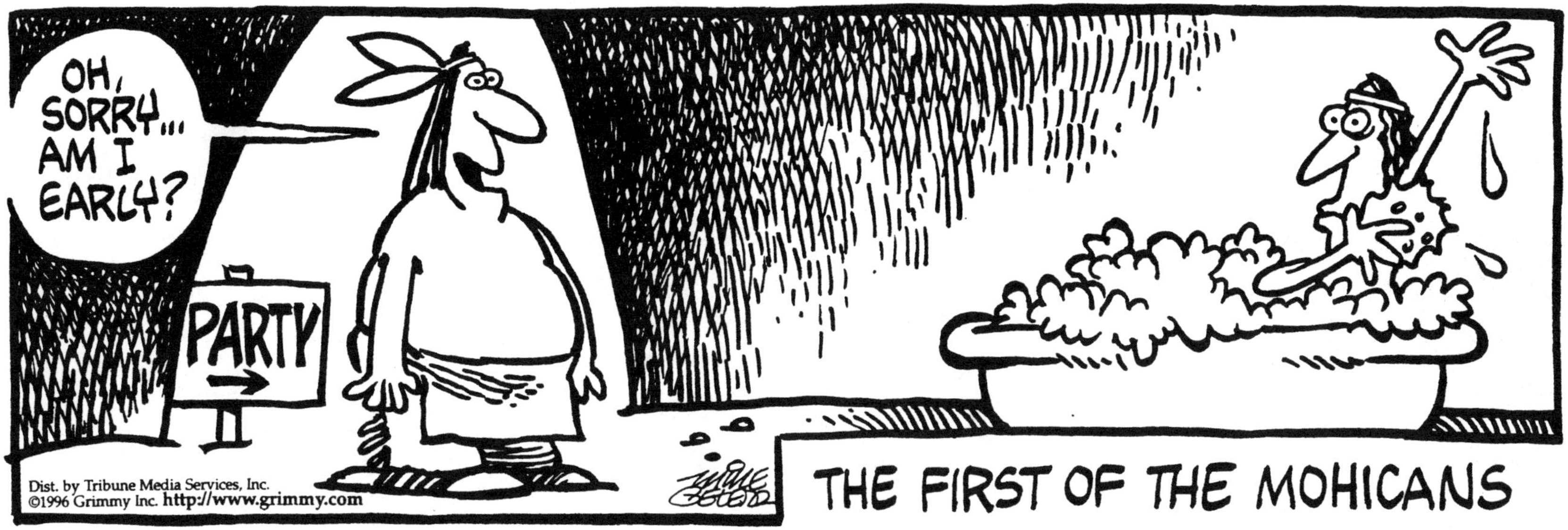
OH, SORRY... AM I EARLY?
PARTY
Dist. by Tribune Media Services, Inc.
©1996 Grimmy Inc. http://www.grimmy.com

THE FIRST OF THE MOHICANS

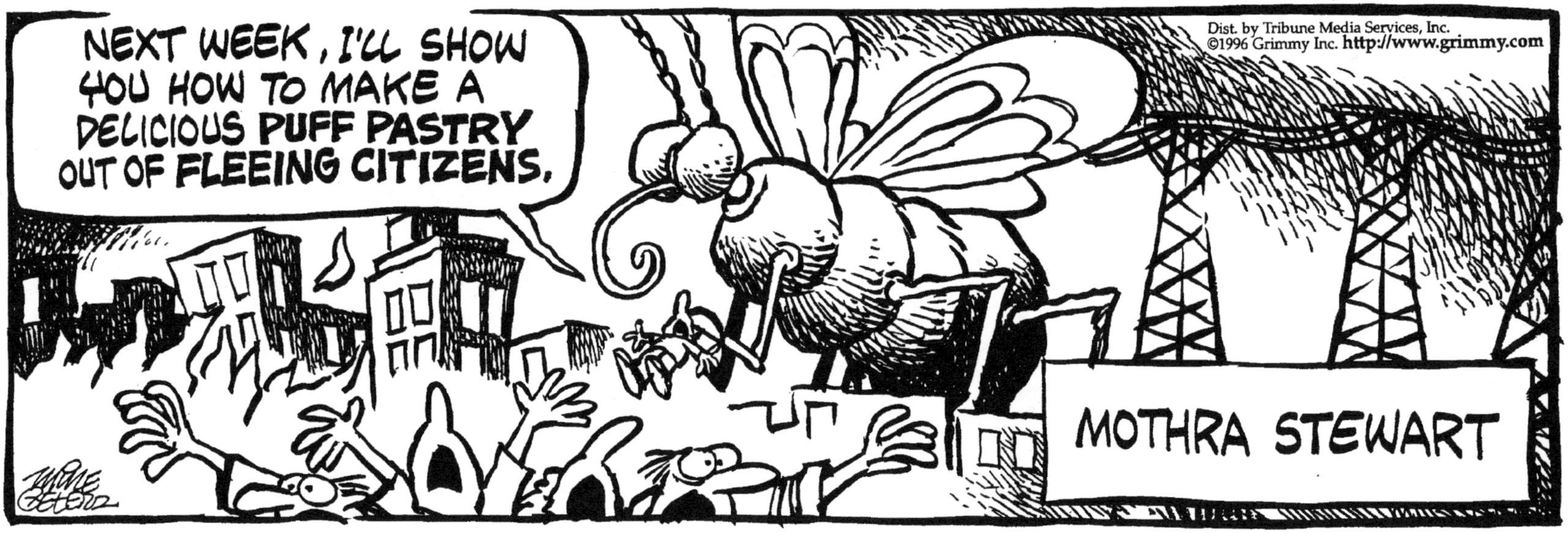
NEXT WEEK, I'LL SHOW YOU HOW TO MAKE A DELICIOUS PUFF PASTRY OUT OF FLEEING CITIZENS.
Dist. by Tribune Media Services, Inc.
©1996 Grimmy Inc. http://www.grimmy.com
MOTHRA STEWART

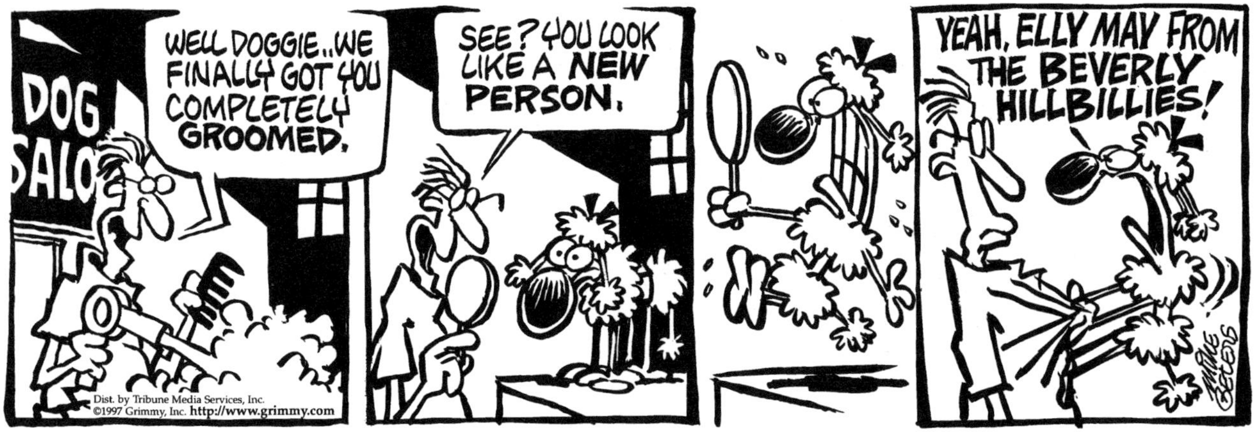
DOG SALO
WELL DOGGIE..WE FINALLY GOT YOU COMPLETELY GROOMED.
SEE? YOU LOOK LIKE A NEW PERSON.
YEAH, ELLY MAY FROM THE BEVERLY HILLBILLIES!
Dist. by Tribune Media Services, Inc.
©1997 Grimmy, Inc. http://www.grimmy.com

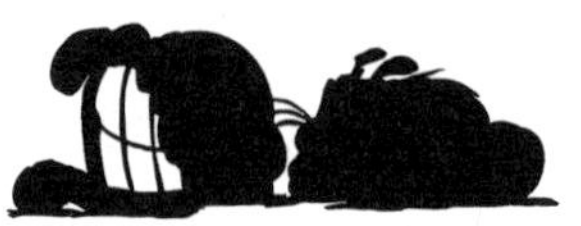

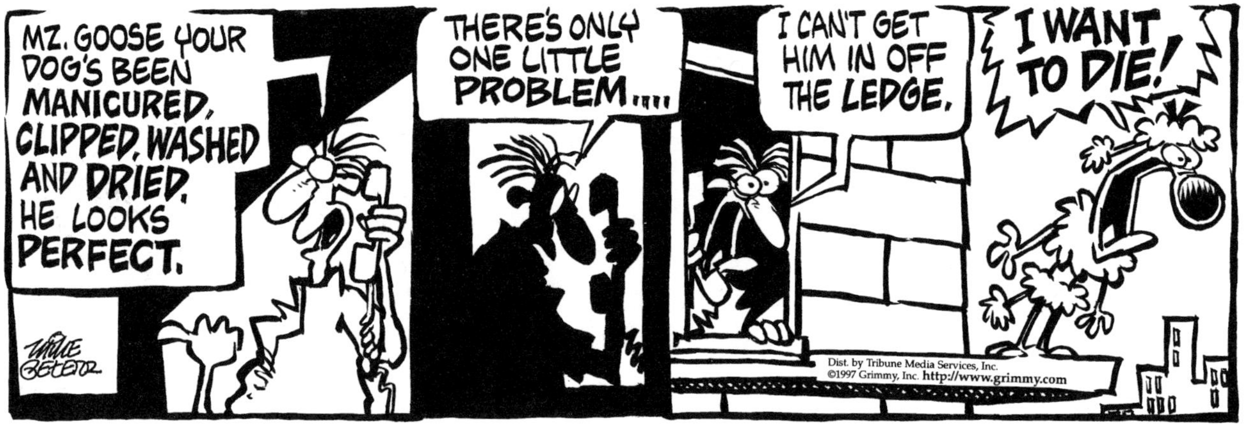
MZ. GOOSE YOUR DOG'S BEEN MANICURED, CLIPPED, WASHED AND DRIED. HE LOOKS PERFECT.
THERE'S ONLY ONE LITTLE PROBLEM.....
I CAN'T GET HIM IN OFF THE LEDGE.
I WANT TO DIE!
Dist. by Tribune Media Services, Inc.
©1997 Grimmy, Inc. http://www.grimmy.com

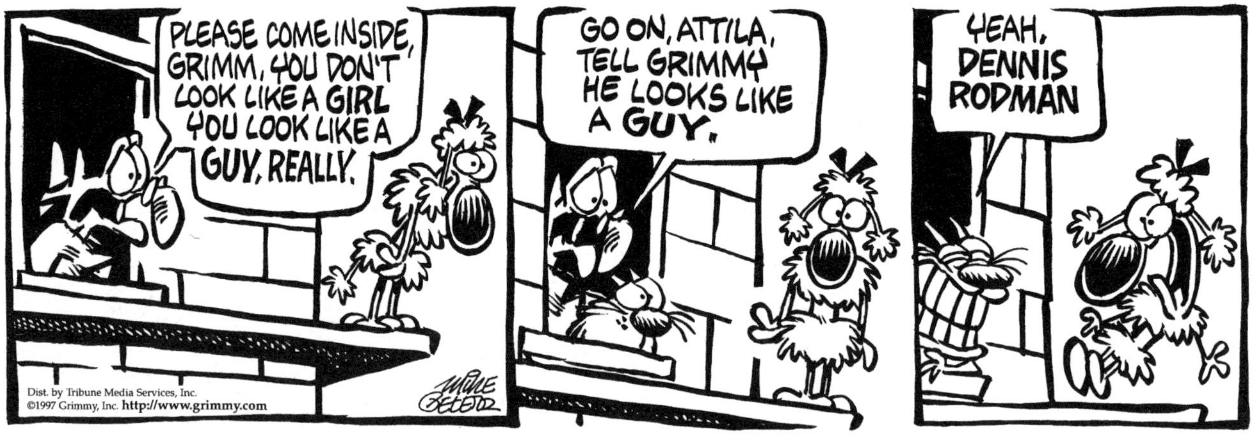
PLEASE COME INSIDE, GRIMM, YOU DON'T LOOK LIKE A GIRL YOU LOOK LIKE A GUY, REALLY.
GO ON, ATTILA, TELL GRIMMY HE LOOKS LIKE A GUY.
YEAH, DENNIS RODMAN
Dist. by Tribune Media Services, Inc.
©1997 Grimmy, Inc. http://www.grimmy.com

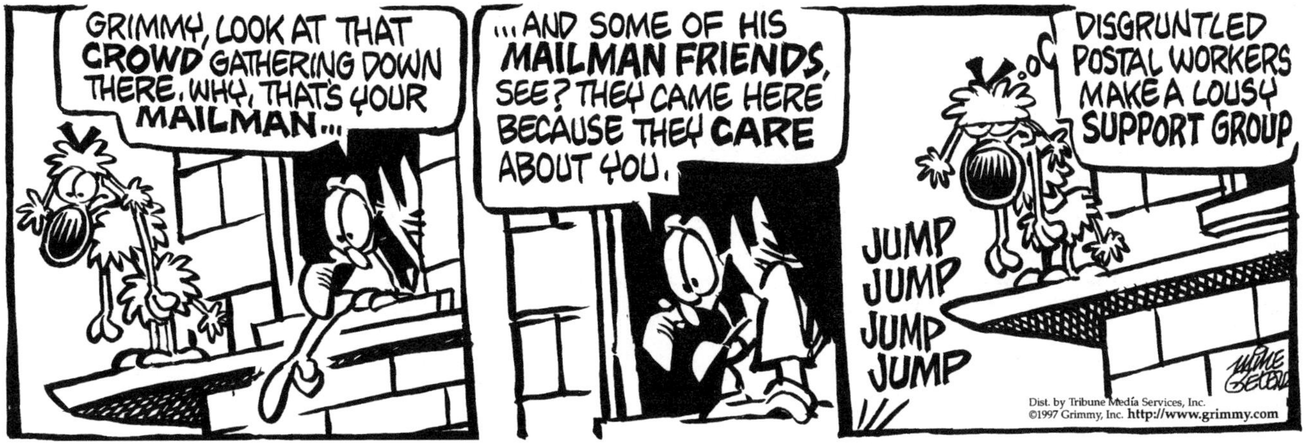
GRIMMY, LOOK AT THAT **CROWD** GATHERING DOWN THERE. WHY, THAT'S YOUR **MAILMAN**...
...AND SOME OF HIS **MAILMAN FRIENDS**, SEE? THEY CAME HERE BECAUSE THEY **CARE** ABOUT YOU.
DISGRUNTLED POSTAL WORKERS MAKE A LOUSY SUPPORT GROUP
JUMP JUMP JUMP JUMP
Dist. by Tribune Media Services, Inc. ©1997 Grimmy, Inc. http://www.grimmy.com

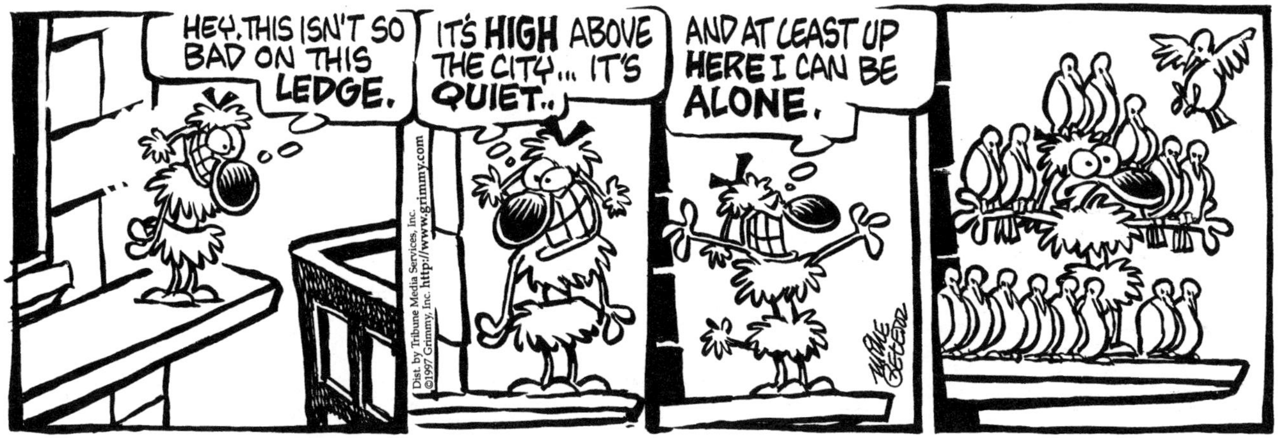
HEY, THIS ISN'T SO BAD ON THIS **LEDGE**.
IT'S **HIGH** ABOVE THE CITY... IT'S **QUIET**..
AND AT LEAST UP **HERE** I CAN BE **ALONE**.
Dist. by Tribune Media Services, Inc. ©1997 Grimmy, Inc. http://www.grimmy.com

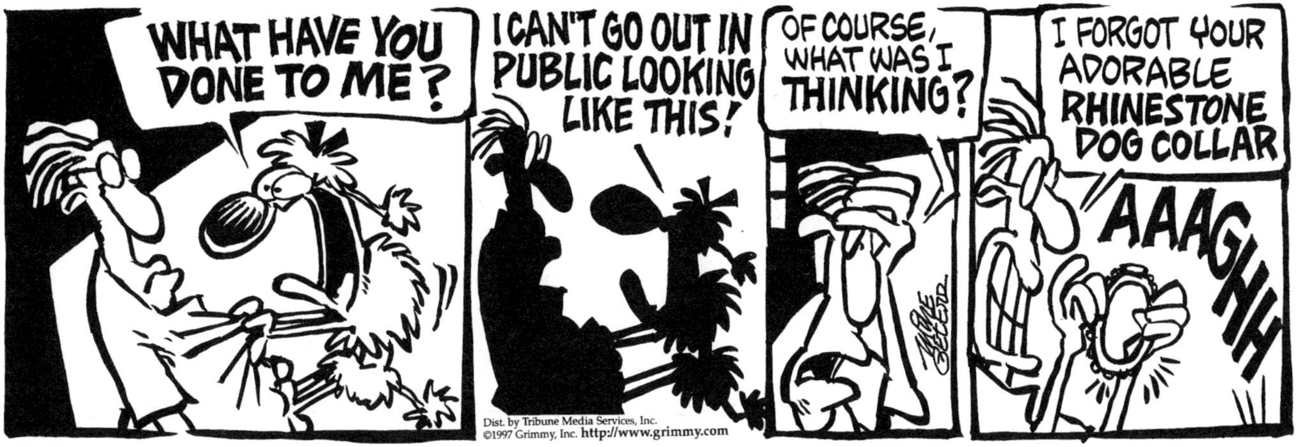
WHAT HAVE YOU DONE TO ME?
I CAN'T GO OUT IN PUBLIC LOOKING LIKE THIS!
OF COURSE, WHAT WAS I **THINKING**?
I FORGOT YOUR ADORABLE **RHINESTONE DOG COLLAR**
AAAGHH
Dist. by Tribune Media Services, Inc. ©1997 Grimmy, Inc. http://www.grimmy.com

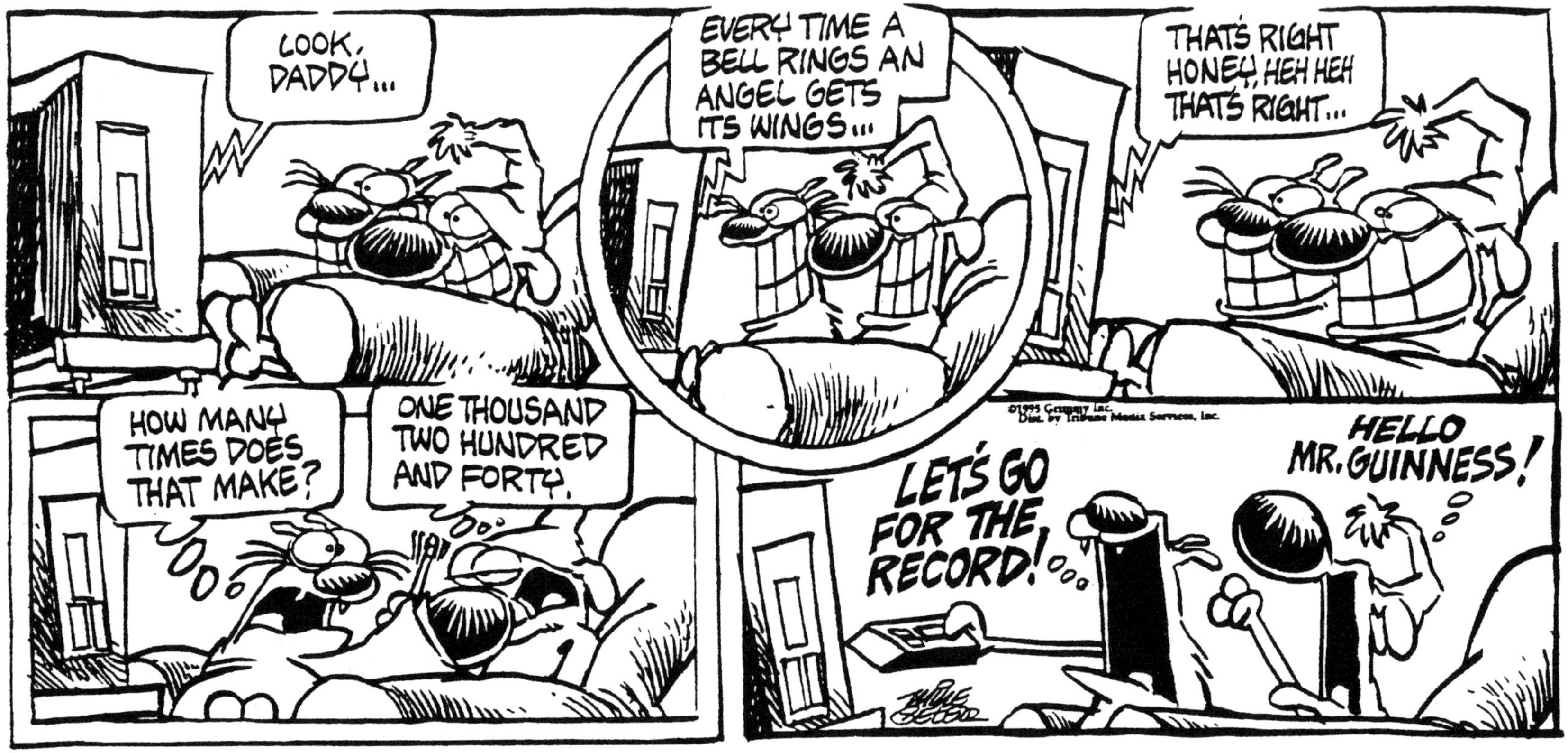
LOOK, DADDY...
EVERY TIME A BELL RINGS AN ANGEL GETS ITS WINGS...
THAT'S RIGHT HONEY, HEH HEH THAT'S RIGHT...
HOW MANY TIMES DOES THAT MAKE?
ONE THOUSAND TWO HUNDRED AND FORTY.
©1995 Grimmy Inc. Dist. by Tribune Media Services, Inc.
LET'S GO FOR THE RECORD!
HELLO MR. GUINNESS!

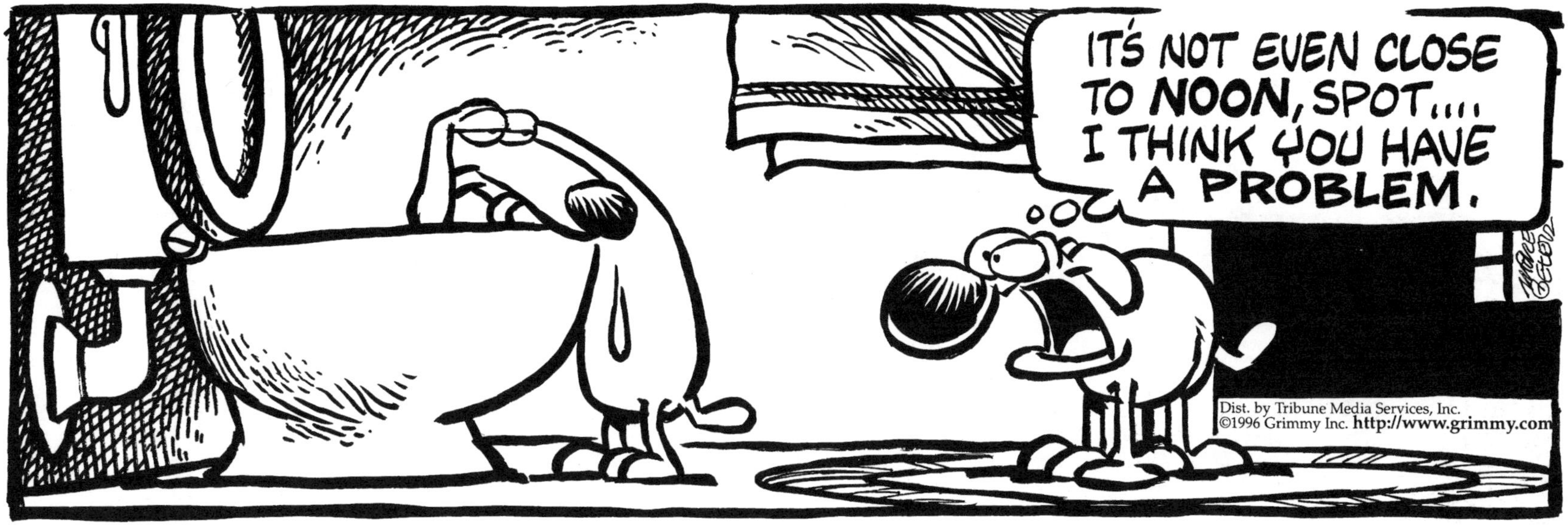
IT'S NOT EVEN CLOSE TO NOON, SPOT.... I THINK YOU HAVE A PROBLEM.
Dist. by Tribune Media Services, Inc.
©1996 Grimmy Inc. http://www.grimmy.com

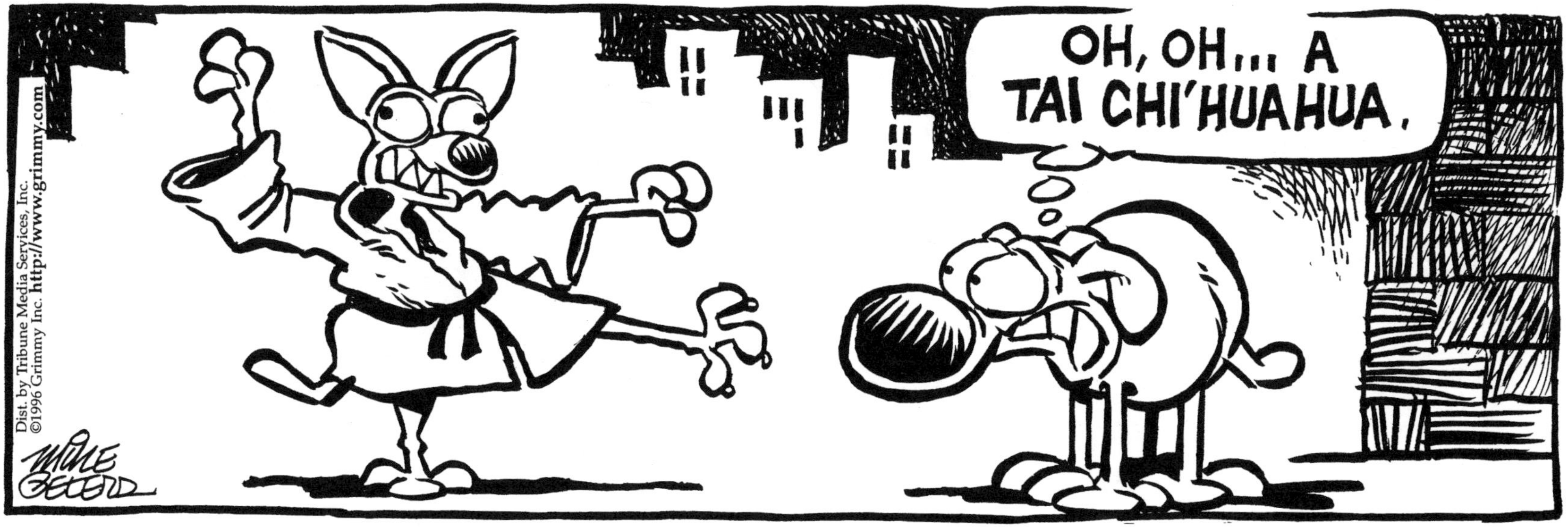
OH, OH... A TAI CHI'HUAHUA.
Dist. by Tribune Media Services, Inc.
©1996 Grimmy Inc. http://www.grimmy.com
MIKE PETERS

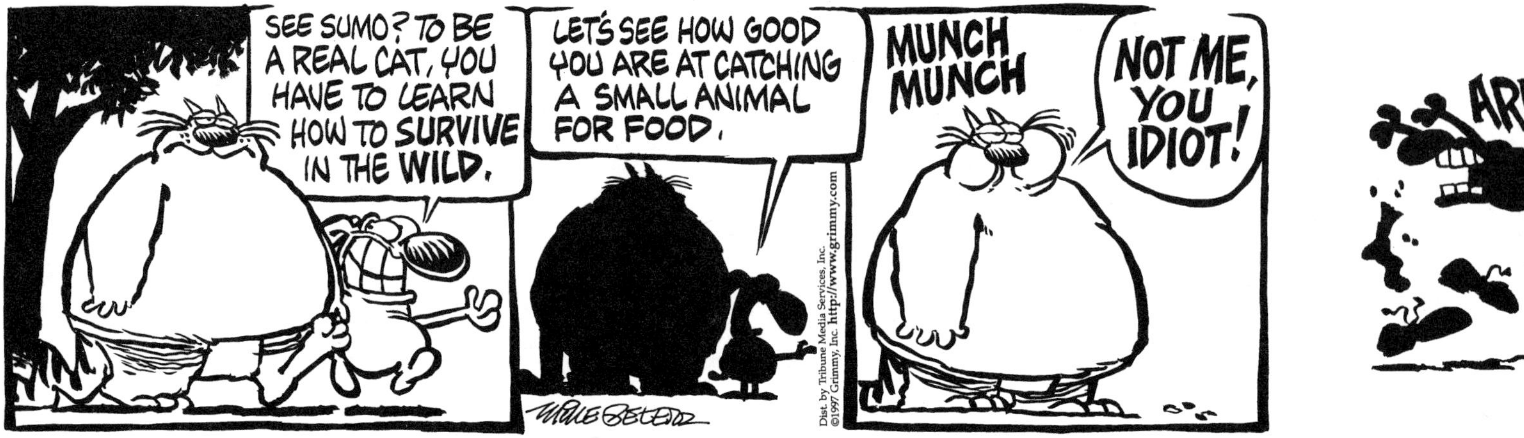
SEE SUMO? TO BE A REAL CAT, YOU HAVE TO LEARN HOW TO SURVIVE IN THE WILD.
LET'S SEE HOW GOOD YOU ARE AT CATCHING A SMALL ANIMAL FOR FOOD.
Dist. by Tribune Media Services, Inc. ©1997 Grimmy, Inc. http://www.grimmy.com
MUNCH MUNCH
NOT ME, YOU IDIOT!
ARUGH!

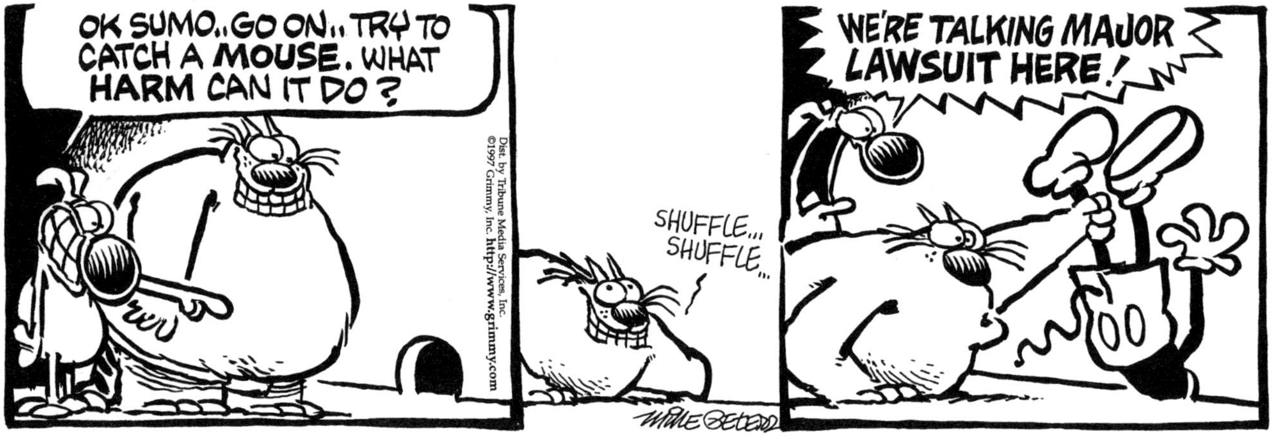
OK SUMO.. GO ON.. TRY TO CATCH A MOUSE. WHAT HARM CAN IT DO?
Dist. by Tribune Media Services, Inc. ©1997 Grimmy, Inc. http://www.grimmy.com
SHUFFLE... SHUFFLE...
WE'RE TALKING MAJOR LAWSUIT HERE!

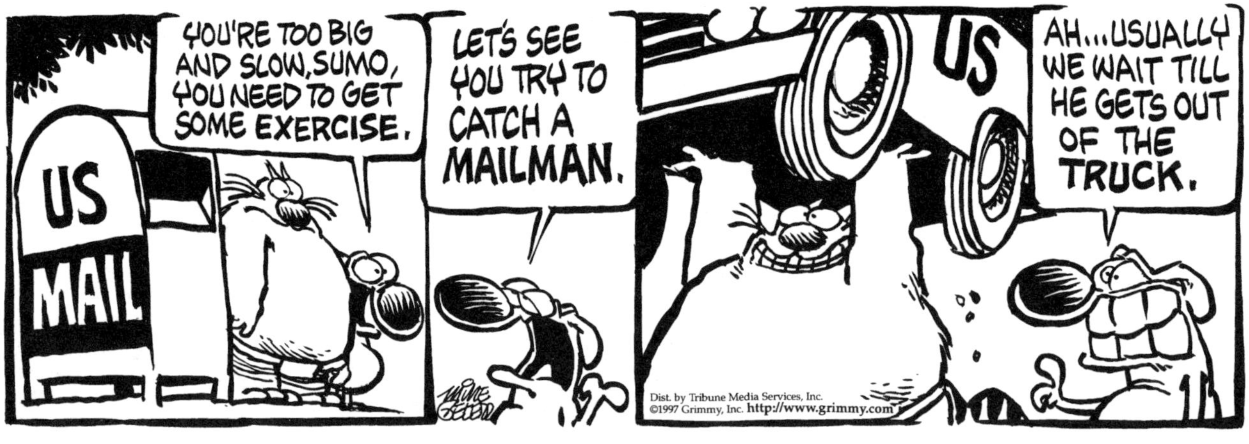
US MAIL
YOU'RE TOO BIG AND SLOW, SUMO, YOU NEED TO GET SOME EXERCISE.
LET'S SEE YOU TRY TO CATCH A MAILMAN.
US
AH... USUALLY WE WAIT TILL HE GETS OUT OF THE TRUCK.
Dist. by Tribune Media Services, Inc. ©1997 Grimmy, Inc. http://www.grimmy.com

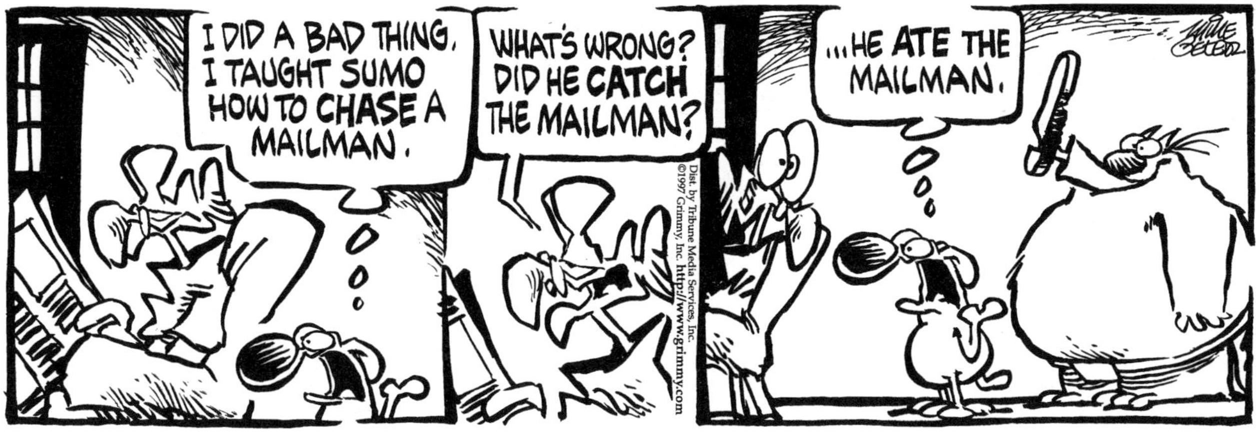
I DID A BAD THING. I TAUGHT SUMO HOW TO CHASE A MAILMAN.
WHAT'S WRONG? DID HE CATCH THE MAILMAN?
...HE ATE THE MAILMAN.
Dist. by Tribune Media Services, Inc. ©1997 Grimmy, Inc. http://www.grimmy.com

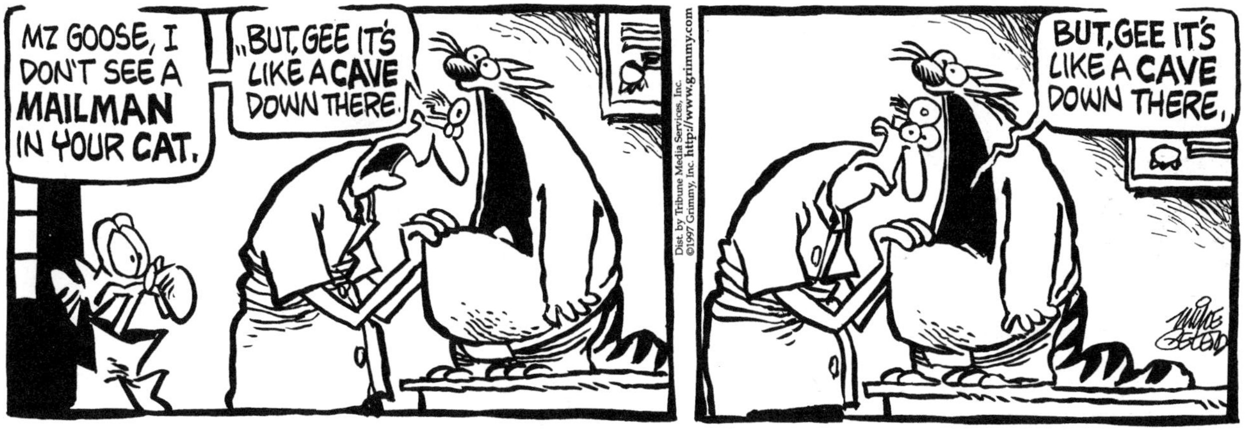
MZ GOOSE, I DON'T SEE A MAILMAN IN YOUR CAT.
..BUT, GEE IT'S LIKE A CAVE DOWN THERE.
BUT, GEE IT'S LIKE A CAVE DOWN THERE.
Dist. by Tribune Media Services, Inc. ©1997 Grimmy, Inc. http://www.grimmy.com

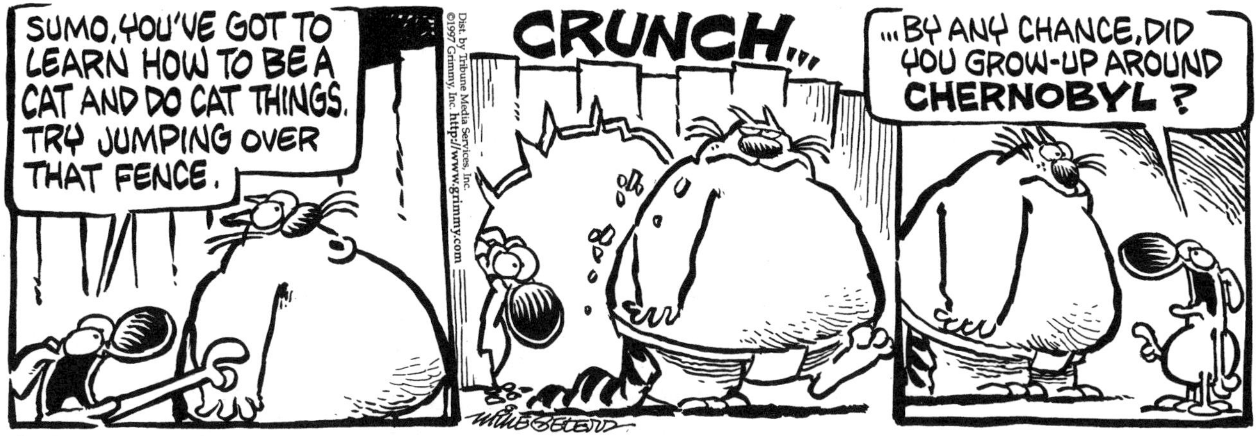
SUMO, YOU'VE GOT TO LEARN HOW TO BE A CAT AND DO CAT THINGS. TRY JUMPING OVER THAT FENCE.
CRUNCH...
...BY ANY CHANCE, DID YOU GROW-UP AROUND CHERNOBYL?
Dist. by Tribune Media Services, Inc. ©1997 Grimmy, Inc. http://www.grimmy.com

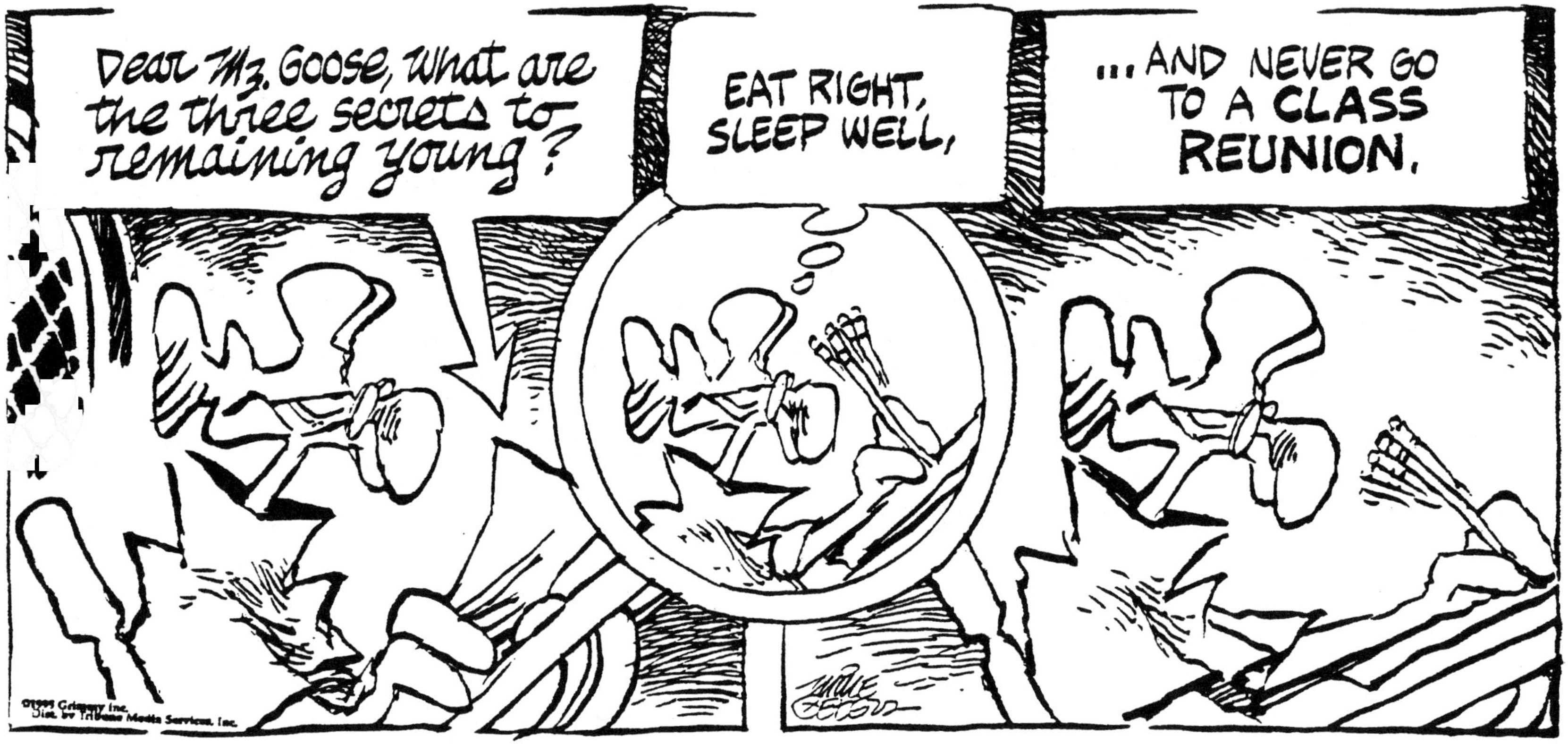
Dear Mz. Goose, what are the three secrets to remaining young?
EAT RIGHT, SLEEP WELL,
...AND NEVER GO TO A CLASS REUNION.

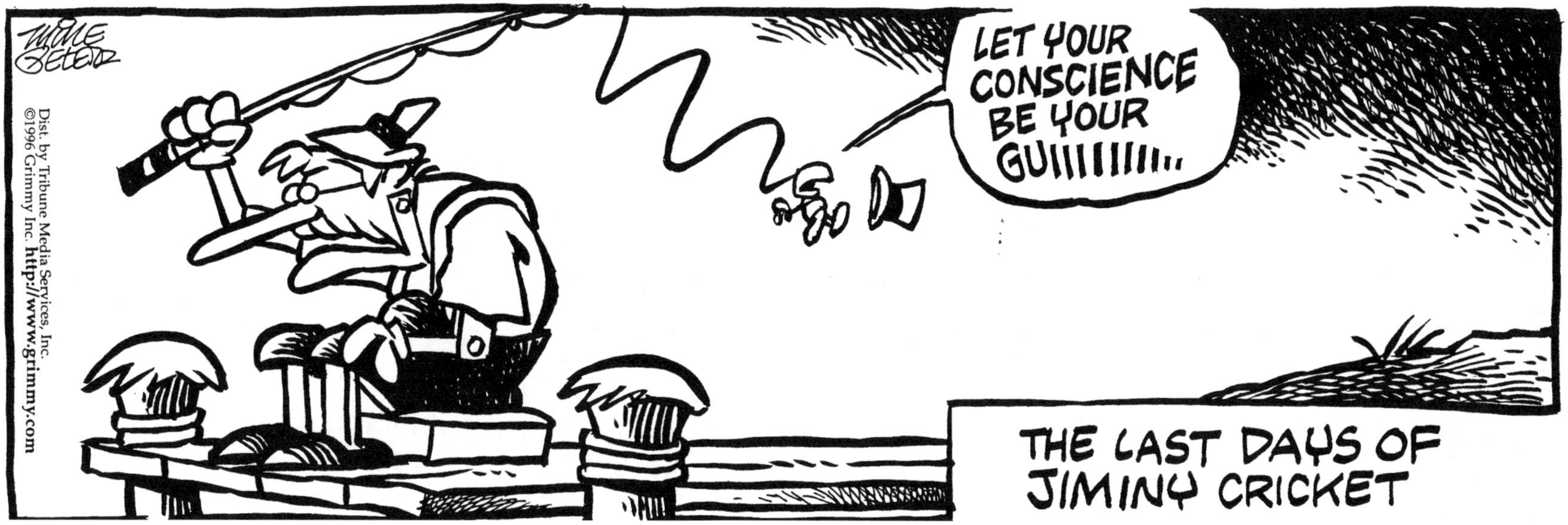
Dist. by Tribune Media Services, Inc. ©1996 Grimmy Inc. http://www.grimmy.com
LET YOUR CONSCIENCE BE YOUR GUIIIIIII...
THE LAST DAYS OF JIMINY CRICKET

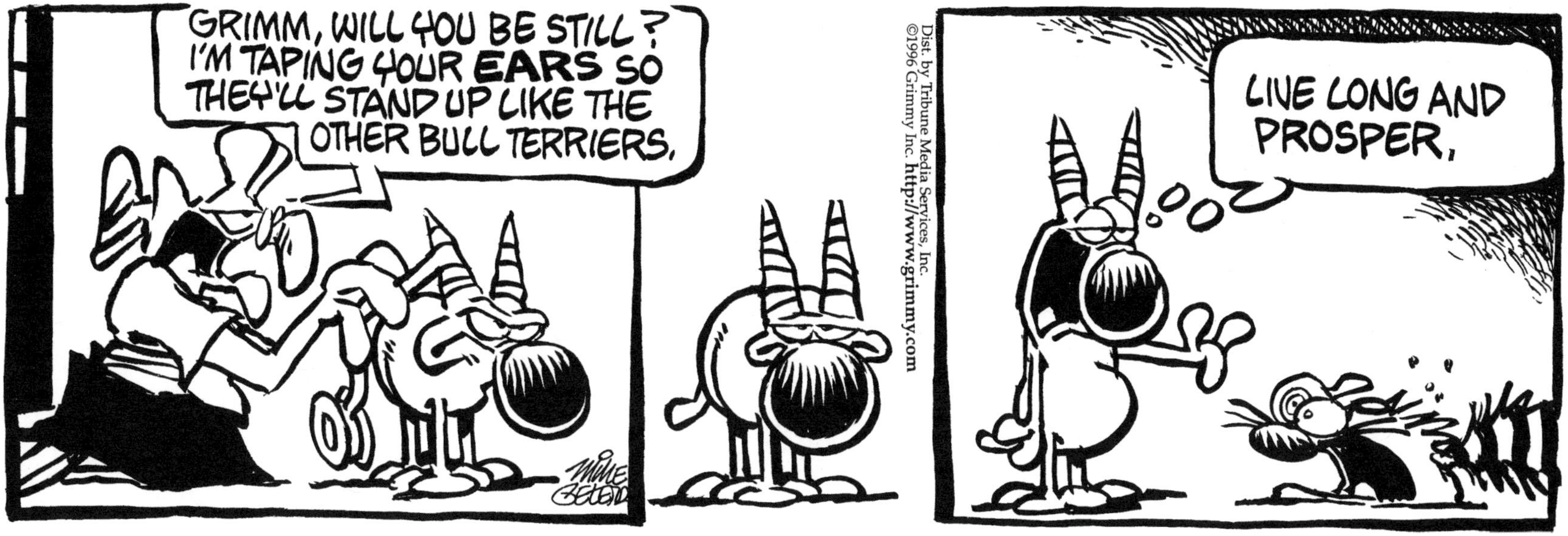
GRIMM, WILL YOU BE STILL? I'M TAPING YOUR **EARS** SO THEY'LL STAND UP LIKE THE OTHER BULL TERRIERS.
Dist. by Tribune Media Services, Inc. ©1996 Grimmy Inc. http://www.grimmy.com
LIVE LONG AND PROSPER.

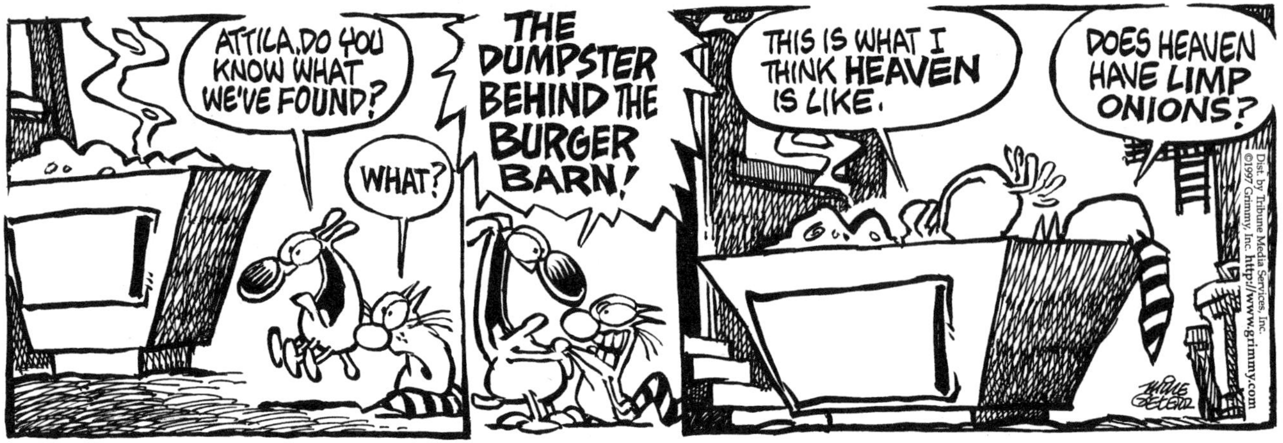
ATTILA, DO YOU KNOW WHAT WE'VE FOUND?
WHAT?
THE DUMPSTER BEHIND THE BURGER BARN!
THIS IS WHAT I THINK HEAVEN IS LIKE.
DOES HEAVEN HAVE LIMP ONIONS?
Dist. by Tribune Media Services, Inc. ©1997 Grimmy, Inc. http://www.grimmy.com

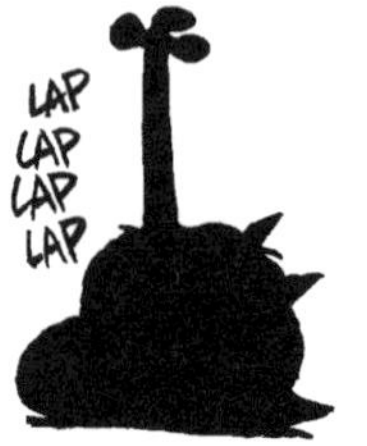
LAP
LAP
LAP
LAP

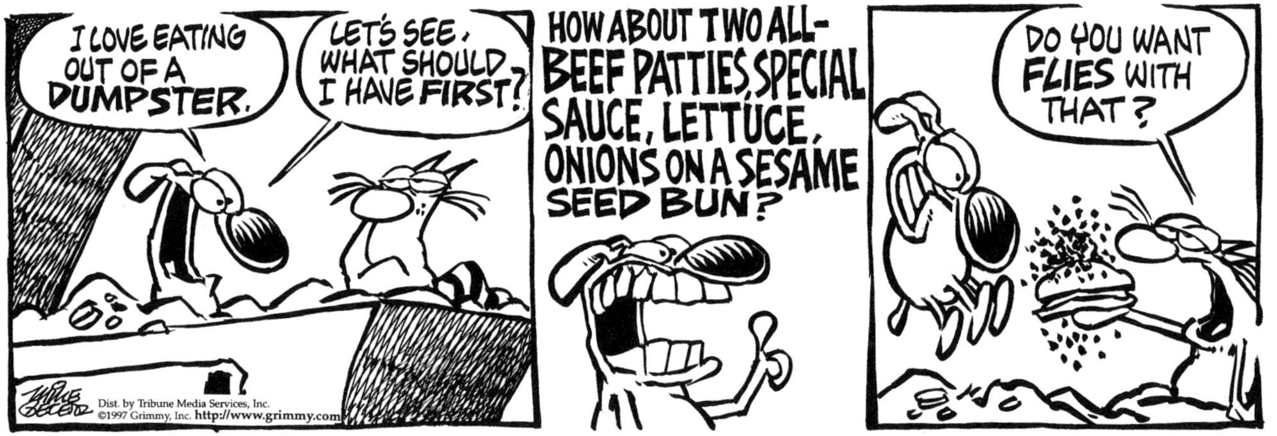
I LOVE EATING OUT OF A DUMPSTER.
LET'S SEE, WHAT SHOULD I HAVE FIRST?
Dist. by Tribune Media Services, Inc. ©1997 Grimmy, Inc. http://www.grimmy.com
HOW ABOUT TWO ALL-BEEF PATTIES, SPECIAL SAUCE, LETTUCE, ONIONS ON A SESAME SEED BUN?
DO YOU WANT FLIES WITH THAT?

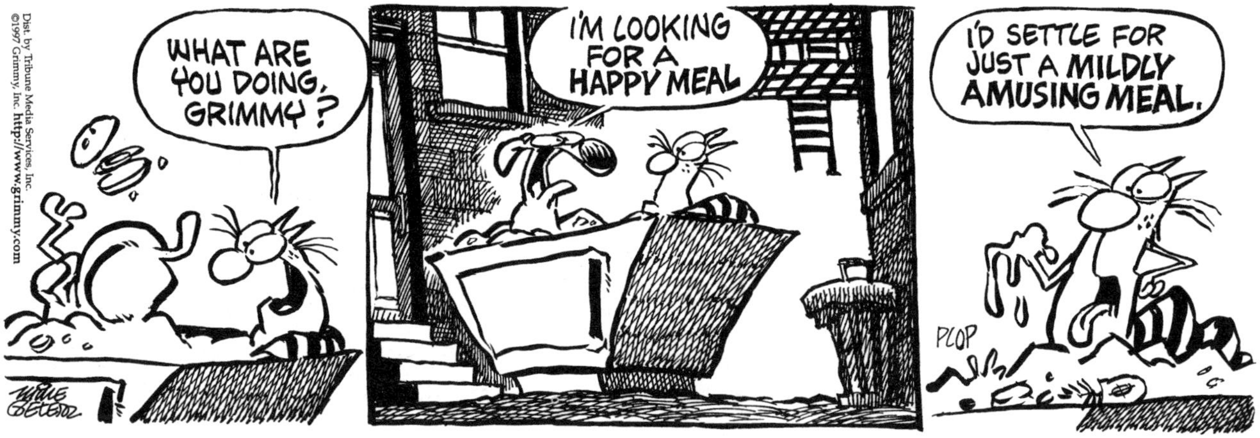
Dist. by Tribune Media Services, Inc. ©1997 Grimmy, Inc. http://www.grimmy.com
WHAT ARE YOU DOING, GRIMMY?
I'M LOOKING FOR A HAPPY MEAL
I'D SETTLE FOR JUST A MILDLY AMUSING MEAL.
PLOP

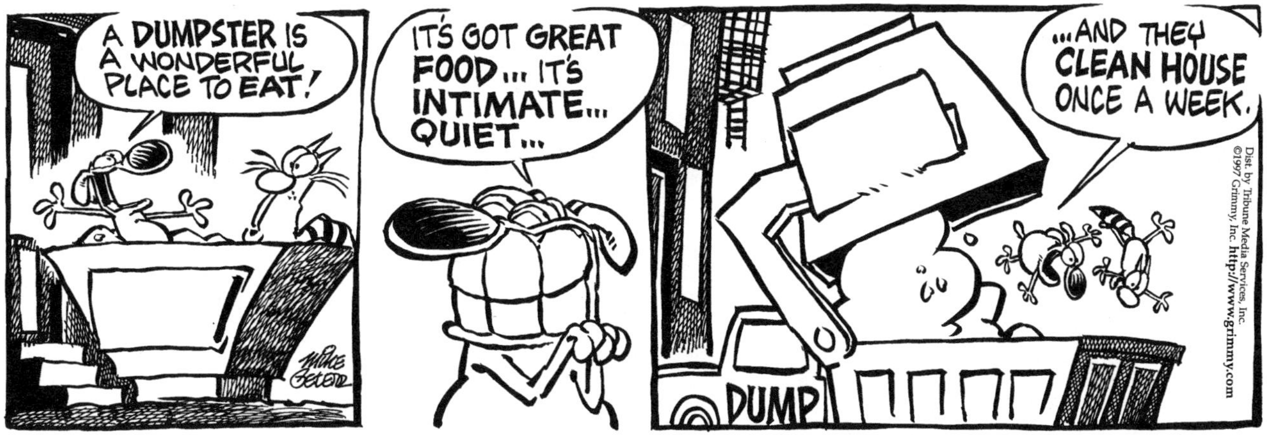
A DUMPSTER IS A WONDERFUL PLACE TO EAT!
IT'S GOT GREAT FOOD... IT'S INTIMATE... QUIET...
...AND THEY CLEAN HOUSE ONCE A WEEK.
DUMP
Dist. by Tribune Media Services, Inc. ©1997 Grimmy, Inc. http://www.grimmy.com

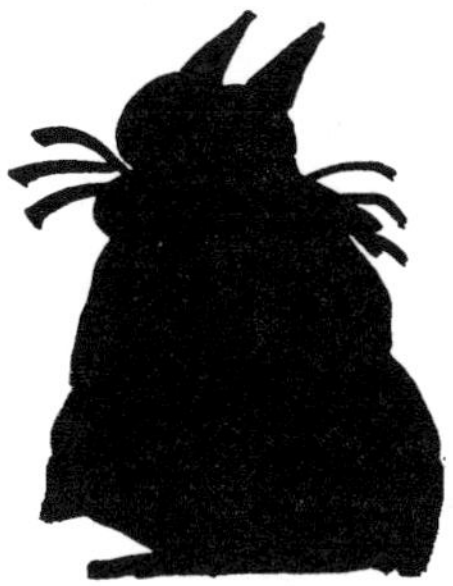

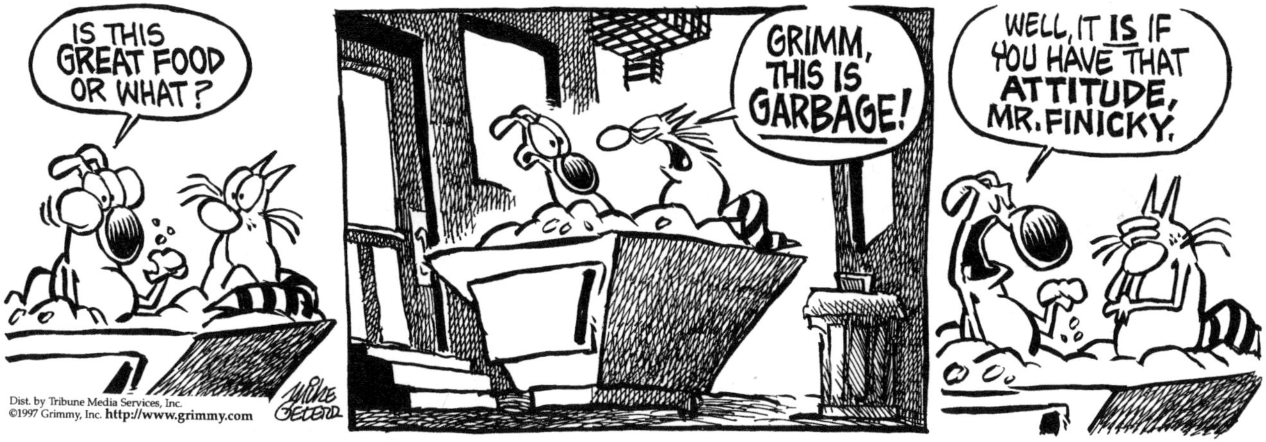
IS THIS GREAT FOOD OR WHAT?
GRIMM, THIS IS GARBAGE!
WELL, IT IS IF YOU HAVE THAT ATTITUDE, MR. FINICKY.
Dist. by Tribune Media Services, Inc. ©1997 Grimmy, Inc. http://www.grimmy.com

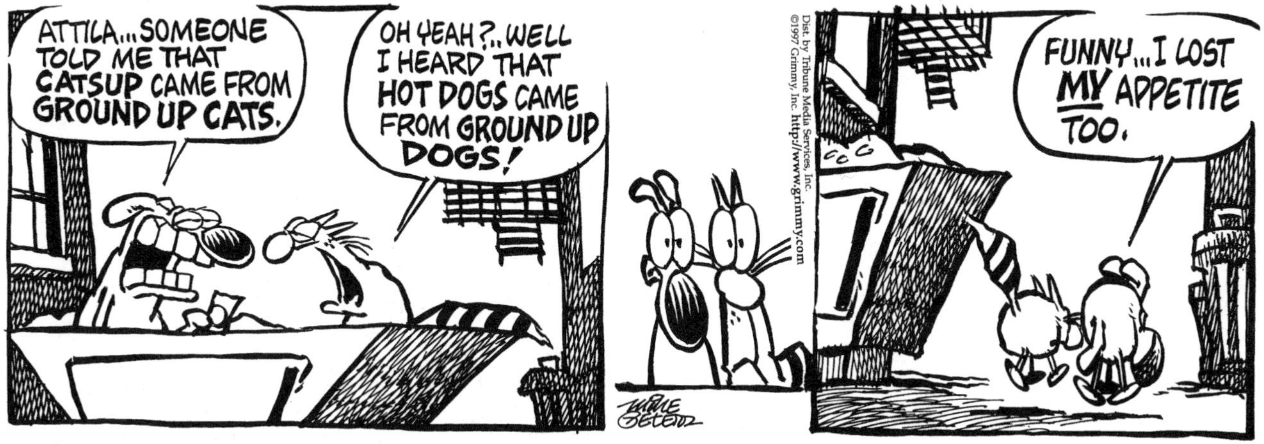
ATTILA... SOMEONE TOLD ME THAT CATSUP CAME FROM GROUND UP CATS.
OH YEAH?.. WELL I HEARD THAT HOT DOGS CAME FROM GROUND UP DOGS!
FUNNY... I LOST MY APPETITE TOO.
Dist. by Tribune Media Services, Inc. ©1997 Grimmy, Inc. http://www.grimmy.com

WHERE ARE THE GOODS?

MANY OF OUR READERS ASK HOW THEY CAN BUY GRIMMY MERCHANDISE.

HERE IS A LIST OF LICENSEES IN THE UNITED STATES AND CANADA THAT CARRY GREAT STUFF!

GIVE THEM A CALL FOR YOUR LOCAL DISTRIBUTOR.

WWW.GRIMMY.COM

Avalanche Publishing
15262 Pipeline Lane
Huntington Beach, CA 92649
PH 800/888-6421
365 Day Box Calendar-Year 2000
www.avalanchepub.com

Classcom, Inc.
770 Bertrand
Montreal, Quebec
Canada H4M1V9
PH 514/747-9492
Desk Art

C.T.I.
22160 North Pepper Rd.
Barrington, IL 60010
PH 800/284-5605
Balloons, Coffee Mugs

Gibson Greetings
2100 Section Rd.
Cincinnati, OH 45237
PH 800/345-6521
Greeting Cards, Party
Papers, Gift Wrap, Egreetings, etc...
www.greetst.com

Linda Jones Enterprises
17771 Mitchell
Irvine, CA 92614
PH 949/660-7791
Cels

Balzout, Inc.
#5 McJunkin Rd.
Nitro, W.V. 25143
PH 800/926-0169
T-Shirts

Pomegranate
210 Classic Ct.
Rohnert Park, CA 94928
PH 800/227-1428
Wall Year 2000 Calendars,
Postcard Booklets
www.pomegranate.com

Tor Books
175 Fifth Ave.
New York, NY 10010
PH 212/388-0100
Paperback Books
www.tor.com

GRiMM iN CYBERSPACE!

Your favorite garbage-eating, toiletwater drinking dog has his own Web site!
Surf through pages of fun!

**Order Grimmy products
Learn about Pulitzer prize winning creator Mike Peters
See favorite strips including Mike s editorial cartoons
Get the inside scoop on all of the main characters**

Explore the world of Grimmy, Mother Goose, Attila, and Mike at:

http: www.grimmy.com

**"One small step for Grimm,
One giant leap for Grimmkind."**